iLife™ ALL-IN-ONE DESK REFERENCE FOR DUMMIES®

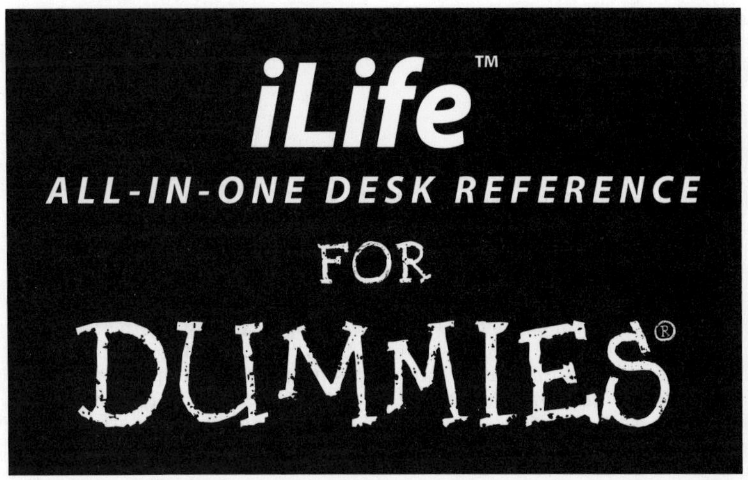

by Tony Bove and Cheryl Rhodes

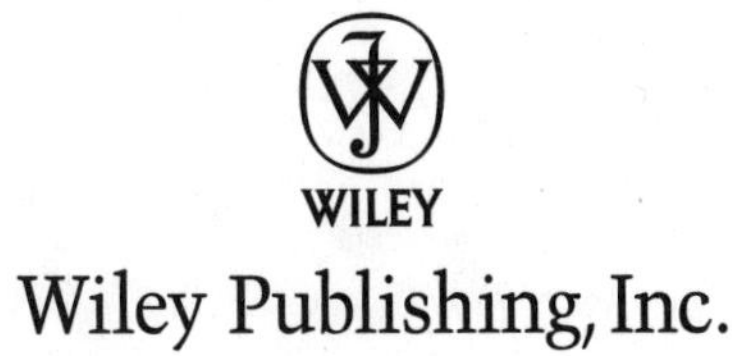

Wiley Publishing, Inc.

iLife™ All-in-One Desk Reference For Dummies®

Published by
Wiley Publishing, Inc.
111 River Street
Hoboken, NJ 07030

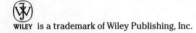

www.wiley.com

Published by Wiley Publishing, Inc., Indianapolis, Indiana

Published simultaneously in Canada

For general information on our other products and services or to obtain technical support, please contact our Customer Care Department within the U.S. at 800-762-2974, outside the U.S. at 317-572-3993, or fax 317-572-4002.

Wiley also publishes its books in a variety of electronic formats. Some content that appears in print may not be available in electronic books.

Library of Congress Control Number: 2003105633

ISBN: 0-7645-4213-3

Manufactured in the United States of America

10 9 8 7 6 5 4 3 2 1

1B/QZ/RQ/QT/IN

About the Authors

Tony Bove and **Cheryl Rhodes** have kicked around the computer industry for decades, acting as pathfinders to new technologies, and surprising folks every few years with new projects. They edited the influential newsletter *Bove & Rhodes Inside Report on New Media,* and wrote weekly and monthly columns and feature articles for computer-industry magazines including *Computer Currents* (for computer users), *Nextworld* (for computer professionals), and *NewMedia* (for multimedia professionals). They also co-founded and edited *Desktop Publishing/Publish* magazine (for publishing professionals).

Tracing the personal computer revolution back to the Sixties counterculture, Bove and Rhodes produced a CD-ROM interactive documentary in 1996, *Haight-Ashbury in the Sixties* (featuring music from the Grateful Dead, Janis Joplin, and the Jefferson Airplane), which garnered critical acclaim and published reviews, such as "An unflinching, nonjudgmental chronicle" (*Wired*), "Inspires then and now connections, fulfilling any historical work's highest calling" (*S.F. Examiner*), "Truly greater than the sum of its parts" (*N.Y. Post*).

Bove and Rhodes have written over a dozen books on computing, desktop publishing, and multimedia, including at least one bestseller, *The Art of Desktop Publishing* (Bantam); a series of books about Macromedia Director that includes *Macromedia Lingo Studio* and *Official Macromedia Director Studio* (Random House); the long-running *Adobe Illustrator: The Official Handbook for Designers* (Random House) now in its fourth edition; *Desktop Publishing with PageMaker* and *PageMaker 4: The Basics* (Wiley Publishing, Inc.); and *The Well-Connected Macintosh* (Harcourt Brace Jovanovich).

Tony Bove has been a director of enterprise marketing for a large software company, as well as a communications director and technical publications manager. He also developed the Rockument music site, `www.rockument.com`, with commentary and radio programs focused on rock music history. As a founding member of the Flying Other Brothers band (`www.flyingotherbros.com`), he has performed at numerous benefit concerts and co-written songs with Hot Tuna keyboardist Pete Sears and Saturday Night Live/Bob Dylan bandleader G.E. Smith.

Cheryl Rhodes is an education specialist, researcher, and advocate. She founded and served as director of the Pacific Community Charter School, and worked as a professional courseware designer for ComputerTown USA (a National Science Foundation project) and the Lawrence Hall of Science, as well as an instructor in computer courses at elementary and high schools.

Dedication

This book is dedicated to our sons, John Paul Bove and James Eric Bove, both of whom contributed tips and spent considerable time testing examples while turning a vacation into a book project. These kids truly live the iLife and should probably get a raise in their allowances, now that you bought this book. Let's send them to college — tell your Mac friends to buy this book! Thank you.

Authors' Acknowledgments

We want to thank our Wiley project editor, Christine Berman, for having the patience of a saint while pulling this project through the process on time. We also thank Wiley editors Rebecca Senninger and Linda Morris for their skills and ongoing assistance that made our job so much easier. Thanks as well to Dennis Cohen for contributing material to this book. A book of this size places a considerable burden on a publisher's production team, and we thank our technical editor, Lisa Spangenberg, and the Production crew at Wiley for diligence beyond the call of reason.

We owe thanks and a happy hour or two to Carole McLendon at Waterside, our agent. And we have acquisitions editor Bob Woerner at Wiley to thank for coming up with the idea for this book and helping us to become professional dummies — that is, dummy authors.

Finally, our heartfelt thanks to members of the Flying Other Brothers (Pete Sears, Barry Sless, Jimmy Sanchez, Bill Bennett, Bert Keely, and Roger and Ann McNamee) as well as Chris Flum for letting us use photographs of the band.

Publisher's Acknowledgments

We're proud of this book; please send us your comments through our online registration form located at `www.dummies.com/register/`.

Some of the people who helped bring this book to market include the following:

Acquisitions, Editorial, and Media Development

Project Editor: Christine Berman

Acquisitions Editor: Bob Woerner

Copy Editor: Rebecca Senninger

Technical Editor: Lisa Spangenberg

Editorial Manager: Leah Cameron

Media Development Manager: Laura VanWinkle

Media Development Supervisor: Richard Graves

Editorial Assistant: Amanda Foxworth

Cartoons: Rich Tennant, `www.the5thwave.com`

Production

Project Coordinator: Maridee Ennis

Layout and Graphics: Amanda Carter, Seth Conley, Joyce Haughey, Stephanie D. Jumper

Proofreaders: Jacqui Brownstein, David Faust, Susan Moritz, Carl William Pierce, Charles Spencer

Indexer: Ty Koontz

Special Help

Linda Morris

Publishing and Editorial for Technology Dummies

Richard Swadley, Vice President and Executive Group Publisher

Andy Cummings, Vice President and Publisher

Mary C. Corder, Editorial Director

Publishing for Consumer Dummies

Diane Graves Steele, Vice President and Publisher

Joyce Pepple, Acquisitions Director

Composition Services

Gerry Fahey, Vice President of Production Services

Debbie Stailey, Director of Composition Services

Contents at a Glance

Table of Contents

Introduction

Remember the Nowhere Man from the Beatles classic animated movie, *Yellow Submarine?* He was the nerdy little fellow always going round in circles, writing books, making music, taking pictures, directing plays, and making movies, always so very busy. But he was also very sad, because no one could see his work; the Blue Meanies had taken art away from the people (and if we speculate on who the Blue Meanies are, we might *really* get in trouble . . .). Nowhere Man just sat in his nowhere land, making nowhere plans for nobody. But as John Lennon pointed out, “Isn’t he a bit like you and me?”

With this suite of software tools, the world is at your command. All of your digital assets — your photos, your songs, your videos, everything — are at your fingertips. The iLife software brings together all your digital assets so that you can use them for creative projects and manage them for the rest of your real life.

A day in the iLife might include ripping some music CDs with iTunes to use with your iPod on the road, or transferring the photos from your digital camera into your iPhoto library to share them with friends by e-mail. You might want to assemble a slideshow of the photos in iPhoto and set it to music, which you have in your iTunes library, and post that on the Web. You can then bring video footage from your DV camcorder into iMovie and make a music video with all these elements. Finally, you can use iDVD to put together eye-popping menus and buttons to show off the music video and slideshow and anything else you may have, and burn a disc that your friends can play on an everyday DVD player. You can find all this and more in this book.

Now you’re getting somewhere, man.

About This Book

We designed this book as a reference. You can find the information you need when you need it easily — this book even has thumbtabs to locate subjects quickly. We organize the information in a linear fashion into five mini-books. You can read each mini-book from beginning to end to find out how to use the software from scratch. You can also dive in anywhere and begin reading, because you find all the info you need to know for each task.

We don't cover every detail of every function of the software, and we intentionally leave out some detail so that we don't spook you with technospeak when it's not necessary. (Really, engineers can sometimes provide too many obscure choices that no one ever uses.) We wrote brief but comprehensive descriptions and included lots of cool tips on how to be productive with iLife.

Conventions Used in This Book

Like any book about computers, this book uses certain conventions.

When we write "Choose iTunes⇨Preferences," you should open the iTunes menu from the toolbar (in iTunes) and then select the Preferences menu item. Some menus have selections that are submenus with more choices. Okay, that's fairly simple, but some commands are very long and complicated, such as View⇨Arrange Photos⇨By Date. If we wrote out each command, this book would be much longer. In an effort to save paper, ink, and your money, we use the command arrows.

It's a relief that we're mostly beyond having to type commands into a computer, even if we have to use something rodent-like in appearance as well as name. You can use a one-button mouse to do just about everything on a Mac. When we write "Click the Import button" you should move the mouse cursor to the button on-screen, and click the mouse button.

Clicking once is not the only way to use a mouse. When we write "Drag the photo over the name of the album" we mean click the photo, hold the mouse button down, and drag the mouse pointer over to the name of the album before lifting your finger off the mouse button.

Sometimes we abbreviate the instruction "click the name of something" to "select something." For example, when we say "Select a photo album" we mean click the name of the photo album. Other times we combine the click-and-drag function — we say "**scroll the Source list**" when we mean clicking and dragging the scroll bar for the Source List window.

Foolish Assumptions

Contrary to popular belief (and rumors circulated by the Blue Meanies), you *don't* need the following to use any of the applications (or this book):

- **A pile of cash for extra equipment and software:** Yes, you need a digital camera for iPhoto, a digital camcorder for iMovie, a DVD-R drive for iDVD, and the iPod for portable music playing, but you can get all of this, including an iMac with a SuperDrive for DVD-R, for under $3,500, which is about one-tenth of what it cost to do the same in 1998. And you don't need any extra software — every important piece of software we describe in this book is either already on your Mac or available for free from the Apple Web site, `www.apple.com`.
- **A better education:** Courses in film, photography, and music can't hurt, but iLife is designed for the rest of us air-guitar players that barely know the difference between a video clip and a still image. You won't need any specialized knowledge to have a lot of fun with this software while building your digital assets.
- **A tech support hotline:** Not once do we ever feel the need to contact the Apple technical support. Everything works as it should. We pinch ourselves daily for this apparent miracle. We never have to wade through inscrutable documentation, either — the built-in help is informative and useful (which you certainly won't need if you have this book).

The iLife software is free, supplied with every Mac. That's really all the software you need.

However, we do make some honest assumptions about your computer skills:

- **How to use the Mac Finder:** You should already know how to use the Finder to locate files and folders, and how to copy files and folders from one disk to another.
- **How to select menus and applications on a Mac:** You should already know how to choose an option from a Mac menu, how to find the Dock to launch a Dock application, and how to launch an application in the Application folder.

For more information on either topic, see that excellent book by Mark L. Chambers, *Mac OS X All-in-One Desk Reference for Dummies* (Wiley Publishing, Inc.).

How This Book Is Organized

We organize this tome into four mini-books representing the four parts of iLife (iTunes, iPhoto, iMovie, and iDVD), one mini-book for the iPod, and an extra mini-book for the extra iLife information.

Book I: iTunes

This mini-book begins with the revolution in digital music and what iTunes does. You find out how to play music CDs like a professional DJ, buy music online from the Apple Music store, rip CDs and import music from many sources, and organize your music library. The mini-book covers everything you need to know about sound quality and disk space trade-offs, as well as how to get the best sound from your computer or CDs you burn yourself.

Book II: iPhoto

This mini-book provides all you need to know about using digital cameras and organizing your photos to produce prints, photo albums, and even professional looking photo books. It shows you how to improve and retouch digital photos, create slideshows, and share photos online and by e-mail.

Book III: iMovie

This mini-book introduces digital video and tells you everything you need to know about using digital camcorders with your Mac to create videos of all kinds, even professional videos. This mini-book shows you how to manage video clips, create movies with photos and clips, and even edit soundtracks and special effects. It also covers sharing movies online and saving movies in professional formats.

Book IV: iDVD

This mini-book describes how to bring all your digital assets together to create exciting DVD discs that can play in DVD players as well as computers. You find out how to create interactive menus and buttons and special effects, such as video backgrounds. Burn DVDs like the pros and save all your precious digital assets — photos, music, movies, slideshows — at their highest quality on DVD.

Book V: iPod

This mini-book tells how to take your entire music library with you on the road with an iPod. You also discover how to use the iPod to look up contacts (addresses and phone numbers) and your calendar and to-do lists, as well as use the iPod as a portable hard disk.

Book VI: iLife Extras

This mini-book talks about integrating the various components of iLife and includes some helpful third-party stuff.

Icons Used in This Book

The icons in this book are important visual cues for information you need.

The Remember icons highlight important things you should remember.

The Technical Stuff icons highlight technical details you can skip unless you want to bring out the technical geek in you.

Tips highlight tips and techniques that save you time and energy, and maybe money.

Warnings save your butt by preventing disasters. Don't bypass a warning without reading it. This is your only warning!

Where to Go from Here

Feel free to begin reading anywhere or skip particular sections or chapters (or go really wild, start on page 1 and continue reading to the index). If you want to know how to tackle a particular task, look it up in the Index or Table of Contents and flip to the page you need. Or if you want to start finding out about one of the products, start with that mini-book. This is your book; dive right in.

Book I

iTunes

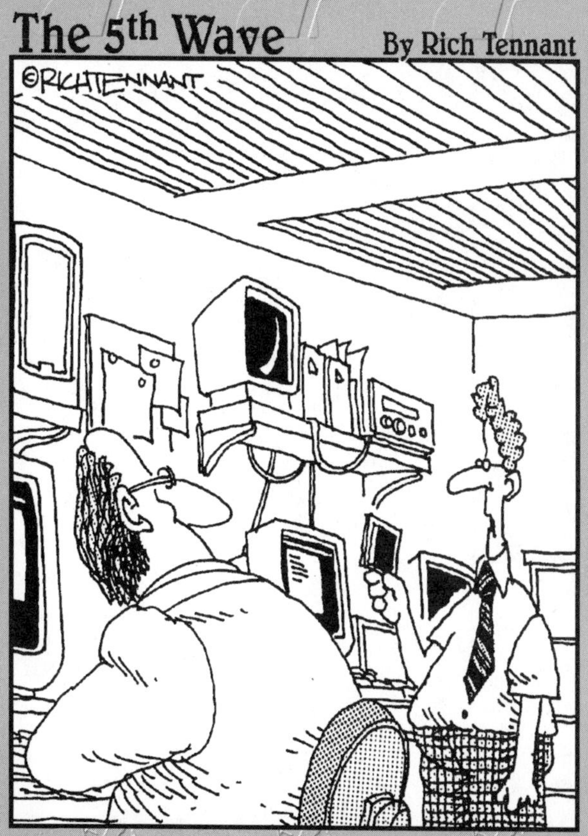

"I ran this Bob Dylan CD through our voice recognition system, and he really is just saying, 'Manaama-manaaabadhaabadha...'"

Chapter 1: iTunes — the Digital Jukebox

In This Chapter

- **Starting iTunes**
- **Playing music tracks**
- **Setting visual effects**
- **Perfecting the sound**
- **Shopping for music online**
- **Importing into iTunes**
- **Listening to Web radio streams**

More than half a century ago, jukeboxes were the primary and most convenient way for people to select the music they wanted to hear and share with others, especially newly released music. Juke joints were hopping with the newest hits every night; however, you still had to insert coins every time you played a song. Possibly, you could afford records and a turntable, but you had to throw a party to share the music with others.

Today, using a computer, you can create a digital jukebox and conveniently click a button to play a song. Connect your Mac to a stereo amplifier in your home, or connect speakers to your Mac, and suddenly your Mac is the best jukebox in the neighborhood.

You can listen to a new song on the Internet and download it immediately. You can also buy music online at the Apple Music Store. iTunes downloads music from the store and puts it in your library, making it immediately available for playing, burning onto a CD, or transferring to an iPod. You can even listen to Web radio stations using iTunes and define your favorite stations.

Transferring songs from CD to your computer is called *ripping a CD* (to the chagrin of the music industry old-timers who think we intend to destroy the disc or steal the songs). Ripping an entire CD's worth of songs is quick and easy, and track information including artist name and title arrives automatically over the Internet.

iTunes gives you the power to organize songs into playlists and burn (or record) CDs of any songs in your library, in any order. You can even set up dynamic smart playlists that reflect your preferences and listening habits. iTunes offers an equalizer with preset settings for all kinds of music and listening environments, and the ability to customize and save your own settings with each song.

This chapter explains how iTunes changes your music playing and buying habits for the better. You'll be able to preserve your music virtually forever without any loss in quality, and use your music in a variety of creative projects made possible by iLife.

Setting Up iTunes

You need to set up iTunes to use with your Internet connection. This happens automatically when you first start iTunes. Follow these steps:

1. **Launch iTunes.**

   Double-click the iTunes application, or click the iTunes icon in the Dock. If this is the first time, the Setup Assistant wizard appears.

2. **Click Next.**

   The Setup Assistant takes you through the process of setting up iTunes for the Internet.

3. **Click Yes or No for the following options:**

   - **"Yes, use iTunes for Internet audio content," or "No, do not modify my Internet settings"**

     We suggest clicking Yes, allow iTunes to handle audio content, because iTunes offers more features than you typically find with browser plug-ins from other companies. On the other hand, if you are happy with your plug-ins and helper applications, you can click No and leave your Internet settings untouched.

   - **"Yes, automatically connect to the Internet," or "No, ask me before connecting"**

     If you use an *always-on* broadband Internet service, you probably want iTunes to connect automatically, and you can click Yes. If you use a modem, if your Internet service is intermittently off, or if your Internet service charges when you use it, you probably *don't* want this connection to be automatic — you can set iTunes to ask first.

     The Setup Assistant also asks if you want iTunes to search your home folder for music files. You may want to click the No button for now, because iTunes may find files you don't want to add to your library (such as music for games). The Setup Assistant also asks if you want to go straight to the Apple Music Store.

4. **In the Setup Assistant window, click Done.**

   The iTunes window appears, as shown in Figure 1-1.

Figure 1-1: Launching iTunes.

If your computer shares a phone line or you pay Internet connection charges by the minute, you probably don't want to connect automatically. If you're modem-bound, you may not want your modem to make a phone call every time you slip a CD into the computer. On the other hand, if your Internet cost isn't based on usage and you're always connected, connecting iTunes automatically is convenient.

Whether or not you set iTunes to automatically connect to the Internet, you should at some point connect to the Internet with iTunes, not only to buy music online and listen to Web radio, but also to retrieve the track information every time you insert a CD new to iTunes so you don't have to type the information yourself.

Playing CD Tracks

To start playing music, just insert any commercial music CD, or even a CD-R disc that someone else may have burned for you. The music tracks appear in the iTunes song/detail list, as shown in Figure 1-2.

You can play CDs without importing the music to your iTunes library if you want to use iTunes as a CD player only. To find out how to get digital music online or import music from CDs, see the sections, "Buying Music Online from Apple" and "Importing into iTunes," later in this chapter.

Figure 1-2: The tracks of an audio CD.

If your Mac is connected to the Internet, iTunes presents the track information from the Internet for each song automatically after you insert the CD, as shown in Figure 1-3.

To play a track on the CD, click the track name, and then click the Play button. The Play button turns into a Pause button and the song plays.

When the song finishes, iTunes continues playing the songs in the list in sequence until you click the Pause button (which turns back into the Play button). You can skip to the next or previous song using the arrow keys on your keyboard, or by clicking the Forward or Back button next to the Play button.

The status display above the list of songs tells you the name of the artist and song (if known), and the elapsed time. If you click the Elapsed Time status, the status changes to the remaining time and then, with another click, to the total time (one more click brings you back to the elapsed time).

Rearranging and repeating tracks

You can rearrange the order of the tracks to automatically play them in any sequence you want — similar to programming a CD player. Click the upward-pointing arrow at the top of the first column in the song list, and it changes to a downward-pointing arrow, with the tracks in reverse order.

Figure 1-3: CD track info appears after iTunes consults with the Internet.

You can change the order of tracks played in sequence. Just press and hold the mouse button on the track number in the first column for the song, and drag it up or down in the list. You can set up the tracks to play in some completely different sequence.

Skipping tracks

To skip tracks so they don't play in sequence, click the box next to the song name to remove the check mark. Unselected songs are skipped when you play the entire sequence.

To remove a series of check marks simultaneously, hold down the ⌘ key while clicking a check mark.

Repeating a song list

You can repeat an entire song list by clicking the Repeat button at the bottom of the Source list on the left side of the iTunes window (or by choosing Controls➪ Repeat All). Click the Repeat button again to repeat the current song (or choose Controls➪Repeat One). Click it once more to return to normal playback (or choose Controls➪Repeat Off).

The Shuffle button, to the left of the Repeat button, plays the songs in the list in a random order, which can be fun. You can then press the arrow keys or the Back or Forward button to jump around in random order. Eject a CD by clicking the Eject button or by choosing Controls⇨Eject Disc.

Displaying Visuals

Visual effects can turn your Mac display into a lightshow for your amusement. You can watch a cool visual display of eye candy while the music plays — or leave it on like a sixties-style lava lamp. Click the Visual Effects button on the bottom right side of the iTunes window (or choose Visualize⇨Turn Visualizer On). The visual animation appears in the iTunes window and coordinates with the music.

In addition to the animation replacing the iTunes song list, an Options button replaces the Import button in the upper-right corner of the iTunes window. You can click the Options button to open the Visualizer Options dialog box, as shown in Figure 1-4.

The Visualizer Options dialog box offers the following options that affect the animation but not the performance of iTunes playing music:

- **Display frame rate:** Displays the frame rate of the animation along with the animation.
- **Cap frame rate at 30 fps:** Keeps the frame rate at 30 fps or lower, which is the speed of normal video.
- **Always display song info:** Displays the song name, artist, and album for the song currently playing, along with the animation.
- **Faster but rougher display:** The animation plays faster, with rougher graphics. Choose this option if your animation plays too slowly.

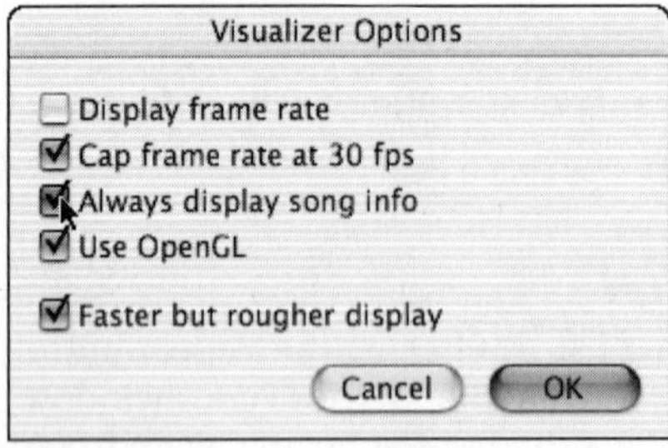

Figure 1-4: Set your options for visual effects.

The Visualizer menu in iTunes gives you even more control over visual effects. You can choose Visualize⇨Small or Visualize⇨Medium to display the visual effects in a rectangle inside the iTunes window, or Visualize⇨Large to fill the iTunes window. Choosing Visualize⇨Full Screen sets the visual effects to take over the entire screen. With full-screen visual effects, you can click the mouse or press the Escape key on your keyboard to stop the display and return to iTunes.

While the animated visual effects play, press Shift+slash (as in typing a question mark) to see a list of keyboard functions. Depending on the visual effect, you may see more choices of keyboard functions by pressing Shift+slash again.

To turn off visual effects, click the Visual Effects button again. You can leave the effects on (except when in full-screen mode) even while opening the equalizer, because you still have access to the playback controls. See the following section to find out how to change the equalizer settings.

Fine-Tuning the Sound

The jumping-bar displays you see on audio equipment are in most cases equalizers. An equalizer (EQ in audiospeak) enables you to fine-tune the specific sound spectrum frequencies. Adjusting bass and treble controls on a radio or stereo are simply cruder ways of adjusting these frequencies. An equalizer gives you far greater control over specific frequencies.

Using an equalizer preset

To see the iTunes equalizer, click the Equalizer button, on the bottom right side of the iTunes window. The Equalizer window appears, as shown in Figure 1-5. Chapter 3 of this book provides more details on enhancing the sound with the iTunes equalizer.

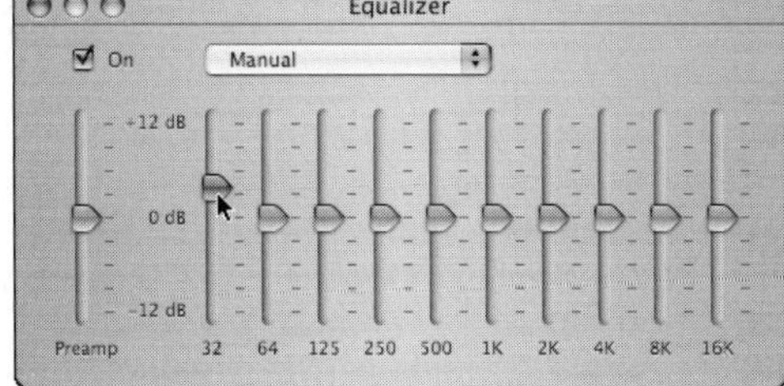

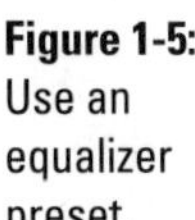

Figure 1-5: Use an equalizer preset.

You can select one of the preset values from the pop-up menu or adjust the frequencies manually by dragging the sliders up and down, just like a professional mixing console. We describe in detail how to use the equalizer in Chapter 3 of this book.

Cross-fading and controlling volume

You can fade the ending of one song into the beginning of the next one to slightly overlap songs, just like a radio DJ. Ordinarily, iTunes is set to have a short cross-fade — a short amount of time between the end of the fade in the first song and the start of the fade in the second song.

You can change this cross-fade setting by choosing iTunes⇨Preferences and then clicking the Effects button. You can turn the Crossfade Playback option on or off, and increase or decrease the amount of the cross-fade.

You can also adjust the volume for all the songs at once by sliding the volume slider in the upper-left section of the iTunes window. The maximum volume of the iTunes volume slider is the maximum set for the computer's sound in the Sound pane of System Preferences.

To adjust the volume of a particular song, click a song to select it, and then choose File⇨Get Info. In the Get Info dialog box, click the Options tab, and then drag the Volume Adjustment slider left or right to adjust the volume.

Some CDs play more loudly than others, and occasionally, individual tracks within a CD are louder than others. To ensure that all the songs in your library play at the same volume level, follow these steps:

1. **Choose iTunes⇨Preferences.**

   The Preferences window appears.
2. **Click the Effects button.**
3. **Select the Sound Check check box.**

   iTunes sets the volume for all songs according to the level of the slider.

Buying Music Online from Apple

When Apple announced its new music service, Apple chairman Steve Jobs remarked that other services put forward by the music industry tend to treat consumers like criminals. Steve had a point. Many of these services cost more and add a level of copy protection that prevents consumers from burning CDs or using the music they bought on other computers or portable MP3 players.

Apple did the research on how to make a service that worked better and was easier to use, and forged ahead with the Apple Music Store. By all accounts, Apple has succeeded in offering the easiest, fastest, and most cost-effective service for buying music for your Mac and iPod.

Visiting the Apple Music Store

As of this writing, the Apple Music Store offers more than 200,000 songs, with most songs $.99 each, and entire albums available at far less than the price you pay for the CD. You can play the songs on up to three different computers, burn your own CDs, and use them on players such as the iPod.

You can preview any song for up to 30 seconds, and if you already established your account, you can buy and download the song immediately. We don't know of a faster way to get a song.

To use the Apple Music Store:

1. **Click the Music Store option in the Source list.**

   The Music Store front page appears (see Figure 1-6), replacing the iTunes song list. The page lets you check out artists and songs to your heart's content, although you can't buy songs until you sign into a Music Store account. You can use the Choose Genre pop-up menu to specify music genres, or click links for new releases, exclusive tracks, and so on — just like any music service on the Web.

Figure 1-6: The Music Store front page.

2. **Click the Sign In button on the right to create an account or sign in to an existing account.**

   You need an account (with a credit card) to buy music. iTunes displays the account sign-in dialog box, as shown in Figure 1-7.

   If you already set up an account in the Apple Store, you're halfway there. Skip Step 3 and type in your Apple ID and password. Apple remembers the information you put in previously, so you don't have to re-enter it. If you forgot your password, click the Forgot Password? button, and iTunes provides a dialog box to answer your test question. If you answer correctly, your password is then e-mailed to you.

Figure 1-7: Signing into the Apple Music Store.

3. **To create an account, click the Create Account button.**

   iTunes displays a new page, replacing the iTunes front page, with an explanation of steps to create an account, and the terms of use.

4. **Click the Agree button, and fill in your personal account information.**

   iTunes displays the next page of the setup procedure, which requires you to type your e-mail address, password, test question and answer (in case you forget your password), birth date, and privacy options.

5. **Click Continue to go to the next page of the account setup procedure, and enter your credit card information.**

   Enter your personal credit card information. The entire procedure is secure, so you don't have to worry. The Music Store keeps your information on file and you don't have to type it again.

6. **Click Done to finish the procedure.**

Previewing a song

You may want to listen to a song before buying, or just browse the Store listening to song previews. Each preview lasts about 30 seconds. When you select an artist or a special offering, the browser window divides and gives you a list of songs you can select to play a preview, as shown in Figure 1-8.

The previews play on your computer off the Internet in a stream, so there may be a few hiccups in the playback.

Buying and playing songs

With an account set up, you can purchase songs and download them to your computer. Select a song and click the Buy button at the far right of the song (you may have to scroll your iTunes window horizontally). The store displays a warning to make sure you want to buy the song, and you can either go through with it or cancel. The song downloads automatically and shows up in your iTunes song list. Purchased songs also appear in a Purchased Music playlist in the iTunes library.

Figure 1-8: Previewing songs online in the Apple Music Store.

If for some reason your computer crashes or you quit before the download finishes, iTunes remembers to continue the download when you return to iTunes. If for some reason the download doesn't continue, choose Advanced⇨Check for Purchased Music to continue the download.

You don't have to use the 1-Click technology. You can instead add songs to a shopping cart in the store, to delay purchasing and downloading until you're ready. If you decide on the shopping cart method, the Buy button for each song changes to an Add Song button. When you're ready to purchase everything in your cart, click the Buy Now button to close the sale and download all the songs at once. To switch from 1-Click to a shopping cart, check out the section, "Setting the Music Store preferences."

All sales are final. If your computer's hard disk crashes and you lose your information, you also lose your songs — you have to purchase and download them again. But you can mitigate this kind of disaster by backing up your music library, which we describe in detail in Chapter 2 of this book. You can also burn your purchased songs onto an audio CD, as we describe in Chapter 4 of this book.

Handling authorization

The computer you use to set up your account is automatically authorized by Apple to play the songs you buy. Fortunately, the songs aren't locked to that computer — you can copy them to another computer and play them from within the other computer's iTunes program. When you first play them, iTunes asks for your Apple Music Store ID and password in order to authorize that computer. You can authorize up to three computers at a time. If you want to add a fourth computer, you can deauthorize a computer by choosing Advanced⇨Deauthorize Account.

After you set up an account, you can sign into the Music Store at any time to buy music, view or change the information in your account, and see your purchase history. To see your account information and purchase history, click the View Account link in the store after signing in with your ID and password. Every time you buy music, you get an e-mail from the Apple Music Store with the purchase information.

Setting the Music Store preferences

Your decision to download each song immediately or add to a shopping cart and download later will likely be based on how your computer connects to the Internet. If you have a slow connection, you probably want to use the shopping cart method.

You can change your preferences with the Apple Music Store by choosing iTunes⇨Preferences, and in the Preferences window, clicking the Store button at the top of the window. The Store Preferences window appears, as shown in Figure 1-9. The Store Preferences window enables you to change from 1-Click to Shopping Cart or vice-versa. You also have a choice of playing songs after downloading, and loading a complete song preview before playing the preview. This last option provides better playing performance (fewer hiccups) with previews over slow Internet connections.

If you use more than one computer with your account, you can set the preferences for each computer differently while still using the same account. For example, your store-authorized home computer may have a faster connection than your authorized PowerBook on the road, and you can set your iTunes preferences accordingly.

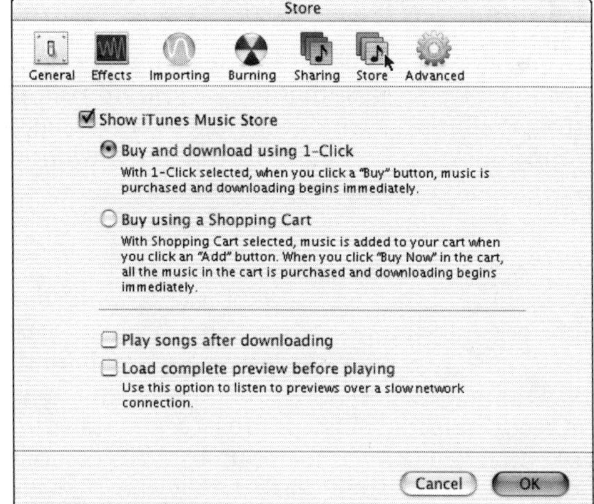

Figure 1-9: Setting your preferences for the Apple Music Store.

Importing into iTunes

To immortalize your music, you need to import it into iTunes from your audio CDs and other sources. After you put music into the iTunes library, you can preserve it forever. You can make backup copies with perfect quality.

Importing from a CD is called *ripping* a CD. We're not sure why it came to be called that, but Apple certainly took the term to a new level with an ad campaign for Macs a while back that featured the slogan "Rip, Mix, Burn." Burning was the hip thing to do a few years ago. Now, you only have to rip and mix — with an iPod, burning CDs to play your music wherever you go isn't necessary.

Ripping, in technical terms, is the process of compressing the song's digital information and encoding it in a particular sound file format. The ripping process is straightforward, but the settings you choose for importing affect sound quality, disk space (and iPod space), and compatibility with other types of players and computers. Chapter 3 of this book provides an in-depth look at these encoders and quality settings; for now, we show you how to do it and provide suggestions for settings.

Ripping music from CDs

Though importing music from an audio CD takes a lot less time than playing the CD, it still takes time. We suggest that before you rip your first CD, you look at the Importing Preferences window by choosing iTunes⇨Preferences, and then clicking the Importing button at the top of the window. The Importing Preferences window appears, as shown in Figure 1-10.

Figure 1-10: Check your preferences for ripping CDs.

Note the type of encoding selected in the Import Using pop-up menu and the quality setting in the Setting pop-up menu and consider these options:

- **Import Using:** Set this to AAC Encoder, which is the same as the format used by the Apple Music Store, or the MP3 Encoder, which is the standard for online music files. The other formats are for higher-quality uncompressed music files. Chapter 3 of this book provides a more in-depth look at these choices.
- **Setting:** Set this to High Quality for most music. You can change this setting to get better quality or use disk space more efficiently, as we describe in Chapter 3 of this book.

To rip a CD, follow these steps:

1. **Insert an audio CD.**

   The songs appear in your song list as generic unnamed tracks at first. If the track names don't appear in a minute, connect to the Internet and choose Advanced⇨Get CD Track Names.

2. **(Optional) Click to remove the check mark next to any songs on the CD that you don't want to import.**

   iTunes imports the songs that have check marks next to them; when you remove the check mark next to a song, iTunes skips that song.

3. **(Optional) To remove the gap of silence between songs that segue together, select those songs and choose Advanced⇨Join CD Tracks.**

   The tracks on many music CDs are separate but the end of one song merges into the beginning of the next song. You don't want an annoying half-second gap between the songs.

   To select multiple songs, click the first one, and then hold down the ⌘ key to click each subsequent song. To click several songs consecutively, click the first one and hold down the Shift key and click the last one.

4. **Click the Import button at the top right of the iTunes window.**

   The status display shows the progress of the operation. To cancel, click the small x next to the progress bar.

   iTunes plays the songs as they import. You can click the Pause button to stop playback. You can also stop the playback by choosing iTunes⇨Preferences and clicking the Importing button. Uncheck the Play Songs While Importing option in the Importing Preferences window.

   As iTunes finishes importing each song, it chimes and displays a green check mark next to the song.

5. **Click the Eject button at the bottom right of the iTunes window after all the songs import.**

   You can also choose Controls⇨Eject Disc to eject the disc.

Importing music files from other sources

The quality of the music you hear depends on the quality of the source. Web sites and services offering MP3 files vary widely. Some sites provide high-quality, legally derived MP3 songs, and some don't. Anyone can create MP3 files, so beware of less-than-high-quality knockoffs and sites that offer free music.

Some sites offer only streaming audio, just like a Web radio station (described in the "Listening to Web Radio" section, later in this chapter). If you download something that turns out to be just a Web address (a URL), you can still use that with iTunes — a broadcast symbol appears next to the song in your library, just like a Web radio station.

Whether you download the music file or copy it from another hard disk, you need to save it on your hard disk. After you save or copy an MP3 file — or for that matter an AIFF or WAV file — on your hard disk, you can simply drag it into the iTunes window to import it to your library. If you drag a folder or disk icon, all the audio files it contains are added to your iTunes Library. Choose File⇨Add to Library as an alternative to dragging.

Adding your own pet sounds

No, we're not talking about sounds your pet may have made. We're referring instead to your favorite music or sounds that can't be found on CD or, believe it or not, on the Internet. The ***Pet Sounds Sessions*** box set by the Beach Boys includes just about every spoken word and sneeze in the studio during the recording, and you may have equally unusual sounds or rare music that can't be found anywhere else. How do you get stuff like that into iTunes?

Sound can be imported from almost anywhere:

- **Internet:** You can import MP3 music files from Web sites by first downloading the MP3 files to your Mac. You can also link to Web radio stations, but you can't capture the songs from Web broadcasts.
- **Professional editing programs:** You can import high-quality AIFF-format or WAV-format files from music editing programs. These programs typically record from any analog source device, such as a tape player or even a turntable for playing vinyl records.
- **Any analog source:** You can record music directly into a digital file from the Mac's line-in connector using the Sound Studio program, found in the Applications folder in Mac OS X systems (you can use it for about two weeks before paying for it). You can connect any music source to the line-in connector, including home stereos with turntables for playing vinyl records, or even a microphone for recording live directly into the Mac. (The Sound Studio program may not be bundled with all systems. You can download an application to check it out at `http://www.felttip.com/products/sound studio/`.)

You can import any sound saved in an MP3, AIFF, or WAV sound file, including your own voice recorded to disk using the Mac microphone and a program such as Sound Studio. You may want to create special sound effects to use with photo slideshows in iPhoto, videos in iMovie, or DVD menus in iDVD. You can import the sound effects file once into your iTunes Library, and use it in all three types of projects.

Voice recordings tend to be low-fidelity, so we recommend using the MP3 Encoder with the Good Quality setting (128 Kbps), rather than higher quality settings. Sound effects and voice recordings are typically mono rather than stereo — but you can also select the Custom setting to force the importing to be mono or stereo, as described in Chapter 3 of this book.

To record directly into your Mac from either a home stereo system, or through a microphone (either the Mac built-in microphone, an external microphone that connects to the Mac, or a USB microphone that connects through the Mac USB port), you can use Sound Studio, which is available free for a two-week trial period. For newer Macs that no longer have the line-in connections, you can purchase a USB audio input device, such as the Griffin iMic or the Roland UA-30.

When you add a song to your iTunes Library, a copy is placed inside the iTunes Music folder, which you can view in the Finder. (The iTunes Music folder lives in the Music folder of your Home directory/folder.) The original is not changed or moved. You can then convert the song to another format — for example, you can convert an AIFF file to an MP3 file — while leaving the original intact. We describe converting songs in Chapter 3 of this book.

Importing Audio Books

Do you like to listen to audio books and spoken magazine and newspaper articles? Not only can you bring these sounds into iTunes, but you can also transfer them to an iPod and take them on the road, which is much more convenient than taking cassettes or CDs.

Audible is a leading provider of downloadable spoken audio files. Audible lets you enable up to three computers to play the audio files, just like the Apple Music Store. Audible does require that you purchase the files.

To import Audible files, follow these steps:

1. **Go to `www.audible.com` and set up an account if you don't already have one.**
2. **Choose and download an Audible audio file.**

   These are files whose names end with ".aa".
3. **Drag the Audible file to the iTunes window.**

   If this is the first time you've added an Audible file, iTunes asks for your account information. You need only to enter this information once for each computer you use with your Audible account.

To disable an Audible account, open iTunes on the computer that will no longer be used with the account, and choose Advanced➪Deauthorize Computer, and in the Deauthorize Computer dialog box, choose the Deauthorize Computer for Audible Account option, and click OK. Remember that you need to be online to authorize or deauthorize a computer.

Listening to Web Radio

Now you can reach radio stations on the Internet that represent nearly every area of the world. You can tune into RadioNorba for the top 40 hits in Italy, or Radio Retro from Moscow, or AryaLive Radio for Persian, Farsi, and Iranian music and talk radio. Check out the local news and sports from your hometown no matter where you are. Listen to talk radio and music shows from all over the country and the world.

You can't record or save a song from a radio broadcast without special software. But you can add your favorite stations to your music library or to a playlist to tune in quickly and easily. You can also tune in any Web radio or streaming broadcast if you know the Web address.

Streaming music from the Internet

Apple provides links within iTunes directly to radio stations on the Internet, so you may want to try these first. Follow these steps:

1. **Click the Radio option in the Source list.**

   The iTunes window displays a list of categories of radio stations, as shown in Figure 1-11.

2. **Click the Refresh button to retrieve the latest radio stations.**

   More Web radio stations are added all the time. The Refresh button in the top-right corner of the iTunes window (taking the place of the Browse button) connects iTunes to the Internet to retrieve the latest list of radio stations for each category.

3. **Click the triangle next to a category name to open the list of radio streams in that category.**

   Radio station broadcasts stream to your computer over the Internet — sections of the audio transfer and play while more sections transfer so that you hear it as a continual stream. Some large radio stations offer more than one stream.

4. **Select a stream and click the Play button.**

   Within seconds you hear live radio off the Web.

If you use a modem connection to the Internet, you may want to choose a stream with a bit rate of less than 56 Kbps for best results. The Bit Rate column shows the bit rate for each stream.

Figure 1-11: Selecting a Web radio station.

iTunes creates a buffer for the audio stream so that you hear continuous playback with fewer Internet-related hiccups than most Web radio software. The buffer temporarily stores as much of the stream as possible, adding more of the stream to the end of the buffer as you play the audio in the buffer. If you hear stutters, gaps, or hiccups when playing a stream, set your buffer to a larger size by choosing iTunes⇨Preferences. In the Preferences window, click the Advanced button, and then choose a size from the pop-up menu for Streaming Buffer Size. Your choices are Small, Medium, or Large (sorry, no X-Large).

Saving your favorite stations

Car radios offer preset stations activated by you pressing a button. Of course, you first need to tune into the station of your choice. You can do the same with iTunes, only the process is much easier:

1. **Select a radio station stream.**
2. **Create a playlist, or scroll the Source list to an existing playlist.**

   See Chapter 2 of this book to discover how to create a playlist.
3. **Drag the stream name over the playlist name.**

   iTunes places the stream name in the playlist with a broadcast icon next to it. You can click the playlist name and rearrange the playlist as you want, dragging stream names as you would drag song names.

Drag as many steams as you like to as many playlists as you like. Radio streams in your playlists play only if you are connected to the Internet.

To quickly create a playlist from selected radio streams, first select the streams (by holding down Shift or the ⌘ key to make multiple selections), and then choose File⇨New Playlist from Selection.

Adding Web broadcasts

Millions of Web sites offer temporary streaming audio broadcasts all the time. A rock group on tour may offer a broadcast of a special concert, available for only one day. You may want to tune in weekly or monthly broadcasts such as high-tech talk shows, news programs, documentaries, or sporting events . . . the list is endless. You may even have access to private broadcasts such as corporate board meetings.

As of this writing, iTunes supports only MP3 broadcasts. You can find lots of MP3 broadcasts at `www.shoutcast.com` and `live365.com`.

All you need to know is the Web address, also known as the URL (Uniform Resource Locator) — the global address of documents and other resources on the Web. You can find most URLs from a Web site or e-mail about a broadcast. Then follow these steps:

1. **Choose Advanced⇨Open Stream.**

   The Open Stream dialog box appears, with a URL text field for typing a Web address.

2. **Type the exact, full URL of the stream, as shown in Figure 1-12.**

   Include the http: prefix as in `http://64.236.34.141:80/stream/1014`.

   If you're connected to the Internet, iTunes automatically retrieves the broadcast and places it at the end of your song list.

Figure 1-12: Enter the URL to play any Web streaming broadcast.

Chapter 2: Organizing Your Library

In This Chapter

- **Browsing the library and searching for songs**
- **Adding and editing song information**
- **Creating custom and automatic smart playlists**
- **Backing up your library and sharing music over a network**

The iTunes library is awesome even by jukebox standards — it can hold up to 32,000 songs depending on your disk space. Finding Chuck Berry's "Maybelline" is a challenge using a rotating dial of 32,000 songs. And its companion, the 30GB iPod portable music player, can hold about 7,500 songs — that's enough music to last two weeks if played 24 hours a day!

Even if you keep your iTunes library down to the size of what you can fit on your iPod, you still have a formidable collection at your fingertips. If you're a music lover, you'll want to organize this collection to make finding songs easier.

In this chapter, we show you how to organize your songs in iTunes. You can find any song in seconds and display songs sorted by artist, album, genre of music, or other attributes. You can grab song information from the Internet and add and edit the information to make organizing more useful. Grabbing and editing the information is important because you don't want your imported CD music to have song titles like "Track 1" — you don't want to mistakenly play "My Guitar Wants to Kill Your Mama" by Frank Zappa when trying to impress your classical music teacher with Tchaikovsky's 3rd Movement, Pathétique Symphony do you?

This chapter also explains how to create *playlists,* which are lists of songs to be played, transferred to an iPod, or burned to a CD. iTunes even offers smart playlists — playlists that generate their own lists without your help — based on the song information (which is another good reason to edit the information). You also find out how to make a backup of your library — a very important operation, especially if you purchase songs that don't exist anywhere else.

I've Been Searching . . . Browsing and Sorting, Too

You rip a few CDs, buy some songs from the Apple Music Store, and you watch your music library fill up with songs. That song list is getting longer and longer, and as a result, your library is harder to navigate. Selecting songs to play in a proper order also is harder. Shouldn't a computer be able to do these things? Of course it can.

Browsing by artist and album

You can switch to the Browse view to find songs more easily. The Browse view is useful as long as you track information for the songs. You aren't overwhelmed by a long list of songs — when you select an album, iTunes displays only the songs for that album.

To select the Browse view, click the Browse button in the upper-right corner. iTunes organizes your music library by artist and album, which makes finding just the right tunes easier, as shown in Figure 2-1. Click the Browse button again to return to List view. The Browse button toggles between the two views.

The Browse view sorts by artist, and within each artist, by album. This type of column arrangement is a tree structure, although it looks more like a fallen tree.

When you click an artist in the Artist column on the left side (as shown in Figure 2-2) the album titles appear in the Album column on the right. At the top of this Album column, the All selection is highlighted, and all of the songs appear in the Song Name list.

Figure 2-1: Click the Browse button to browse the iTunes library.

Figure 2-2: Select an artist in the Browse view to see the list of albums for that artist.

To see more than one artist's albums at a time, hold down the ⌘ key and click each artist's name. iTunes displays all of the albums.

As you click different albums in the Album column, the Song Name list displays the songs from that album. The songs are listed in proper track order, just as the artist intended them.

This is great for selecting songs from albums, but what if you want to look at all the songs in the library at once? See all the songs in the iTunes library by selecting the All option in the Album column. You can return to the default List view by clicking the Browse button.

Understanding the song indicators

As you make choices in iTunes, it displays an action indicator next to each song to show you what iTunes is doing. Here's a list of indicators and what they mean:

- **Moving zigzag:** iTunes is importing the song.
- **Green check mark:** iTunes finished importing the song.
- **Exclamation point:** iTunes can't find the song. You may have moved or deleted the song accidentally. Drag the song from the Finder to the iTunes window.
- **Broadcast icon:** The song is on the Internet, and iTunes plays it as a music stream.
- **Black check mark:** Songs marked for the next operation, such as importing from an audio CD or playing in sequence.
- **Speaker:** The song is currently playing.

✦ **Chasing arrows:** iTunes is copying the song from another location or downloading the song from the Internet.

Changing viewing options

iTunes gives you the ability to customize a song list. The list starts out with the Song Name, Time, Artist, Album, Genre, My Rating, Play Count, and Last Played categories — you may have to drag the horizontal scroll bar along the bottom of the song list to see all these columns. You can display more or less information, or different information, in your song list; you can also display columns in a different order from left to right, or with wider or narrower column widths.

You can make a column fatter or thinner by dragging the dividing line between the column and the next column. As you move your cursor over the divider, it changes to a double-ended arrow; you can click and drag the divider to change the column's width.

You can also change the order of columns from left to right by clicking a column header and dragging the entire column to the left or right.

Maybe you don't like certain columns — they take up valuable screen space. Or perhaps you want to display some other information about the song. You can add or remove columns such as Size (for file size), Date and Year (for the date the album was released, or any other date you choose for each song), Bit Rate, Sample Rate, Track Number, and Comment. To add or delete columns, choose Edit⇨View Options.

The View Options window appears as shown in Figure 2-3, and you can select the columns you want to appear in the song list. To pick a column, click the check box next to the column header so that a black check mark appears. Any unchecked column headers are columns that do *not* appear. ***Note:*** The Song Name column always appears in the listing and can't be removed. You can also view the same options by ⌘+clicking any of the column headings.

The viewing options you choose depend on your music playing habits. You may want to display the Time column to know at a glance the duration of any song. You may want the Date or Year columns to differentiate songs from different eras, or the Genre column to differentiate songs from different musical genres.

You can also browse by genre in the Browse view, rather than by artist. To add a Genre column to the Browse view, choose iTunes⇨Preferences and click the General button at the top of the Preferences window. In the General Preferences window that appears, select the Show Genre When Browsing option.

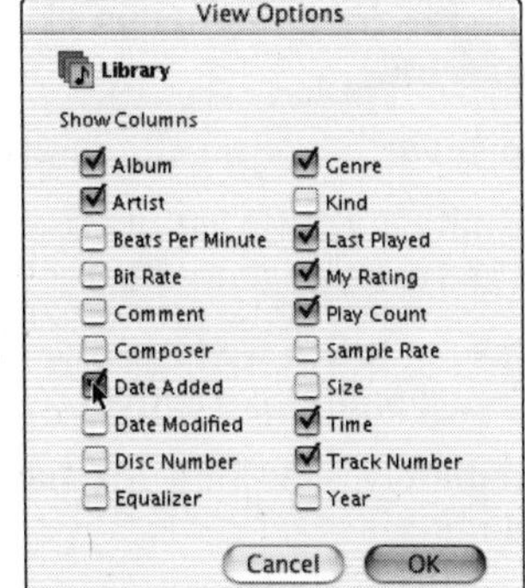

Figure 2-3: The viewing options for the song list.

Sorting songs by viewing options

Knowing how to set viewing options is a good idea because you can then sort the listing of songs by them. Whether you're in Browse view or viewing the song list in its entirety, the column headers double as sorting options.

For example, if you click the Time header, the songs reorder by their duration in ascending order — starting with the shortest song. If you click the Time header again, the sort is reversed, starting with the longest song. This can be useful if you are looking for songs of a certain length — for example, looking for a song to match the length of a slideshow in iPhoto (see Book II) or a movie clip in iMovie (see Book III).

You can tell which way the sort is sorting — ascending or descending order — by the little arrow indicator in the header. When the arrow is pointing up, the sort is in ascending order; when down, it is in descending order.

You can sort the song list in alphabetical order. Click the Artist header to sort all the songs in the list by the artist name, in alphabetical order (the arrow points up). Click it again to sort the list in reverse alphabetical order (the arrow points down).

Searching for songs

As your music library grows, you may find locating a particular song by the usual browsing and scrolling methods that we describe earlier in this chapter time consuming. So . . . let iTunes find your songs for you!

Locate the Search field — the oval field in the top-right corner, to the left of the Browse button — and follow these steps:

1. **Click in the Search field, and type the first characters of your search term, using these tips for best searching.**
   - You can search for a song title, an artist, or an album title.
   - Typing very few characters results in a long list of possible songs, but the search narrows down as you type more characters.
   - The Search features ignores case — when we type *miles*, it finds "Eight Miles High" as well as "She Smiles Like a River."

   The search operation works immediately, searching for matches in the Song Name, Artist, and Album columns.
2. **The results display as you type.**

   If you're in Browse view with an artist and a particular album selected, you can't search for another artist or song. Why not? Browsing *with* searching narrows your search further. The song you are looking for isn't on the selected album you are browsing.

If you want to search the entire library, first click the All selection at the top of the Artist column to browse the entire library, before using the Search field. Or if you prefer, turn off the Browse view by clicking the Browse button again, and use the Search field with the library's song list.

To back out of a search so that the full list appears again, you can either click the circled X in the Search field, or delete the characters in the Search field. You then see the entire list of songs in your library, just as before. All the songs are still there, and remain there unless you explicitly remove them. Searching only manipulates your view of them.

The Singer, Not the Song: Adding and Editing Information

Organization depends on information. You expect the computer to do a lot more than just store this music with "Untitled Disc" and "Track 1" as the only identifiers. Song names, album titles, composer credits, and release dates may seem trivial. But you can use the song information to search for songs or sort song lists, and the information is absolutely necessary for making smart playlists.

Adding all the song information seems like a lot of trouble, but that ol' Mac magic comes through for you. You can get most of the information automatically, without typing.

Automatic dialup

If your computer uses a modem, iTunes triggers the modem automatically (like a Web browser). It can call your service provider and complete the connection process before retrieving the track information.

At that point, your Internet service may still be on until the service hangs up on you. You may want to switch to a browser, without quitting iTunes, and surf the Web to make use of the connection — iTunes continues to import or play the music while you surf.

You can *stop* an automatic modem connection as quickly as possible — if your service provider or phone service charges extra fees based on timed usage. When iTunes finishes importing, switch to your remote connection program without quitting iTunes, terminate the Internet connection, and then switch back to iTunes.

Retrieving information from the Internet

Why type song information if someone else has typed it? You can get information about most commercial CDs from the Internet. However, you need to check your Internet connection first.

During the setup process you can control whether iTunes connects automatically or manually to the Internet. In Chapter 1 of this book we describe how, when you first start iTunes, the Setup Assistant helps you through the process of setting it up. You can change of the setup of your Internet connection at any time, by following these steps:

1. **Choose iTunes⇨Preferences.**
2. **Click the General button.**
3. **Select the Connect to Internet When Needed option.**

   When on, iTunes connects automatically; when off, iTunes asks first.

You can connect to the Internet at any time, if you're not automatically connected, and get the song information when you need it. After you connect, choose Advanced⇨Get CD Track Names from the iTunes menu.

Even if you automatically connect to the Internet, the song information database on the Internet (known as CDDB) may be momentarily unavailable, or you have a delayed response. If at first you don't succeed, choose Advanced⇨Get CD Track Names.

Long distance information: The CDDB database

The first time we popped an audio CD into the Mac was like magic. iTunes, after thinking for less than a minute, displayed the song names, album title, and artist names automatically. How did it know? This information isn't stored on a standard music CD — you have to either recognize the disc somehow or read the liner notes.

The magic is that the software knows how to reach out and find the information on the Internet, in a music database known as CDDB. The site (`www.cddb.com`) that hosts CDDB on the Web offers the ability to search for music CDs by artist, song title, and other methods. The iTunes software already knows how to use this database, so you don't have to!

iTunes finds the track information by first looking up a key identifying number on the audio CD — a secret number stored on every publicly released music CD. iTunes uses this number to find the information within the CDDB database. The CDDB database keeps track information for most of the music CDs released in the global commercial market.

While the database doesn't contain any information about personal or custom CDs, people can submit information to the database about CDs that the database doesn't know about. You can even do this from within iTunes — type the information for each track while the audio CD is in your Mac, and then choose Advanced➪Submit CD Track Names. The information you typed is sent to the CDDB site, where the good people who work tirelessly on the database check out your information before including it. In fact, if you spot a typo or something erroneous in the information you receive from CDDB, you can correct it, and then use the Submit CD Track Names command to send the corrected version back to the CDDB site. The good folks there appreciate the effort.

Editing artist and band names

At some time or another you may want to edit artist and band names that come in from the Internet. When the artist is a single individual — a solo artist — we like to list the artist by last name rather than first name, as CDDB does. For example, we routinely change the name of the artist derived from CDDB, which comes in as, "Miles Davis" and we'd rather have it be "Davis, Miles."

Other annoyances, such as bands that normally have "The" in front of their names, often occur. "The Who," for example, is listed that way in the CDDB database, and so are The Band, The Beatles, and The Beach Boys. We dislike having "The" before the band name, so we routinely change it.

You can edit a song's information in either Browse view or the song list view. Edit a song's track information by clicking directly in the field, and clicking again so that the mouse pointer turns into an editing cursor. You can then select the text and type over it, or use ⌘+C (copy), ⌘+X (cut), and ⌘+V (paste) to move tiny bits of text around within the field. As you can see in Figure 2-4, we changed the Artist field to be "Beck, Jeff."

TIP

We prefer working directly with the song list (with Browse view turned off) when editing song information.

Figure 2-4: Click inside the Artist field to edit the information.

You can edit the Song Name, Artist, Album, Genre, and My Ratings fields right in the song list. But editing this information with File⇨Get Info is easier. Keep reading to find out more info.

Speed editing multiple songs

Editing in the song list is fine if you're editing the information for one song, but typically you need to change all the tracks of an audio CD. For example, if a CD of songs by Bob Dylan is listed with the artist as "Bob Dylan" you may want to change all the songs at once to "Dylan, Bob." Changing all the song information in one fell swoop, of course, is fast and clean, but like most powerful shortcuts, you need to be careful because it can be dangerous.

You can change a group of songs in either Browse view or the song list view. To change a group of songs at once, follow these steps:

1. **Select a group of songs by clicking the first song and holding down the Shift key while you click the last song.**

   The last song, and all the songs between the first and last, highlight at once. You can add to a selection by Shift-clicking other songs, and you can remove songs from the selection by holding down the ⌘ key when clicking (*Command-click* in Mac jargon).

2. **Choose File⇨Get Info, or press ⌘+I.**

   A warning message displays `Are you sure you want to edit information for multiple items?`

   Like speed skating, speed editing is dangerous. If, for example, you change the song name, *the entire selection* then has that song name. Be careful about what you edit when doing this. We recommend leaving the Do Not Ask Me Again warning option unchecked, so that the warning appears whenever you try this.

3. **Click the Yes button.**

   The Multiple Song Information window appears, as shown in Figure 2-5.

4. **Edit the field you want to change (typically the Artist field) for the multiple songs.**

   When you edit a field, a check mark appears automatically in the box next to the field. iTunes assumes you want that field changed throughout the song selection. Make sure no other box is checked except the field you want, which is typically the Artist field (and perhaps the Genre field).

5. **Click OK to make the change.**

   iTunes changes the field for the entire selection of songs.

You can edit the song information *before* importing the audio tracks from a CD. The edited track information for the CD imports with the music. (What's interesting is that when you access the library without the audio CD, the edited version of the track information is still there — iTunes remembers CD information from the CDs you inserted before. Even if you don't import the CD tracks, iTunes remembers the edited song information until the next time you insert that audio CD.)

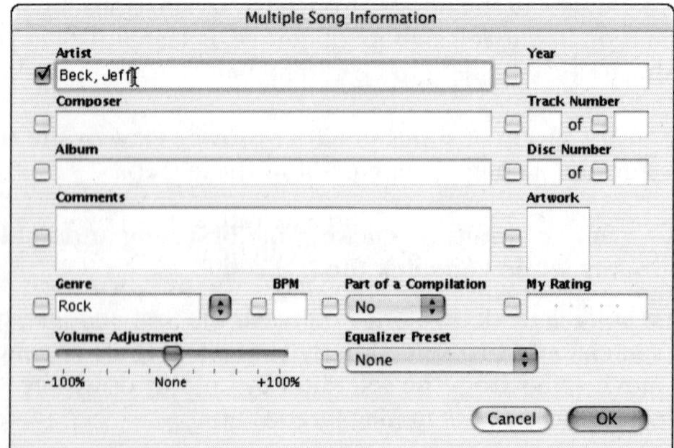

Figure 2-5: Change the artist name for multiple songs at once.

Adding liner notes and ratings

While the track information grabbed from the Internet is usually enough, you probably won't find it complete, or that it matches your personal taste. Your ratings and Genre choices make creating playlists automatically possible (as described later in this chapter).

Some facts, such as composer credits, may not be included in the information grabbed from the Internet. However, composer information is important for iPod users, because the iPod allows you to scroll music by composer as well as by artist, album, and song. Adding composer credits is usually worth your while because you can then search, sort, and create playlists based on this information.

After your songs import into the music library, locate a single song and choose File⇨Get Info (or ⌘+I). You see the Song Information window, as shown in Figure 2-6. The Song Information window offers the following tabs to click for different panes:

✦ **Summary:** The Summary tab offers useful information about the music file's format and location on your hard disk, its file size, as well as information about the digital compression method (bit rate, sample rate, and so on), which you can read about in Chapter 3 of this book.

✦ **Info:** The Info tab allows you to change the song name, artist, composer, album, genre, and year, and you can add comments.

✦ **Options:** The Options tab offers volume adjustment, choice of equalizer preset, ratings, and start and stop times for each song. We describe these settings in Chapter 3 of this book. You can assign up to five stars to a song (your own rating system, equivalent to the Top 40 charts).

✦ **Artwork:** The Artwork tab allows you to add or delete artwork for the song (the Apple Music Store supplies artwork with most songs).

You may have noticed the My Top Rated playlist in the Source list. This playlist is an example of a *smart playlist* — a playlist that updates itself when ratings are changed. The My Top Rated playlist plays all the top-rated songs in the library.

The cool thing about ratings is that they're *yours*. You can use them to mean anything you want. For example, you may rate songs based on how much you like them, or whether your mother can hear them, or how they blend into a work environment. Then you can use the My Top Rated playlist to automatically play the top-rated songs in the library. You find out more about playlists later in this chapter, in the section, "Comprising a Smart Playlist."

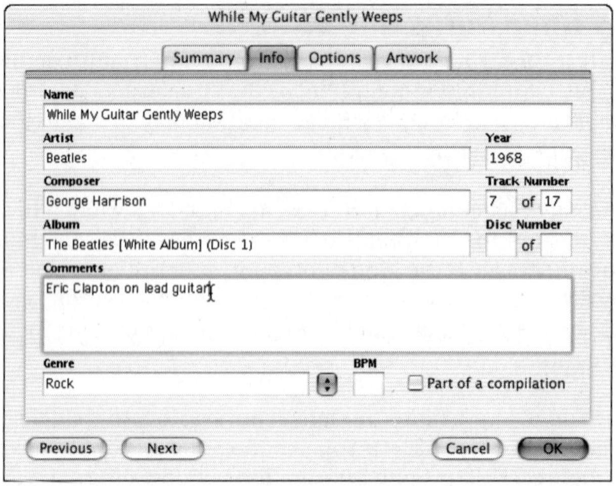

Figure 2-6: View and edit the song information.

Play It Again, Sam: Using Playlists

To organize your music for different operations, such as copying to an iPod or burning a CD, you make a list of the songs called a *playlist.* You can also use playlists to organize your music and play DJ. Select love songs from different albums to play the next time you need a romantic mood. Compile a list of surf songs for a trip to the beach. We create playlists specifically for use with an iPod on road trips, and others that combine songs from different albums based on themes or similarities.

You can create as many playlists of songs, in any order, as you want. The files don't change, nor are they copied — the music files stay right where they are, only their names are stored in the playlists. You can even create a smart playlist that automatically adds songs to itself based on the criteria you set up.

Creating a playlist of multiple songs

The Mac was made for this: dragging items visually to arrange a sequence. Save yourself a lot of browsing time by creating playlists — which, by the way, can really improve the way you use music with an iPod. You can drag individual songs and entire albums into a playlist and rearrange the songs quickly and easily. To create a playlist, follow these steps:

1. **Click the + button or choose File⇨New Playlist.**

   The + button, in the bottom-left corner of the iTunes window under the Source list, creates a new playlist in the Source list named "untitled playlist."

2. **Type a name for the playlist.**

   The playlist appears in the Source list, as shown in Figure 2-7. After you type a new name, iTunes automatically sorts it into alphabetical order in the Source list, underneath the preset smart playlists and other sources.

3. **Select the library in the Source list, and drag songs from the library to the playlist.**

Figure 2-7: Creating a playlist and adding songs.

4. **Select the playlist in the Source list, and drag songs to rearrange the list.**

   The order of songs in the playlist is based on the order in which you drag them to the list. To move a song up the list and scroll at the same time, drag it over the up-arrow in the first column (the song number); to move a song down the list and scroll, drag it to the bottom of the list. You can move a group of songs at once by selecting them (using click and Shift-click or ⌘+click).

You can drag songs from other playlists to a playlist. ***Remember:*** Only links are copied, not the actual files. Besides dragging songs, you can also rearrange a playlist by sorting the list — click the Song Name, Time, Artist column headings, and so on. And when you double-click a playlist, it opens in its own window, displaying the song list.

To create a playlist quickly, select multiple songs at once (using Shift-click or ⌘+click), and then choose File➪New Playlist from Selection. You can then type a name for the playlist.

Creating a playlist of multiple albums

You may want to play entire albums of songs without having to select each album as you play them. You may want to use an iPod, for example, on that long drive from London to Liverpool, and play Beatles albums in the order they were released (or perhaps the reverse order, reversing the Beatles' career from London back to Liverpool).

To create a playlist of entire albums in a particular order, follow these steps:

1. **Create a new playlist.**

   Create a playlist by clicking the + sign under the Source list, or choosing File➪New Playlist. Type a name for the new playlist.

2. **Select the library in the Source list, and click the Browse button to find the artist.**

   The Album list appears in the right panel.

3. **Drag the album name over the playlist name.**

4. **Select and drag each subsequent album over the playlist name.**

   Each time you drag an album, iTunes automatically lists the songs in the proper track sequence.

You can rename a playlist at any time by clicking its name and typing a new one, just like any filename in the Finder.

Generating a Smart Playlist

At the top of the Source list, indicated by a gear icon, you can find what Apple (and everyone else) calls smart playlists. iTunes comes with a few sample smart playlists, such as the My Top Rated playlist we mention earlier in this chapter, and you can create your own. Smart playlists add songs to themselves based on prearranged criteria. For example, as you rate your songs, the My Top Rated playlist changes to reflect your new ratings. You don't have to set anything up — My Top Rated is already defined for you.

The smart playlists are actually ignorant of your taste in music. You can create one that grabs all the songs from 1966, only to find that the list includes "Eleanor Rigby," "Strangers in the Night," "Over Under Sideways Down," and "River Deep, Mountain High" (in no particular order) — which you may not want to hear at the same time. You may want to fine-tune your criteria.

Viewing and editing a smart playlist

To view and edit a smart playlist, select the playlist and choose File➪Edit Smart Playlist. The Smart Playlist window appears, with the criteria for the smart playlist. You may want to modify the smart playlist so songs with a higher rating are picked — simply add another star or two to the My Rating criteria. You can also choose to limit the playlist to a certain number of songs, selected by various methods such as random, most recently played, and so on.

Setting up a new smart playlist

To create a new smart playlist, choose File➪New Smart Playlist. The Smart Playlist window appears, giving you the following choices for setting criteria:

- **Match the Following Condition:** You can select from the first pop-up menu any of the categories used for song information, and select an operator, such as the greater than or less than operators from the second pop-up — combine them to express a condition: `Year is greater than 1966` or something like that. You can also add multiple conditions by clicking the + button, and then deciding whether to match all or any of these conditions.
- **Limit To:** You can make the smart playlist a specific duration, measured by the number of songs, time, or size in megabytes or gigabytes. Limiting a smart playlist to what can fit on a CD, or for the duration of a drive or jogging exercise with an iPod is useful. You can select the songs by various methods such as random, most recently played, and so on.
- **Match Only Checked Songs:** This selects only songs that have a black check mark beside them, along with the rest of the criteria. Checking and unchecking songs is an easy way to fine-tune your selection for a smart playlist.
- **Live Updating:** This allows iTunes to automatically update the playlist continually, as you add or remove songs from the library.

After setting up the criteria, click OK to create the smart playlist. iTunes creates the playlist with a gear icon and the name "untitled playlist." You can click in the playlist and type a new name for it.

Setting up multiple criteria gives you the opportunity to create playlists that are way smarter than the ones supplied with iTunes. For example, we created a smart playlist with criteria shown in Figure 2-8 that does the following:

- ✦ Adds any song added to the library in the past week that *also* has a rating greater than three stars.
- ✦ Limits the playlist to 72 minutes of music to fit on an audio CD, and refines the selection to the most recently added if the entire selection becomes greater than 72 minutes.
- ✦ Matches only checked songs and performs live updating.

Figure 2-8: Create a smart playlist with multiple conditions.

You can export a playlist and import it into a different computer, in order to have the same playlist in both places: Select the playlist and choose File➪Export Song List, and choose the XML option from the Format pop-up menu in the Save: iTunes dialog box. When you export a playlist, you get a list of songs in the XML (Extensible Markup Language) format. You can then import the playlist into the other computer by choosing File➪Import and selecting the XML file. The playlist shows only songs located on the other computer's hard disk. You can also export all the playlists in your library at the same time by choosing File➪Export Library.

Gimme Shelter: Consolidating and Backing Up

If you hate to be disorganized, you'll love iTunes and its nice, neat file storage methods. You can install iTunes anywhere, and iTunes remembers the location of its own folder. People typically install it inside their home folders — the path to this folder is typically *your home folder*/Music/iTunes/. Inside this folder is a iTunes Music folder. All songs you import are stored in this folder. Even music files you drag to the iTunes window are stored here — iTunes makes a copy and stores the copy in the iTunes Music folder.

If you access Web radio and shared libraries on a network, you probably have music in your library that is not actually *in* your library at all — it can be streamed to your computer over the Internet, or be part of a shared library or playlist on a network, as we describe later in this section.

You can find the location of any song by selecting the song and choosing File➪Get Info, and then clicking the Summary tab in the Song Information window. Look in the Kind section. If you see `remote`, then the song is not on your hard disk. If you have songs in different locations — on different hard disks connected to the same Mac, or shared over a network, you can have iTunes consolidate your music library by copying everything into the iTunes Music Library folder. By consolidating your library first, you make sure that your backup is complete.

To consolidate your music library, choose Advanced➪Consolidate Library. The original songs remain where they are, but copies are made in your music folder.

To copy your music library to another disk, locate the iTunes folder using the Finder. Drag this entire folder to another hard disk or backup device, and you're all set.

The copy operation may take some time if the library is huge — you can stop the operation anytime, but the newly copied library may not be complete. Allowing the copy operation to finish is always best.

If you subscribe to the Apple .Mac service, you can use its hassle-free Backup software. With Backup, which comes with a .Mac membership, you can quickly and easily store important files on your iDisk. For information about Mac OS X backup procedures and the .Mac service, see the excellent book titled *Mac OS X All-in-One Desk Reference For Dummies* by Mark L. Chambers.

To copy your entire music library to another Mac, follow these steps:

1. **Locate your iTunes Music folder in the Finder in your old Mac.**

   Locate your iTunes folder, which is usually within the Music folder in your home folder. Inside the iTunes folder is the iTunes Music Folder, containing your music library.

2. **If the new Mac has a music library, move the music folders inside the iTunes Music folder to another folder, or copy them to another disk and delete the original files.**

   If the music library is empty, you can skip this step.

3. **Copy the iTunes Music folder from the old Mac to the iTunes folder of the new Mac.**

   You can replace the old one if it is empty. This folder contains all the music files.

4. **Choose File➪Export Library to export the Library.xml file from the iTunes folder of the old Mac to the new Mac, using any folder other than the iTunes folder.**

When you export your entire library, iTunes creates an XML file that contains all the playlist information and links to music files.

5. **Start iTunes on the new Mac.**
6. **Choose File⇨Import and import the Library.xml file.**

   The music library is now available on the new computer.

Sharing Music (Legally)

You want to protect your investments in music. If you buy music online, you want to be able to play the music anywhere, and even share the music with your friends. You can easily share the music you rip yourself from CDs. You can also share, to a limited extent, the music you buy online from Apple.

Apple uses a protected form of the AAC encoder for the songs in its online store. The rights of artists are protected while also giving you more leeway in how to use the music more than most other services (though by the time you read this, other services may have adopted this format with similar privileges).

Some of the features Apple offers through the Apple Music store are the following:

- **Creating backups:** Easily create backups by copying music several times.
- **Copying music:** Play songs on three separate computers. See Chapter 1 of this book for more info.
- **Sharing music over a network:** Everyone on a network can play the music, such as the Apple wireless AirPort network.

Whether or not you manage files on your hard disk on a regular basis, you may want to know where these songs are stored, so that you can copy music to other computers and make a backup of the entire library. You may also want to move the library to another Mac — after all, these Macs just keep getting better year after year. You can play your purchased music on any authorized computer, and you can authorize up to three at once, and deauthorize ones you don't use.

Copying songs to other computers

You can copy as much music as you want. If the songs are in the protected AAC format (bought from the online music store), you can copy them, but you can't play them unless, of course, the computer is authorized to do so.

I fought the law and the law won: Sharing and piracy

Apple CEO Steve Jobs gave personal demonstrations of the Apple Music Store, iTunes, and the iPod to Paul McCartney and Mick Jagger. According to Steven Levy at *Newsweek* (May 12, 2003), Jobs said, "They both totally get it." The former Beatle and the Stones frontman are no slouches — both conduct music-business affairs personally and both have extensive back catalogs of music. They know all about the free music swapping services on the Internet, but they agree with Jobs that you will be willing to pay for high-quality music rather than download free copies of questionable quality.

We agree with the idea, also promoted by Jobs, that technology should not be treated as the culprit with regard to violations of copyright law. Conversely, technology should not be used as a solution to piracy, because determined pirates will circumvent it with newer technology, and only consumers are inconvenienced.

We're not lawyers, but we think the law already covers the type of piracy that involves counterfeiting CDs. The fact that you are not allowed to copy a commercial CD and sell the copy to someone else makes sense. You also can't sell the individual songs of a commercial CD.

Giving music away is, of course, the subject of much controversy, with services such as Napster closed by court order while others flourish in countries that don't have copyright laws as strict as the United States. Nothing in the Apple realm of technology enables the sharing of music at this level — you have to hack it somehow — so we don't need to go into it, except to provide one observation: The songs we hear from free sharing services such as KaZaa have, for the most part, been low in quality — on a par with FM radio broadcasts. Nice for listening to new songs to see if we like them, but not useful for acquiring as part of our real music collection. The Apple Music Store is clearly superior in quality and convenience, and we prefer the original, authorized version of the song, not some knock-off that may have been copied from a radio broadcast.

As for making copies for personal use, the law is murky at best. It depends on what you *mean* by personal use. The iLife package allows you to use these music files in creative projects. You can, for example, put together a music video to show your friends, using iMovie, some video footage you shot with your camcorder, and the latest hit by Eminem. But don't expect to see it on MTV or *American Idol*. Your local public access cable TV station cannot even play it, unless you obtained the broadcast rights (which typically includes contacting the music publisher, the record label, and the artist — good luck).

Can you legally use a pop song as a soundtrack for a high school yearbook slideshow? It sounds legal to us, given the ability to use music for educational purposes, but that is a question only a lawyer can answer. If you're interested in obtaining the rights to music to use in semi-public or public presentations, or even movies and documentaries for public distribution, you can contact the music publisher or a licensing agent. Music-publishing organizations, such as the Music Publishers' Association (`www.mpa.org/`), offer information and lists of music publishers, as well as explanations of various rights and licenses.

You can copy songs freely from your iTunes Music folder to other folders, other disks, and other computers using the Finder, and to devices such as the iPod using iTunes itself. We describe the iPod in Book V.

The files are organized in folders by artist name, and by album, within the iTunes Music folder. Copying an entire album, or every song by a specific artist, is easy. You can find the location of any song by selecting the song and choosing File⇨Get Info. Click the Summary tab in the Get Info window to see the Summary pane.

To use iTunes music with iPhoto, iMovie, or iDVD, you don't have to copy anything or do anything. When you open any of the iLife applications, your iTunes music library is automatically available from within the iLife application.

You can export a playlist of the songs by selecting the playlist and choosing File⇨Export Song List, picking XML from the Format pop-up menu in the Export Song List window. When you export a playlist you get a list of songs in the XML (Extensible Markup Language) format with the song information. You can then import the playlist into the other computer by choosing File⇨Import and selecting the XML file.

Sharing music in a network

If you live like the Jetsons, the TV cartoon family of the future — with a Mac in every room, connected by wireless or wired network — iTunes is made for you. You can share the music in your library with up to five other computers in the same network. You can even do this with music from the Apple Music Store.

When you share songs on a network, the song is *streamed* from the library Mac to your computer over the network — the song is not copied to your music library. From your computer, you can't burn a CD, or copy to an iPod, songs shared on the library Mac. You can, of course, do those things on the library Mac.

You can share radio links, MP3, AIFF, and WAV files, and even AAC files and music purchased from the Apple Music Store, but not Audible spoken word files or QuickTime sound files. If you have a large network (such as an office network), check to make sure the computers share the same subnet. The computers need to be within the same subnet to share music.

To share your music library, turning your Mac into the library Mac, follow these steps:

1. **Choose iTunes⇨Preferences and click the Sharing button.**

   The Sharing pane of the Preferences window appears, with options for sharing music.

2. **Select the Share My Music option.**
3. **Select either the Share Entire Library option or the Share Selected Playlists option and choose the playlists to share.**
4. **Type a name for the shared library and add a password if you want.**

   The name you choose appears in the Source list for other computers that share it. The password restricts access to those who know it.

On the other computers on the network, you can access the music by following these steps:

1. **Choose iTunes⇨Preferences and click the Sharing button.**

   The Sharing pane of the Preferences window appears, with options for sharing music.

2. **Select the Look for Shared Music option.**

   The shared libraries or playlists appear in the iTunes Source list.

3. **Click the shared library or playlist to play it.**

This can be incredibly useful for playing music on laptops such as PowerBooks that support the wireless AirPort network.

Chapter 3: Enhancing the Audio

In This Chapter

- **Importing and converting music using custom import settings**
- **Getting the best quality and space trade-offs with music files**
- **Using the equalizer and assigning presets to songs**

Just a century ago, people would gather at *phonography parties* to rent a headset and listen to a new invention called a phonograph, the predecessor to the record player. Before records, radio, and jukeboxes, these parties and live performances were the only sources of music, and the quality of the sound must have been awful by today's standards.

The choices of formats for sound have changed considerably from the fragile 78-rpm records from the phonography parties and the scratchy 45-rpm and 33-rpm records of the later half of the century to today's CDs. Consumers had to be on the alert then, as you do now, for dead-end formats that could lock up music in a cul-de-sac of technology, never to be played again. You know what we're talking about — dead-end formats like the ill-fated eight-track cassette, or the legendary quadraphonic LP.

You want your digital music to last forever, and play at high quality on future players as well as today's. You also want to take advantage of the compression technology that squeezes more music onto players than ever before. This chapter provides our suggestions for the importing preferences for ripping CDs that provide the highest quality and the best use of compression technology. You may be quite happy with the results using these suggestions. But listening pleasure depends entirely on the listener, and some people can hear qualitative differences that others don't hear or don't care about.

You can specify quality settings to your liking, but as you discover more about digital audio technology, you'll find that you have decisions to make about your music library. This chapter helps you make them. For example, you may be tempted to trade quality for space — import music at average-quality settings that allow you to put more songs on your hard disk and iPod than if you chose higher-quality settings. This may make you happy today, but what about tomorrow, when iPods and hard disks double or triple in capacity?

On the other hand, you may be very picky about the sound quality and, with an eye toward future generations of iPods and cheap hard disks, decide to trade space for quality, importing music at the highest possible quality settings and then converting copies to lower-quality, space-saving versions for iPods and other uses. Of course, you need more disk space to accommodate the higher-quality versions.

This chapter explains which music encoding and compression formats to use for higher quality, and which to use for cramming more songs into the same disk space. It also covers importing sounds other than music, converting songs from one format to another, enhancing music with the built-in equalizer, and saving equalizer settings with songs. You'll impress your audiophile friends, even ones who couldn't believe that iTunes is capable of reproducing magnificent music.

Deciding Your Encoding Format

The encoding format and settings you choose for importing music when ripping a CD affect sound quality, disk space (and iPod space), and compatibility with other types of players and computers. You may want to change your import settings before ripping CDs depending on the type of music, the source of the recording, or other factors, such as whether you plan to burn a CD or use the music in a portable player such as the iPod. We describe in detail how to change your import settings in the section, "Changing Encoders and Settings," later in this chapter.

Some encoding formats compress the music, whereas others do not. Compression reduces the sound quality because it throws away information to make the file smaller. The amount of compression depends on the bit rate you choose, as well as the encoding format and other options.

Without getting too technical (as we do later in this chapter), more compression means the files are smaller but music quality is poorer. Less compression means better quality, but the files are larger. You can therefore trade quality for space, and have more music, or trade space for quality, and have higher-quality music with less space.

Power also is an issue. In iPods, playing larger files takes more power because the hard disk inside the iPod has to refresh its memory buffers more quickly to process more information as the song plays.

We prefer a higher-quality sound overall, and we typically don't use the lower-quality settings for encoders except for voice recordings. We can hear differences in music quality at the higher compression levels and would rather go out and buy more hard disks if necessary. But iTunes gives you the choice in the Import Using pop-up menu in the Import pane of the Preferences window. This is perhaps the most important choice. You can choose one of four encoders (see the sidebar, "AAC, MP3, and AIFF" for more detailed descriptions):

✦ **AAC Encoder:** Used for songs in the Apple Music Store, we recommend it for all uses except when ripping your own CDs in order to burn new audio CDs (see AIFF).

✦ **AIFF Encoder:** Use AIFF if you plan on burning the song to an audio CD, because it offers the highest possible quality. The files occupy lots more space than AAC or MP3 files because they are not compressed.

✦ **MP3 Encoder:** Supported everywhere — use the MP3 format for songs you intend to send to others or use with MP3 players.

✦ **WAV Encoder:** WAV is the high-quality sound format used on PCs (like AIFF). The files occupy lots more space than AAC or MP3 files because they are not compressed. Use WAV if you plan on burning the song to an audio CD, or use with PCs.

If you use an MP3 player other than an iPod, you want to either import or convert songs with the MP3 Encoder. If you use an iPod or play music on the Mac, you can use the higher-quality AAC Encoder to produce files that are either the same size as their MP3 counterparts but higher in quality, or at the same quality but smaller in size.

To have the best possible quality you can have for future growth, you may consider not using compression at all, and not compromising on quality. You can import music at the highest possible quality — using the uncompressed AIFF or WAV encoders — and then convert the music files to a lesser-quality format for use in the iPod or other devices. We describe how to convert music later in this chapter in the section, "Converting songs to other encoders."

You can import a CD using one encoder, and then import the CD again using a different encoder as long as you change the name of at least one of the imported CDs to identify it (you can always tell by its settings, as described in Chapter 2 of this book). You can always delete the repetitive album after you transfer it into another application (such as the iPod) to reclaim disk space.

AAC, MP3, and AIFF

We intend to leapfrog years of technospeak about digital music file formats and get right to the ones you need to know about:

AAC: The Apple music file format, known as MPEG-4 Advanced Audio Coding, is a higher quality format than MP3, comparable to CD quality (*MPEG* stands for Moving Pictures Experts Group, a body that recognizes compression standards for video and audio). We think it offers the best trade-off of space and quality. All your purchased music from the Apple Music Store comes in this format. It is suitable (though not as good as AIFF) for burning to an audio CD, and excellent for playing in an iPod or from hard disk. However, as of this writing, only Apple supports it.

AIFF: The Audio Interchange File Format is the standard digital format for uncompressed sound on a Mac, and provides the highest quality representation of the sound. Use AIFF if you plan to burn songs to an audio CD. Mac-based digital sound editing programs import and export AIFF files, and you can edit and save in AIFF format with absolutely no loss in quality. AIFF files take up enormous amounts of disk and iPod space because they're uncompressed.

MP3: The MPEG-1, Layer 3 format, also known as MP3, is supported everywhere. Use the MP3 format for songs you intend to send to others or use with MP3 players. The MP3 format offers quite a lot of different compression and quality settings, so you can fine-tune the format to get better quality, sacrificing disk (and iPod) space as you dial up the quality. Use the MP3 format for a song you intend to burn on an MP3 CD (AIFF or WAV formats are better for regular audio CDs).

WAV: Waveform Audio File Format is a digital audio standard that Windows-based PCs can understand and manipulate. Like AIFF, WAV is uncompressed and provides the highest quality representation of the sound. Use WAV if you plan on burning the song to an audio CD or using it with PC-based digital sound editing programs, which import and export WAV files. WAV files take up enormous amounts of disk and iPod space because they're uncompressed.

DVD-audio: DVD-audio is a relatively new digital audio format developed from the format for DVD video. DVD-audio is based on PCM recording technology but offers improved sound quality by using a higher sampling frequency and longer word lengths. iTunes does not yet directly support the DVD-audio format, but you can import a digital video file containing DVD-audio sound into iMovie (as described in Book III, Chapter 2), extract the sound, and export the sound in AIFF or WAV format, which can be used with iTunes.

Super Audio CD (SACD): The Super Audio CD is a new format developed from the past audio format for CDs. The SACD format is based on Direct Stream Digital (DSD) recording technology that closely reproduces the shape of the original analog waveforms to produce a more natural, higher quality sound. Originally developed for the digital archiving of priceless analogue masters tapes, DSD is based on 1-bit sigma-delta modulation, and operates with a sampling frequency of 2.8224 MHz (64 times the 44.1 kHz used in audio CDs). Philips and Sony have adopted DSD as the basis for SACD, and the format is growing in popularity among audiophiles. However, iTunes does not support SACD. If you buy music product in the SACD format, choose the hybrid format that offers a conventional CD layer and a high-density SACD layer. You can then import the music from the conventional CD layer.

Changing Encoders and Settings

If you want to change your encoder and quality settings before you rip an audio CD, follow these steps:

1. **Choose iTunes⇨Preferences, and then click the Importing button.**

   The Importing Preferences window appears, where you can make changes to the encoding format and its settings.

2. **Choose the encoding format you want to convert the song into, and the settings for that format.**

   Use the pop-up menus to make your changes. The Setting pop-up menu offers different settings depending on your choice of encoder in the Import Using pop-up menu. See the sections on each encoding format later in this chapter for details on settings.

3. **Click OK to accept changes.**

   After changing your importing preferences, and until you change them again, iTunes uses these preferences whenever it imports or converts songs.

Using the AAC Encoder

TIP

We recommend using the AAC Encoder for everything except music you intend to burn on CD. AAC offers the best trade-off of space and quality for hard disks and iPods.

The AAC Encoder offers only two choices: High Quality and Custom. You may want to use the High Quality setting for most music (see Figure 3-1), but for very complex music (such as jazz and classical), you may want to fine-tune the AAC Encoder settings.

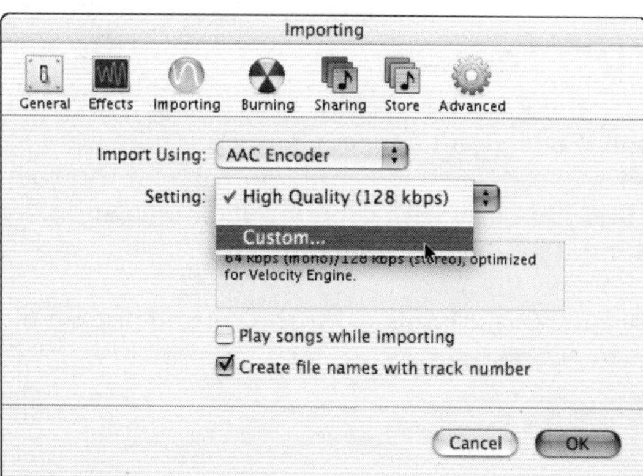

Figure 3-1: Set the AAC Encoder to import with the highest bit rate and automatic detection of sample rate and channels.

To customize your AAC Encoder settings, choose Custom from the Setting pop-up menu. The custom settings for AAC, as shown in Figure 3-2, allow you to change the following:

- **Stereo bit rate:** Measured in kilobits per second (Kbps), use a higher bit rate for higher quality, which, of course, increases the file size. 320 Kbps is the highest-quality setting for this format; 128 is considered high quality.
- **Sample rate:** The sample rate is the number of times per second the sound waveform is captured digitally (or *sampled*). Higher sample rates yield higher quality sound and large file sizes. However, never use a higher sample rate than the rate used for the source. CDs use a 44.100 kHz rate, so choosing a higher rate is unnecessary unless you convert a song that was recorded from digital audiotape (DAT) or directly into the Mac at a high sample rate, and you want to keep that sample rate.
- **Channels:** Stereo, which offers two channels of music for left and right speakers, is the norm for music. Mono — monaural or single-channel — was the norm for pop records before the mid-1960s. (Phil Specter was known for his high-quality monaural recordings, and the early Rolling Stones records are in mono.) Monaural recordings take up half the space of stereo recordings when digitized. Choose the Auto setting to have iTunes use the appropriate setting for the music.

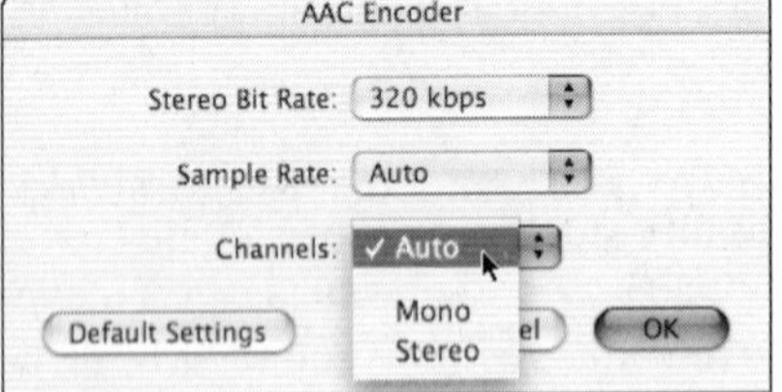

Figure 3-2: Customize the settings for the AIFF encoder.

Using the MP3 Encoder

Although we prefer the AAC Encoder for quality, most MP3 players as of this writing, other than iPods, don't support AAC. You may want to use the MP3 Encoder for other reasons, such as more control over the compression parameters and compatibility with other applications and players that support MP3.

The MP3 Encoder offers four choices for the Setting pop-up menu in the Importing Preferences window:

- **Good Quality (128 Kbps):** Certainly fine for audio books, comedy records, and old scratchy records. You may even want to go lower in bit rate (Kbps stands for kilobits per second) for voice recordings.
- **High Quality (160 Kbps):** Most people consider this high enough for most popular music, but we go higher with our music.
- **Higher Quality (192 Kbps):** High enough for just about all types of music.
- **Custom:** To fine-tune the MP3 Encoder settings, choose the Custom setting, as shown in Figure 3-3. Customizing your MP3 settings increases the quality of the sound while also keeping file size low.

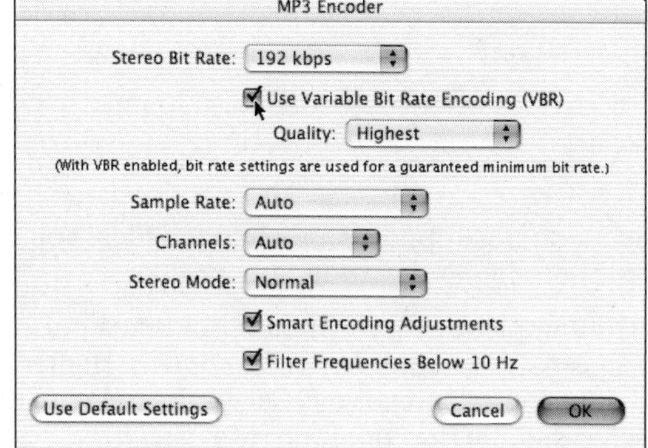

Figure 3-3: Customize the settings for the MP3 encoder.

The MP3 Encoder offers a raft of choices in its custom settings window (refer to Figure 3-3):

- **Stereo bit rate:** Measured in kilobits per second (Kbps), use a higher bit rate for higher quality, which, of course, increases the file size. The most common bit rate for MP3 files you find on the Web is 128 Kbps. Lower bit rates are more appropriate for voice recordings or sound effects. We recommend at least 192 Kbps for most music, and we use 320 Kbps, the maximum setting, for songs we play on our iPods.
- **Variable Bit Rate Encoding (VBR):** This option helps keep file size down, but quality may be affected. VBR varies the number of bits used to store the music depending on the complexity of the sound. If you use the Highest setting for VBR, iTunes encodes at up to the maximum bit rate of 320 Kbps in sections of songs where the sound is complex enough to require a high bit rate, while keeping the rest of the song at a lower bit rate to save file space. The lower limit is set by the rate you chose in

the Stereo Bit Rate pop-up menu (shown in Figure 3-4). Some audiophiles swear by it, others don't ever use it. We use it only when importing at low bit rates, and we set VBR to its highest quality setting.

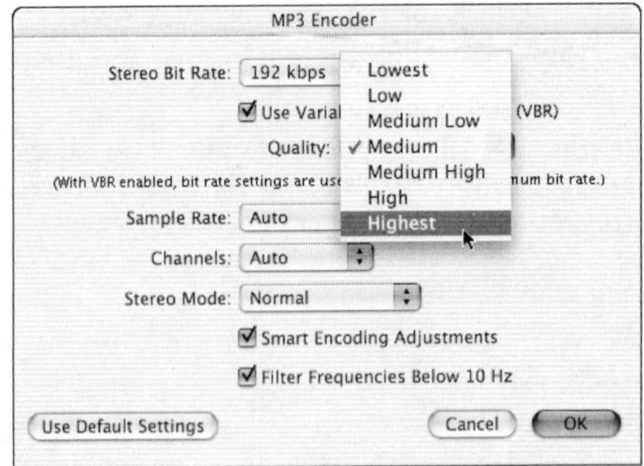

Figure 3-4: Use Variable Bit Rate Encoding for MP3 to get high quality using less file space.

Many MP3 players do not support VBR-encoded files. You can use VBR-encoded MP3 files on the iPod without any problem.

- **Sample rate:** The sample rate is the number of times per second the sound waveform is captured digitally (or *sampled*). Higher sample rates yield higher quality sound and large file sizes. However, you should never use a higher sample rate than the rate used for the source — CDs use a 44.100 kHz rate, so choosing a higher rate is unnecessary, unless you convert a song that was recorded from DAT or directly into the Mac at a high sample rate, and you want to keep that sample rate.
- **Channels:** Stereo, which offers two channels of music for left and right speakers, is the norm for music. Monaural recordings take up half the space of stereo recordings when digitized. Choose the Auto setting to have iTunes use the appropriate setting for the music.
- **Stereo mode:** Normal mode is just what you think it is — normal stereo. Choose the Joint Stereo setting, as shown in Figure 3-5, to make the file smaller by removing information that is identical in both channels of a stereo recording, using only one channel for that information, while the other channel carries unique information. At bit rates of 128 Kbps and below, this mode can actually improve the sound quality. However, we typically don't use the Joint Stereo mode when using a high-quality bit rate.
- **Smart Encoding Adjustments:** Select this option to have iTunes analyze your MP3 encoding settings and music source and change your settings as needed to maximize the quality of the encoded files.

✦ **Filter Frequencies Below 10 Hz:** Frequencies below 10 Hz are hard to hear, and most people don't notice if they're missing. Filtering inaudible frequencies helps reduce the file size with little or no perceived loss in quality. However, we think removal detracts from the overall feeling of the music, and we prefer not to filter frequencies.

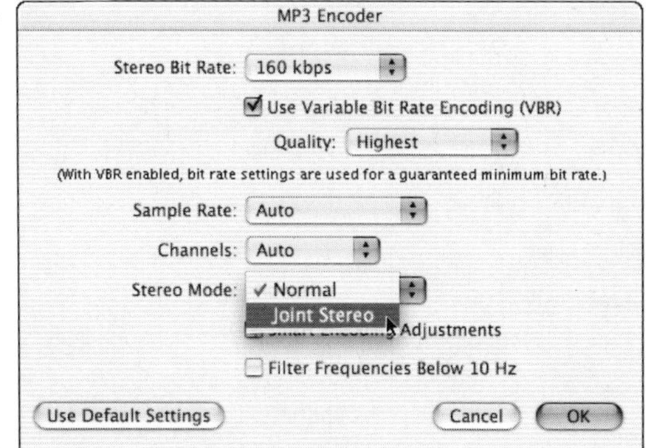

Figure 3-5: Choose the Joint Stereo setting for MP3 encoding to reduce file size without noticeably affecting quality.

Using AIFF or WAV encoders

With the exception of Apple Music Store songs provided in the protected AAC format (which you can't convert anyway), use the AIFF or WAV encoders for songs from audio CDs if you want to burn your own audio CDs with the music. You get the best possible quality with either encoder because the music is not compressed.

The difference between the encoders is only that AIFF is the standard for Mac applications and computers, and WAV is the standard for PC applications and computers.

You can import music with AIFF or WAV at the highest possible quality and then convert the music files to a lesser-quality format for use in the iPod or other devices.

AIFF and WAV files take up huge amounts of disk space, and although you can play them on an iPod, they take up way too much space and battery power to be convenient for anyone but the most discerning audiophile who can afford multiple iPods. Disk space you can handle by adding more disks, and by backing up portions of your music library onto other media, such as a DVD-R disc (which can hold 4.7GB). But if multiple disk drives and backup scenarios scare you, you should use the AAC or MP3 encoders to compress files for lower quality.

Both the AIFF Encoder and the WAV Encoder offer the same Custom settings window, shown in Figure 3-6, with settings for sample rate, sample size, and channels. You can choose the Auto setting for all three settings, and iTunes automatically detects the proper sample rate, size, and channels from the source. If you choose a specific setting, such as the Stereo setting, for the Channels setting, iTunes imports in stereo regardless of the source. Audio CDs typically sample at a rate of 44.1000 kHz, with a sample size of 16 bits, and stereo channels.

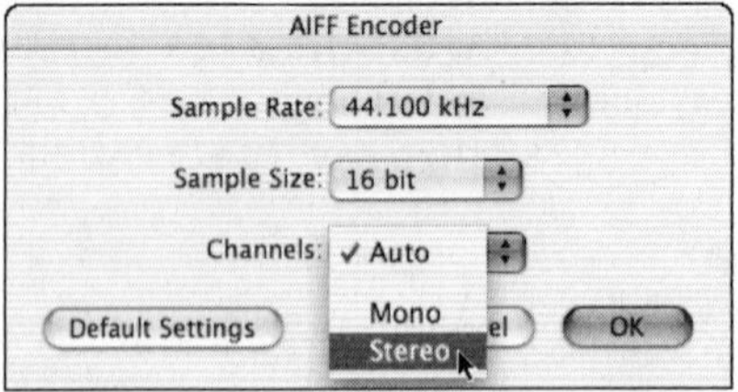

Figure 3-6: Set the AIFF Encoder to import in stereo no matter what the source.

The AIFF and WAV custom settings windows offer more choices than AAC in sample rates, down to a very low sample rate of 8.000 kHz suitable only for voice.

Import settings for voice and sound effects

Audio books are available from Audible (www.audible.com) in a special format that doesn't require any further compression. But you can also import audio books in the MP3 format, spoken-word titles, comedy CDs, and other voice recordings.

If the recording has any music at all, or requires close listening to stereo channels (like a Firesign Theatre or Monty Python CD), you should treat the entire recording as music and skip this section.

Sound effects CDs offer sound effects at CD quality, which you may want to treat as normal music; but you may also want to reduce the sound file if you intend to incorporate the sound effect into movies in iMovie to keep the overall movie from getting too large.

By fine-tuning the import settings for voice recordings and sound effects, you can save a significant amount of space without reducing quality. We recommend the following settings depending on your choice of encoder:

- **AAC Encoder:** AAC allows you to get away with an even lower bit rate than MP3 to get the same quality, thereby saving more space. We recommend a bit rate as low as 80 Kbps for sound effects and voice recordings.

✦ **MP3 Encoder:** Use a low bit rate (such as 96 Kbps). You may also want to reduce the sample rate to 22.050 kHz for voice recordings. Filter frequencies below 10 Hz because voice recordings don't need such frequencies.

Converting songs to other encoders

Converting a song from one encoder to another may be useful if you want to use one encoder for one purpose, such as burning a CD, and another encoder for another purpose, such as playing on an iPod.

You want to use different encoding formats if you have a discerning ear and you want to burn a CD of songs, and also use the songs in your iPod. You can first import and then burn AIFF-encoded songs to a CD, and then convert the songs to AAC or MP3. You can then save space by deleting the AIFF versions.

Converting a song from one compressed format (MP3 or AAC) to another (AAC or MP3) is possible, but you may not like the results. When you convert a compressed file to another compressed format, iTunes compresses the music *twice,* reducing the quality of the sound. Start with an uncompressed song, imported using either the AIFF or WAV format, and convert that to the compressed AAC or MP3 format.

You can tell what format a song is in by selecting it and choosing File➪Get Info. The Summary tab displays what kind of music file the song is and the format it's in.

You can't convert songs bought from the Apple Music Store, because they are encoded as protected AAC files. If you could, they wouldn't be protected, would they? You also can't convert Audible books and spoken-word content to another format.

To convert a song to another format, follow these steps:

1. **Choose iTunes➪Preferences, and then click the Importing button.**

   The Importing Preferences window appears.

2. **Choose the encoding format you want to convert the song into, and the settings for that format.**

   For example, if you are converting songs in the AIFF format to the MP3 format, you choose the MP3 format and its settings.

3. **Select one or more songs and choose Advanced➪Convert Selection to convert the songs**

The encoding format you chose in Step 2 appears in the menu: Convert Selection to MP3, Convert Selection to AAC, Convert Selection to AIFF, or Convert Selection to WAV. Choose the appropriate menu operation to perform the conversion.

Manic compression has captured your song

Everyone hears the effects of compression differently. You may not hear any problem with compressed audio that someone else says is tinny or lacking in depth.

But too much compression can be a bad thing. Further compressing an already-compressed music file — by converting a song — reduces the quality significantly. Not only that, but once your song is compressed, you can't uncompress the song back to its original quality. Your song is essentially locked into that format.

The audio compression methods that are good at reducing space (and if you're not going to reduce space significantly, why bother?) have to throw away information. In technospeak, they are *lossy* (as opposed to loss-less) compression algorithms. Lossy compression loses information each time you use it, which means if you compress something already compressed, you lose more information than before.

MP3 and its new, advanced Apple-sponsored cousin AAC, use two basic methods to compress audio: removing non-audible frequencies, and removing the less important signals.

For non-audible frequencies, the compression removes what you supposedly can't hear (although this is a subject for eternal debate). For example, if a background singer's warble is totally drowned out by a rhythm guitar playing a chord, and you can't hear the singer due to the intensity of the guitar's sound, the compression algorithm loses the singer's sound while maintaining the guitar's sound.

Within the sound spectrum of frequencies that can be heard by humans, some frequencies are considered to be less important in terms of rendering fidelity, and some that most people can't hear at all. Removing specific frequencies is likely to be less damaging to your music than other types of compression, depending on how you hear things. In fact, your dog may stop getting agitated at songs that contain ultra-high frequencies only dogs can hear (such as the ending of "Day in the Life" by the Beatles).

Another option in MP3 compression is the Channel choice. Most likely you want to keep stereo recordings in stereo, and mono recordings in mono, and the Auto setting guarantees that. But you can also use the Joint Stereo mode of the MP3 Encoder to reduce the amount of information per channel. Joint Stereo mode removes information that is identical in both channels of a stereo recording, using only one channel for that information, while the other channel carries unique information. At bit rates of 128 Kbps and below, this mode can improve the sound quality.

Variable Bit Rate Encoding (VBR) is a technique that varies the number of bits used to store the music depending on the complexity of the sound. While the quality of VBR is endlessly debated, it's useful when set to the Highest setting, because VBR can encode at up to the maximum bit rate of 320 Kbps in those rare cases where the sound requires it, while keeping the rest at a lower bit rate.

iTunes creates a copy of each song and converts the copy to the new format. Both the original and the copy are stored in your music library.

If you convert songs obtained from the Internet, you'll find that the most common bit rate for MP3 files is 128 Kbps, and choosing a higher stereo bit rate won't improve the quality — it only wastes space.

This automatic copy-and-convert operation can be useful for converting an entire music library to another format — hold down the Option key and choose Advanced⇨Convert Selection, and all the songs copy and convert automatically. If you have a library of AIFF tunes, you can quickly copy and convert them to AAC or MP3 in one step, and then assign the AIFF songs to the AIFF-associated playlists for burning CDs, and MP3 or AAC songs to MP3 or AAC playlists that you intend to copy to your iPod.

Equalize It!

When you turn up the bass or treble on a stereo system, you are actually increasing the volume, or intensity, of certain frequencies while the music is playing — as you know, you aren't really changing the music itself, just the way it is playing back. If you are a discerning listener, you may change these bass and treble settings a lot — perhaps even for each song. Wouldn't it be nice if you could save these settings with each song? You can with iTunes.

The iTunes equalizer (EQ) allows you to fine-tune the specific sound spectrum frequencies in a more precise way than with bass and treble controls. You can use the equalizer to improve or enhance the sound coming through a particular stereo system and speakers — for example, you may pick entirely different equalizer settings for car speakers, home speakers, and headphones.

With the iTunes EQ you can adjust the frequencies directly, or use one of more than 20 built-in presets for various types of music from classical to rock. You can then assign the equalizer settings to a specific song or set of songs. With the equalizer settings you can customize playback for different musical genres, listening environments, or speakers. You can even save your own presets.

To see the iTunes equalizer, click the Equalizer button, which is on the bottom right side of the iTunes window or choose Window⇨Equalizer.

Adjusting the preamp volume

The preamp in your stereo is the component that offers a volume control that applies to all frequencies equally. (Volume knobs generally go up to ten, except, of course, for Spinal Tap's preamps, which go to eleven.)

The iTunes equalizer, shown in Figure 3-7, offers a Preamp control on the far left side. You can increase or decrease the volume in 3-decible increments up to 12 dB. Decibles are units that measure the intensity (or volume) of the frequencies. You can adjust the volume while playing the music so that you can hear the result right away.

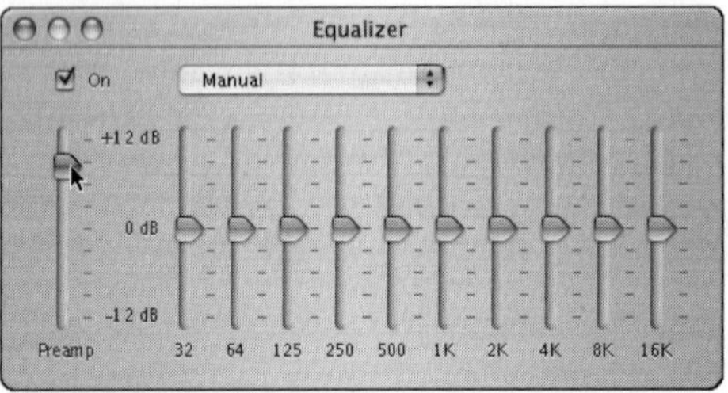

Figure 3-7: Use the equalizer's Preamp slider to adjust volume across all frequencies.

You may want to increase the preamp volume for songs that are recorded too softly, or decrease it for songs that are so loud you can hear distortion. If you want to make any adjustments to frequencies, you may want to adjust the preamp volume first if volume adjustment is needed, and then move on to the specific frequencies.

Using presets

iTunes offers *presets,* which are equalizer settings made in advance and saved by name. You can quickly switch settings without having to make changes to each frequency slider. iTunes comes with more than 20 presets of the most commonly used equalizer settings.

To use an equalizer preset, click the Equalizer button, which is on the bottom right side of the iTunes window. The Equalizer window appears, and you can click the pop-up menu at the top of the equalizer, as shown in Figure 3-8, to select a preset. If a song is playing, you hear the effect in the sound immediately after choosing the preset.

You can also create your own presets. Choose the Manual option in the pop-up menu to make setting changes in the equalizer, as described in the next section, "Adjusting frequencies." Then choose the Make Preset option from the pop-up menu to save your changes. The Make Preset window appears, as shown in Figure 3-9. Give your new preset a descriptive name. The name appears in the pop-up menu from that point on — your very own preset.

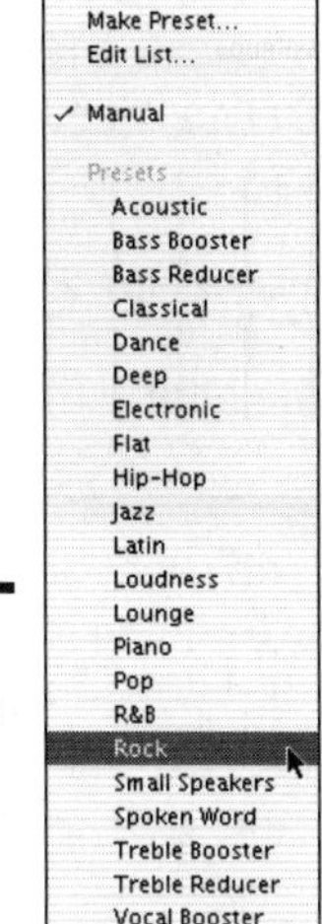

Figure 3-8: Choose one of the built-in equalizer presets.

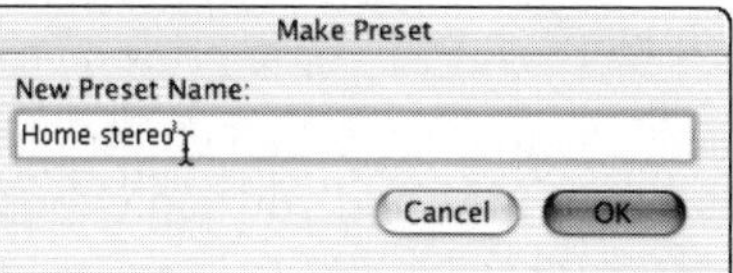

Figure 3-9: Save your adjustments as your own preset.

You can rename or delete the presets by choosing the Edit List option from the pop-up menu, which displays the Edit Presets window for renaming or deleting presets, as shown in Figure 3-10. You can rename or delete any preset, including the ones supplied with iTunes.

Figure 3-10: Edit the preset pop-up list.

Adjusting frequencies

You can adjust the frequencies in the iTunes equalizer by clicking and dragging sliders that look like mixing-board faders.

The horizontal values across the equalizer represent the spectrum of human hearing. The deepest frequency ("Daddy sang bass") is 32 hertz (Hz); the mid-range frequencies are 250 Hz and 500 Hz, and the higher frequencies go from 1 kHz (kilohertz) to 16 kHz (treble).

The vertical values on each bar represent decibels (dB), which measure the intensity of each frequency. Increase or decrease the frequencies at 3-decibel increments by clicking and dragging the sliders up and down. You can drag the sliders to adjust the frequencies while the music is playing, and hear the effect immediately.

Assigning equalizer presets to songs

One reason why you go to the trouble of setting equalizer presets is to assign the presets to songs. Then when you play the songs, the preset for each song takes effect for that song.

You can also use the same presets in an iPod. When you transfer the songs to the iPod, the preset stays assigned to it, and you can choose whether or not to use it when playing the song on the iPod.

You can assign any preset directly to a song. Assign a preset to songs by following these steps:

1. **Choose Edit⇨View Options.**

   Or ⌘+click any column heading in the song list and choose the Equalizer option from the shortcut menu.

   The View Options window appears, as shown in Figure 3-11.

2. **Select the check box next to the Equalizer option and click OK.**

3. **Locate a song in the song list, and scroll the song list horizontally to see the Equalizer column.**

   You can open a playlist or scroll the entire song list in List or Browse view.

4. **Choose a preset from the pop-up menu in the Equalizer column.**

   The Equalizer column has a tiny pop-up menu that allows you to assign any preset to a song.

When you transfer songs with presets to the iPod, use the presets for playback. See Book V, Chapter 2 for lots of great suggestions on using equalizer settings with the iPod.

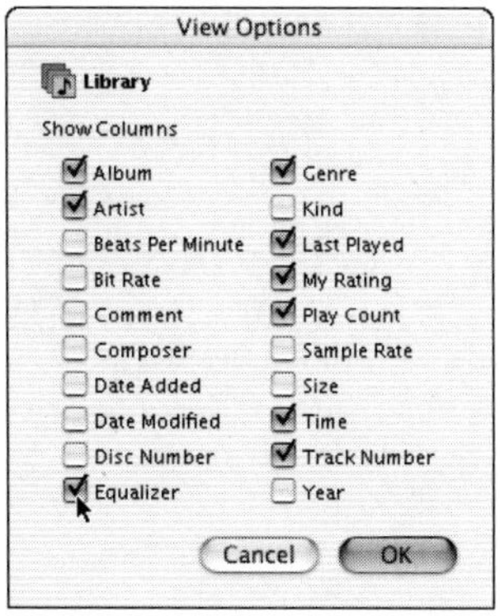

Figure 3-11: Assign an equalizer preset to a song.

Chapter 4: Burning CDs

In This Chapter

- **Choosing the proper disc media**
- **Preparing a playlist for burning**
- **Choosing the sound and format settings**
- **Burning CDs**

When vinyl records were popular, rock radio disk jockeys who didn't like disco would hold *disco meltdown* parties. People were encouraged to throw their records into a pile to be burned up or steamrolled into vinyl glop. This chapter isn't about that, nor is it about anything involving fire or heat.

Burning a CD actually refers to the process in which the recorder's laser meets the surface of the disc and creates a new impression loaded with digital information.

Contrary to the beliefs of some record company executives, burning CDs is not a global pastime simply because people want to steal music. People burn CDs for a lot of reasons. Maybe you want to bring a CD of your special party songs to the local DJ club to mix in with the night's music. Maybe having your 12 favorite love songs on one CD for your next romantic encounter is convenient. Or maybe you want to burn a few CDs of obscure songs to impress your friends on your next big road trip. Blank discs are cheap — pennies to the dollar compared with the older technology of cassette tapes for taking music on the road.

This chapter boils everything down for you by telling you what kind of discs to use, where the discs play, how to get your playlist ready for burning, what settings to use for burning, and so on. You find out what you need to know to make sure that your burns are not meltdowns — the only melting is the music in your ears.

Using CD-Recordable Discs

If you don't have an iPod or similar player, you can't take music with you unless you burn a disc. Even if you have a player, you may still want to make a CD that plays on any CD player or make a CD backup of your music files.

After importing music into your iTunes library, you can arrange any songs in your library into a playlist and burn a CD using that playlist. If you have an Apple-supported CD-R, CD-RW, or DVD-R drive (such as the Apple Super Drive), and a blank CD-R ("R" is for "recordable") disc, you can create your own music CDs that play in most CD players.

Blank CD-R discs are available in most electronics and computer stores. You can also get them online from the Apple Store. Choose iTunes⇨Shop for iTunes Products to reach the Apple Store online.

The discs are called CD-R discs because they use a recordable format related to commercial CDs (which are not recordable, of course). You can also create a disc in the new MP3 format, and create a CD-R disc with data rather than music, which is useful for backing up a music library.

Where you can play CD-R discs

CD-R discs play just like commercial CDs in most CD players, including car CD players and portables. The CD-R format is the most universal and compatible with older players.

The Apple SuperDrive also creates CD-RW (recordable, read-write) discs that you can erase and reuse, but CD players don't recognize them as music CDs. The SuperDrive can create data DVD-R and DVD-RW discs also, which are useful for holding data files, but you can only use these discs with computers — most commercial DVD players won't read data DVD-R or DVD-RW. To create DVD titles for commercial players, see Book IV.

CDs encoded in the MP3 format can play on the new consumer MP3 disc players and combination CD/MP3 players, as well as on computers that recognize MP3 CDs (including Macs with iTunes).

What you can fit on a CD-R disc

You can fit up to 74 minutes of music on high-quality CD-R discs (some can go as high as 80 minutes). You measure the amount of music in minutes (and seconds) because the Red Book encoding format for audio CDs and CD-R discs compresses the music information. Although CD-R discs (and CD-RW discs) hold about 650MB of data, the actual storage of music information varies. The sound files on your hard disk may take up more space but still fit within the 650MB confines of the CD.

MP3 discs can hold more than 12 hours worth of music. You read that right — 12 hours on one disc. Now you know why MP3 discs are popular. MP3 discs are essentially CD-R discs with MP3 files stored on them.

The little Red Book that launched an industry

The typical audio CD and CD-R disc uses the CD-DA (Compact Disc-Digital Audio) format, which is known as *Red Book* — not something from Chairman Mao, but a document, published in 1980, that provides the specifications for the standard compact disc (CD) developed by Sony and Philips. According to legend, this document was in a binder with red covers.

Also according to legend, in 1979, Norio Ohga, honorary chairman and former CEO of Sony who's also a maestro conductor, overruled his engineers and insisted that the CD format be able to hold Beethoven's *Ninth Symphony* (which is 74 minutes and 42 seconds).

CD-DA defines audio data digitized at 44,100 samples per second (44.1 KHz) and in a range of 65,536 possible values (16 bits). Each second of hi-fi stereo sound requires almost 1.5 million bits of storage space. Data on a CD-DA is organized into sectors (the smallest possible separately addressable block) of information. CD data is not arranged in distinct physical units; data is organized into frames that are each 1⁄75 of a second. These frames are intricately interleaved so that damage to the disc does not destroy any single frame, but only small parts of many frames.

To import music into the computer from an audio CD, you have to convert the music to digital sound files by a program such as iTunes. When you burn an audio CD, iTunes converts the sound files into the CD-DA format as it burns the disc.

If you have a DVD (Digital Versatile Disc) burner, such as the Apple SuperDrive, you can burn data DVD-R or DVD-RW discs to use with other computers. This approach is suitable for making backup copies of music files (or any data files). DVD-R discs can hold about 4.7GB.

To burn a CD-RW or DVD-RW disc that already has data on it, you must first erase it by reformatting it using the application supplied with the drive. CD-RW and DVD-RW discs work with computers but won't work with consumer players.

Creating a Burn Playlist

To burn a CD, you must first define a playlist for the CD. See Chapter 2 of this book for how to create a playlist. You can use songs encoded in any format that iTunes supports; however, you get higher quality music with the uncompressed formats AIFF and WAV.

If your playlist includes music purchased from the Apple Music Store or other online stores in the protected AAC encoding format, some rules may apply. For example, the Apple Music Store allows you to burn ten copies of the same playlist containing protected songs to an audio CD, but no more. You can, however, create a new playlist and copy the protected songs to the new playlist, and then burn more CDs with the songs.

Calculating how much music to use

When you create a playlist, you find out how many songs can fit on the CD, by totaling the durations of the songs, using time as your measure. You can see the size of a playlist by selecting the playlist and the number of songs, the amount in time, and the amount in megabytes all appear at the bottom of the iTunes window, as shown in Figure 4-1.

Figure 4-1: Check the duration of the playlist.

In Figure 4-1, the selected playlist has 23 songs that total 1.1 hours and 724.1MB. You may notice the discrepancy between the megabytes (724.1) and what you can fit on an audio CD (650). While a CD holds only 650MB, the music is compressed and stored in a special format known as CD-DA (or Red Book). Thus, you can fit a bit more than 650MB of AIFF-encoded sound, because AIFF is uncompressed. We can fit 1.1 hours (66 minutes) of music on a 74-minute or 80-minute CD-R disc with many minutes to spare.

You should always use the actual duration, in hours, minutes, and seconds, to calculate how much music you can fit on an audio CD — either 74 or 80 minutes for blank CD-R discs. Leave at least an extra minute for gaps between songs.

You should do the *opposite* for an MP3 CD — use the actual megabytes to calculate how many songs to fit — up to 650MB for a blank CD-R disc. You can fit lots more music on an MP3 CD-R disc, because you use MP3-encoded songs rather than uncompressed AIFF songs.

Importing music for audio CD-R discs

Before you rip an audio CD of songs you want to burn to an audio disc, you may want to change the importing settings, as described in Chapter 3 of this book.

With the exception of Apple Music Store songs provided in the protected AAC format (which you can't convert anyway), you should use AIFF or WAV for songs from audio CDs if you want to burn your own audio CDs with music.

AIFF is the standard digital format for uncompressed sound on a Mac, and you can't go wrong with it. WAV is basically the same thing for Windows. Both the AIFF Encoder and the WAV Encoder offer the same Custom settings window, with settings for sample rate, sample size, and channels. You can choose the automatic settings, and iTunes automatically detects the proper sample rate, size, and channels from the source.

The Apple AAC music file format is a higher quality format than MP3, comparable to CD quality. We think it offers the best trade-off of space and quality. All your purchased music from the Apple Music Store comes in this format. It is suitable (though not as good as AIFF) for burning to an audio CD.

Importing music for MP3 CD-R discs

MP3 discs are essentially CD-R discs with MP3 files stored on them. Consumer MP3 CD players are now on the market, including hybrid models that play both audio CDs and MP3 CDs.

You can fit up to 12 hours of music on a CD using the MP3 format. The amount of music varies with the encoding options and settings you choose, as does the quality of the music. If you rip an audio CD, you can set the importing options to precisely the type of MP3 file you want, as we describe in Chapter 3 of this book.

You can use only MP3-encoded songs to burn an MP3 CD-R disc. Any songs not encoded in MP3 are skipped. Audible books and spoken-word titles are provided in an audio format that uses security technologies, including encryption, to protect purchased content. You can't burn an MP3 CD-R disc with Audible files — any Audible files in a burn playlist are skipped when you burn an MP3 CD-R disc.

Setting the Burning Preferences

Burning a CD is a simple process, and getting it right the first time is a good idea — when you burn a CD-R disc, it's done, right or wrong. You can't erase content as you can with a CD-RW disc. But you can't play a CD-RW disc in most CD players. Fortunately CD-R discs are cheap.

Setting the sound check and gaps

Musicians do a sound check before every performance to check the volume of microphones and instruments and its effect on the listening environment. The aptly named Sound Check option in iTunes allows you to do a sound check on your tunes to bring them all in line, volume-wise.

To have all the songs in your library play at the same volume level all the time, choose iTunes⇨Preferences, and click the Effects button to see the Effects preferences window, as we describe in Chapter 1 of this book. Select the Sound Check check box, which sets all the songs to the current volume controlled by the iTunes volume slider.

After turning on the Sound Check option, you can burn your audio CD-R so that all the songs play back at the same volume, just like they do in iTunes. Choose iTunes⇨Preferences, and then click the Burning button. Select the Use Sound Check option, as shown in Figure 4-3. This option is only active if you already selected the Sound Check option in the Effects preferences.

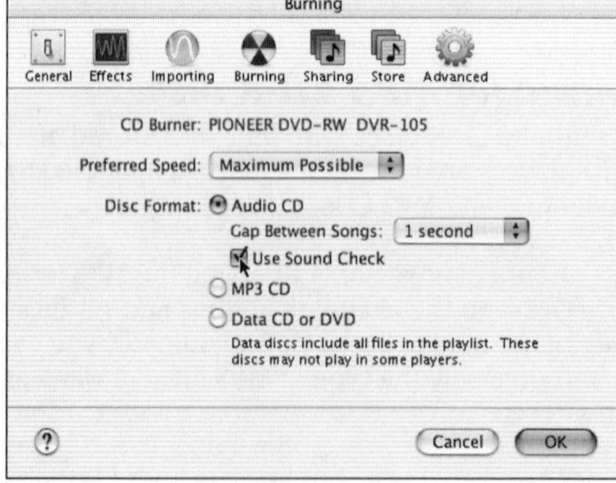

Figure 4-2: Select the Sound Check option for the CD-R disc burn.

Consistent volume for all tracks makes the CD-R disc sound professional. Another professional touch is an appropriate gap between songs, just like commercial CDs. Follow these steps to control the amount of the gap between the songs on your audio CD-R discs (not MP3 CD-R discs):

1. **Choose iTunes⇨Preferences, and then click the Burning button in the Preferences window.**

   The Burning Preferences window displays, as shown in Figure 4-3.

2. **Choose an amount from the Gap Between Songs pop-up menu.**

   You can choose from a gap of none to five seconds.

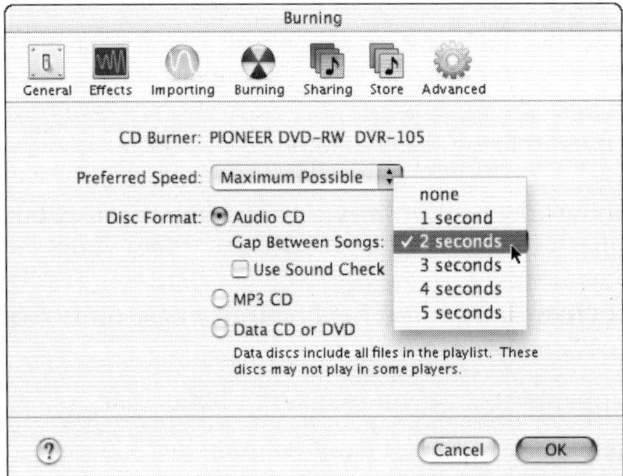

Figure 4-3: Set the gap between songs for an audio CD.

Setting the format and recording speed

Before burning a CD-R disc, you have to set the disc format and the recording speed. Choose iTunes⇨Preferences and then click the Burning button in the Preferences window.

The Disc Format setting in the Burning Preferences window (refer to Figure 4-2) offers three choices:

- **Audio CD:** You can burn a normal audio CD of up to 74 or 80 minutes (depending on the type of blank CD-R disc) using any iTunes-supported music files, including songs bought from the Apple Music Store. While connoisseurs of music may use AIFF-encoded or WAV-encoded music to burn an audio CD, you can also use songs in the AAC and MP3 formats.
- **MP3 CD:** You can burn an MP3 CD with songs encoded in the MP3 format, but no other formats are supported.
- **Data CD or DVD:** You can burn a data CD-R, CD-RW, DVD-R, or DVD-RW with the music files. You can use any encoding formats for the songs. Data discs don't play on most consumer CD players — they are meant for use with computers.

Blank CDs are rated for recording at certain speeds. Normally iTunes detects the rating of a blank CD and adjusts the recording speed to fit. But if your blank CDs are rated for a slower speed than your burner, or you are having problems creating CDs (see the section, "Dealing with Trouble in Paradise," later in this chapter), you can change the recording speed setting to match the CD's rating. Choose iTunes➪Preferences, and then click the Burning button in the Preferences window. Choose a specific recording speed from the Preferred Speed pop-up menu in the Burning Preferences window, or choose the Maximum Possible option to set the recording speed to your burner's maximum speed.

Burning a Disc

After you set the burning preferences, you're ready to start burning. Follow these steps to burn a CD:

1. **Select the playlist designated for burning a disc and click the Burn Disc button.**

   A message appears telling you to insert a blank disc.

2. **Insert a blank disc.**

   iTunes immediately checks the media and displays a message in the status window that the disc is ready to burn.

3. **Click the Burn Disc button *again*.**

   This time, the button has a radioactive symbol. After clicking the Burn Disc button, the process begins. The radioactive button rotates while the burning takes place, and a progress bar appears, displaying the names of the songs as they burn to the disc.

Burning takes several minutes. You can cancel the operation at any time by clicking the X next to the progress bar. But canceling the operation isn't like undoing the burn. Once the burn starts, you can't use the CD-R disc or DVD-R disc again.

If the playlist has more music than fits on the disc using the chosen format, iTunes burns as much as possible from the beginning of the playlist, cutting off the end. If you didn't calculate the amount of music right the first time, turn to the section, "Calculating how much music to use," earlier in this chapter.

If you choose the MP3 CD format, iTunes skips over any songs in the playlist that are not in the MP3 format.

Exporting song information for liner notes

Don't delete the playlist yet! You can export the song information for all the songs in the playlist to a text file, and edit liner notes for the CD.

iTunes exports all the song information for a single song, all the songs in a playlist, an album, by an artist, or in the library into a text file. Select the songs or playlist and choose File⇨ Export Song List (or ⌘+click and choose Export Song List from the shortcut menu). In the Export Song List window, select the Plain Text option from the Format pop-up menu (unless you use a double-byte language, such as Japanese or Chinese, for which the Unicode option is the right choice).

You can open this text file in a word-processing program, such as the free TextEdit program supplied with the Mac. iTunes formats the information in order for you to easily imported it into a database or spreadsheet program. You can change the formatting by manipulating the tab settings (tabs are used between pieces of information).

iTunes exports all the song information, which may be too much for your liner notes. Edit the liner notes by following these steps:

1. **Open the word-processing program while you are using iTunes.**
2. **Switch to iTunes, select the playlist, and choose Edit⇨View Options.**

   The View Options window opens.
3. **Select the columns you want to appear in the song list.**

   To pick a column, click the check box next to the column header so that a check mark appears. Any unchecked column headers are columns that do not appear. ***Note:*** The Song Name column always appears in the listing and can't be removed.
4. **Select all the songs in the playlist and choose Edit⇨Copy.**

   To select all the songs in the playlist, click the first song, and hold down Shift while clicking the last song to highlight all the songs.
5. **Switch to your word-processing program and choose Edit⇨Paste.**

   The liner notes appear in your word-processing program, as shown in Figure 4-4.

Dealing with Trouble in Paradise

Murphy's Law applies to everything, even something as simple as burning a CD-R disc. Don't think for a moment that you are immune to the whims and treacheries of Murphy, who in all his infinite wisdom (no one really knows who Murphy was), pronounced that if anything *could* go wrong, it would go wrong. We cover some of the most common problems in this section.

The best way to test your newly burned disc is to pop it right back into your SuperDrive or any CD-ROM drive, or try it on a CD player. Audio CD-R discs play just like any commercial audio CD. MP3 CDs play fine on MP3 CD players and also work in computers with CD-ROM and DVD drives.

If the CD works on the Mac but not on a CD player, you may have a compatibility problem with the player and CD-R discs. We have a five-year-old CD player that doesn't play CD-R discs very well, and car players sometimes have trouble with them.

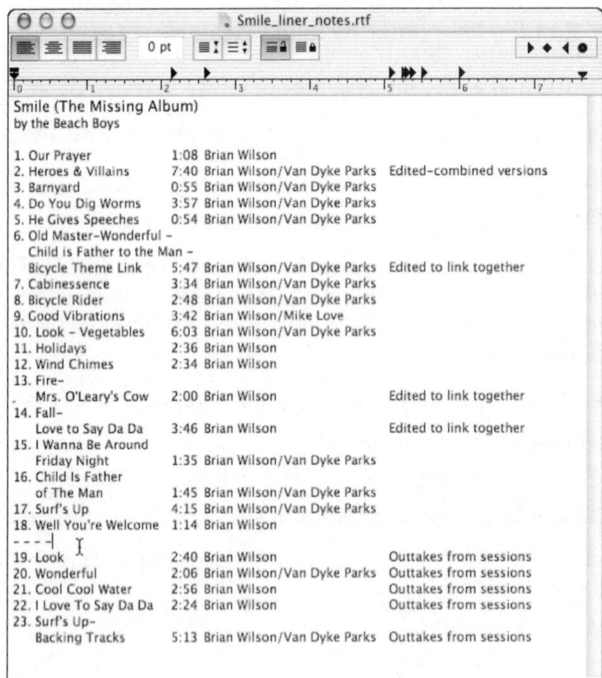

Smile (The Missing Album)
by the Beach Boys

1. Our Prayer	1:08	Brian Wilson	
2. Heroes & Villains	7:40	Brian Wilson/Van Dyke Parks	Edited-combined versions
3. Barnyard	0:55	Brian Wilson/Van Dyke Parks	
4. Do You Dig Worms	3:57	Brian Wilson/Van Dyke Parks	
5. He Gives Speeches	0:54	Brian Wilson/Van Dyke Parks	
6. Old Master-Wonderful - Child is Father to the Man - Bicycle Theme Link	5:47	Brian Wilson/Van Dyke Parks	Edited to link together
7. Cabinessence	3:34	Brian Wilson/Van Dyke Parks	
8. Bicycle Rider	2:48	Brian Wilson/Van Dyke Parks	
9. Good Vibrations	3:42	Brian Wilson/Mike Love	
10. Look - Vegetables	6:03	Brian Wilson/Van Dyke Parks	
11. Holidays	2:36	Brian Wilson	
12. Wind Chimes	2:34	Brian Wilson	
13. Fire- Mrs. O'Leary's Cow	2:00	Brian Wilson	Edited to link together
14. Fall- Love to Say Da Da	3:46	Brian Wilson	Edited to link together
15. I Wanna Be Around Friday Night	1:35	Brian Wilson/Van Dyke Parks	
16. Child Is Father of The Man	1:45	Brian Wilson/Van Dyke Parks	
17. Surf's Up	4:15	Brian Wilson/Van Dyke Parks	
18. Well You're Welcome	1:14	Brian Wilson	
----			
19. Look	2:40	Brian Wilson	Outtakes from sessions
20. Wonderful	2:06	Brian Wilson/Van Dyke Parks	Outtakes from sessions
21. Cool Cool Water	2:56	Brian Wilson	Outtakes from sessions
22. I Love To Say Da Da	2:24	Brian Wilson	Outtakes from sessions
23. Surf's Up- Backing Tracks	5:13	Brian Wilson/Van Dyke Parks	Outtakes from sessions

Figure 4-4: Edit the exported playlist text in TextEdit.

- ***Problem:*** The disc won't burn.

  Solution: Perhaps you have a bum disc (it happens). Try another one.

- ***Problem:*** The disc doesn't play, or stutters when playing, with a CD player.

  Solution: This happens often with older players that don't play CD-R discs well. Try the disc in your Mac CD-ROM, DVD-ROM, or SuperDrive. If it works there, and you set the format to Audio CD, then you probably have a compatibility problem with your CD player.

- ***Problem:*** The disc doesn't show tracks on a CD player, or ejects immediately.

  Solution: Be sure to use the proper disc format — choose iTunes➪Preferences, and click the Burning button to see the Disc Format setting in the Burning Preferences window. The Audio CD format works in just about all CD players that play CD-R discs. MP3 CDs work in MP3 CD players and computer CD-ROM and DVD drives. Data CD or DVD discs work only in computer drives.

- ***Problem:*** The eMac went to sleep while burning and never woke up.

  Solution: You have found one strange glitch that fortunately only applies to eMacs set to go into sleep mode. As a safety precaution, turn off sleep mode in the Energy Saver preferences (in System Preferences) before starting a burn.

- ***Problem:*** Some songs in a playlist were skipped and not burned onto the disc.

  Solution: Audio CD-R discs burn with songs encoded in any format, but you can use only MP3-encoded songs to burn an MP3 CD-R — any songs not encoded in MP3 are skipped (any Audible files are also skipped). If your playlist for an audio CD-R disc includes music purchased from the Apple Music Store or other online stores in the protected AAC encoding format, some rules may apply — see the section, "Creating a Burn Playlist," in this chapter.

Burning CDs is a personal matter. Piracy is not a technology issue — it is a behavior issue. Don't violate copyright law.

Book II

iPhoto

"Remember–if you're updating the family album, no more animated GIFs of your sister swinging from a tree, scratching her armpits!"

Chapter 1: Getting to Know iPhoto

In This Chapter

- **Features to look for in digital cameras**
- **What iPhoto can do for you**
- **Opening images in iPhoto**

Taking photos has never been easier. Digital cameras and Apple software have combined to turn the Macintosh into a digital darkroom without the need for a dark room with smelly chemicals and film processing equipment. In fact, you no longer need film. What a relief! You can take all the pictures you want without having to find a store to buy another roll of film.

This chapter tells you all you need to know about digital cameras, and provides an overview of what you can do with iPhoto. You find out how to get around in iPhoto and look at your pictures in detail.

Living in the Digital World

Maybe your vacation photos bore other people, but to you they're priceless, preserving special memories. Family pictures, vacations, weddings . . . these events don't happen every day and you don't want your photos to deteriorate due to weather and other environmental factors, such as kids with peanut-butter fingers. But film negatives eventually deteriorate. Photographic prints don't last forever and are costly to replace, if they can be replaced at all. The cost of film also limits the number of pictures you may want to take.

In the digital world, these limitations don't exist. The ones and zeroes that make up digital information don't change, and the image remains perfect — for all eternity. In fact, you can't tell how old a digital image really is.

Digital information can be destroyed, however. Your computer may fail, taking the hard disk with it (or vice versa). A virus can take over your computer and wreak havoc, destroying files in the process. Your laptop can be stolen. You may drop the computer while moving. Stuff happens, even in the digital world.

USB versus FireWire for digital cameras

USB (Universal Serial Bus) is used for everything from keyboards to pointing devices, hard disks, and scanners. USB connectors are plug-and-play: You can plug them in at any time while your computer is on or off. Many devices get their power directly from the Mac through the USB connection.

Like USB, FireWire also supplies power to a device, such as a camera, through the same cable that connects to the computer. FireWire devices are also plug-and-play. But FireWire can handle data transfer speeds of more than 30 times faster than USB — at least that's true of the first versions of USB and FireWire. USB version 1, which is used in every Mac model sold at the time of this writing, offers a transfer rate of 12 megabits per second (Mbps). FireWire version A offers a rate of 400 Mbps. However, the more advanced generation of USB, version 2, is 40 times faster than the first version. While Mac OS X supports USB 2.0 with an eye toward the future, only the G5 desktops, at the time of this writing, sport the actual 2.0 connectors. Meanwhile, the FireWire spec (IEEE-1394) hasn't stood still: Version B offers 800 Mbps, twice as fast as Version A. Again, OS X supports both, but as of this writing, older Mac models offer Version A. The new G3 and 17-inch PowerBook G4 offer Version B.

Even though FireWire is faster, USB is the connection of choice for most digital cameras (very high quality cameras that offer FireWire are the exception). USB is generally fast enough for transferring images. Digital camera manufacturers need to make cameras that work with all types of computers, and many computers have USB, not FireWire.

But you can protect information a number of ways. With iPhoto, you can archive all of your photos to CD or DVD, creating multiple copies easily. You can, for example, store archives of your photos on separate DVDs, storing one copy at home and another at work for safekeeping — all for just the price of a few blank DVD discs.

Why digital is better: Instant pictures

Everything about digital photography is easier and costs less than traditional photography. Digital photography is truly instant gratification — you see the results immediately and can then take more pictures based on what happened an instant before.

With a film camera, you pay for every picture, including the accidental shot of your foot. The entire roll, no matter what's on it, has to be processed before you even see the photos. And if you want extra prints of the good photos, you need to reorder them, and pay for them again.

With a digital camera, you see your pictures in seconds, and you can delete bad shots and reshoot them. You can archive what you like, and you can delete what you don't like. If you have a color printer, obtaining extra prints is as easy as using the Print command. You can even e-mail the photos to a service for high-quality prints. You never have to run to a store to buy film, nor waste money again on perishable film you don't use.

Features of digital cameras can be intimidating. Camera buffs speak a different language with their F-stops, optical zoom, and fish-eye lenses. You may want to base your choice of digital cameras on features such as optical zoom, which offers a higher-quality close-up than digital zoom, or the type of memory card available for the camera.

If you're an amateur photographer (like us), you probably don't need to be too picky about which camera to buy. You can get excellent results from just about any digital camera. You need only know two important facts when picking out a digital camera:

- **Your camera must be compatible with the Mac USB (a.k.a. Universal Serial Bus) or FireWire (a.k.a. IEEE-1394) connectors.**
- **Image quality is measured by the pixel resolution of the digital camera.**

Resolution — the image quality factor

All you need to know about image quality with a digital camera is the number of pixels — specific points of information in a picture. Digital cameras are often described by the image resolution in millions of pixels, or *megapixels*. Higher megapixel counts usually result in better images. A 2-megapixel camera produces good 4 x 6-inch prints and acceptable 8 x 10-inch prints. A 3-megapixel camera produces very good 4 x 6-inch prints and magazine-quality 8 x 10-inch prints. A 5-megapixel camera produces good quality 10 x 14-inch prints. And so on.

Improving and enhancing your photos

If you aren't a professional photographer, the chances that your pictures come out perfect every time are very slim. Some of the pictures may not be as vivid as you thought they would be. That postcard-perfect view from the highway may show a bit of road litter and guardrail, and you want to cut that part out. Or maybe the light was too bright or too dim, or your flashbulb put red spots in your subject's eyes (red-eye).

No problem. iPhoto is a digital darkroom, offering a number of easy ways to improve and enhance your photos, such as the following:

- **You can instantly correct any photo that's too dark, too light, or overexposed.** iPhoto provides editing tools for automatically correcting that red-eye effect.
- **You can crop any image.** *Cropping* is a process in which you draw a smaller rectangle inside the image and omit everything outside the rectangle. You can improve a postcard-perfect view of a highway by removing, for example, the road litter and guardrail at the bottom edge.
- **You can change color photos to black and white (actually gray).** This feature is very handy for printing in books, newspapers, newsletters, or documents that don't use color.
- **You can make blemishes disappear like magic.** (And with some creative editing in programs such as Adobe Photoshop, you can even make people look thinner.)

You don't have to load any special software to do the kind of improvements to your pictures that make them more effective as photographs. Chapter 4 of this book provides details on how to make improvements.

Storing, printing, and sharing your photos

iPhoto acts as your own processing lab and photo service. iPhoto allows you to use your Mac to keep track of photos with titles and keywords and comments. You can quickly display them on-screen, in any size ranging from thumbnails to full screen.

The iPhoto photo library holds any number of photos — limited only by how much disk space you have. Even if you store thousands and thousands of photos in your library, find the one you want quickly and easily by searching by titles or comments. Even better, you can organize the photos in separate photo albums — and in each album, you can arrange the photos exactly in the sequence you want for slideshows and photo books.

You can produce slideshows, photo portfolios, and even nicely bound coffee-table photo books and school yearbooks. All you have to do is organize the photos in an album, select a theme and a layout, and bingo, iPhoto creates the book in electronic format. You can then print out the pages on your own printer, or order professionally-printed and bound books from a service directly from iPhoto. In the case of a school yearbook, you could get last-minute pictures into it and still make the graduation-day deadline.

Photos are just the beginning of the iLife experience. iPhoto connects to the other iLife applications, and if you explore them you find uses for your digital photos you hadn't thought of before, such as creating a DVD of a slideshow using music from your iTunes library, or using photos in an iMovie project along with video clips and music.

More pixels mean higher quality

When digital cameras take a picture, they divide the image in the lens into many tiny squares, or pixels, to represent the image. There are two factors with pixels that affect image quality. The first factor, controlled by the digital camera or scanner, is the spatial resolution of the image. The *spatial resolution* is the number of pixels in the image both horizontally and vertically. With a pixel dimension of 300 x 300, for example, an image has a total of 90,000 pixels. With a pixel dimension of 1,000 by 1,000, the image has a million pixels, or a *megapixel*. The more pixels, or specific points of information in a picture, the more detail that is represented, as shown in the following figure. The photo on the left shows less detail than the photo on the right, which was taken with a higher-resolution camera.

The second factor is the number of colors your Mac can display, which is controlled by the Display setting in the System Preferences. When you set the Display setting to the Millions option, you are actually getting over 16 million colors. You get 16 million colors because a pixel in a typical image can represent 256 levels of red, green, and blue, which gives a possible tonal range of over 16 million colors (256 x 256 x 256). Anything less than that can cause the image to appear with splotches of the same color rather than a subtle tonal range of color.

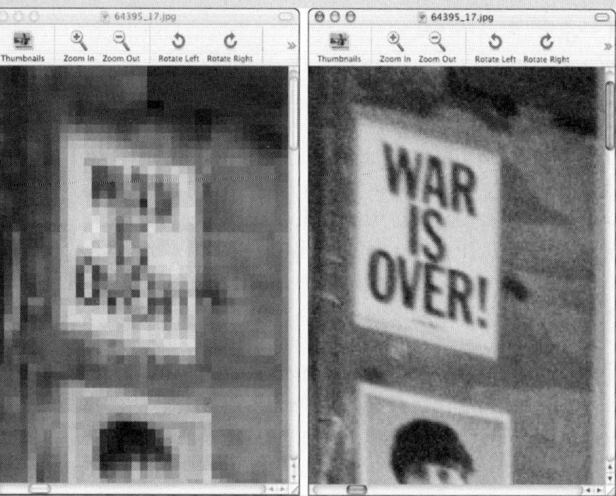

Saving your photos has never been easier. You can copy your entire photo collection to another hard disk, or burn CDs or DVDs with your images to keep archives. Archiving saves all the information you have about each photo, including date, album, film roll, keywords, and comments. After you archive your photos on CD or DVD, you can still view them in iPhoto directly from the disc — when you insert the disc, the archived library on the disc appears automatically in iPhoto with its titles, keywords, and photo albums.

You can also share photos. E-mail them directly from iPhoto if you use the standard Mac OS X Mail application, or even Eudora or Microsoft Entourage. You can even share entire slideshows with others on the Internet using the .Mac service, or post photos on Web pages. Essentially everyone can have a copy of your photos.

We describe slideshows in detail in Chapter 5 of this book. You can read all about printing photos and photo books, and sharing photos online in Chapter 6 of this book.

Opening Images in iPhoto

This section provides a tour of iPhoto. If you're using iPhoto for the first time, you won't have photos in your photo library until you import them, which we cover in Chapter 2. If you already have photos on your hard disk (either scanned images or files from a digital photo service), you can drag the files directly to the iPhoto window after starting iPhoto to add them to your photo library.

Starting iPhoto

The iPhoto icon is available in the Dock, which appears typically at the bottom of the desktop. To start iPhoto, click the iPhoto icon.

When you start iPhoto, its window takes up a good portion of your desktop, but you may want to make it as large as possible to see all your thumbnails and view individual images with as large a viewing area as possible. To do this, choose Window➪Zoom Window. The Zoom Window command fills the desktop with the iPhoto window. To make the iPhoto window smaller, choose Zoom Window again.

To make the window invisible but accessible from the Dock, choose Window➪Minimize Window. (If you do this and then can't find iPhoto, click either the iPhoto icon or the newly created minimized document icon in the Dock, and the window reappears.) iPhoto works like all the other "i-applications" in Mac OS X.

Changing your display settings

When you start iPhoto, you may get the message `Caution: The current screen resolution is not optimal for iPhoto`. Whether accidentally or intentionally, your color display setting is set to fewer colors than the display can actually handle, or your display's resolution is set to a lower number than possible. Either one of these settings, if not set to its highest value, causes this message to appear. And in particular, if you use an older iBook, the settings provided for the iBook display always causes this message to appear.

If you're unlucky enough to get this message, don't panic. iPhoto still works properly, but colors in images may appear in solid splotches rather than smooth gradients, and the images themselves may not appear as good as they would at the higher settings. The images aren't changed, of course — the digital information is still there. All you need to do is change your display settings.

You can change your display settings at any time in OS X and your settings take effect immediately. However, you should first quit iPhoto before doing so.

Follow these steps to change your display settings:

1. **Choose ⇨System Preferences from the Finder menu.**

   The System Preferences window displays.

2. **Click the Displays icon.**

   The icon appears in the Hardware row of icons (and also, typically, in the top row of most-used icons).

   The Display Preferences window appears.

3. **Click the Display tab.**

   The Display pane appears.

4. **Choose the highest pixel resolution setting in the Resolutions list.**

   The resolution settings are on the left side of the Display pane. Your display may be capable of 1024 x 768 pixels; you should choose that setting or a higher one if available.

5. **Choose the Millions option from the Colors pop-up menu.**

   The Colors pop-up menu is to the right of the list of resolution settings, in the Display pane. Your display should be capable of displaying millions of colors; choose that setting so that your photos look their best.

6. **Close the System Preferences window by choosing System Preferences⇨Quit System Preferences.**

Now your display settings offer the best quality viewing for your photos.

Getting around in iPhoto

The iPhoto window is split into three major sections, or *panes* (as in windowpanes), as shown in Figure 1-1.

- **Tools pane:** The iPhoto tools pane acts like a control center, offering one-click access to the iPhoto tools. These tools change when you switch modes by clicking the mode buttons, which are Import, Organize, Edit, and Book.

- **Album list pane:** The list of albums appears in a pane on the left side of the window. You use this list to organize your photo albums and select them for viewing. Beneath this pane are buttons for creating a new album, playing a slideshow, showing information about the selected photos, and rotating the selected photos.
- **Viewer pane:** The largest windowpane — the viewer — displays your photo thumbnails when you are in Organize mode. Individual photographs show when you select one for viewing or editing.

Figure 1-1: The iPhoto window is split into three panes.

When you first use iPhoto, the photo library appears in the viewer pane. As you organize photos into photo albums, the names of the albums appear in the album list pane. You can change the viewer pane to show only a single album's photos by selecting the album's name in the album list pane. To view the entire photo library, click the photo library at the top of the album list pane.

Use the mode buttons to switch modes of operation:

- **Import:** Transfer photos from your digital camera.
- **Organize:** View your photo library and organize photo albums.
- **Edit:** View a single photo to make improvements, such as removing red-eye and changing brightness and contrast.
- **Book:** Organize photos into a book layout for printing books.

Viewing photos

The viewer pane of the iPhoto window shows thumbnail images of your photos. You can change the size of the thumbnail images — make them shrink or grow larger to see more detail — by dragging the size control slider (beneath the viewer pane) to the right, as shown in Figure 1-2. The size control slider has an icon of a large photo on one side and a small one on the other.

Figure 1-2: Drag the size control slider to make thumbnails larger or smaller.

To look at a single image, double-click the thumbnail of the image, or click it once (to select it) and click the Edit mode button. Either way, the image fills the viewer pane, and the tools in the toolbar change into the Edit mode tools, as shown in Figure 1-3.

As you see in Figure 1-3, even in Edit mode the size control slider is available to make the image larger or smaller, so you can zoom into an image to see more detail, or zoom out to see the entire picture.

For optimum viewing, check out the following tips:

✦ **Open a photo in a separate window:** Hold down the Option key while double-clicking a photo's thumbnail, for an even better way to view a photo, as shown in Figure 1-4. iPhoto scales the photo in its proper proportions, rather than stretching it to fit the iPhoto viewer pane, so the image looks exactly as it should.

If you like the separate window approach to view your photos, and you want iPhoto to do this every time you double-click a photo (rather than using the viewer pane in Edit mode), choose iPhoto⇨Preferences, and in the Preferences window that appears, switch the Double-click option to the Opens in Separate Window option.

- **Compare several photos side by side:** Open several photos, each in separate windows, by holding down the Option key while double-clicking the thumbnails. This is where a large display comes in handy.

You can tell how large the photo is, too — whether it is a small photo scaled to display at 100 percent magnification, which is its actual size, or if it is a very large photo scaled at 50 percent or less in order to display it. iPhoto displays, in the window's title bar, the percent the photo is scaled — for example, in Figure 1-4, the photo is scaled to 39 percent of its actual size.

- **Zoom in and out of photos:** The Zoom buttons on the left side of the photo window's special toolbar (at the top of the window) allow you to zoom in or out of the photo. You can also scale the photo by dragging the window's lower-right corner to make the window larger or smaller. The Fit button in the window's toolbar automatically scales the photo to fit the window. The window's toolbar offers many of the Edit mode tools including cropping and rotating in the toolbar.

Figure 1-3: Double-click a thumbnail to see the image in detail.

Figure 1-4: Option + double-click opens the photo in its own window.

You can experiment freely with the Edit mode tools to improve your photos, as we describe in Chapter 4 of this book. You can, for example, click the B & W button to turn the photo into black and white (actually shades of gray). You can adjust brightness and contrast, and even experiment with retouching and cropping. It doesn't matter how much you experiment — if you don't like a change you make, don't worry: iPhoto stores originals of every photo in its library. Simply choose File⇨Revert to Original and your original photo is restored in pristine condition.

Chapter 2: Importing Photos

In This Chapter

- **Importing your photos from a digital camera**
- **Using a photo service to import photos**
- **Importing images from your hard drive**
- **Scanning images into iPhoto**

With iPhoto, you can import pictures directly from your digital camera. Don't have a digital camera? You still like to use that old Brownie your grandmother gave you? Don't worry. You can use a scanner to scan photographic prints, or send your film rolls to a photo service that can convert your film to digital images on a CD or the Web. (Odds are the photo service you already use offers this service. Next time you're there, ask about it.) iPhoto has no problem importing images from CD or hard disk. In this chapter, you find out how to import your photos — even those musty photos of grandma you found in the attic — into iPhoto.

Importing Photos from Digital Cameras

If you ever need to show somebody how much easier it is to use a Mac, all you need to do is open iPhoto, connect your digital camera to the USB port, and click the Import button. That's all there is to it. Your photographs appear in the iPhoto viewer pane, ready to edit, print, archive, or whatever you want to do.

Your picture-taking skills may improve with iPhoto as you experiment more, without the limitations of film. Because digital cameras don't use film, you'll find yourself taking many more pictures than usual, dumping them into your Mac, viewing them, deleting the truly bad ones, and taking more pictures. As your collection of photographs grows, you will appreciate how easy importing and organizing your photos in iPhoto is. The photo library allows you to view all the photos you import from your digital camera.

Connecting a digital camera

USB (Universal Serial Bus) is the connection of choice for most digital cameras — the exceptions are very high quality cameras that offer FireWire. Fortunately, both types of connections work the same way.

To import pictures from a digital camera, follow these steps:

1. **Connect the camera to the Mac using a USB or FireWire cable.**

   Digital cameras typically come with a special USB or FireWire cable that has a very small connector on one end for the camera, and a larger connector on the other end for the computer's USB or FireWire port. If both ends are the same, it doesn't matter which end is plugged into the camera or the computer.

2. **Power up your digital camera by pushing the power button.**

   Most cameras also have a power-on switch to save battery life. (Many smart people, including ourselves, have sat there waiting for the photos to appear, only to find that the camera was still asleep.)

   Connecting your camera first is usually better, and then turn the camera on, because the Mac may not recognize some camera models unless they are turned on while connected. If the Mac doesn't recognize your camera, try turning the camera off, and then turning it on again.

3. **Click the iPhoto icon to start iPhoto (if it hasn't already started).**

   When you connect and power on your digital camera, the iPhoto icon becomes animated (or *dancing* in the Dock), awaiting your click. Depending on how you configure your Mac, iPhoto may automatically start when the computer detects the camera. If you are running iPhoto for the first time, a dialog box pops up asking if you want to always run iPhoto when you connect a camera. Click the Yes button.

   iPhoto opens displaying the iPhoto window.

4. **Click the Import mode button.**

   The tools pane changes to show the Import tools, as shown in Figure 2-1.

   When you start iPhoto, you may get the message `Caution: The current screen resolution is not optimal for iPhoto`. Whether accidentally or intentionally, your color display setting is set to fewer colors than the display can actually handle, or your display's resolution is set to a lower number than possible. See Chapter 1 of this book to change your display settings.

5. **Choose whether or not to delete the photos in your camera after importing.**

   If you want to delete photos from your camera as soon as they are imported, click the Erase Camera Contents after Transfer option in the tools pane (located at the bottom of the iPhoto window). Many cameras have a delete function, so you don't need to use this option, but this option makes importing and deleting photos in the camera all in one step possible. With the photos in the photo library, you no longer need to keep copies in your camera or memory card, and you can make room for new photos.

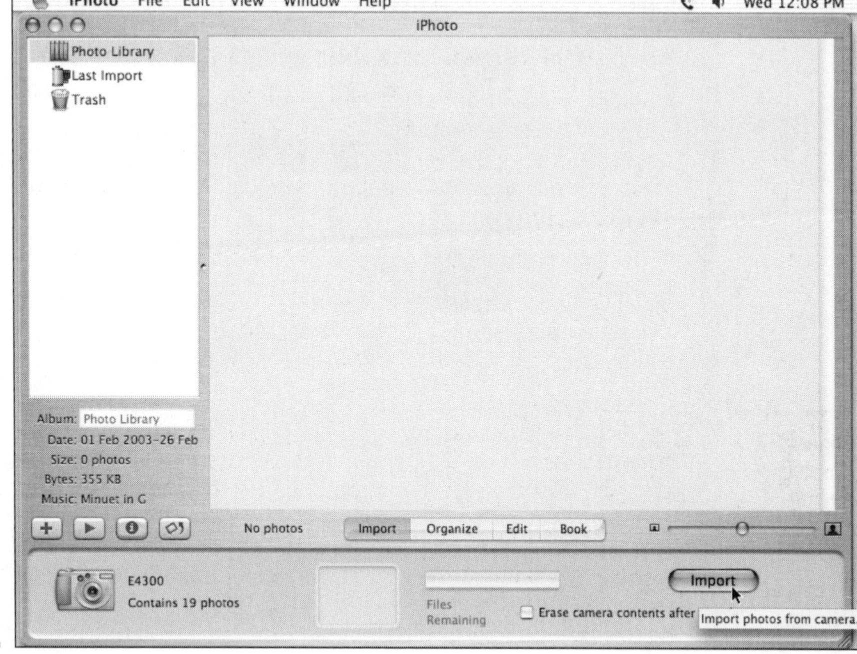

Figure 2-1: iPhoto is in import mode, ready to import photos from a digital camera.

6. **Click the Import button.**

   iPhoto displays a small thumbnail image for each photo as it imports the photo, as shown in Figure 2-2. Each photo imports into the photo library, where all images reside. While the importing occurs, the Import button changes to a Stop button; to cancel the photo transfer at any time during your import, click the Stop button.

   If your camera has a sleep mode, make sure you disable or set it to a time increment long enough to allow your images to import into the Mac. Importing 24 photos generally takes about one minute with most digital cameras.

7. **Disconnect the camera (eject it first if necessary).**

   If ejecting is required, the camera's icon appears on the desktop. To eject the camera, click the camera's icon and hold down the mouse button. The Trash icon changes to the Eject icon. You can then drag the camera icon over the Eject icon to eject the camera properly. While nothing really happens (nothing actually ejects from the machine, nor do any doors open), you may find that if you don't eject as required with some cameras, your images may not delete from the camera even if you have the delete option enabled.

Figure 2-2: Imported photos appear as thumbnails in the photo library.

Wait until all photos transfer into iPhoto or click the Stop button before disconnecting your camera.

Of course, if you don't like to drag icons (such as when you use a laptop in an airline seat and dragging may cause you to elbow your neighbor), you can click the camera icon and press ⌘+ E. When the camera ejects properly, you can then disconnect the camera.

If you disconnect your camera and suddenly get a message from OS X telling you that the device isn't properly disconnected, you didn't drag its icon over the Trash icon. Other USB devices may be in trouble if you did this — with hard disks, for example, you could lose data if the disk is disconnected improperly.

Importing from memory card readers

Additional memory cards are like extra rolls of film. A memory card reader is useful if you take lots of pictures and use additional cards. Rather than connecting your camera to your Mac every time you want to transfer pictures, leave the card reader connected to the USB port of your Mac and put the camera's memory card in the card reader. If you use multiple memory cards, this method is especially convenient.

Many cameras come with relatively small memory cards — 16MB or less, enough to hold about 24 pictures. Memory card formats include Compact Flash, SmartMedia, and Memory Stick. They all function in a similar manner, but they're different physical sizes and shapes.

If you want to get more memory cards for your camera, be sure to ask for the right kind of card, as the wrong type won't work with your camera. Generally, a sample memory card is provided with your new digital camera, along with information about which type of cards to buy.

iPhoto imports photos from a card reader just as it does with a camera, using the same steps:

1. **Connect the card reader to the Mac.**

   Standard USB cables generally work with card readers, so either end of the cable can be plugged into the card reader and the computer. If you use a memory card reader that doesn't offer a USB connection, it may provide a PCMCIA card for a PCMCIA slot often found in computers, especially PCs. Some Mac models also offer PCMCIA slots, and you can insert the PCMCIA card for the memory card reader into a slot and use it like any other device.

2. **Power up your card reader and insert a card.**

   Use the power button on your card reader if you have one; many card readers power themselves on by sensing power from the USB cable.

3. **Start iPhoto.**

   The iPhoto icon is available on the desktop in the Dock. Simply click the iPhoto icon, and the iPhoto window appears.

4. **Click the Import mode button.**

   The tools pane changes to show the Import tools (refer to Figure 2-1).

5. **Click the Import button in the tools pane.**

   If your card reader is connected and powered on, iPhoto displays the card icon in the tools pane, along with the number of photos on the card and the Import button. While importing, the Import button changes to the Stop button. To cancel the photo transfer at any time during your import, click the Stop button. If you want to delete photos from the memory card as soon as they are imported, click the Erase Camera Contents After Transfer option in the tools pane. With the photos in the photo library, you no longer need to keep copies on your memory card, and you can make room for new photos.

6. **Eject and disconnect the card reader.**

   Wait until all the photos transfer into iPhoto or click the Stop button before disconnecting your card reader. After you finish importing your photos, drag the card reader's icon from the desktop to the Trash icon in the Dock. However, you may find leaving your card reader connected to your Mac useful, and just switch memory cards to import more photos.

Transferring Images from Other Sources

If you don't have a digital camera, don't worry. You can turn your film into digital images in many ways. You can continue to use your favorite film camera and probably even continue using whatever services you use now for film processing.

If your camera uses 35mm film, you can have your pictures developed by a digital imaging service, such as PhotoWorks (`www.photoworks.com`) or the "You've Got Pictures" service on America Online (sponsored by Kodak). Many services offer digital processing of film and choices on how to deliver the digital images — on a floppy disk or CD, or posted on the Web for easy downloading to your Mac.

Suppose you have photographic prints or slides. You may think that prints or slides can't be included in the photo library. But you'd be wrong. In fact you can not only include them and organize them into albums, but you can improve these photos. Then you can create new prints and do anything with them that you can do with your digital images.

Using a photo service

Many photo services offer photos on CDs, which can be mailed to you or picked up at your convenience. Typically the service offers either the Kodak Picture CD or Photo CD formats, but it may offer a special format that requires software from the service.

We should mention here that professional photographers using film cameras should investigate professional services that offer at least the Photo CD format. Services offering high-resolution film scanning most likely offer Photo CD discs that you can use with your Mac and iPhoto, as well as high-resolution digital files that can be transferred by network or high-speed Internet connection. The Photo CD format offers resolutions high enough for even magazine-quality photo prints.

If the format is Photo CD or Picture CD, you import the photos by following these steps:

1. **Insert the CD into your CD-ROM drive.**

   An icon representing the CD appears on the desktop.

2. **Click the CD icon to view the files in the Finder.**
3. **Open iPhoto by clicking its icon on the desktop.**

   iPhoto opens displaying the iPhoto window.

4. **Drag the individual files (or folder of files) containing the photos to the iPhoto viewer pane (as shown in Figure 2-3).**
5. **Close the Finder window by clicking the button in the right corner of the title bar when the files finish copying.**
6. **Drag the CD icon to the Trash icon to eject the CD from the CD-ROM drive.**

If you drag a folder, a film roll is created with the folder's name. If the folder you import contains subfolders, film rolls are created with each subfolder's name. We describe how to edit the film roll information in Chapter 3 of this book.

If a service offers images on floppy disk, you may want to choose that medium. However, floppies hold only about 1MB of image data, compared to nearly 600MB available on a CD. You also need to have a floppy disk drive for your Mac, which is not included in the newest Mac models.

If a service offers a format that is not Photo CD or Picture CD, it most likely offers software you can download that extracts the images from the CD and save them as image files on your hard disk. While having every service use the same or similar format would be convenient, some services offer proprietary formats. For example, PhotoWorks offers a CD format that requires use of the service's special software, but this software offers the ability to organize photos into albums, much like iPhoto itself. PhotoWorks offers this software not to compete with iPhoto, but to provide iPhoto-like functions for people who use PCs and older Macs that can't run iPhoto. The software is free and very easy to download, and it is also supplied with the CD in case you don't want to download it.

When a service offers a proprietary format with special software, make sure the software can save the image in one of the following formats: TIFF, PICT, JPG (or JPEG), or EPS. You don't need to know anything about these formats to import them, except that TIFF is the preferred format for photos because it guarantees the highest quality without compression. iPhoto can import images in any of these formats automatically.

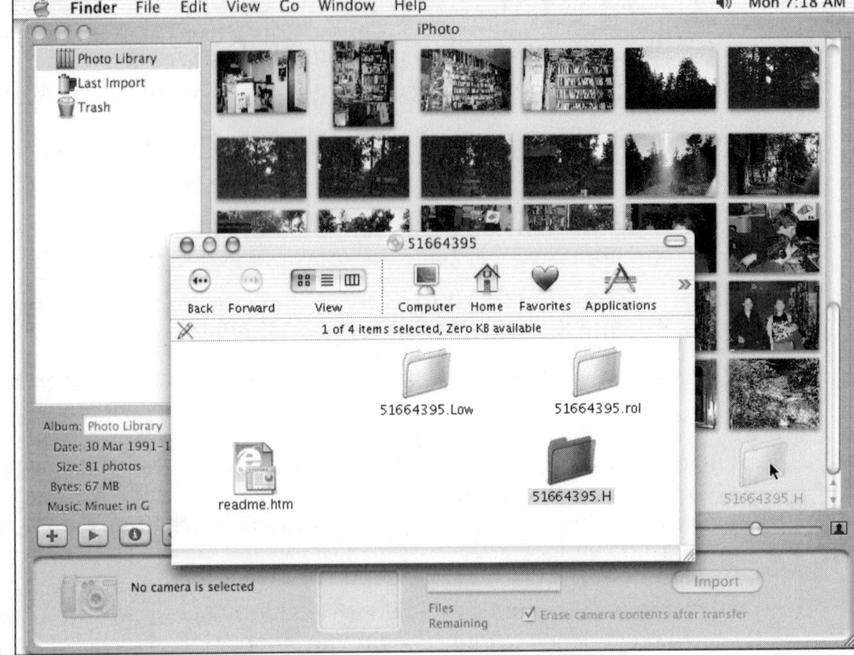

Figure 2-3: Import photos from a CD by dragging files to the iPhoto window.

Importing images from your hard drive

If you save images to your hard disk in one of the appropriate formats, you can then import each file or a folder of files. Follow these steps to import files:

1. **With iPhoto open, choose File⇨Import.**

   The File Import dialog box appears.

2. **Use the Mac Finder browser to find the folder containing the image files.**
3. **Select the image file or files to import.**
4. **Click the Import button.**

   Your images import to the photo library.

You can delete the image files from your hard disk after importing them.

Using a scanner

A scanner optically scans a photographic print, slide, or negative, and creates a digital image. A scanner can be controlled directly by a Mac using the Image Capture application.

Unless you have a consistent need for scanning, you may get by with using a scanning service at a local copy shop, such as Kinko's. Many shops offer self-service scanning with instructions, and others do the scanning for you. All you need to know to order scans of photographic prints is the following:

- **Ask for the highest color depth.** The Mac can handle millions of colors, which is also known as 32-bit color in the world of PCs.
- **Ask for the highest affordable resolution.** Many services offer scanning at 600 dots-per-inch (dpi), which is acceptable for most personal uses.
- **Select the TIFF file format.** TIFF files are better than any other compressed file format (such as JPEG) for images that you still want to work on — to edit or retouch, as we describe in Chapter 4 of this book.

If your scanner is connected to your Mac (most likely with a USB cable), install the Mac OS X software that was provided with it. If you don't have the software, check with the manufacturer of the scanner to see if it works with Mac OS X. If it does, you can use the Image Capture application, located in the Applications folder to scan photos:

1. **Open Image Capture and click the Full Screen button to see the whole image.**
2. **Use the selection tool in the toolbar to zoom in and define the image scan area.**

   Select a portion of the image to scan, or the entire image.
3. **When you're satisfied with the results, click the Scan button to create a TIFF file, and save the file on your hard disk.**

   Image Capture provides a dialog box for saving the TIFF file in a folder on your hard disk.

Use the Options button in the toolbar to change the scanner's settings to set image-related options, such as resolution if you don't like the outcome of the file. Check the documentation that came with your scanner for more information about its capabilities.

If you want Image Capture to open automatically when you press a button on your scanner, choose the Preferences option from the Image Capture menu. In the Preferences dialog box, select the Image Capture option from the When a Scanner Button Is Press, Open menu.

Finally, import the TIFF file into iPhoto by following these steps:

1. **Choose File⇨Import.**

   The File Import dialog box appears.

2. **Navigate to the folder containing the image files.**
3. **Select the image file to import.**
4. **Click the Import button.**

   The files are imported into iPhoto.

After you import image files, the images in those files become part of the photo library. You can then delete the image files after importing them.

Scanner talk

Once upon a time, before digital cameras became widely available, the only way to get a photo into digital form was to use a scanner — a machine that optically scans a photographic print or slide in the same way that a copier can optically scan a piece of paper and reproduce it.

In fact, most copiers are essentially scanners, and many of today's office copiers double as image scanners when connected to a computer. The typical flatbed scanner is popular because you can put anything on the scanning surface — a photographic print, a book page, a newspaper, an object, or even a body part such as your hand — and scan the material. Sheet-fed scanners look more like copiers and accept only flat pieces of paper, making them not as useful for scanning photographic prints.

Slide scanners designed for scanning 35mm slides are a bit more expensive than your average flatbed scanner. If you have slides that need to be scanned, you may want to instead use a photo service, as many of them offer slide scanning. Slide scanners aren't convenient to buy because of the expense and because digital cameras are cheaper and easier to use. If you really need slides, a photo service can take your digital photos and create slides from them.

If you are even semi-serious about getting a scanner, check out *Scanners For Dummies* by Mark L. Chambers (published by Wiley Publishing, Inc.). Image Capture works with scanners that have driver software for Mac OS X. Image Capture also works with TWAIN drivers that are Mac OS X-compatible. TWAIN is a standard protocol for controlling scanners from computers, and has nothing to do with Mark Twain, nor is it an acronym — it refers to Rudyard Kipling's "The Ballad of East and West" and its famous line, ". . . and never the twain shall meet . . ." — an ironic reflection on the difficulty, at that time, of connecting scanners and personal computers.

Chapter 3: Organizing Photos

In This Chapter

- Organizing photos into photo albums
- Using iPhoto as a digital contact sheet
- Arranging, sorting, and searching for photos
- Backing up your photo library

Free photos are a wonderful thing. After you see how easy taking pictures with a digital camera is, and how you can save your photos on the Mac without spending money on film, and share them with others by printing them yourself or sending them by e-mail, you'll start experimenting at will. Go ahead, take another shot. If you run out of exposures on your digital film card, connect your camera or card reader to your Mac and offload the photos to the photo library, and delete them from the memory card. Then go back and take more pictures!

The iPhoto photo library can hold any number of photos; the number is limited only by available hard disk space. At an average size of 1MB per photo (and many photos occupy less space), you can store 20,000 photos in a 20GB hard disk. And, of course, you can expand a photo library over multiple disks or create multiple libraries. The number of digital photos you can manage has no practical limit, using backup storage devices and media, such as DVDs. For all practical purposes, you can keep shooting pictures forever.

Fortunately, you can organize even massive quantities of photos in the photo library. You can add keywords, titles, and film roll information to each photo automatically, to make locating a particular photo very easy. iPhoto also provides a very convenient organizing metaphor for assembling sets of related photos: the *photo album*. You can organize hundreds or thousands of photos into albums to make the photos easier to locate. This chapter shows you how to organize your photo library and photo albums, assign titles and keywords to photos, and manage your library.

Photo Albums for All Occasions

You've probably seen photo albums with plastic sleeves for holding photographic prints. A *digital* photo album is similar in concept but holds digital photo files instead of prints. In both cases, an album is simply a way of organizing photos and placing them in a proper sequence. You select the photos from your photo library and arrange them in the order you want.

You can use photo albums to assemble photos from special events, such as a vacation, or to display a particular subject, such as your favorite nature photos. You can also use albums to organize photos for a slideshow, QuickTime movie, or Web page. Students on a class trip can contribute photos from their cameras to the same photo library, and you can create a set of albums that document the trip, and post the documentary as a slideshow on the Web. You can organize a photo album of a band on tour, and add music from the tour to create a slideshow — just like a rockumentary!

You can make as many albums as you like using any images from your photo library. Because the albums are *lists* of images, they don't use up disk space by copying the images — the actual image files remain in the photo library. You can include the same photo in several albums without making multiple copies of the photo and wasting disk space. You can delete a photo from an album without actually removing it from your library. As we show in this chapter, you actually have to select the photo library itself, and find the photo in order to delete it entirely.

Creating albums and adding photos

To create a new photo album and add a photo to it in iPhoto, follow these steps:

1. **Click the Organize mode button.**

   The photos appear as thumbnails in the viewer pane, as shown in Figure 3-1.

Figure 3-1: Add a new photo album.

2. **Click the + button.**

   The + button is underneath the album list pane (refer to Figure 3-1). Alternatively choose File⇨New Album or ⌘+N.

   The New Album dialog box appears.

3. **Type the album name and click OK.**

   The default name appears highlighted in the New Album dialog box. Type a name for the album (other than "Album 01" — something descriptive) as shown in Figure 3-2.

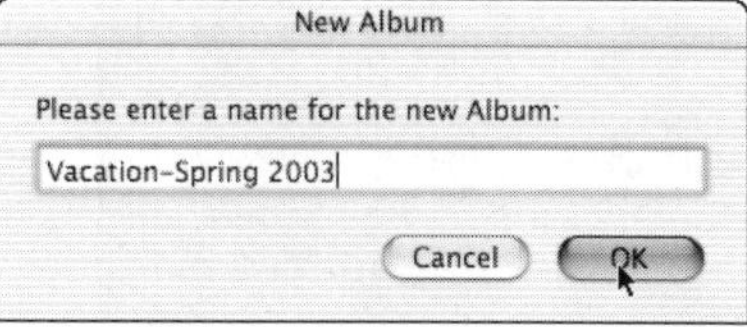

Figure 3-2: Type the new photo album's name.

4. **Click a photo and drag it into the album.**

   You know the photo is selected when an outline appears around it — drag it over the name of the album in the album list.

5. **Repeat Step 4 until you drag all the photos you want for this album.**

6. **Click the photo album name in the album list pane to see the photos in the album.**

   Only the photos you dragged to the album appear in the viewer pane, not the entire library. Find out how to organize your album later in this chapter in the "Arranging photos in albums." To view the entire photo library again, select the photo library in the album list pane.

You can select multiple photos for dragging by clicking the first one and holding down the Shift key while clicking the last one — the first, last, and all the photos between them are selected automatically. You can then drag the selection over the name of the album in the album list, as shown in Figure 3-3. A number appears, showing the number of selected photos in the range.

The same selection rules that apply to files in the Finder also apply to photos in the iPhoto viewer:

- ✦ **Click the photo once to select it.** You can then drag the photo.
- ✦ **Click the first photo, and then Shift-click the last photo (hold down the Shift key), to select a range of photos.** You can then drag the entire selected range.

- **After making a selection (single or a range), you can add a nonconsecutive photo to the selection by ⌘+clicking a photo (holding down the ⌘ key).** You can also ⌘+click a selected photo to remove it from the selection.

Figure 3-3: Add multiple photos at one time to an album.

Another way to select multiple photos is to first reduce the thumbnail size with the size slider, and then drag a selection rectangle around all the thumbnails. You can then drag the selection over the album name to add all the photos at once. Of course, with thumbnails that small, you may not be able to determine which photos belong and which don't. Don't worry — in the next section, "Arranging photos in albums," we show how to remove unwanted photos from an album.

You can also create an album by dragging a folder of photos from the Finder into the iPhoto album list. iPhoto creates an album with the folder's name and imports all photos contained in the folder. Using the Finder you can add a photo to an album directly from a CD, or from another location on your hard disk.

Arranging photos in albums

To see the photos gathered into an album, click the name of the album in the album list, as shown in Figure 3-4.

All your photos are still in the library; the viewer pane shows only the photos you added to the album. You can organize the photos within your album without having to wade through all the other photos.

Figure 3-4: View the photos in a single album.

The order your photos appear in the album is important — it defines the order of photos in a slideshow or a book layout. You will probably always want to change the order of photos after you create an album. To change the order of photos in an album, follow these steps:

1. **Click the album name in the album list.**
2. **Click the Organize mode button.**

   iPhoto switches to organize mode, with organization tools in the tools pane, and photo thumbnails in the viewer pane.
3. **Click a photo and drag it to a new location, or select multiple photos and drag them to a new location.**

   The three sunset photos in Figure 3-4 are dragged to a new location near the end of the photo album, shown in Figure 3-5.
4. **Repeat Step 3 until all your photos are arranged as you want them in the album.**

You can also use the Cut, Copy, and Paste commands in the Edit menu to organize your photos. Use the Cut command (Edit⇨Cut) to move one or more selected photos from one location into another location (Edit⇨Paste). Use the Copy command (Edit⇨Copy) to leave the selected images in the original location and repeat them in the new location. Using the Copy and Paste commands, you can repeat images throughout an album as many times as you like.

Figure 3-5: Arrange the photos in an album in a certain order.

To use the same photo in more than one album, simply drag the thumbnail for that photo over one album, and then select and drag the thumbnail over another album. The photo appears in both albums without having to create duplicates and waste disk space.

You can also duplicate an entire photo album, in case you want to arrange the photos in different ways. You don't duplicate the photos themselves, so disk space is not wasted. To duplicate an album, select the album name in the album list, and choose File➪Duplicate. A new album is created with the same name and "—1" added to the name. You can then rename the album if you want.

Removing photos from albums

You may have been a bit hasty with your selections in the photo library when dragging them over to the new photo album. Or perhaps you just noticed that useless shot you accidentally took of the side of a barn. Never mind — just select the photo, and press the Delete key on your keyboard.

If you are squeamish about using the Delete key (and who isn't?), choose File➪Remove from Album.

When you remove a photo from an album, the photo is not deleted. It remains intact in your photo library. The only way to delete a photo from the library is to select the photo in the photo library, and then press the Delete key or choose File➪Move to Trash.

In all cases, if you delete something that you didn't want to delete, you can usually undo the operation by choosing Edit➪Undo. If you perform some operations after deleting the photo, you may have to choose Edit➪Undo several times and undo all the subsequent operations before you can undo the deletion.

Using an album for desktop and screen effects

One of the surest ways to demonstrate your skills with a Mac is to personalize your Desktop and Screen Effects settings to show your own pictures. The Desktop is the background image behind the Finder. The Screen Effects function acts like a *screen saver* — it displays animation when your computer is inactive.

To protect your display, you can set the Screen Effects setting to display animation if your computer hasn't been used for several minutes. Apple provides a set of effects, but you can use an album from your photo library as your screen saver — the photos appear one after the other, like a slideshow.

To set your Desktop and Screen Effects settings to a photo album, follow these steps:

1. **With iPhoto open, select an album or group of photos.**
2. **Click the Organize mode button in the toolbar.**
3. **Click the Desktop icon in the tools pane.**

   The Screen Effects dialog box appears, as shown in Figure 3-6, with the album you selected in Step 1 listed. If the album isn't correct, click the arrow and select a new album from the drop-down menu.
4. **Click OK.**

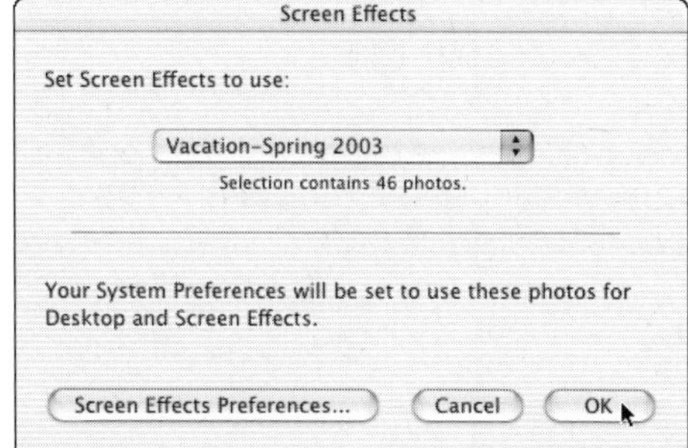

Figure 3-6: Select the photo album for Screen Effects.

Your pictures are now used for the screen effects; to see them working, just leave your computer inactive for the time it takes to launch the screen effects.

If you're impatient, you can see the effects right away, and control the animation settings as well. Before clicking OK in the Screen Effects dialog box, click the Screen Effects button to open the Screen Effects Preferences window (which is also accessible by opening the System Preferences window and clicking the Screen Effects icon). The Screen Effects Preferences window, shown in Figure 3-7, provides a preview of the effect. Click the Configure button, to access the display options, as shown in Figure 3-8. Control cross-fading between slides, zooming back and forth, cropping slides to fit the display, and so on by clicking the check boxes.

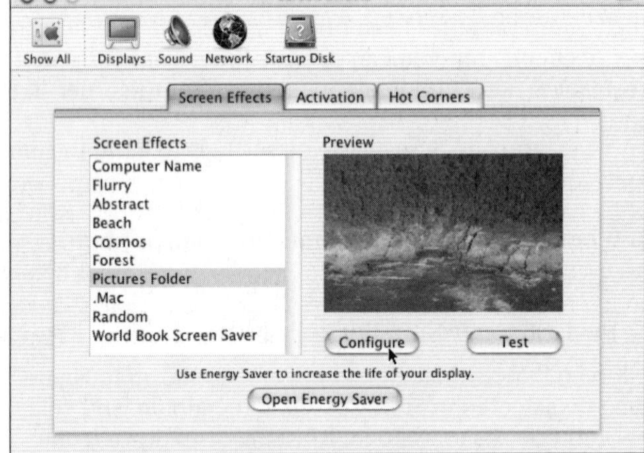

Figure 3-7: The Screen Effects Preferences window controls screen effects.

Figure 3-8: Change the display options for screen effects.

Notice the following settings are already set:

- ✦ **Cross-Fade between Slides:** On. A cross-fade is a smooth transition from one image to another.
- ✦ **Zoom Back and Forth:** On. The screen effect zooms into the image to show more detail, and zooms out to show the entire picture.
- ✦ **Crop Slides to Fit on Screen:** On. This option draws a smaller rectangle inside the image and cuts away everything outside the rectangle, in order to fit the image on-screen.
- ✦ **Keep Slides Centered:** Off. When you turn this on, the pictures are always centered on-screen without the need for cropping.
- ✦ **Present Slides in Random Order:** Off. When you turn this setting on, the images appear in random order rather than in the sequence you arranged for the photo album in iPhoto.

The Screen Effects Preferences window also offers controls over activation with the Activation pane, and the ability to set hot corners in the Hot Corners pane that activate the screen effect when you drag your mouse into the corner. Click the Activation tab for the Activation pane to change the time you have to wait until the screen effects starts, as shown in Figure 3-9. You drag the pointer in the timeline to set the number of minutes before the screen effects turn on.

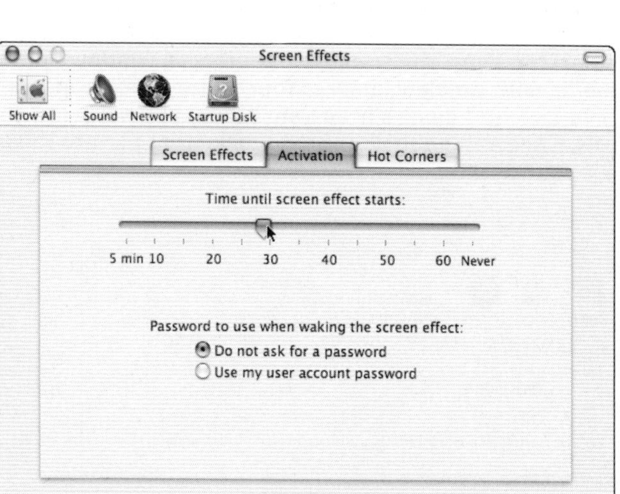

Figure 3-9: Change the activation setting for screen effects.

You can also set the screen effect to ask for a password when waking from the screen effect. With a password, you can leave your computer inactive on your desk, running the screen effects, and prevent any unauthorized use. Select the Use My User Account Password option in the Activation pane.

Why use screen effects?

Screen effects are primarily eye candy, but they can also be useful with older desktop monitors (which is why they were once called "screen savers").

Unlike most of the other parts of your computer, your display is vulnerable to prolonged use: Pixels can burn out over time if they do not change their color values. The pixel "freezes" on a certain color value and stays that way. When this happens, the pixel appears in a strange color in the context of the other pixels around it. Eventually, if enough pixels die, your display won't look so good.

With animation, each pixel of the display changes over time, so that it doesn't burn out and freeze on one color. Therefore, you want to use a screen effect that changes every pixel of the display over time. Photos are good to use because, typically, every pixel in a photo has a different color value. The best animation for screen saving is switching from one photo to another (as in a slideshow), because the switching exercises all the pixels in the display.

Screen effects do not protect LCD displays in laptops. The most important display part in a typical laptop is the backlighting, which is not affected by screen effects. In laptops, use the Sleep and Energy Manager settings to protect hardware and save energy.

You can also place images from your photo album into the collection of images used with the Desktop Preferences settings. The Desktop Preferences settings control the background displayed behind the Finder. To access the Desktop Preferences settings, open the System Preferences window and click the Desktop icon. The Desktop Preferences window appears, as shown in Figure 3-10, with preview images. Your album name appears in the Collection menu, and images from your album appear below that menu in thumbnails. Click a thumbnail image to make that picture the background picture for your desktop.

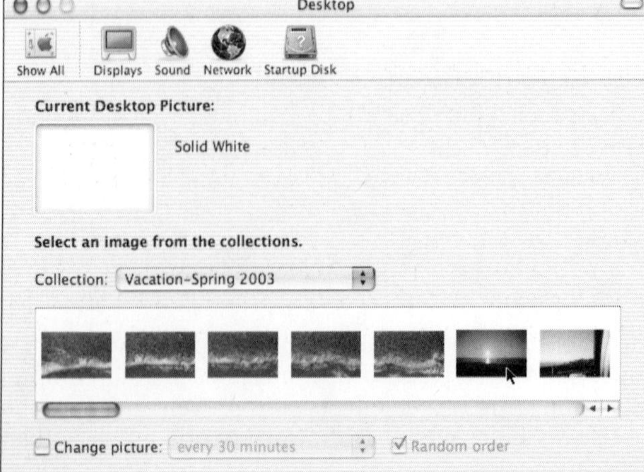

Figure 3-10: Use a photo album for the Desktop background images.

The Digital Contact Sheet

In commercial photography, a *contact sheet* is a quick print of photos in a thumbnail size with titles and information about the negatives. If you were ordering wedding pictures, for example, you may be presented with a contact sheet for choosing the pictures you want developed. You may mark a few pictures for large prints that can be framed, and several dozen more to be developed at normal size for your photo album, and tell the photographer to discard the rest in order to save money.

If all this sounds familiar, it's because you can perform all these functions (and more) with iPhoto — and you wouldn't even have to discard any to save money. In fact, iPhoto is set up to look like a contact sheet, with thumbnail images arranged in any order you choose. A huge difference exists, however: iPhoto is a digital contact sheet. You can find photos faster, sort them easier, and save the information about them more securely than with an old-fashioned contact sheet.

Every picture tells a story, but you still need words to describe your pictures. A title, for example, may be all you really need to identify a particular photo. iPhoto allows you to arrange the photos by title, so you can easily find the photo you're looking for. You can also sort your photos by film roll information.

Amateur and professional photographers can use the iPhoto sorting and searching functions and assign keywords to photos, turning your photo library into a simple database. With keywords, you can search and display photos related by topic, or assign a check mark or "favorite" label to certain photos and find them instantly. After a keyword search you can quickly arrange the found photos in a certain order to create a new photo album. You can also add comments to each photo that can be useful as descriptions in a book of photos (we describe how to create photo books in Chapter 6 of this book).

Displaying photo information

When iPhoto imports pictures from a digital camera, it finds out how the picture was taken. The photo information includes the type of camera, shutter speed, aperture, focal length, exposure data, whether the flash was on, the resolution of the image, and so on.

To see information about a photo, select the photo in Organize mode (either in the photo library or in a photo album), and choose File⇨Show Photo Info. iPhoto opens the Photo Info window, shown in Figure 3-11.

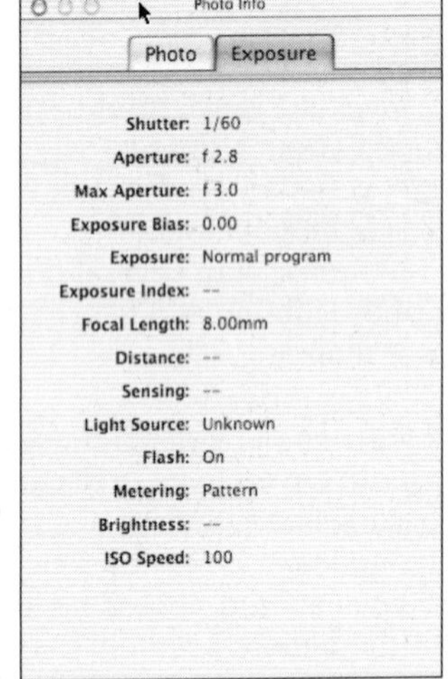

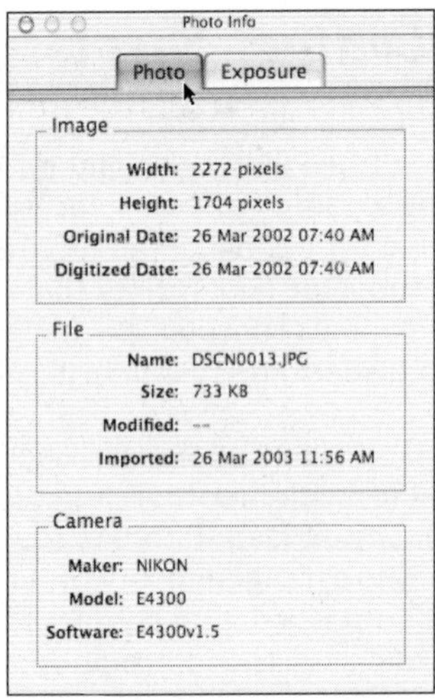

Figure 3-11: Show the photo info.

The Exposure tab (on the left in Figure 3-11) provides information about the camera's shutter, aperture, exposure bias, and so on. The Photo tab (on the right in Figure 3-11) offers the image resolution in pixels, the date the photo was taken, the dates it was digitized and imported, the filename and file size, and the camera make and model. A lot more information is found in iPhoto than is found on a typical contact sheet, and the information is useful for learning how to take better pictures, or for choosing photos to use in projects.

Adding and editing titles

Titles are the most convenient way to identify photos. A *title* is the name or a short description of a photo. Every photo has a title when imported — iPhoto simply assigns the film roll and photo number to the title, usually in an eight-character name that also doubles as the filename (with a JPG extension, as in "DSCN0015.JPG").

Of course, DSCN0015.JPG is not descriptive. You can edit the title of each photo by typing directly into the Title box that appears below the album list pane in either Organize or Edit mode, as shown in Figure 3-12. You can change the title of a photo assigned to an album, and it automatically changes the title of the same photo in the photo library. If the Title field is not visible, click the "i" button in the toolbar, which displays brief information including titles and comments.

Editing a photo's title changes it in the photo library and in all albums and books where the title appears.

Figure 3-12: Type a title for a photo in the Title box.

Titles can be useful for sorting purposes. You can arrange your photos alphabetically by title, which can be quite useful if your titles are "Beach 1," "Beach 2," "Beach 3," "Trail A," Trail B," and so on, but not quite so useful if your titles are more like "Several Species of Small Furry Animals Gathered Together in a Cave and Grooving with a Pict" (your titles can be quite long if you want).

To see titles under each thumbnail image in the viewer pane, choose View⇨Titles to turn on the viewing of titles. (Choose it again to turn it off.)

To see titles properly in the viewer pane, you may want to increase the size of the thumbnails in the pane by dragging the size slider on the right side of the iPhoto window under the viewer pane.

You don't necessarily have to type a title for every photo. You may be happy with using the filename supplied by iPhoto, which usually consists of three letters identifying the source, and a film roll number and picture number. However, one very cool feature of iPhoto is the ability to automatically assign a title to a set of photos.

For example, you can assign the date and time to a set of selected photos by following these steps:

1. **Select the photos you want to assign titles to.**

   You can select photos in the photo library or in a photo album.

2. **Choose Edit⇨Set Title To⇨Date/Time.**

   The Set Title to Date/Time dialog box appears, as shown in Figure 3-13.

Set Title To Date/Time

Select the Date and Time format to be used for setting the titles of the selected photos.

Include Date: Short / Abbreviated / Long

Include Time: 12-Hour clock / 24-Hour clock / Show Seconds

29 Mar 2003 05:47 PM

Cancel OK

Figure 3-13: Choose date and time formats useful for photo titles.

3. **Select the date and time formats.**

   You have choices for short, abbreviated, or long date formats, and 12-hour or 24-hour clock formats with or without seconds.

4. **Click OK.**

   The photos now have titles consisting of the date and time, as shown in Figure 3-14. Find out how to sort photos by date and time, later in this chapter, in the "Arranging and sorting photos" section.

Figure 3-14: The date and time as part of a photo title.

Keeping track of film rolls

After taking lots and lots of pictures, you will want iPhoto to help you keep track of them. iPhoto already knows which picture came from which film roll or camera. Even though you are not actually using *film* with digital cameras, iPhoto still uses the quaint language of photography and refers to a set of pictures from a memory card (or any import operation) as a *film roll.*

You can keep track of each film roll by viewing the thumbnail images in the photo library with film roll information. First select the entire photo library (select the photo library in the album list pane), and then choose View➪Film Rolls. iPhoto separates the display of thumbnails into film rolls, as shown in Figure 3-15.

Figure 3-15: Keep track of photos by film roll.

Viewing your photo library by film roll gives you a useful way of sorting photos by film roll. Click the triangle next to a film roll to hide photos. As shown in Figure 3-16, iPhoto displays a list of film rolls, just like Finder folders. The photos are still there — just click the triangle again to see them.

If you have a lot of photos and begin to experience slow performance, view your photos by film roll, and hide the photos you don't need to look at. Viewing photos by film roll increases performance because iPhoto won't have to display so many thumbnails.

Arranging and sorting photos

Although you can't rearrange the photos in the photo library by dragging them, as you can in a photo album, you can view them by different methods, including by title, by date, and by film roll.

After initially importing photos, the iPhoto viewer pane displays thumbnails arranged by film roll (View➪Arrange Photos➪by Film Roll). You can view each film roll separately by choosing View➪Film Rolls (choose it again to view all the film rolls).

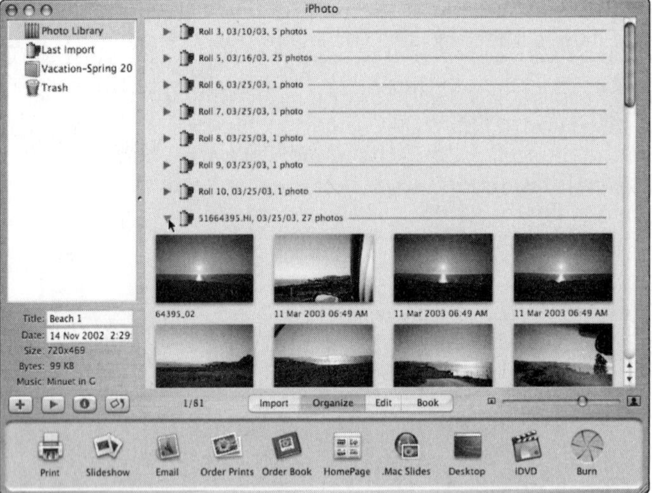

Figure 3-16: Hide photos to view the list of film rolls in the photo library.

To arrange your photos by title, choose View➪Arrange Photos➪by Title.

Arranging by date is just as easy: Choose View➪Arrange Photos➪by Date. The photos are arranged by the date you imported them into iPhoto.

Adding comments

An old Chinese proverb, often misquoted, says that "one picture is worth more than ten thousand words." But sometimes a few words can help explain the picture. Those photos you took years or even months ago — do you remember what was so important about them? You may want to share information with others about each photo, or simply add comments to photos to remind yourself what was so important about them or what details to look for in them.

You may want to use comments as descriptive captions, as in magazines and books. The comments you add to photos can optionally appear as captions in printed photo books and as messages accompanying the photos you send by e-mail, as well as on Web pages. You can even search for photos by your comments, as we describe later in this chapter, in the section "Searching for photos."

To add a comment to a photo, follow these steps:

1. **Select a photo in Organize or Edit mode.**

   You can select any photo appearing in the viewer pane for an album or for the entire photo library.

2. **Click the "i" button in the toolbar.**

   Typically the Comment field is not visible, even when the Title and Date fields are showing. Clicking the "i" button once shows the Title and Date fields, and clicking it again shows the Title, Date, and Comment fields, as shown in Figure 3-17. Clicking it a third time makes them all disappear.

3. **Type the comment in the Comment field.**

   Each line of text wraps to the next line as you type.

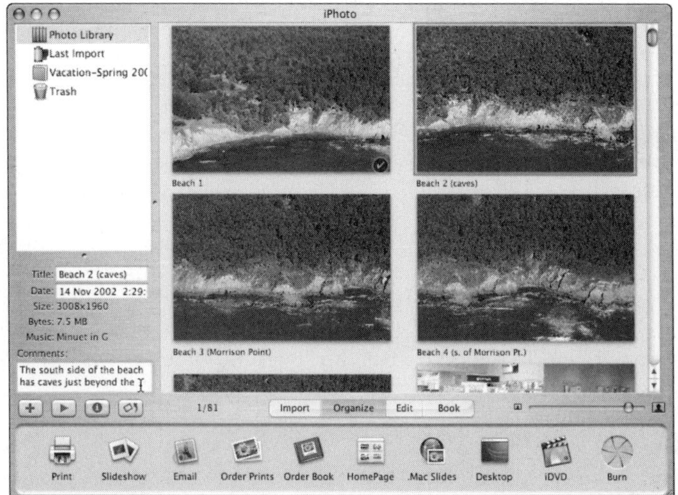

Figure 3-17: Add a comment to a photo in the Comment field.

Adding and using keywords

Titles are useful for identifying individual photos, and film roll and date information can be useful for identifying sets of photos taken at the same time or with the same type of camera. Photo albums serve nicely as collections of photos. But you can organize photos in another way: by keyword.

Keywords give you the power to organize your photos by topics or other characteristics that likely appear throughout your photo library — photos of your kids, vacations, and so on. The larger your photo library, the more useful keywords can be. After you assign keywords, you can quickly search and locate photos using the keywords.

For example, you can assign the keyword "Birthday" to photos related to birthdays, and find all the birthday shots in one search. All the photos related to vacations can have the keyword "Vacation" assigned to them. And what if a birthday occurred during a vacation? You can assign both keywords to those special photos, so that a search on either "Vacation" or "Birthday" finds those photos — indeed, a search on "Vacation" and "Birthday" finds only those photos.

Apple thoughtfully included a set of keywords that most people find useful, but you can rename any of them and add your own keywords as well. To see the keywords list (shown in Figure 3-18), edit the keywords, and assign keywords to photos, choose Edit➪Keywords (or press ⌘+K).

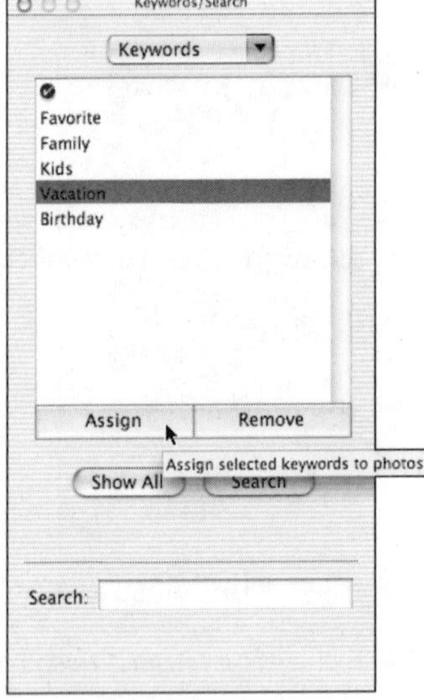

Figure 3-18: Assign a keyword to a selected photo.

To assign a keyword to one or more selected photos, follow these steps:

1. **Click the Organize mode button to switch to Organize mode (if you're not all ready in Organize mode).**
2. **Select one or more photos.**

   Use Shift-click to select a range of photos, and ⌘+click to add photos to a selection.
3. **Choose Edit➪Keywords (or press ⌘+K).**

   iPhoto displays the keywords list (refer to Figure 3-18).
4. **Select one or more keywords.**

   Use Shift-click to select a range of keywords and ⌘+click to add keywords to a selection.
5. **Click the Assign button.**

   The selected photo or photos are assigned keyword or keywords.

You don't have to add all the keywords at once. You can, for example, add the keyword "Vacation" to a set of photos, and then go back and add "Kids" to a subset of those photos. The subset has two keywords: "Vacation" and "Kids."

The supplied keywords may not be as useful as your own would be, so iPhoto gives you a way to rename the supplied keywords, delete keywords, and create your own keywords.

Renaming a keyword changes that keyword in any photos to which you assigned it. Be sure you truly want to rename the keywords assigned to the photos, because it happens automatically.

To rename an existing keyword, follow these steps with the keyword list open:

1. **Select the keyword in the keyword list.**
2. **Choose the Rename option from the Keywords menu at the top of the keywords list.**

   The keyword becomes highlighted.
3. **Type the new keyword replacing the old one, and click outside the keyword's text field to finish.**

   The new keyword replaces the old keyword wherever it is used.

To create a new keyword, follow these steps with the keywords list open:

1. **Choose the New option from the Keywords pop-up menu at the top of the keywords list.**

   A new "untitled" keyword becomes highlighted.
2. **Type the new keyword in the empty text field, and click outside the keyword's text field to finish.**

   If you previously selected a keyword, the new keyword is inserted right after it. You can add as many keywords as you want. Although previous versions of iPhoto supported only 14 keywords, the current version allows a lot more (we stopped at about 30, which is way more than we needed).

You can't rename or delete one keyword: the check mark keyword, at the top of the list. When you assign the check mark to one or more photos, a small check mark appears superimposed over the bottom-right corner of the thumbnail image. (The check mark doesn't change the photo in any way — it appears only on the thumbnails in Organize mode.) You can then easily search for all the photos marked with a check mark. Marking photos with a check mark is simply the electronic version of marking photos on a contact sheet with a magic marker or felt-tip pen.

Searching for photos

After assigning keywords to photos, you can search your photo library for photos that match your keyword selections. iPhoto assembles the thumbnails of the located photos in the viewer pane so that you can easily add them to a photo album, edit and improve them, assemble a slideshow with them, and so on.

To search by keyword, follow these steps:

1. **Click the Organize mode button to switch to Organize mode (if you're not all ready in Organize mode).**
2. **Select the photo library in the album list pane.**
3. **Choose Edit⇨Keywords (or press ⌘+K).**

   iPhoto displays the keywords list (refer to Figure 3-18).
4. **Select one or more keywords.**

   In this case we're searching for all the photos that have the keyword "band-tour."
5. **Click the Search button.**

   iPhoto locates one or more photos that have the selected keywords assigned to them (in this case, "band-tour"), and displays thumbnails in the viewer pane, as shown in Figure 3-19.

By assigning the "Vacation" and "Kids" keywords to photos that show the kids on vacation, you can search for either "Vacation" or "Kids" to locate them, and narrow your search by looking for photos that match both keywords. You can then sort the photos by title, date, or film roll.

By creating your own keywords, you can set up a hierarchical organization for photos. A photographer may use client names for keywords, and thereby quickly locate photos for clients and create several photo albums for a single client. Titles can be used to sort specific projects for clients, while the photographer can still sort by date or film roll.

You can also search for photos by text found in titles and comments by following these steps:

1. **Click the Organize mode button to switch to Organize mode (if you're not all ready in Organize mode).**
2. **Choose the photo library in the album list pane to view the entire library.**
3. **Choose Edit⇨Keywords (or press ⌘+K).**

   iPhoto displays the keywords list.

4. **Type text in the Search field.**

   For example, we typed "cave" in the Search field, as shown in Figure 3-20.

Figure 3-19: Search for photos using keywords.

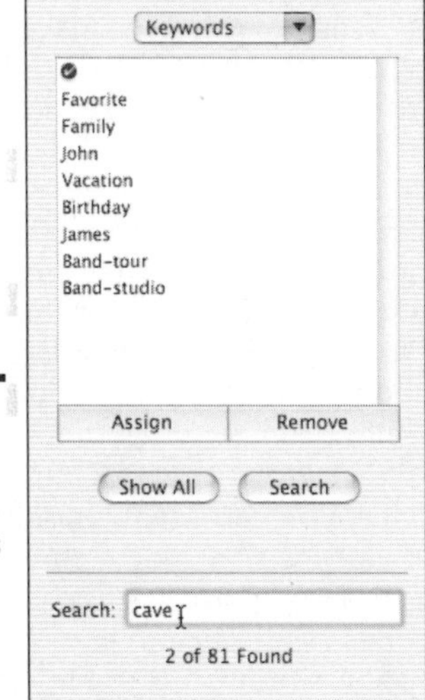

Figure 3-20: Search for photos using words found in comments and titles.

As you type characters in the Search field, iPhoto automatically starts locating photos that have those characters in the comment or title fields, and displays thumbnails in the viewer pane. You may not even have to type the entire word you are looking for, as iPhoto may find the photos with only a word fragment.

Maintaining a Photo Archive

Whether or not you manage files on your hard disk, you may want to know where these photos are stored, so that you can go about your usual file management tasks — such as backing up current files and archiving files you no longer need at hand.

You may also want to move the whole photo library to another Mac — after all, these Macs just keep getting better year after year. You may also want to make more copies of all your photos and create CDs or DVDs as archives. They're your photos, and why shouldn't you have multiple copies of them? The cost of a single blank CD or DVD is very low compared to the cost of the film you used to buy just to take pictures (not to mention the fact that some of your photos are undoubtedly priceless).

The operations we describe in this section make use of the Mac Finder and the iPhoto Library folder, which is the folder that contains the individual photo files that comprise your entire photo library. If you move, delete, rename, or otherwise tamper with files or folders inside the iPhoto Library folder, you may be unable to see your photos in iPhoto.

Backing up your library

Routinely copying your photo library to another hard disk or removable storage device, or using the backup services provided by .Mac to back up the photo library is a good idea. You can also burn a CD or DVD with your photo library, as we describe, later in this chapter, in the section "Burning a CD or DVD."

To copy the photo library to another disk, locate the iPhoto Library folder using the Finder. The folder is usually located within the Pictures folder in your User folder. Drag this folder to another hard disk or backup device, and you're all set. The copy operation may take some time if the library is huge — you can stop the operation anytime, but the newly copied library may not be complete. For best results, allow the copy operation to finish.

If you subscribe to the Apple .Mac service, you can use its hassle-free Backup software. With Backup, which comes with a .Mac membership, you can quickly and easily store important files on your iDisk. Backup allows you to save the latest versions of your files regularly and automatically, so you never have to worry about losing photos or any other important documents.

To use Backup with the .Mac service, follow these steps:

1. **Download the Backup software.**

   Go to the .Mac main page (`www.mac.com`), click the Backup button, and click the Download Backup link. (You need to stay connected to the Internet to complete the next steps.) Locate a folder on your hard disk to receive the downloaded installation file.

2. **Read the instructions.**

   Instructions are available on how to download and install your Backup software. These instructions have probably changed since we wrote this — the helpful people at .Mac always try to make things easier for you. When the installation completes, a Backup icon is created in your chosen folder on your hard disk.

3. **Double-click the Backup icon.**

   The Backup software launches.

4. **Select the iPhoto Library folder.**

   Locate and select the iPhoto Library folder, which is usually within the Pictures folder in your User folder. You may also want to select other files and folders at this time to back up several files at the same time.

5. **Click the Backup Now or Schedule Backup button.**

   The Backup Now button saves your files to your iDisk immediately. To arrange for an automatic backup, click the Schedule Backup button to automatically back up your data at the intervals of your choice.

Moving and switching between libraries

Moving a photo library involves copying it to a new location (and then deleting the original version if you wish). You can copy the iPhoto Library folder to any other hard disk, placing the folder inside the Pictures folder of anyone's User folder, replacing the existing iPhoto Library folder.

When you buy a new Mac, its iPhoto Library folder is most likely empty. You can copy your library folder from your regular Mac to the new Mac, replacing the empty library folder on the new Mac. When you start iPhoto on the new Mac, it automatically opens the library you copied over.

If you don't want to replace the library on the new Mac, you can rename the new Mac's library folder, or move it to a new location on the hard disk, to preserve it. Then you can copy the older iPhoto Library folder into the Pictures folder of your User folder on the new Mac without copying over the new photo library. When you start iPhoto on the new Mac, it automatically opens the older library you copied.

You can also switch between two or more photo libraries. To open another photo library, follow these steps:

1. **Quit iPhoto by choosing iPhoto⇨Quit iPhoto**
2. **In the Finder, rename the current iPhoto Library folder, or move it to another location.**

   Essentially you are hiding the library folder from iPhoto, tricking it to start a new one.
3. **Open iPhoto.**

   iPhoto can't find the library folder, so it asks if you want to find it, or create a new one.
4. **Click the Find Library button.**
5. **Choose the library you want to use, and click Open.**

You can also start a new library with the Create Library button.

Burning a CD or DVD

A great way to maintain several photo libraries is to burn CDs or DVDs with them. If you have an Apple-supported CD-RW or DVD-R drive (such as the Apple SuperDrive), you can create your own CDs and DVDs to store your photos. This process is called burning because when you save (or write) information to a disc, your drive burns the information onto the disc's surface with a laser.

To burn your own CD or DVD, follow these steps:

1. **Click the Organize mode button.**
2. **Select the photo library.**

   You can select the entire library, a specific album, or individual photos to burn to a disc. You can fit quite a lot of photos on a CD or DVD, so you may want to select your entire photo library for a CD or DVD burn operation to use up the entire CD or DVD space.
3. **Click the Burn icon.**

   The Insert Disc dialog box appears, prompting you to insert a blank disc.
4. **Insert a blank disc and click OK.**

   A disc icon appears on the information panel. The green area on the disc icon (on the left side) represents the amount of disc space your photos require.

5. **Click the Burn button in the tools pane a second time.**

   Clicking the Burn button two times is a safety precaution.

   The Burn Disc window appears, as shown in Figure 3-21.

6. **Click the Burn button in the Burn Disc window.**

   The burn operation starts. You can cancel the operation before starting. It may take several minutes to burn the disc; when it is done, you hear a chime and the disc automatically ejects. You can cancel the burn by clicking the Cancel button next to the progress bar, but if you're using a CD-R disc, you may not be able to use the CD after canceling.

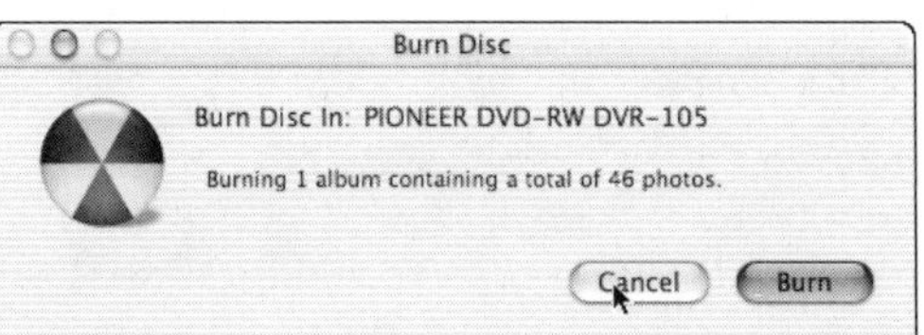

Figure 3-21: Burn a CD of the photo library.

You can show other photo libraries you burned to a CD or a DVD while using your current photo library. You can't modify the photo libraries on the CD or DVD, but you can view and copy any photos and albums they contain.

To open a photo library on a CD or a DVD, follow these steps:

1. **Insert the CD or DVD disc into your Mac.**

   An icon for the disc appears in the photo library list, as shown in Figure 3-22.

2. **Click the disc's icon in the photo library list.**

   iPhoto displays the photos and albums on the disc. Click the triangle next to the CD's title to see the photo albums on the CD, as shown in Figure 3-22. You can copy them to your current library to work on them.

If you want to edit the entire photo library on the disc, you can copy the library to your hard disk and then switch to that library, as described earlier in this chapter, in the section "Moving and switching between libraries."

You can use photos and DVDs in many ways, including assembling documentary-style slideshows. We cover these and many other DVD topics in Book IV.

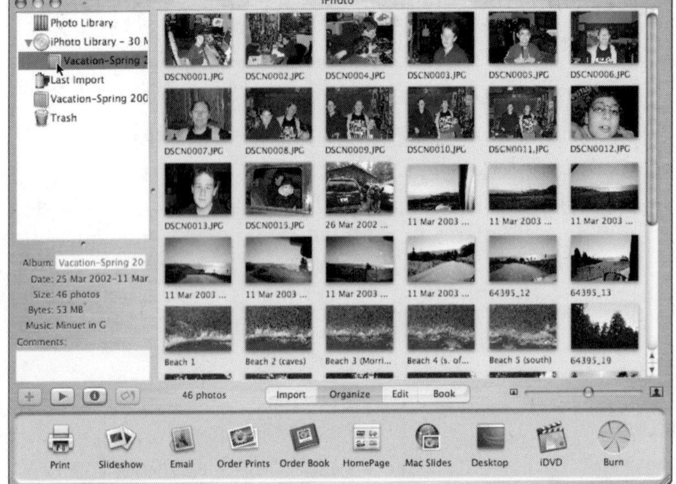

Figure 3-22: Select a photo library on CD and view its albums.

Chapter 4: Improving Photos

In This Chapter

- Rotating and cropping
- Changing brightness and contrast
- Removing red-eye and retouching

Photos are records of reality, but reality doesn't always comply with your wishes — the sun may be too bright, or the forest too dark, the subject too far away, or the combination of light, shadows, and distance make the scene too blurry to show details. Cameras offer automatic settings for taking pictures that compensate for some of these factors, but these settings don't always give you the best pictures.

Digital photography, on the other hand, offers unlimited ways to change images without adversely affecting the quality of the image. Unlike the technology involved with developing film, in which successive modifications to the film degrade the image quality, digital technology allows you to experiment with images at will, and we encourage experimentation. Not only can you save the original version of the image in pristine condition, you can also directly change the pixels of an image without changing its resolution. The image resolution remains as high as when you started.

So go ahead and have fun with your photos. This chapter is all about using iPhoto to its fullest potential for improving and enhancing images. You find out how to adjust the brightness and contrast, remove the annoying red-eye effect in the photo subject's eyes, and retouch photos to remove blemishes and image artifacts. As influential writer Arthur C. Clarke once said, "any sufficiently advanced technology is indistinguishable from magic." He could have easily been talking about the editing capabilities of iPhoto.

Modifying Photos

The most obvious advantage digital photos have over prints is the fact that you can change your digital photo instantly. You can also make copies quickly and easily, and make changes to the copies without affecting the originals.

Whether you're viewing photos within a photo album (after selecting the album in the album list), or in the entire photo library (after selecting the photo library in the album list) doesn't matter when you change them. The changes are recorded in the original photo stored in the library.

You can make some changes while in Organize mode, but certain changes are easier to make in Edit mode. For example, you can rotate a group of photos quickly in Organize mode. But if you want to see the images up close while rotating, or if you want to make other changes and see those changes in detail, use Edit mode by selecting the photo and clicking the Edit mode button. Alternatively, you can open the photo in a separate window, as we describe in Chapter 1 of this book.

Keep the following tips in mind when enhancing photos:

- ✦ Any changes you make to a photo, such as cropping, rotating, or changing a photo's brightness or contrast, changes the photo's appearance in the photo library and in every album where it appears.
- ✦ To change a photo without changing it everywhere, make a duplicate of the photo by selecting the photo and choosing File➪Duplicate (or ⌘+D). Then you can change the duplicate without changing the original.
- ✦ If you make a mistake, you can always revert a photo to its original version by choosing File➪Revert to Original.
- ✦ To quickly compare the adjusted version of the photo with the original, press and hold down the Control key. iPhoto displays the original version as long as you hold down the Control key. By holding and releasing the Control key, you can toggle back and forth to compare the original to the adjusted version.

Cropping and Rotating Photos

In traditional commercial printing and photography, a *light table* — a translucent piece of plastic or glass fitted on top of a box with internal light — is used for trimming photographic film negatives or positives and preparing them for printing in magazines, newspapers, books, and so on. Because light illuminates the film from below, the image can be seen and trimmed.

The professionals who know how to trim photos on a light table wield precision knives with wild abandon, and most importantly, they know how to cut in straight lines. They uses words such as cropping to describe cutting away the outer edges of a photo, bringing the center of the photo to the forefront; and retouching to describe brushing away artifacts in the image.

The fact that iPhoto uses the same terms as professional photographers and provides all of the functionality of a light table in the digital world is no accident. You can crop a photo to frame it better and show only what you want it to show; rotate a vertical photo horizontally; and combine cropping and rotating to show only part of an image at the proper angle. And you don't need to be able to draw or cut a straight line.

Rotating photos

If you hold your camera sideways to take a picture of something tall, such as a redwood tree, you end up with a photo that is horizontally oriented (the tree is on its side). You probably want to rotate the photo to be vertically oriented.

You may want to rotate a photo for other reasons as well — for example, you may want to rotate photos shot by a camera held upside down or pointed down.

You can quickly and easily rotate photos right in Organize mode in the viewer pane. You can also rotate a photo after selecting it and clicking the Edit button to edit it. Either way, iPhoto rotates the entire image in 90-degree increments (right angles).

To rotate a photo, follow these steps:

1. **Select a photo by clicking its thumbnail in the viewer pane of Organize mode.**
2. **Click the Rotate button.**

   The photo rotates 90 degrees, as shown in Figure 4-1. Each time you click the Rotate button, the photo rotates 90 degrees.

   Choose File⇨Revert to Original if you don't like how the rotation turns out.

You can rotate a photo in Edit mode as well as Organize mode. The rotate button is available in both modes and also in the toolbar of a photo opened in a separate window. When you rotate a group of photos and you don't need to see them up close, you can rotate them in Organize mode; if you want to see them up close while rotating, use Edit mode by clicking the Edit mode button, or open the photo in a separate window, as we described in Chapter 1 of this book.

Figure 4-1: Rotate a photo by 90 degrees.

Cropping photos

Cropping enables you to keep only a rectangular portion of the photo and remove the outer edge. You can use cropping to do the following:

- **Get rid of something you don't want.** You can eliminate the outer portions of a photo to remove wasted space, crop out an ex-boyfriend that shouldn't be in the picture, or remove the fuzzy outline of a car window in a photo shot from a car.
- **Focus on the subject.** By cropping a photo you can adjust where your subject appears in the frame of the picture, drawing more attention to your subject and improving the overall composition. Professional photographers, for example, may crop tightly around a person's face, removing most of the background.
- **Fit the photo to a specific proportion.** You may want to adjust the proportions of your photo to fit sizes for book layout or prints, which iPhoto makes easy with a Constrain feature that draws exactly the right proportions for you. Cropping is often better than stretching or resizing a photo, because the pixels within the cropped area do not change. By constraining the cropping selection, you get better results with prints and books because the picture is framed properly for the size of the print or book layout.

Make a copy before cropping the photo. Find out how to make a copy and other tips in the "Modifying Photos" section, earlier in this chapter.

To crop a photo to get rid of the outer edges and improve the composition (without using the Constrain feature):

1. **Click the thumbnail image for the photo in the viewer pane.**
2. **Click the Edit mode button for Edit mode.**

   After switching to Edit mode, the selected photo fills the entire viewer pane.
3. **Click a starting point and drag diagonally across the photo in the viewer pane to create a cropping rectangle.**

   Click at the top left corner of the photo in the area you want to crop, and drag down and across the image. The cursor's pointer turns into a crosshair. As you drag, the portions of the photo outside the selected area dim to show that it will be cut from the photo, as shown in Figure 4-2.

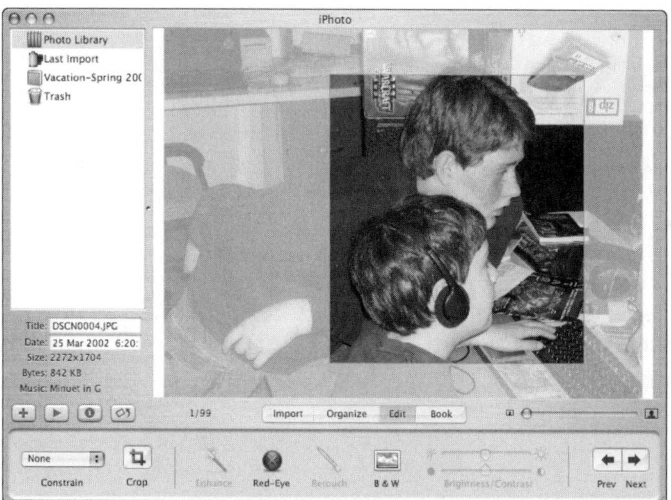

Figure 4-2: Crop the photo in Edit mode.

4. **Adjust the edges of the cropping rectangle, as shown in Figure 4-3.**

   If your cropping rectangle isn't perfect the first time, move your mouse pointer close to the edge or corner of the cropping rectangle and drag to reshape the rectangle.

   See how we dragged the top edge up a little bit in Figure 4-3? We didn't like our original cropping area in Figure 4-2, so we adjusted the cropping area a little more.

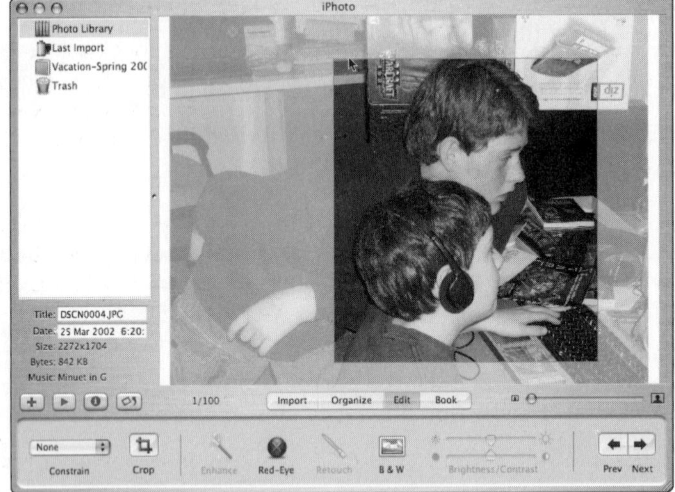

Figure 4-3: Reshape the cropping rectangle by dragging its edges.

Cropping changes the actual photo. Be sure you define the edges perfectly before clicking the Crop button in the next step.

5. **Click the Crop button in the tools pane at the bottom left of the iPhoto window.**

   The Crop button reduces the photo dimensions to the selected area, as shown in Figure 4-4.

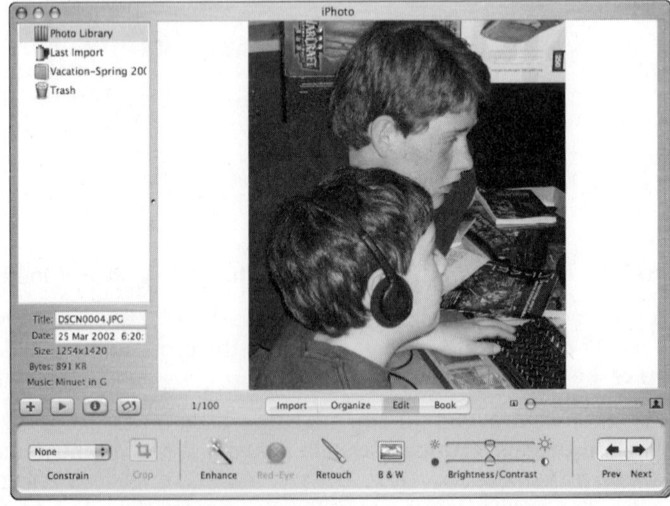

Figure 4-4: Use the Crop button to crop a photo.

Constraining cropping for print sizes

You can use the Constrain feature to crop a photo to a specific proportion. Constrain keeps the proportions accurate while you drag the cropping rectangle, so you don't need rulers, math expertise, and graphics skill to get it right for specific print dimensions. As you drag, the constrain feature keeps the rectangle accurate.

The Constrain pop-up menu, to the left of the Crop button, offers a list of print sizes like 4 x 6 (Postcard), 4 x 6 (Portrait), standard 8 x 10, 8 x 10 (Portrait), and so on. You even find sizes such as 1024 x 768 pixels, for desktop pictures and screen effects. Using the preset choices from the Constrain menu guarantees the cropped photo fits nicely in the format you need.

To crop a photo with the Constrain feature, follow these steps:

1. **Click the thumbnail image for the photo in the viewer pane.**
2. **Click the Edit mode button for Edit mode.**

   The selected photo fills the entire viewer pane.
3. **Click the Constrain pop-up menu and choose a format.**
4. **Click the top-left corner of the area you want to crop and drag the mouse down and across the image in the viewer pane.**

   The mouse pointer turns into a crosshair. As you drag, the portion of the photo outside the area dims to show that it will be cut from the photo (see Figure 4-5).
5. **Adjust and resize the cropping rectangle.**

   If your cropping rectangle isn't perfect the first time, move your pointer anywhere inside the cropping rectangle until the pointer turns into a finger, and drag to adjust the rectangle's position. You can also drag the edges of the cropping rectangle to make it larger or smaller, but still in the same proportion, because the Constrain feature is on: Move your pointer close to the edge or corner of the cropping rectangle and drag to make it larger or smaller.

   We adjusted the area in our photo in Figure 4-6. Notice how smaller the area is now compared to the original selection in Figure 4-5.

6. **Click the Crop button.**

   Be sure you want to crop the photo. Cropping changes the photo everywhere it appears.

   The Crop button reduces the photo dimensions to the selected area, which, due to the Constrain feature, is in the correct proportion for your print or display choice. After clicking the Crop button, the photo consists of only the selected area; the rest of the photo is thrown away.

Figure 4-5: The crop constrains to the proper proportions.

Figure 4-6: Adjust the position of the cropping rectangle before cropping.

While many of us don't need to be extremely precise with cropping our photos, graphic artists and print-layout specialists may want very precise image sizes for reproducing on printing presses. iPhoto allows you to do highly precise cropping when you open your photo in a separate window. Open the photo in a separate window by holding down the Option key while double-clicking the photo. The Crop button and Constrain pop-up menu are available in the window's toolbar. (If you don't see the Crop button on the right, click the double-arrow on the far right side of the toolbar to reveal the Crop function and other functions not visible due to the size of the window.)

Solving printing problems with cropped images

Problems can crop up, if you'll forgive the pun, when you try to print photos that have been cropped or resized. The Constrain feature is useful because prints typically come in specific sizes such as 4 x 6, 5 x 7, and 8 x 10 inches. However, photos from most digital cameras are sized at proportions of 4 (width) to 3 (height) pixels, which is fine for computer displays, DVDs, and iPhoto book layouts, but not the right proportion for typical prints. If you pay no attention to the Constrain feature, you may find some photos have unintended white margins at the sides of the finished prints. Use the Constrain feature if you're cropping for a print.

Although cropping has no effect on the cropping area, the other parts of the photo are removed, reducing the overall size of the photo. A photo at low resolution may, after cropping, be too low to print well at large sizes. The printer resizes the photo to fill the paper size, which makes the pixels larger and produces jagged edges. High-resolution cameras produce higher-quality prints at large sizes, even if you crop them.

Follow the same steps in the "Cropping photos" section to crop your photo. However, in this window, you can zoom into the photo to see more detail while cropping, as shown in Figure 4-7. Notice also that the Custom fields fill in with the proportions for your Constrain choices (4 x 6 in Figure 4-7). After opening a photo in an individual window, the Custom fields allow you to specify your own proportions for constraining the cropping, so you can be as precise as you want.

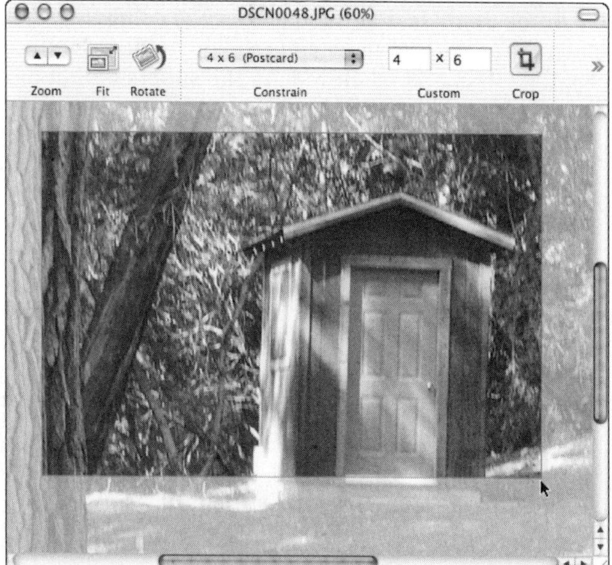

Figure 4-7: Crop a photo in its own window.

Fine-Tuning Photos

Your vacation is over, and you're looking over your photos. The beach shots look washed out from way too much sunlight, and the forest shots look as dark as inside a cathedral. And your youngest son is in the gift shop impersonating a red-eyed Martian.

You can work magic with the iPhoto editing tools, improving photos that would otherwise be fuzzy, too dark, or too bright. Poor lighting is often the biggest problem with photos. But the iPhoto Brightness and Contrast controls can make photos look better, with more saturated colors, or with sharper, crisper details. The iPhoto Red-Eye button removes the red spots in your subject's eyes created by your flash. The Red-Eye button also reduces the amount of red in any selected area of a photo.

Improving brightness and contrast

Some of the best indoor photos are taken with light streaming through a window, using only ambient light. (Why, then, when you sit for a portrait photo, the photographer spends more time on lights than anything else?) With natural, ambient light, your camera reads the lighting for the entire room and reveals more depth in the background and surroundings. Ambient light from various sources, such as lamps and overhead lights, produces a softer, more balanced photo with less contrast. With a flash, only about ten feet in front of the camera is illuminated, and everything beyond fades to black.

However the lighting conditions are when you take your photos, you can regain some of the detail lost in the darkness by using the Brightness and Contrast sliders. The sliders allow you to change the brightness and contrast and see the effect immediately. Find the sliders in Edit mode and also in the toolbar of a photo opened in a separate window.

When in Edit mode, the Brightness or Contrast sliders are located in the tools pane. Drag the sliders left or right, as shown in Figure 4-8. The top slider controls the brightness and the bottom slider controls the contrast.

With the Brightness and Contrast sliders, you can bring out details in photos taken in poor lighting conditions. The sliders allow you to make incremental adjustments the following ways:

- **Adjust each slider gradually until you get the effect you want.**
- **Click the icons at either end to set minimum or maximum brightness and contrast settings.** For example, in Figure 4-9, we clicked the dim sun icon on the left side of the Brightness slider for minimum brightness, and then moved the Contrast slider to get the desired effect.
- **Click anywhere along the slider bar to jump directly to a setting.**

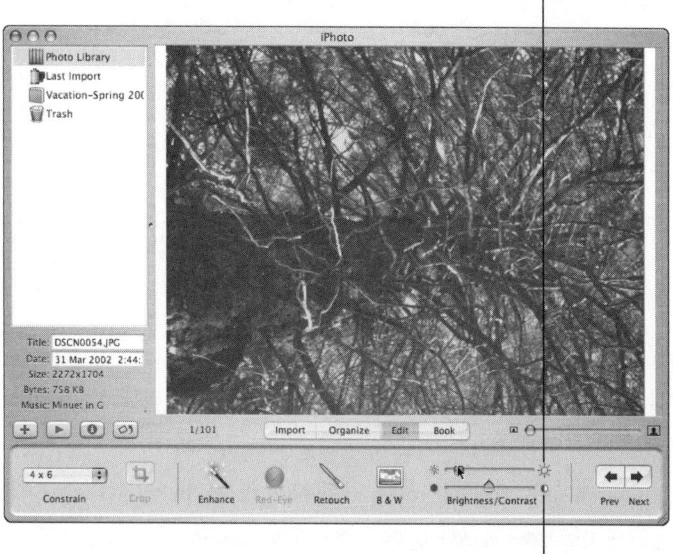

Figure 4-8: Drag the Brightness slider to decrease brightness.

Figure 4-9: We dragged the Contrast slider to increase contrast, with brightness set to minimum.

Removing red-eye and red tint

Red-eye is light from the camera's flash, reflected back. Red-eye happens even with your dog's eyes, making docile Spot look quite vicious. The red is the color of the eye's retinal tissue. (Presumably you'd get green-eye from a creature whose retinal tissue is green.) Red-eye can be more prominent in photos shot in dim rooms, because the eye's pupils are dilated and exposing more retina.

The red-eye effect is a common problem in flash photography — so common that many digital cameras come with built-in red-eye reduction. But our shots prove that our digital camera still zaps people's eyes with red even with this reduction feature; either that or it proves that we don't know how to use the camera's reduction feature.

It doesn't matter. You have a magic wand that zaps red-eye. Follow these steps:

1. **Click the thumbnail image for the photo in the viewer pane.**
2. **Click the Edit mode button for Edit mode.**

   The selected photo fills the entire viewer pane.
3. **Zoom into the photo.**

   In Edit mode, use the size control slider to zoom in, as we have in Figure 4-10. When viewing a photo in a separate window, use the Zoom buttons.
4. **Click and drag with your mouse across an eye to select the image area.**

   Be sure the Constrain pop-up menu is set to the None option, so that you select an image area of any shape.

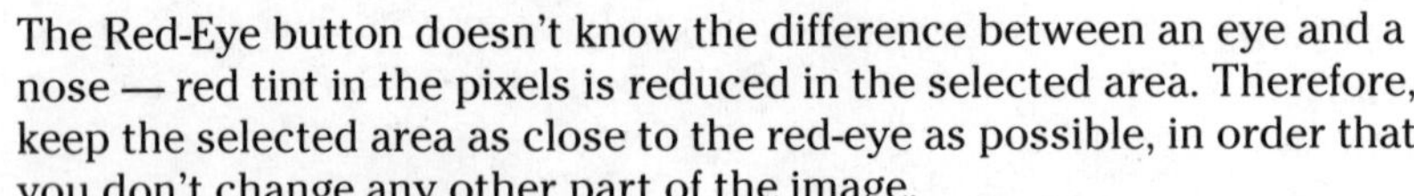

   The Red-Eye button doesn't know the difference between an eye and a nose — red tint in the pixels is reduced in the selected area. Therefore, keep the selected area as close to the red-eye as possible, in order that you don't change any other part of the image.

5. **Click the Red-Eye button.**

   Be absolutely sure you're ready to remove the red-eye. Removing red-eye changes the photo in the photo library and in every album.

   The Red-Eye button, found in the tools pane, removes red tint from the selected area (as shown in Figure 4-10). The eyes may now be a lot darker than before, but at least they don't look bright red.

You can use the Red-Eye button to remove red from any part of a photo. The Red-Eye tool simply removes some of the red from each pixel.

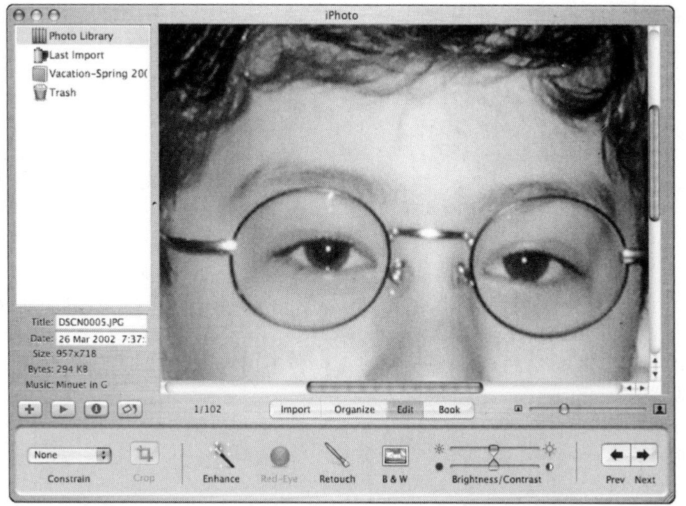

Figure 4-10: Remove red-eye from a photo.

Compare the photo with the red-eye version by pressing and holding the Control key.

Retouching and enhancing photos

Here's where photos can depart from reality. (Removing red-eye is, after all, just removing something the camera put there.) You can literally alter the photo with iPhoto in such a way that even a judge and jury couldn't tell the difference. You can remove anomalies and blemishes with the Retouch brush and enhance the colors in a photo with the Enhance wand. Both tools are available in Edit mode and when viewing a photo in a separate window.

Before making any changes, make a copy of the photo in case you make any changes you don't like. We cover this and other tips in the section, "Modifying Photos," earlier in this chapter.

To use the Retouch brush, follow these steps:

1. **Click the thumbnail image for the photo in the viewer pane.**
2. **Click the Edit mode button for Edit mode.**

   The selected photo fills the entire viewer pane.
3. **Zoom into the photo.**

   In Edit mode, use the size control slider to zoom in as much as possible. When viewing a photo in a separate window, use the Zoom buttons.
4. **Click the Retouch brush.**

The Retouch brush icon is in the center of the tool.

The pointer turns into a crosshair.

5. **Use your mouse pointer as a brush and repeatedly stroke a small area.**

   Repeatedly drag over a small area as if using a brush and slowly the area blends into the surrounding pixels. The blemish or spot disappears, as shown in Figure 4-11. Life would be so much easier if getting rid of real blemishes was this easy.

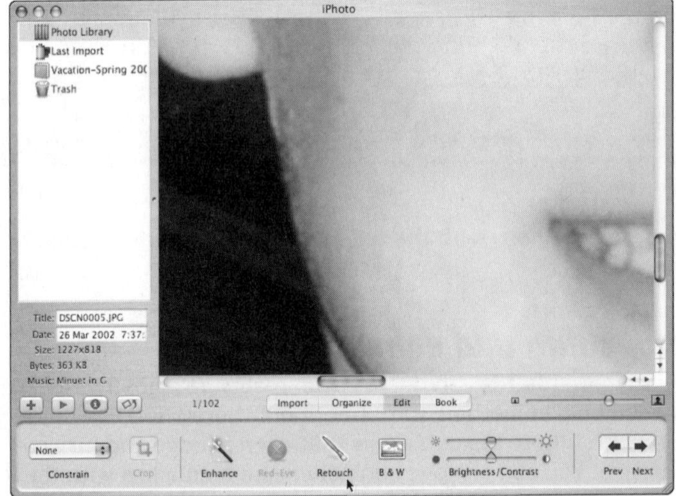

Figure 4-11: Retouch a photo.

The Retouch tool actually *clones* neighboring pixels and uses them to replace the pixels you are brushing over, blending them in by manipulating color values. (And you thought cloning was for sheep!)

The Enhance wand works on the entire photo. It performs a combination of operations, including subtle adjustments to the brightness and contrast and other changes to the colors to bring out more clarity and saturated color in the image. The essential effect of Enhance is to make the colors, and the overall photo, more vivid.

To use the Enhance wand, follow these steps:

1. **Click the thumbnail image for the photo in the viewer pane.**
2. **Click the Edit mode button for Edit mode.**

   The selected photo fills the entire viewer pane.

3. **Click the Enhance wand.**

   The Enhance wand icon is toward the right in the tools pane.

Converting to black and white

Some scenes just look better in black and white. Technically, the photo uses multiple shades of gray, but we call it black and white, or B&W. Gray images can evoke a moody atmosphere. Gray can also be effective for portraits, for obtaining greater contrast and enhanced starkness, and for trying to achieve an Ansel Adams look.

To convert a color photo into gray, choose the photo in the viewer pane, click the Edit mode button for Edit mode, and click the B & W icon toward the right in the tool pane.

Make a copy before you make any irreversible changes to your photo. Find out how to do this and other tips in the "Modifying Photos" section, earlier in this chapter.

Chapter 5: Making Slideshows

In This Chapter

- Creating a slideshow
- Controlling slideshow playback and adding music
- Sharing slideshows online
- Exporting slideshows to QuickTime and iDVD

You may remember the old days when slides were projected onto white walls or sheets and the click-clack sound of the slide carousel on the projector drowned out everything else. Slideshows of this sort were the only way to exhibit photos to a group of people.

Photos can display on computers, and with laptops to connect directly to video projectors, you can put on shows that are nothing like your grandfather's slideshows. Not only do the photos look fantastic, but you can set them to music, fade between each photo, repeat the slideshow in a loop endlessly, and generally look as good as a professional slideshow in a kiosk or boardroom. In this chapter, you discover how to change these and other settings to fine-tune your slideshow. We also describe how to choose the best pictures, how to share slideshows with friends, and how to create a movie from a slideshow.

Playing a Slideshow

Words are inadequate to express the feeling you have when you first look at the photos you've taken in a full-screen slideshow. Your display fades to black, and your entire photo library (or the album you select) starts to appear, photo by photo, filling the screen for two seconds before fading out while the next photo fades in. You hear the music of J.S. Bach — "Minuet in G" — which is the default setting for music during slideshows.

You create and play slideshows within Organize mode. Follow these steps to play a slideshow with a particular selection of photos in mind:

1. **Select the photos for the slideshow in the viewer pane.**
2. **Click the Play button in the toolbar.**

   The Play button looks like a CD-player play button.

Click the mouse, or the Esc key, to stop the slideshow, or it continues to play in an endless loop. Of course, running in an endless loop, with two seconds per slide, may not be the ideal setting for your slideshow, but don't worry. We describe how to change that that setting later in this chapter, in the section "Changing Playback Settings."

If your slideshow doesn't look as good as you expect, check your display settings. To find out how to change your display settings, see Chapter 1 of this book.

iPhoto offers different ways to play a makeshift slideshow on the fly:

- **Show your entire library or an entire album from the beginning:** Select either the photo library or the photo album in the album list pane, without selecting any photos, and click the Play button. The slideshow consists of all the photos in the viewer pane, starting with the first.
- **Show your entire library or an entire album starting at a photo (not at the beginning):** Click a single photo, in either the photo library or an individual album in the viewer pane. The slideshow starts with the photo immediately following the selected photo. (We know, starting on the selected one is logical, but it doesn't work that way.) The show continues and then loops back to the first photo in the viewer pane.
- **Show selected photos only:** Select multiple photos in the viewer pane — either a range of photos in consecutive order, or individual photos in nonconsecutive order. The slideshow uses only those photos, endlessly repeating them.

You may want to play a makeshift slideshow of selected photos just to experiment with them to see if they would work well in the final version of the slideshow. Not all photos are cropped or rotated properly for slideshow viewing. You can preview parts of the show you want to create.

Pausing and playing

When playing a slideshow, you can pause the slideshow and resume playing whenever you want.

To pause a slideshow while playing, press the spacebar. When you pause a show, the music keeps playing. A pause indicator appears briefly on-screen and then disappears, leaving the slideshow paused on the photo.

To resume playing again, press the spacebar again. When the show resumes, a play indicator appears briefly and then disappears, and the slideshow continues.

Advancing manually and controlling the speed

Slideshows run in auto-play mode with timing you can adjust in the Slideshow Settings window, which we describe in the section, "Changing Playback Settings," later in this chapter. However, you can override the settings by manually advancing or reversing the slides and increasing or decreasing the speed of the slideshow.

To advance manually, slide-by-slide, press the right-arrow key on your keyboard. To go backwards, press the left-arrow key.

When you press either of the arrow keys, the slideshow jumps to the next or previous slide. The slideshow then pauses while the music continues playing. You can then manually move forward or backward, slide-by-slide, with the left and right arrow keys.

To return to normal playback speed, press the spacebar to bring it out of pause mode.

You can speed up or slow down a slideshow temporarily, by pressing the up-arrow or down-arrow keys. The up-arrow speeds a slideshow up, decreasing the time to show each slide, while the down-arrow slows a slideshow down, increasing the time to show each slide. The slideshow continues at that speed until you change the speed again with the up or down-arrow. However, this speed change is temporary — speeding up or slowing down the slideshow does not affect the slide playback timing you define in the Slideshow Settings window, covered later in this chapter, in the section "Changing Playback Settings." When you rerun the slideshow after stopping it, iPhoto uses the saved settings for timing the presentation.

Assembling a Slideshow

While playing a slideshow of the photos in your library is easy, in whatever order those photos are sorted, you probably want to create slideshows for others that are at least interesting, if not dazzling. You can do this by choosing the best pictures and the most appropriate music.

Arranging a photo album for a slideshow

Arranging photos in an album allows you to determine the order of your photos in a slideshow.

After you chose the photos you want for a particular slideshow, the best way to organize that slideshow is by assigning the photos to an album. You can make a separate photo album for each slideshow, because albums are just lists of images that don't use up disk space.

Creating a photo album for a slideshow is no different than creating a photo album for any other reason. We describe how to create and arrange photos in photo albums in more detail in Chapter 3 of this book.

The order of your photos in the album defines how your slideshow plays. Photo albums are convenient for this process because you can rearrange your photos any way you like. The final arrangement determines the order in which people see the images in the show.

Choosing photos that display well

The important thing to remember about photos in slideshows is that not all photos fill the screen properly. You may want to use only photos that look good at full-display dimensions.

iPhoto uses the entire display resolution when putting on a slideshow, and for many Mac users, that means at least 1024 x 768 pixels. If your photos are smaller, iPhoto stretches them to fill the display, often with undesirable results (jagged lines and visible pixels, to name a couple).

You can determine whether a photo works well in a slideshow in two ways:

- Select the photo you want to check and select another photo (it doesn't matter which one), and then click the Slideshow button. The slideshow consists of just those two slides, over and over, and you see not only how the photo looks at full-screen resolution, but also when fading in and out.
- When looking at a single image in Edit mode, hold down the Option key and double-click the photo to open it in a separate window. Make the window as large as you can to see how the photo looks at full screen.

You can tell the size of a photo by opening it in a separate window. iPhoto scales the photo in its proper proportions, rather than stretching it to fit the viewer pane. You can tell how large the photo is by the percentage displayed in the title bar — whether a small photo scaled to display at 100 percent magnification or a very large photo scaled at 50 percent or less.

To make sure your photos are large enough to look good in a full-screen slideshow, you can check the size in two ways:

- Select a photo in the viewer pane. The Size field on the far left side of the iPhoto window displays something like 2272 x 1704, which is the size of the photo (2272 pixels wide by 1704 pixels high).
- Select a photo in the viewer pane. You can also use this method if the photo is open in a separate window. Choose File⇨Show Photo Info. iPhoto lists the Width and Height, in pixels, in the Photo tab of the Photo Info window, shown in Figure 5-1.

Size matters

When the iPhoto slideshow function enlarges a narrow image to show it full screen, the photo maintains the correct horizontal-to-vertical aspect ratio. As a result, some images may appear with black borders on either the horizontal or vertical edges, similar to a wide-screen movie on television (*letterboxing*).

When you include low-resolution images in a slideshow, they may stand out as jaggy-edged and fuzzy, which is fine if you are going for some artistic effect. But if you plan ahead and you know you want to use the pictures you are about to take in a slideshow, make sure your digital camera is set to capture photos a pixel resolution of at least 1024 x 768 pixels, preferably higher.

But if you are stuck with photos that are too small, fixing the problem is possible with an image editing program such as Adobe Photoshop. With Photoshop and iPhoto open, drag a photo directly from iPhoto into the Photoshop window and make changes, such as scaling the image to be larger, or surrounding a small image with a black border. You can then save the image as a TIFF or Photoshop file, and choose File➪Import in iPhoto to bring the revised photo back into your photo library.

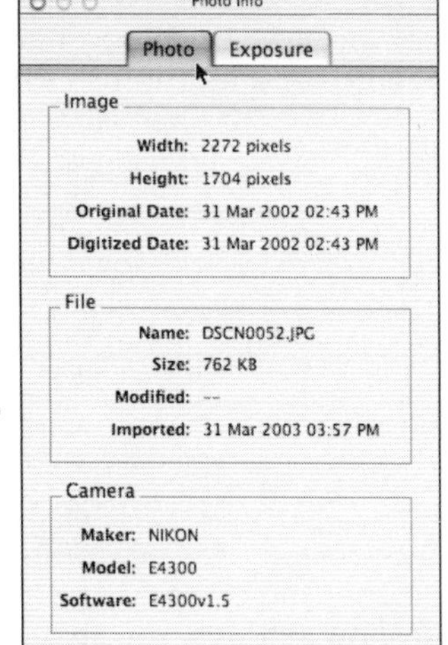

Figure 5-1: Check the size of the photo in pixels.

Changing Playback Settings

Are you ready for a performance? Possibly not — you may want to show each photo for longer than two seconds, change the music, or even set the show to play photos in random order. These choices are available in the Slideshow Settings window.

To open the Slideshow Settings window, follow these steps:

1. **In Organize mode, select the photo album from the albums list.**

   To define slideshow settings, you have to use a photo album as the basis for your slideshow.

2. **Click the Slideshow icon in the tools pane (second icon from the left).**

   The Slideshow Settings window appears, as shown in Figure 5-2.

3. **Make any changes you want.**

   You can change the time each photo plays, the order, and the music.

4. **Click the Save Settings button to save your settings.**

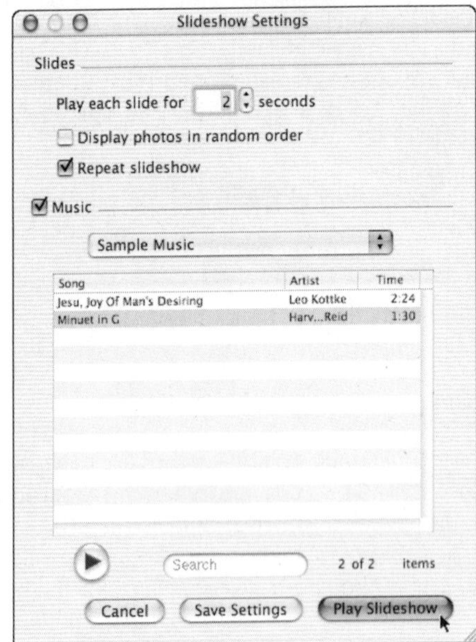

Figure 5-2: Change the settings in the Slideshow Settings window.

Saving your settings

When you are satisfied with your slideshow settings, you should save them by clicking the Save Settings button in the Slideshow Settings window (refer to Figure 5-2). iPhoto saves the slideshow settings for the entire photo album. When viewing your photo album, the slideshow information appears in the viewer pane, as shown in Figure 5-3.

What's cool about saving your settings is that any new photo you drag into the album uses those settings while in the album. Meanwhile, the photo in the photo library remains unchanged, and you can drag it to other albums and use the other album's slideshow settings.

To play the slideshow, select the photo album, and click the Play button. The slideshow runs exactly as you set it up to run.

Slide show info

Figure 5-3: Find info about your slideshow in the viewer pane.

Timing your slideshow

Your slideshows don't have to be fixed to run endlessly, or to show only two seconds per slide. Do you really want your audience to fidget in their seats and keep asking for you to go back to another slide? With the slideshow options, you're in control — set the slideshow so the audience has a chance to really look at each photo or make the photos go by in a flash.

In the Slideshow Settings window, you can change the Play Each Slide For . . . Seconds setting, so that slides appear on-screen for the duration you want before fading. The up and down arrows allow you to adjust the number of seconds with a maximum of 30 seconds between photos.

If you want more than 30 seconds between photos, you can type a number higher than 30, but not higher than 60 seconds (if you do, iPhoto pays no attention to the silly human request and refuses to highlight the Play Slideshow button until you come to your senses).

The number of seconds you choose applies to each slide in the slideshow — you can't set different timings for different slides (if you need that level of control, try iMovie, which we describe in Book III).

The timing is saved with the photo album used for the slideshow. You can try different timings by setting up multiple photo albums, and changing the settings for each one.

The number of seconds you choose for playing each slide also affects the transition time between slides. Choosing a long playing time produces longer, more appealing cross-fades as the photos blend into each other. We prefer setting the timing to 20 or 30 seconds per photo.

You can turn on the option to repeat the slideshow, if you want the slideshow to repeat in a loop. If you turn off the Repeat Slideshow option (click its box in the Slideshow Settings window to toggle the option off), iPhoto plays the slideshow and, at the end, returns to the viewer pane in Organize mode. This may be useful for previewing, but you may want your slideshows to repeat, especially if you are using a slideshow in an exhibit or on a demonstration table. You can always end a slideshow by clicking the mouse or pressing the Esc key.

Changing the music

Apple thoughtfully provided very nice music to go along with your slideshows. Music makes a slideshow come alive, turning your ordinary (and extraordinary) photos into something that resembles parts of a Ken Burns documentary. (Okay, so maybe your family vacation doesn't rank up there with a Ken Burns documentary, no matter what you may think.)

The Slideshow Settings window offers the option to play music. To open the Slideshow Settings window, select a photo album in Organize mode, and click the Slideshow icon in the tools pane.

The pop-up menu in the Music section offers sample music, and the songs available in this category (as of this writing) are from J.S. Bach: "Jesu, Joy of Man's Desiring" performed by Leo Kottke (our favorite), and "Minuet in G" performed by Harvey Reid. After selecting one in the song list, click the Play button at the bottom of the Slideshow Settings window to play just the music (refer to Figure 5-2).

Using iTunes music

Although the default songs, "Minuet in G" and "Jesu, Joy of Man's Desiring," are exquisite, you may become sick of them. Apple only provides them as suggestions, anyway. You can select a tune from your iTunes library. If you don't have any music yet in your iTunes library, read all about importing music into iTunes in Book I, Chapter 1.

To play a tune from the iTunes library, follow these steps:

1. **Open the Slideshow Settings window by selecting a photo album in Organize mode, and clicking the Slideshow icon in the tools pane.**

   The Slideshow Settings window appears.

2. **Select the Music option.**

   A check should be in the check box next to the Music option.

3. **Click the Music option's pop-up menu to select an iTunes playlist, or select iTunes itself to see the entire music library.**

   Selecting a playlist is useful if you already defined a playlist for slideshows in iTunes (Book I, Chapter 2). The songs stored in the playlist appear in the box below the menu, as shown in Figure 5-4.

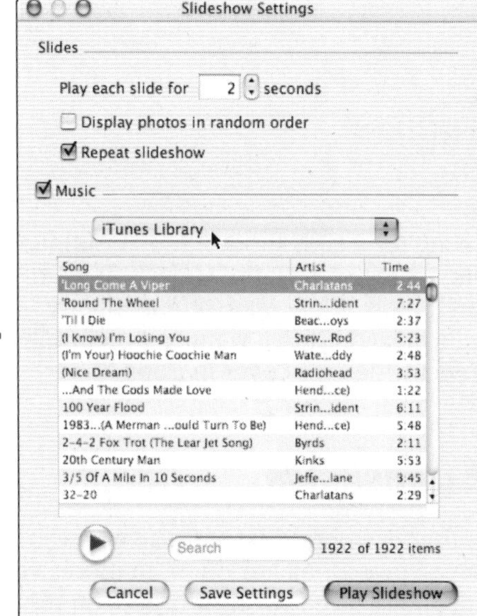

Figure 5-4: Select a tune from an iTunes playlist for the slideshow's music.

4. **Select a song within the playlist.**
5. **Click the Play button to hear your selection.**

If you select the entire iTunes library in Step 3, the list of songs is initially sorted alphabetically by song title, but you can sort the list alphabetically by artist by clicking the Artist column header, or sort the songs by duration (from shortest to longest) by clicking the Time column header. If you know the specific song you want to add to the slideshow, type the title in the Search box to narrow the choices. Figure 5- 5 shows our iTunes library playlist sorted alphabetically by artist.

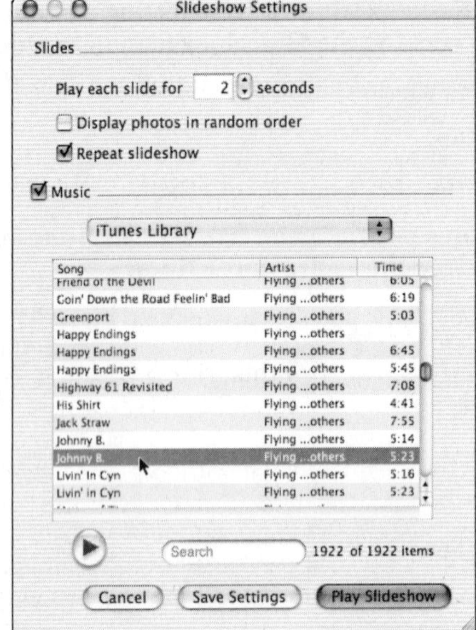

Figure 5-5: View the iTunes playlist by artist rather than by title.

You can choose only one song for a slideshow. iPhoto continues playing the song until it ends or the slideshow ends. If the slideshow repeats endlessly, the song also repeats when it ends. They play independently — the song and the slides are not synchronized. (If you want to synchronize sound with photos or images, use iMovie, which we cover in Book III.)

Sharing and Exporting Slideshows

A slideshow on your computer is wonderful for those who can pull up a seat and watch. If you have a PowerBook laptop or an iBook, you no doubt already appreciate the slideshows you can show others on the spot, thanks to the portability of your machine. But to reach a larger audience, or different audiences at different times, you have some options:

✦ **Share your slideshow online with the .Mac service.**

  The entire slideshow is available online for others to use as a screen effect (anyone using .Mac, that is).

✦ **Export your slideshow to a QuickTime movie.**

  You can post a QuickTime movie on a Web page and including it with other scenes in an iMovie presentation, described in Book III.

✦ **Create a DVD of the slideshow.**

You can export the entire slideshow, including music, to iDVD, which gives you tools to improve the slideshow and burn a DVD disc. We describe iDVD in more detail in Book IV.

In addition, you can share individual photos with others via e-mail, or publish individual photos on a Web page. We describe how to do both in Chapter 6 of this book.

Sharing slideshows online

You can really impress your friends with this trick. You can provide your slideshow online for others to use as a screen effect (that is, a screen saver).

Apple offers the .Mac service for all Mac users (for a fee, of course). One of its major benefits is the capability of sharing iPhoto slideshows with others over the Internet. With the .Mac Slides feature on the .Mac service, others can use your slideshow as a screen effect. The Screen Effects function acts like a *screen saver* — animation displays on your desktop when your computer is inactive.

You can subscribe in advance to the .Mac service, or you can go ahead and click the .Mac Slides icon in the tools pane, and iPhoto automatically connects to the Internet and checks to see if you have a .Mac account. If you don't, iPhoto gives you the option to join the service, and launches your Internet browser to the .Mac sign-up page.

Of course, if you aren't connected to the Internet through a network or high-speed modem that provides always-on service, iPhoto won't automatically connect to the Internet works until you connect manually by modem. Connect to the Internet using your usual method before clicking the .Mac icon.

To share your slideshow with others over the Internet using the .Mac service, follow these steps:

1. **In Organize mode, select the photo album or individual photos in the slideshow.**
2. **Click the .Mac Slides icon in the tools pane.**

   The .Mac Slides icon displays a warning: `Are you sure you want to publish a slideshow as .Mac Slides?` Transferring an entire slideshow can take a bit of time if your slideshow contains a lot of photos.

3. **Click the Publish button to publish the slideshow.**

   iPhoto copies the photos in the slideshow to your iDisk on the .Mac service, as shown in Figure 5-6. You can cancel the operation by clicking the Cancel button.

Figure 5-6: Copy a slideshow to the .Mac service for sharing online.

When the slideshow finishes copying, iPhoto displays a dialog box notifying you that the photos are online, and as an option, gives you the opportunity to announce your slideshow to others who use the .Mac service. If you click the Announce button in the dialog box, your e-mail application appears with a new message ready to send — all you need to do is fill in the addresses. Don't do this unless you're ready to announce your slideshow and send the e-mail.

You can control which e-mail program iPhoto uses by choosing iPhoto➪Preferences and selecting an e-mail application in the Mail pop-up menu.

The message provides instructions to others on how to subscribe to the slideshow using the .Mac service. To use the slideshow, others have to be running Mac OS X version 10.2 or a newer version. They need to connect to the Internet, and then perform the following steps:

1. **Open System Preferences and click the Screen Effects icon.**

   The Screen Effects window appears, shown in Figure 5-7.

2. **Select .Mac in the list of available screen effects.**
3. **Click the Configure button.**

   The screen saver options appear, as shown in Figure 5-8.

4. **In the .Mac Membership Name box, enter the user name of the member who published the slideshow, and click OK.**
5. **Choose System Preferences➪Quit System Preferences to close System Preferences.**

Screen Effects offers settings for playing the screen saver, which you can find out about in Chapter 3 of this book.

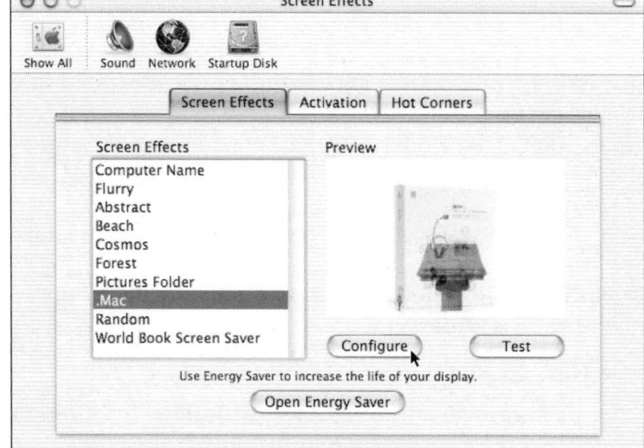

Figure 5-7: Use a shared-online slideshow as a screen effect.

Figure 5-8: Set the screen saver options.

Sharing your slideshows this way is cool. What's cooler is the fact that you can change your slideshow, publish a new version, and your friends automatically see the new version as part of their screen effects. Keep your friends and family abreast of events and changes in your life, as told with photos, through slideshows.

Exporting to a QuickTime movie

Your slideshow is so fantastic you want to share it with the world. But only .Mac users can see your slideshow.

QuickTime to the rescue! QuickTime is like a container for multimedia built into every Mac and available to any PC user intelligent enough to know what's best. When you create a QuickTime movie file, even those dudes with Dells and geeks with Gateways can play it. You send it to them on a CD or DVD or you can also publish a QuickTime file on a Web site for anyone to play.

To put your slideshow into a QuickTime file, follow these steps:

1. **In Organize mode, select an album from the album list or individual photos used in a slideshow.**
2. **Choose File⇨Export.**

   The Export Photos window displays, with tabs for different types of export functions, as shown in Figure 5-9.

   - **File Export:** Export versions of your photos using file formats such as JPG (for JPEG, the standard image format for Web pages) and TIFF (the standard format for desktop publishing software). You can discover more about file formats in Chapter 6 of this book.
   - **Web Page:** Export photos or an entire album to a Web page, as we describe in Chapter 6 of this book.
   - **QuickTime:** Export photos, or an album set up as a slideshow, to the QuickTime format.
3. **Click the QuickTime tab.**

   The QuickTime pane appears.
4. **Change the movie options as you wish, especially the Images section.**

   In the QuickTime pane's Images section, specify the pixel resolution of your movie. If you make a movie as an experiment, go ahead with the suggested resolution settings of 640 x 480 pixels. We outline the different resolutions in the sidebar "The QuickTime resolution."
5. **Click the Export button to create the QuickTime movie.**

   The Save As dialog box opens.
6. **Type a name for the QuickTime movie, and choose where to save it on your hard disk, and then click the Save button.**

The QuickTime resolution

You have some choices to make about how you plan to use this movie, before setting the image resolution and exporting the QuickTime movie. Although you can go with the default resolution of 640 x 480 pixels, you also have the capability of making a movie as large as your monitor (which is how iPhoto typically plays slideshows).

If you do increase the pixel resolution, you may run into a problem. Pixel resolution affects file size dramatically and you need to make a movie that everyone can play. If you specify 1,024 x 768 pixels (the typical display setting for slideshows on an iMac), the resulting movie may be too large to send as an e-mail attachment — if that's what you want to do with it. Your movie's screen size may also be too large for other people's monitors, such as older iBooks.

Although you can type any number you want as a pixel dimension, you should maintain the 4:3 aspect ratio that digital cameras and displays use. You can, however, reverse the ratio and specify 480 x 640 pixels, if all the photos in the slideshow are vertically oriented.

A resolution of 800 x 600 is okay for just about all computer displays, but 640 x 480, the suggested resolution, is by far the most commonly used. With 640 x 480 pixels, the resulting file size is small and easy to handle by e-mail or other means (such as publishing on a Web page). For example, a slideshow of 10 photos, at a 640 x 480 pixel image size, creates a QuickTime file that is 1MB; the same slideshow at 800 x 600 pixels creates a 1.5MB file, and at 1,024 x 768 pixels at 2.3MB file.

Remember: Music takes up considerable space. A slideshow saved as a QuickTime file with music (such as the sample song "Minuet in G") is a lot larger than the same file saved without music. With music, the file size jumps up to 1.6MB for a slideshow with 10 photos at a 640 x 480 resolution. Of course, then you'd have a silent movie. You can reduce the music's sampling rate in iTunes before using the music with the slideshow, but that's another topic, which we cover in Book I.

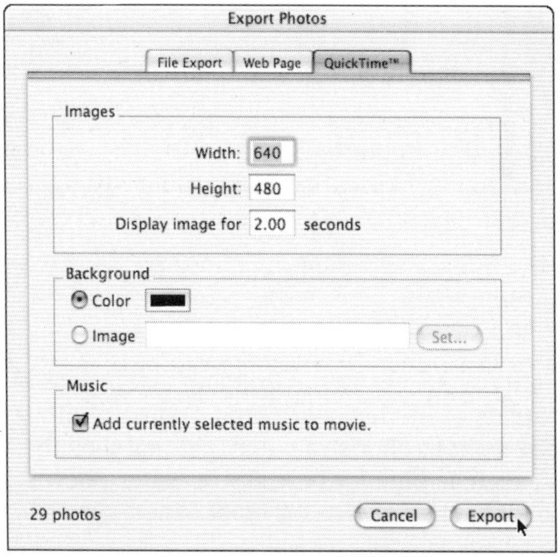

Figure 5-9: Export a slideshow as a QuickTime movie.

You can change the following settings in the QuickTime pane of the Export Files window:

- **Time to display each photo:** You can also control the time each photo takes to show by typing a number in the Display Image For . . . Seconds option box in the Images section of the QuickTime pane. (This setting overrides the settings for the slideshow in the Slideshow Settings window.) You can be precise about the number of seconds for displaying the image, to hundredths of a second. In fact, you can make a QuickTime movie that displays images so fast it could pass for a light show at a rock concert. The maximum is 60 seconds.
- **Background color:** To add a background color, click the Color button in the Background section of the QuickTime pane, and then click the color preview box. The Colors window appears, as shown in Figure 5-10. The Colors window gives you multiple ways to select a color. The color wheel includes a slider for selecting the color's intensity. You can try other ways to select a color — the icons along the top row of the Colors window offer color-value sliders, color swatches, a spectrum, and a set of crayons. To set a color, drag the color you chose in the Colors window to the preview box in the QuickTime pane.

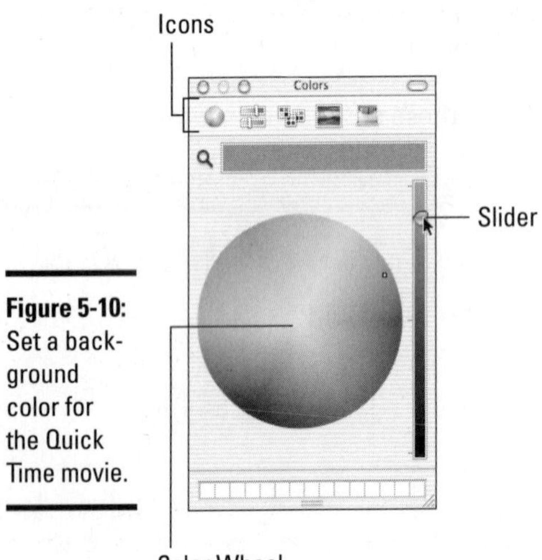

Figure 5-10: Set a background color for the Quick Time movie.

The color you choose serves as the first and last frames of the movie and fills the margins of vertically oriented photos or other odd-shaped photos. You may want to choose a color that matches the backgrounds of your photos, such as blue for blue sky or water photos. However, black is the most effective choice for most slideshows.

✦ **Background image:** An alternative to a background color is a background image, preferably one that doesn't clash with the photos themselves (unless you are trying for a special clashing effect). To set an image as the background, click the Image button in the Background section of the QuickTime pane, and then click the Set button to select an image from your hard disk.

✦ **Music:** Decide whether to include the music you set in the Slideshow Settings window, keeping in mind that the alternative is a silent movie and a smaller file.

To view the finished movie, open the movie file using QuickTime Player or any other application that plays QuickTime movies. Your slideshow looks like a professional presentation and now you can share it with the world.

Exporting a slideshow to iDVD

A great way to share your slideshow is to burn a DVD, to be shown with any type of DVD player. If you have an Apple-supported CD-RW or DVD-R drive (such as Apple's SuperDrive), you can create your own DVDs with slideshows, menus, and video clips — a process called *burning*.

iDVD offers tools for creating DVD discs with menus for selecting material on the disc. You can transfer a slideshow, including its music, directly from iPhoto to iDVD to create a DVD slideshow.

To export a slideshow to iDVD, follow these steps:

1. **In Organize mode, select an album or individual photos used in a slideshow.**
2. **Click the iDVD icon in the tools pane (available if you have iDVD).**

   The iDVD application opens, as shown in Figure 5-11.
3. **Choose Project⇨Show Customize Panel from the iDVD toolbar.**

   The panel to the right of the stage in the iDVD window opens.
4. **Click the Photos icon.**

   Your albums from iPhoto appear, ready for use with iDVD. The photos from your library, while remaining in your library, are now linked to an iDVD project. You don't need to export and import photos; in fact, you can still make changes to the photos in your library and albums in iPhoto, while keeping them linked to this iDVD project.

Creating DVDs is a much bigger topic than we can cover here — look for the iDVD story in Book IV.

Figure 5-11: Your iPhoto albums automatically export to iDVD.

Chapter 6: Printing and Publishing Photos and Books

In This Chapter

- Printing photos
- Ordering prints from services
- Assembling a photo book
- Sharing photos by e-mail
- Publishing Web pages

People generally save photos for posterity, nostalgia, history, and hundreds of other reasons, but for the most part people save photos so that others can see them.

Paper is still the most useful medium for showing photos. You still want prints to put in frames, scrapbooks, and wallets. Your grandmother still hasn't figured out e-mail, let alone how to save a photo attached to an e-mail. With iPhoto, you can create prints on your own color printer and print as many as you want without using a service. And if you want real photographic prints, you can order them directly through iPhoto by using the Kodak online service.

You can go much further with iPhoto: You can even publish a photo book that looks professional. After organizing photos into a book layout that can include titles and captions, you can order professionally printed books worthy of the Library of Congress.

And publishing photos on the Web is easy with the iPhoto HomePage feature. Not only can you connect to a Web site where you can publish your photos, but you can also produce a layout of the Web page automatically and add text, such as titles and captions. You can also export photos into other file formats for use with other programs, such as Web authoring programs, and for posting to Web sites using methods other than HomePage. You can even export an entire photo album to share with others.

This chapter walks you through all the details of printing your own photographic prints and things such as greeting cards, ordering prints from online services, ordering photo books, and publishing photos on the Web.

Setting Up Your Printer

The trees may not like it, but paper remains the most universal medium for showing photos. True, with digital photography, the noxious chemicals of film processing are gone, and the darkroom has been turned into a walk-in closet, but you still need to make prints of some kind.

In fact, digital photography makes it easier than ever to get exactly the prints you want without wasting money on the prints you don't want. For example, you can print your own *contact sheets,* which are quick prints of photos in a thumbnail size. Or you can simply use iPhoto as a digital contact sheet. As an added bonus, you can print individual photos on your own color printer to see how they look in print form before ordering a high-quality print on photographic paper. You can even print your own greeting cards.

Read through this section to discover how to easily set up your printer to take advantage of printing your own photos.

Picking a desktop printer and paper

Printing photos from iPhoto is just about the easiest thing you can do. However, your results may be low quality, especially if you use a standard office printer. Office printers used for invoices and documents are not going to do justice to your color photos. To achieve the result that you want, you have to spend a little money.

First, we recommend that you buy a *color* printer. You need at least a decent inexpensive color printer, available from manufacturers such as Epson, Hewlett-Packard, and Canon for less than $200. Higher-quality color printers are surprisingly affordable, such as the Canon i950 Color Photo Printer for about $250. ***Note:*** Make sure that you factor in the number prints that you can make with a single ink cartridge and the cost to replace the cartridge. Desktop printers designed to print photos, such as the aforementioned Canon i950, typically use six different ink colors rather than just the four colors used by most color inkjet printers. The extra colors make photo prints look outstanding.

A second factor to consider is the type of paper used for printing. The plain typing paper that you use with a laser printer or copier is too thin and can't absorb enough ink to show colors well. You can still use regular copy paper, however, to show how large a photo print is or for contact sheets. Still, so-called "high resolution" paper used with inkjets is heavier and might do better for test prints — it's not glossy, but it has a smooth finish on one side. The best paper for finished prints or greeting cards is either glossy photo paper or, if you can afford it, glossy film, made with polyethylene rather than paper.

Setting up pages for your desktop printer

When using a printer with iPhoto, like with most Mac applications, you can access printer quality features by choosing File➪Page Setup. Different printers offer different features (or sometimes, just different terminology for the same types of features). You can access the printer's settings by clicking the Settings pop-up menu in the Page Setup dialog box, as shown in Figure 6-1, which offers these settings:

- ✦ **Page Attributes:** Choose the size of your paper. You can also set the orientation of the page to portrait style (horizontal), or landscape style (vertical facing left, or vertical facing right). You can also resize the page to fit the paper.
- ✦ **Custom Paper Size:** You can specify custom sizes, depending on your printer. Color photo printers typically offer sizes for precut photo paper, such as 4 x 6. Your printer may also have choices for paper, such as plain, inkjet paper, glossy photo paper, and so on.
- ✦ **Summary:** Displays a summary of the page attributes, including the document page size, paper dimensions, orientation, scale, and paper margins.

If you have more than one printer that you can choose from, switch printers by choosing the one that you want in the Format For pop-up menu in the Page Setup dialog box.

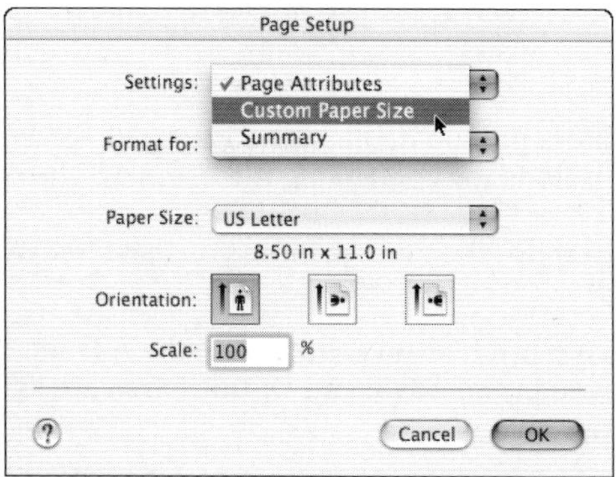

Figure 6-1: Change the printer settings in the Page Setup dialog box.

Printing Photos

After you set up your printer settings, you're ready to print. Follow these steps:

1. **Select one or more photos in Organize mode.**

2. **Choose File➪Print or click the Print button in the tools pane.**

   Click the Print button, *not* the Order Prints button, which connects you to the Kodak service.

   The Print dialog box appears with the photo that you selected displayed in a preview pane, as shown in Figure 6-2.

3. **Make any changes to the settings.**

   For example, in Figure 6-2, we set the Style setting to the Full Page option to get a full-page print of a single photo, and we also specified one copy. A preview of the printed photo appears on the left side of the dialog box.

4. **Click the Print button.**

Figure 6-2: Print from the Print dialog box.

The Print dialog box offers pop-up menus for page styles, presets, and printers, and various options for controlling the printing:

✦ **Printer:** If you have more than one printer, you can choose a different printer.

✦ **Presets:** You can save print settings if you use the Advanced Options button. Presets saved in the Advanced Options area are listed in the Preset menu for easy selection.

✦ **Style:** Set the specific types of pages that iPhoto handles for any type of color printer. When you choose a different style, the preview image in the dialog box changes to show that style. Some of these styles are described in more detail in this chapter. The styles available from the Style menu are

- **Contact Sheet:** A quick print of photos in a thumbnail size.
- **Full Page:** The photo occupies a full page. You can drag the Margins slider to increase the size of the margins of the page.

- **Greeting Card:** The photos are laid out in the standard greeting card format, either single-fold or double-fold.
- **N-Up:** You can use this style to place from 4 to 16 photos on a single page or to place the same photo several times on the same page.
- **Sampler:** This style offers two templates for layouts that are attractive for printed photos.
- **Standard Prints:** This style provides sizes and layouts for prints just like the ones that you get from a photo service.

✦ **Copies:** Specify the number of copies to print. If you print a set of photos, this number specifies the number of copies of the entire set.

✦ **Preview button:** Click to see a full-screen preview of the page that you're printing.

✦ **Save As PDF button:** You can save the pages as a PDF (Portable Document Format) file that others can open with Adobe Acrobat.

✦ **Advanced Options button:** Click to access the Advanced Options area of the Print dialog box. These settings vary from printer to printer. You can use the Presets pop-up menu to save your settings by choosing Save As in the pop-up menu and typing a name for the preset. The preset appears from that point on in the Presets menu. The Advanced Options area include the Copies & Pages, Layout, Output Options, Error Handling, Paper Feed, and Printer Features settings. (These settings are described in detail in a book about Mac OS X such as *Mac OS X All-in-One Desk Reference For Dummies* by Mark L. Chambers, published by Wiley Publishing, Inc.)

Printing standard prints

Standard prints are what you get from a photo service. iPhoto makes conforming to standard print sizes with your color printer easy because it automatically resizes images to fit properly for the settings you choose. These settings are useful if you intend to use store-bought picture frames, which are measured for specific sizes like 4 x 6 or 8 x 10.

To select a standard print size when printing to your desktop printer, choose these settings from the Print dialog box:

1. **Choose the Standard option from the Presets pop-up menu, as shown in Figure 6-3.**
2. **Choose the appropriate size from the Size pop-up menu.**

   iPhoto can print two 4 x 6 copies on a single page, which is useful if you select more than one photo for printing.

Don't choose a very large print size, such as 8 x 10, for a low-resolution image because the picture stretches over a large area and doesn't look as good as it does at smaller print sizes. You need a resolution of at least 1800 x 2200 pixels for a decent 8 x 10 print. If you choose a large size for an image that is lower in resolution than quality demands, iPhoto kindly signals you with a yellow warning sign in the preview pane of the Print dialog box.

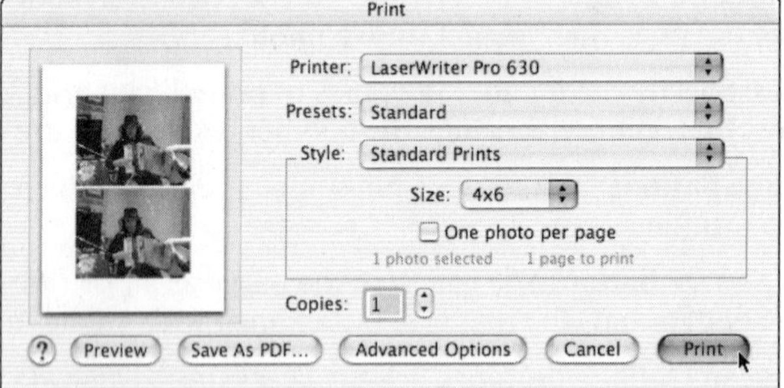

Figure 6-3: Print standard prints.

Although the Print dialog box offers many choices for printed photo sizes, you may need to adjust the proportions of your photo to fit certain sizes. Photos from most digital cameras are sized at proportions of 4 (width) x 3 (height) pixels, which is fine for computer displays, DVDs, and iPhoto book layouts but isn't the right proportion for standard prints. If you don't adjust the proportions, you may find that some photos have unintended white margins at the sides of the finished prints. iPhoto makes this adjustment easy with the Constrain feature for cropping.

The Constrain pop-up menu in iPhoto offers choices for standard print and display formats. When cropping is constrained, the cropped photo fits the format properly. To find out more about cropping with the Constrain feature, see Chapter 4 of this book.

Printing greeting cards

iPhoto provides a style for greeting cards with two different layouts for folding them. To select a greeting card layout when printing to your desktop printer, choose the Greeting Cards option from the Style pop-up menu the Print dialog box.

iPhoto rotates and places your photo properly on the page so that you can fold the page into a proper greeting card. You can click the option to print in single-fold or double-fold style. The preview pane shows what the photo looks like in either style.

✦ **Single-fold:** The photo appears upside down at the top of the page, making a large greeting card with a single horizontal fold easy to create, as shown in Figure 6-4.

✦ **Double-fold:** The photo appears in the top-right corner of the page facing to the right, making a standard-sized greeting card with both a horizontal and a vertical fold easy to create, as shown in Figure 6-5.

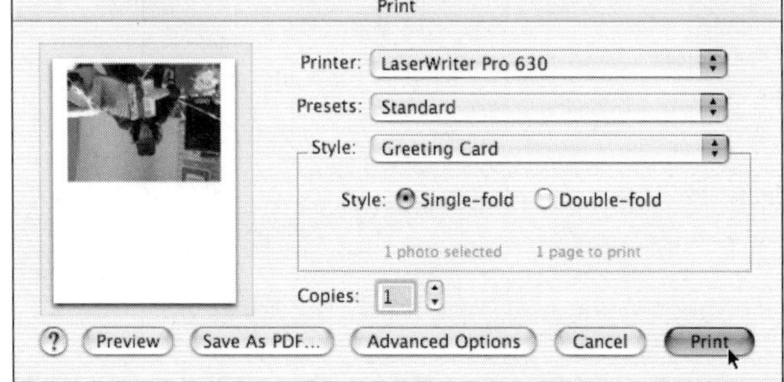

Figure 6-4: Print a greeting card with a single fold.

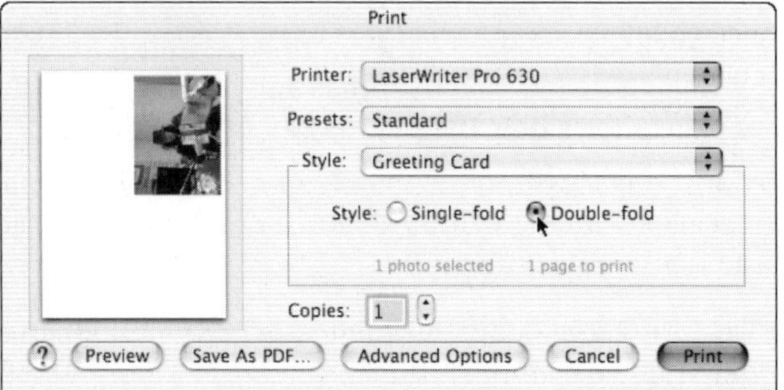

Figure 6-5: Print a greeting card with a double fold.

You can use the special glossy paper stock for greeting cards that is already scored and perforated for easy folding.

Printing contact sheets for albums

In commercial photography, a *contact sheet* is a quick print of photos in a thumbnail size. You can order contact sheets when you process film rolls so that you can choose which ones to use for full prints.

Of course, in iPhoto, you can print your own contact sheets, just like a commercial photo service. Contact sheets can be useful for comparing the quality of several photos at once, making test prints of an entire album, or even repeating the same photo in a grid for cutting up wallet-sized prints.

To print a contact sheet, choose the Contact Sheet option from the Style pop-up menu the Print dialog box, as shown in Figure 6-6.

Figure 6-6: Choose a contact sheet and adjust the number of photos in a row.

The Contact Sheet style offers the following settings:

- **Across:** Use the slider to choose how many slides you want across the page. You can print up to eight photos in a row (although you need a magnifying glass to see them).
- **Save Paper:** Select the Save Paper option to print photos with thinner margins. Keep it unselected to spread the photos out on the page. The preview pane shows how the photos will print.

Ordering Prints

You can order prints from the Kodak photo service directly from iPhoto that are much higher quality than the prints you can make with a color printer. You can set up an account with your credit card, and Apple remembers your account information the next time that you order prints. Select the size and quantity of the photos to be printed, and in one click, transmit the photos directly to Kodak. Your finished photos are printed on high-quality glossy photographic paper and are mailed or express-delivered to you.

To order prints, you need to connect to the Internet. Then follow these steps:

1. **Select the photos to print in Organize mode.**

   You can also select an album to order prints of all the photos in the album.

2. **Click the Order Prints button in the tools pane.**

   The photos that you selected appear in the Kodak Order Prints window, as shown in Figure 6-7.

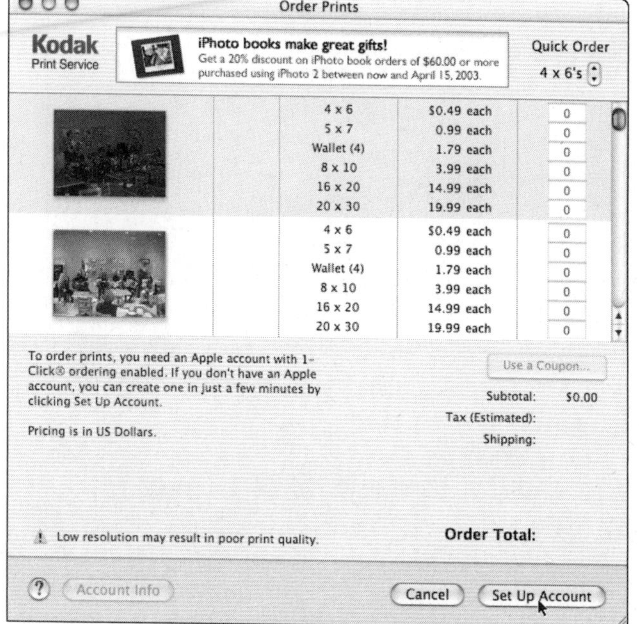

Figure 6-7: Order prints from Kodak with the Order Prints window.

3. **Click the Set Up Account button.**

   The Set Up Account window appears, as shown in Figure 6-8.

   - **If you already have an account,** sign in with your Apple ID and password. You can skip Steps 4 through 7 if you already have an account.
   - **To create a new account,** click the Create Account button, which takes you to another page in the Set Up Account window, as shown in Figure 6-9.

4. **Fill in your personal information and click the Continue button.**

   The information includes your e-mail address, a password, and a question and answer that you can easily remember to help verify your identity in case you forget your password.

Set Up Account

Apple Account Sign-in

To continue with your order, enter an Apple ID and Password. If you don't have an Apple account, create one.

Create Account

Learn More

Apple ID:

Example: steve@mac.com

Password:

Forgot Password?

Cancel

Sign In

Figure 6-8: Log into your Apple account in the Set Up Account window.

Set Up Account

Step 1 of 3: Create an Apple Account

Please enter the following information to create your new Apple account.

Email Address: bove@ — This is your Apple ID.

Password: •••••••• — This must be at least 6 characters.

Verify: •••••••• — Retype your password.

Enter a question and answer that you can easily remember to help us verify your identity in case you forget your password.

Question:

Answer:

Please enter your date of birth.

Month: January Day: 5

I would like to receive Apple news, software updates, special offers, and information about related products and services from other companies.

Privacy Policy

Cancel Continue

Figure 6-9: Create a new account with your personal information.

5. **Click the Accept button to accept the Terms of Use agreement for the service.**
6. **Enter your billing information and click the Continue button.**

   This includes your billing address, phone number, credit card information, and preferred shipping method (standard or express).
7. **Enter your shipping address and phone number and click the Continue button.**
8. **Enter the quantity of prints in the far right column of the Order Prints window for each print size.**

   To quickly fill in a quantity of one for a specific print size for multiple photos, click the Quick Order button at the top-right corner of the Order Prints window. Alternatively, you can scroll down and specify different numbers and sizes for each photo. The total cost updates as you make your selections.
9. **Click the Buy Now button to finish your order.**

A low-resolution warning (exclamation point in a yellow triangle) appears if your photo is not high enough in resolution for a particular print size. You can still order that print size for that photo, but the quality will probably be poor. You get the same warnings when you print at these sizes on your own printer — if you do test prints first, you know in advance which photos work best at which sizes. We suggest that you use the 8 x 10 size with photos 1536 x 1024 pixels or higher in resolution.

You may already have realized that the Order Prints function, which is connected to the Kodak service, is not the only way to order prints. Other services may be less expensive or offer better choices. You can easily burn a CD with a photo album (as we describe in Chapter 3 of this book) and send the CD to a photo service. Many services on the Internet accept photos attached to e-mails or uploaded directly to a Web site — we describe both methods later in this chapter.

Services may accept only certain file formats for photos. You can export photos from iPhoto in appropriate file formats by selecting one or more photos, or an entire album, and choosing File⇨Export. We explain more about how to do this later in this chapter, in the "Exporting to a photo service" section.

Making Photo Books

Inexpensive desktop publishing technology provided freedom for many small presses and publishers and also paved the way for digital photography and other multimedia pursuits. But it was not just the graphical interface of the computer and the rise of laser printers that brought about this change — it was most importantly the introduction of *layout tools* that everyone could use. Overnight, anyone could be a newsletter publisher, or even a magazine or book publisher, because tools were available to help you lay out elements on pages.

iPhoto provides an automatic book layout capability that helps anyone become a photo book publisher. You can assemble a book from a photo album and have it professionally printed and bound to look as good as most books on library shelves (better, in fact, because yours hasn't been mishandled yet). You can create catalog-style books, picture books, portfolios, story books, and yearbooks, or use any of the layout themes for books that defy category.

Choosing a book layout theme

With iPhoto, you can choose from among several book layout themes and place photos in pages automatically. Your first step is to choose the photos that you want for the photo book and assemble them into a photo album, as we describe in Chapter 3 of this book.

Book layouts are based on photo albums — the sequence of photos in the album defines the sequence of the pages in the book. If you want to change the sequence, rearrange the photos in the album. You can create different types of books with the same photos by creating separate photo albums for each book. Creating a photo album for a book is no different than creating a photo album for any other reason. We describe how to create and arrange photos in photo albums in more detail in Chapter 3 of this book. To start the process of creating a book, you choose a book layout theme:

1. **Select a photo album and arrange the photos in the sequence that you want in Organize mode.**

   Flip to Chapter 3 of this book if you need help arranging your photos.

2. **Click the Book mode button.**

   iPhoto displays the layout of the book with photos from the selected album with the Picture Book theme. A preview of the cover page appears at the top, and thumbnails of subsequent pages arranged below it, as shown in Figure 6-10.

Figure 6-10: The Picture Book layout theme.

   The Picture Book theme appears by default when you first click the Book mode button. As you can see in Figure 6-10, photos of different sizes work well in this format, and iPhoto makes semi-intelligent choices based on photo sizes — page 3, for example, places two photos side-by-side. We describe how to fine-tune the design of pages in the next section "Fine-tuning page layouts."

3. **Choose a book layout theme in the Theme pop-up menu in the tools pane.**

   The themes define the photo layout for the pages:

   - **Catalog:** This theme places more photos on each page than other themes. It is often used for catalogs and directories.
   - **Classic:** The Classic theme is a standard layout for coffee-table books with room for captions and commentary.

* **Picture Book:** The default setting, Picture Book is commonly used for printed photo albums and does not include any text, such as titles or comments.
* **Portfolio:** This theme presents photos with accompanying captions and text in a layout suitable for commercial portfolios, used by artists and photographers to show their work.
* **Story Book:** With photos placed at angles and combined on the page, this theme offers attractive choices for page layouts that allow enough room for text.
* **Year Book:** This variation of the Catalog theme provides a standard layout for college and high school yearbooks, with multiple photos on each page.

All the themes offer special title pages and variations of the layout in order for you to customize your book.

4. **Optional: Select a page to preview and click the Preview button in the tools pane.**

   To really look at the way a theme works its magic on pages, select a page from the row of thumbnails — scroll the row of thumbnails horizontally to see more pages. The page that you selected appears in a separate window, as shown in Figure 6-11.

By choosing themes and previewing pages, you can see right away what the book looks like.

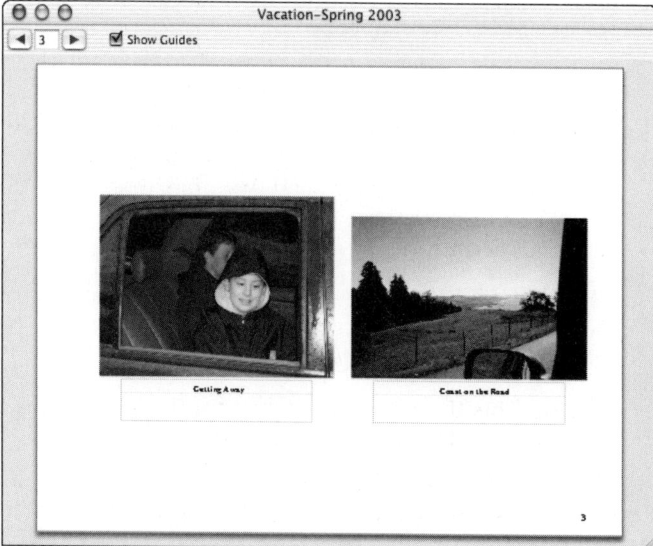

Figure 6-11: Preview for the Classic photo book theme.

Fine-tuning page layouts

After selecting a book layout theme for your photo album, you can fine-tune the design of each page. You can even rearrange the photos in your book while designing — you may not realize that certain photos don't look good together until you see the page sequence in Book mode.

When you rearrange pages in Book mode (as in moving page 5 before page 3, and so on), the photos on those pages are also automatically rearranged in the photo album. You can set the photo sequence for your book in either Organize mode by rearranging photos in the album or in Book mode by rearranging pages. If you change the arrangement in the album, the book changes as well, and vice-versa. However, you can't delete a photo in Book mode — use Organize mode to delete a photo from the photo album used for the book.

To rearrange pages, click the page and drag it to the new location in the sequence. While you drag, the sequence scrolls horizontally to reveal more pages, so you can drag a page from the beginning to the end.

Each theme offers options for laying out pages. For example, in Figure 6-12, page 3 shows two slides on the page, but by changing the number of photos in the page in the Page Design pop-up menu in the tools pane, you can add or delete a photo to this page.

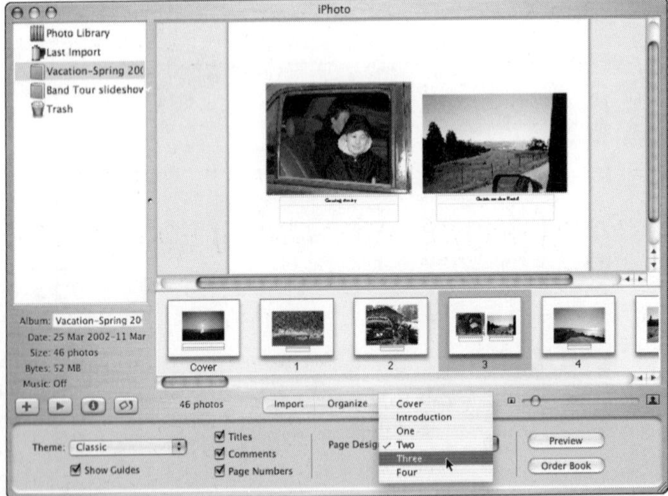

Figure 6-12: Change the number of photos per page.

The Page Design pop-up menu, available for each theme, provides layouts for

- **Cover:** The cover page of the book
- **Introduction:** The introduction page, which may have room for text.
- **One:** A book page layout with one photo on the page
- **Two**, **Three**, **Four**, and so on: Book page layouts with two, three, four, or more photos on the page (menu options change depending on theme)

Options that also appear in the tools pane for each theme include the following:

- **Titles:** Check the Title box to include titles. By default, the title (or caption) for each photo in the book is the photo's title in the photo library.
- **Comments:** Check the Comments box to add comments to your book. Comments for photos in your photo library are, by default, used as comments in layouts that offer space for them.
- **Page Numbers:** iPhoto automatically numbers the pages of your book, but you can opt not to use page numbers by unchecking the Page Numbers box.

Editing titles and captions

The titles and comments that you assign to your photos can automatically be used as titles and captions in books. In each layout theme, you can also add more text — to the title and introduction page, and in some themes, to captions. If your comments are like ours, ("Daddy falls in the creek to much applause") and not meant to be real captions, adding more text is useful. And if you are ordering a print of this book, check it first for spelling errors and typos.

Locking pages and saving your work

As you change the number of photos on a page, or change the order of pages that have multiple photos, the change affects the pages that come afterwards. The best way to design pages is to work forward in sequence from the cover page and page one. When you make changes that ripple across the page sequence, you can decide whether you like the changes, and if you do, you can lock the page by checking the Lock Page check page in the tools pane. From that point, changes made to other pages do not affect the locked page.

As for saving your work, you don't have to. iPhoto keeps track of your Book mode settings for the photo album you select. But if you want to change the book layout while preserving the layout you just created, you can do this by making a duplicate copy of the photo album: Choose File➪Duplicate.

You can edit the text on pages by clicking directly in the text fields of the layout in the preview pane. The preview pane increases the size of the image within the pane, so you can see clearly to type. You can increase or decrease the size by dragging the size control slider on the right side under the row of page thumbnails.

To change the text font and style:

1. **Drag over the text in the field to select it.**
2. **Choose Edit⇨Font⇨Show Fonts or press ⌘+T.**

   The Fonts window appears, as shown in Figure 6-13.

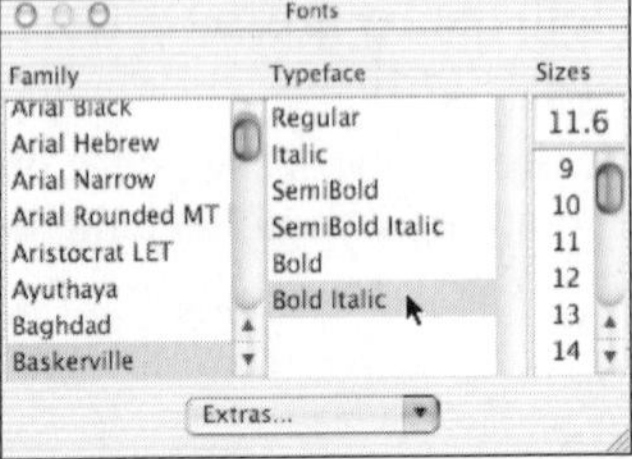

Figure 6-13: Change the font in the Fonts window.

3. **Select a different font and/or style.**

   The selections that you make in the Fonts window change the appearance of the text in the preview pane in Book mode. You can't increase the size of the text beyond the text field length because these layouts adhere strictly to the themes. In general, the font changes that you make to a caption on a page affect all the captions on all the pages.

   To select a font, choose a family (such as Baskerville), a typeface style within that family (such as Bold Italic), and the size of the font.

   The Extras pop-up menu provides many font options for using fonts with Mac OS X applications. Some of these options are useful for text in iPhoto, including

   - **Show Preview/Hide Preview:** Shows or hides a preview of the font settings right in the Fonts window. (You can drag the window to be larger to see both the preview and the font settings.)
   - **Show Characters:** Displays the Character Palette window with Japanese, Chinese, Cyrillic, Greek, and special symbols that you can insert into your text.
   - **Color:** Assigns a color to the text.
   - **Get Fonts:** Launches your Web browser and takes you to the page on the Apple site for buying fonts for the Mac.

4. **Click the Close button to close the Font window.**

If you want to create a more flexible page layout, well, that's what page layout programs are for! (We recommend Adobe PageMaker.)

Previewing and printing books

Previewing your book on your Mac is the best way to see quickly whether the photos look right on the page. Printing is the best way to see whether the photos print well and to catch any spelling errors or typos.

To preview the book, select any page from the row of thumbnails, and click the Preview button in the tools pane to see that page in a separate window, as shown in Figure 6-14. You can jump page by page with the arrow buttons, and you can turn on the Show Guides option at the top of the window to see the text box outlines.

Figure 6-14: Previewing the book page after making text changes.

To print the book, first set up the pages for your printer using File➪Page Setup, as we describe earlier in this chapter, in the section "Setting up pages for your desktop printer." Then follow these steps:

1. **Choose File➪Print in Book mode.**

   The Print dialog box appears with the first page from the book displayed in a preview pane.

2. **Make changes to the settings.**

   The Print dialog box for printing books offers the following settings: Printer, Presets, Copies, Preview button, Save As PDF, and Advanced Options. See the section, "Printing Photos," earlier in this chapter for more on printing options.

3. **Click the Print button.**

You can save the book as a PDF file, which is accepted by many printing and publishing services. You can save an entire book as a PDF file and then attach that PDF to an e-mail message. You can also post PDF files on Web sites.

Ordering professionally printed books

iPhoto links you directly to an online print service where you can order professionally printed and bound versions of your book. When you first use the service, you can either log into your existing Apple account or set up an account with your credit card, as we describe earlier in this chapter, in the "Ordering prints" section.

The books are hardback and covered in elegant linen, at 9 x 11.25 inches. ***Note:*** The minimum number of pages for a book is ten pages; if you order a book with less, you end up with blank pages. You can duplicate a photo in the album and create another introduction page, add more photos, or reduce the number of photos per page to create enough pages.

To order books, you need connect to the Internet. Then follow these steps:

1. **Click the Order Book button in Book mode or the Order Book icon in Organize mode.**

   iPhoto converts your book layout into a form that can be transferred to the book printing service. Depending on how big your book is, transferring may take a few minutes. The Apple Order Book window appears, as shown in Figure 6-15.

   If you get a warning message about low-quality images, it means that you ignored previous warning indicators about printing those images at certain sizes. The photos might be cropped and lower in resolution than their original versions; if so, you can revert back to the original version of the photo by selecting it in Organize mode and choosing File➪Revert to Original. If the photos were taken at low resolution, one work-around is to increase the number of photos on the page, using the Design Page pop-up menu for that page (in Book mode). Using more photos on the page reduces the size of the photo but doesn't reduce its resolution, so the photo looks and prints better.

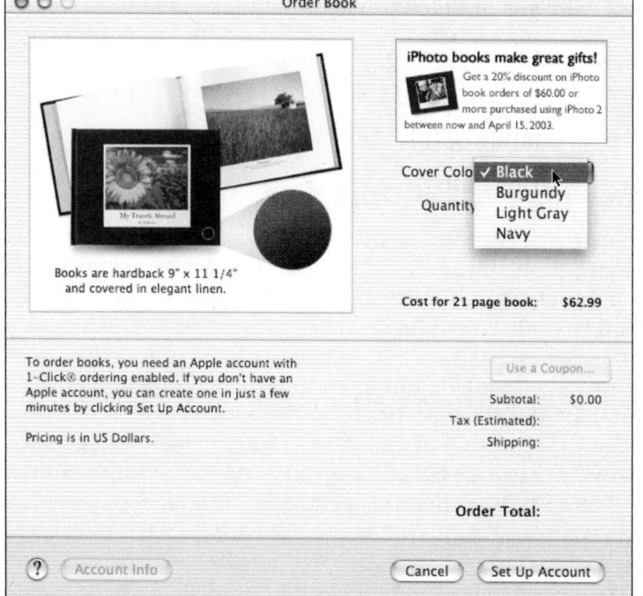
Order Book
iPhoto books make great gifts!
Get a 20% discount on iPhoto book orders of $60.00 or more purchased using iPhoto 2 between now and April 15, 2003.
Cover Colo
✓ Black
Burgundy
Light Gray
Navy
Quantity
Books are hardback 9" x 11 1/4" and covered in elegant linen.
Cost for 21 page book: $62.99
To order books, you need an Apple account with 1-Click® ordering enabled. If you don't have an Apple account, you can create one in just a few minutes by clicking Set Up Account.
Pricing is in US Dollars.
Use a Coupon...
Subtotal: $0.00
Tax (Estimated):
Shipping:
Order Total:
Account Info
Cancel
Set Up Account

Figure 6-15: Use the Apple online book ordering service to order a book.

2. **Select the cover's color and the quantity in the Color Cover pop-up menu.**

   You can make color choices such as black, burgundy, light gray, or navy, for the cover of the book.

3. **Click the Set Up Account button.**

   You need to set up your account with a credit card for billing, as we describe earlier in this chapter, in the "Ordering prints" section.

4. **Follow the on-screen instructions to make the purchase.**

   Follow the instructions (the helpful folks at Apple are always improving them) to finish the purchase process.

Sharing Photos Online

Did you jump right to this section of the book when you first opened it? Going online creates a whole new set of possibilities with your photos. You can do projects you never considered before — a school play, the family vacation, even business opportunities. Whatever you use photos for, you can probably do it cheaper and easier online.

The fastest and easiest way to get photos in the hands of others is through e-mail. But you can also share photo albums by using online photo services (many of which also offer high-quality prints of digital photos). You can even publish your photos on a Web page whether you have a site of your own or not.

Sending photos as e-mail attachments

Besides browsing the Web, sending e-mail with a photo is perhaps the most common use of the Internet. E-mail is a great way to send a photo to one person or a thousand people (although we discourage spamming — please don't send us your baby photos unless we know you). Of course, you can even combine several photos in one e-mail, but if you send high-resolution photos, the e-mail may be too large to send. Adding one photo to an e-mail is easy and almost always works.

iPhoto works with your e-mail program. You can set up your e-mail program by choosing iPhoto➪Preferences and selecting an e-mail application in the Mail pop-up menu. We use the Mail application provided with Mac OS X.

If you have an e-mail account and you're ready to send a message, attaching a photo is simple. Follow these steps:

1. **Select a photo in Organize mode.**
2. **Click the Email icon in the tools pane.**

   The Mail Photo window appears, as shown in Figure 6-16.

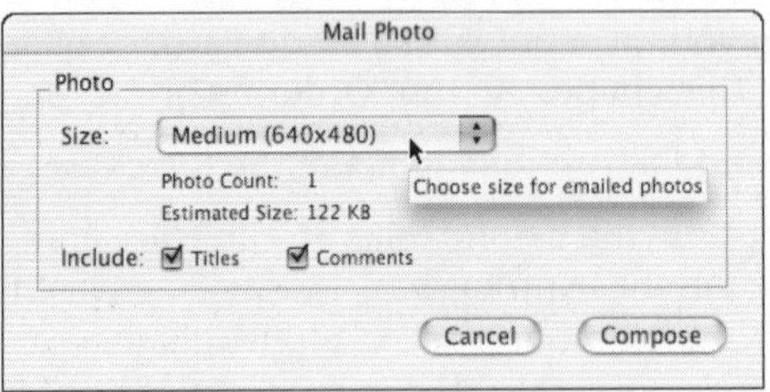

Figure 6-16: Choose a size for photos to e-mail in the Mail Photo window.

3. **Choose a size for the image in the Size pop-up menu.**

   Choose from the following sizes: Small (240 x 320), Medium (640 x 480), Large (1280 x 960), or Full Size (full quality). To find out more about sizing photos for e-mail, see the sidebar "Sizing photos for e-mail" elsewhere in this chapter.

4. **Select the Titles and the Comments check boxes to include titles and comments if you want.**

   iPhoto includes the title and comment in the text part of the e-mail message. iPhoto also puts the title into the subject field of the e-mail.

5. **Click the Compose button.**

   iPhoto processes your photos into the standard JPEG format for e-mail attachments and then launches your mail application with a new message featuring the photo, as shown in Figure 6-17.

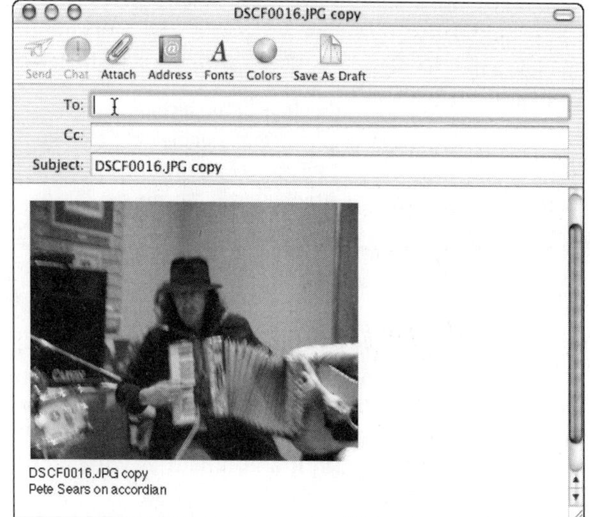

Figure 6-17: An e-mail message ready to send with a photo.

6. **Add the e-mail recipient's address and a subject line.**
7. **Save or send the e-mail message.**

If you want to send the photo in its original file format or use PDF as a file format (for a photo book, for example), don't use the Email icon. First create a new e-mail message and leave its window open. Then switch to iPhoto and drag the thumbnail for the photo (to copy a photo in its original format) directly into the message window to attach the file. To attach a PDF file, you have to save it on disk first from iPhoto by choosing File➪Print and then clicking the Save As PDF button. You can then use the Mail application to attach the PDF file to the message.

Sizing photos for e-mail

The Size pop-up menu in the Mail Photo window offers size choices, and we recommend the following:

Choose the Small setting (240 x 320) to keep e-mail attachments small. The photo resizes to 240 x 320 pixels, which is good enough for many tasks, such as announcing a new baby or sending someone a birthday photo.

Choose the Medium setting (640 x 480) if you want to send photos that occupy a nice portion of a typical monitor but not create too large of an attachment.

Choose the Large setting (1280 x 960) if you are sending samples of your photos to others who will print them. The higher the resolution for printing, the better quality the print result — and the attachment is probably still small enough to pass under the attachment size limits of most Internet service providers.

Choose the Full Size (full quality) setting only when sending photos to photo services for making prints, or when high quality is absolutely necessary, such as the rare occasion when you publish photos in a magazine. The attachment may be too large for some Internet service providers. E-mail servers choke on large attachments, and you may get a polite message from your service provider informing you that the attachment is too large.

Exporting to a photo service

Apple offers the .Mac service for all Mac users (for a fee, of course). One of its major benefits is the capability to share photos with others over the Internet. Online photo services would also love your business. Besides offering prints, many offer online photo albums that you can publish on the Internet to share with friends.

To send your photos to an online service, you must follow the instructions provided by the service. Many services accept photos attached to e-mails or uploaded directly to their sites. Before sending photos, be sure that your photos are in the format the service accepts. You can export photos from iPhoto into the appropriate format.

Follow these steps for exporting photos to photo services:

1. **Select one or more photos, or an entire album, in Organize mode.**
2. **Choose File⇨Export.**

   The Export Photos window appears, as shown in Figure 6-18.
3. **Click the File Export tab.**

   The File Export pane appears, with options for exporting photos into different file formats.

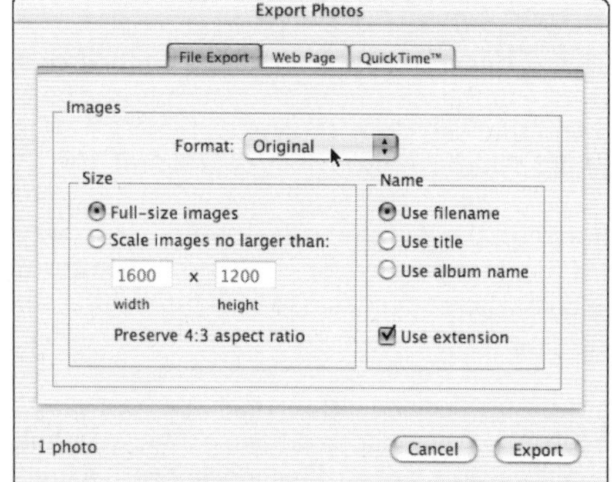

Figure 6-18: Export a photo with the Export Photos window.

4. **Select the appropriate file format from the Format pop-up menu.**

   The Format pop-up menu provides the following formats:

   - **Original:** The original format for the photo (used by the digital camera, typically JPEG).
   - **JPG:** Short for JPEG (Joint Photographic Experts Group), the standard image format for Web pages. Use this choice to make sure the photo is in a standard version of JPEG (if your digital camera's Original format is specialized).
   - **TIFF:** Tagged Image File Format, the standard format for desktop publishing software.
   - **PNG:** Portable Network Graphics format, a new standard designed to replace the GIF format used extensively on the Web for graphics.

   Be sure to select the format that the photo service requires. Most services support the JPEG and TIFF formats.

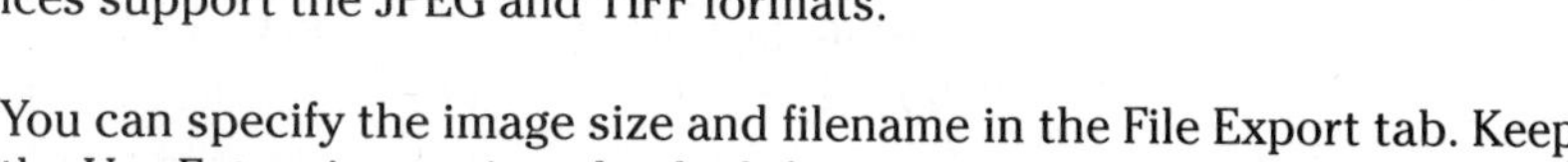

   You can specify the image size and filename in the File Export tab. Keep the Use Extension option checked if you want the filename to have a standard extension that identifies the file's format — this is usually the case, especially with online services.

5. **Click the Export button and choose a folder for saving the file.**

After exporting photos to your hard disk, follow the instructions from the online service to upload the files to the service.

Publishing photos on Web pages

Publishing on the Web is by far the most universal method of distributing photos online. Everyone in the world can see your photos on a Web page — as long as they can find the Web page. (You can create a Web page whose address you never tell anyone, but Google may still find it!)

You can publish photos on the Web by using iPhoto in two ways: Use the HomePage feature of the .Mac service, or export your photos to the Site folder on your hard disk where you can use Web publishing software to post it.

With HomePage on the .Mac service, others can see your photos on your Web page hosted by Apple. You must first have a .Mac account, which you can set up by visiting the Apple site and registering with a credit card, as described in the "Ordering prints" section, earlier in this chapter.

Follow these steps to use the HomePage feature of the .Mac service:

1. **Select the photos you want to publish in Organize mode.**

   You can select multiple photos or an entire photo album. You can even publish an entire library.

2. **Click the HomePage icon in the tools pane.**

   The Publish HomePage window appears, with the photos that you selected.

3. **Choose a Layout option for the Web page.**

   The Layout options, at the bottom-left corner of the Publish HomePage window, offer two choices: two-column or three-column.

4. **Edit the title and caption for the Web page.**

   You can edit the title and caption for the page by clicking inside the text area and selecting the text, and then typing your own, as shown in Figure 6-19. By default, the text comes from the titles and comments in your photo library.

5. **Drag photos to change their locations on the page if you want to change the photo sequence.**

6. **Check the Send Me a Message check box if you want iPhoto to add a Feedback button on your HomePage.**

   Anyone viewing your Web page can send you an iCard with the Feedback button.

7. **Check the Counter check box to display a counter on your HomePage.**

   A counter keeps track of how many times the page is viewed.

Figure 6-19: Edit the title and caption of the Web page.

8. **Select a HomePage site to publish to in the Publish To pop-up menu.**
9. **Click the Publish button.**

iPhoto automatically sends the photos to the Web site and creates the Web page. A message displays telling you publishing was successful and gives you the address of the HomePage so that you can tell others.

To view your HomePage, type the address into your Internet browser. The address is homepage.mac.com/*membername* (substitute *membername* with your name). Figure 6-20 shows an example.

To make changes to your HomePage or to set up a password to protect access to your HomePage, go to `www.mac.com` and click the HomePage icon. You can make changes, preview the page, and re-publish the page from your browser.

If you already have a Web site, use the Export command to create HyperText Markup Language (HTML) pages with your photos included, and then use your usual method of uploading the pages to your site.

The Export function does not use layouts — its no-frills design is simple and easy to modify with any HTML editing program. To publish a Web page of photos by using the Export button, follow these steps:

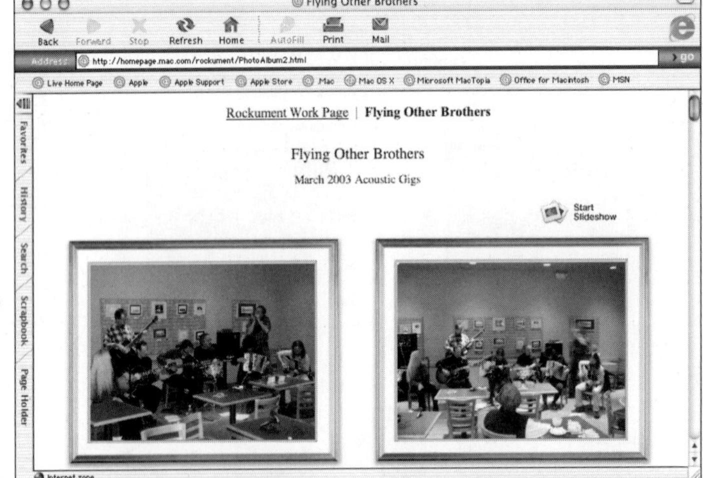

Figure 6-20: The published HomePage on the Web.

1. **Select one or more photos, or an entire album, in Organize mode.**
2. **Choose File⇨Export.**

   iPhoto displays the Export Photos window.
3. **Click the Web Page tab.**

   The Web Page pane appears, as shown in Figure 6-21.

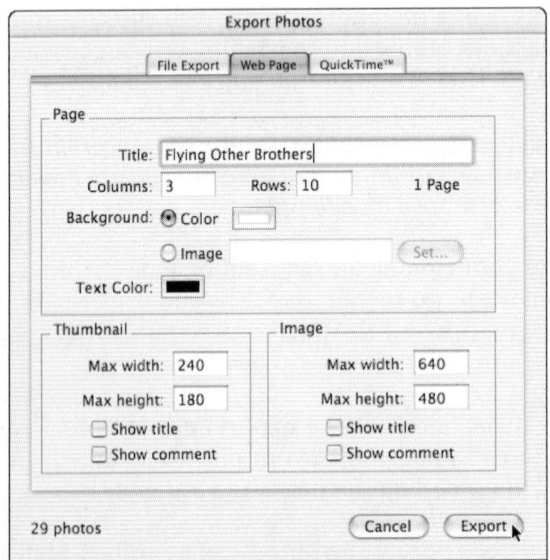

Figure 6-21: Export a Web page with photos to any site.

4. **Customize the page layout.**

   You can specify the number of columns and rows for the photo thumbnails, and the background color and text color. The Web page uses thumbnails as links to larger-size photos. You can specify the size of the thumbnails in the Thumbnails section, and the size of the larger image in the Image section. You can also choose to show titles and comments.

5. **Click the Export button and save the page on your hard disk.**

   The main page with thumbnails, and the associated photos, are saved in files ready to be uploaded to your Web site. You can open the pages in a Web browser, even though they exist only on your hard disk until you upload them to your site. Figure 6-22 shows the main page with thumbnails — viewers click a thumbnail to see the larger version of the photo.

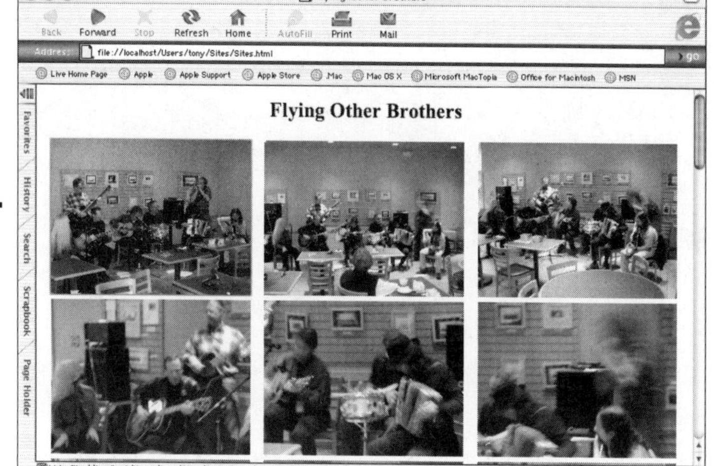

Figure 6-22: The page offers thumbnails that link to larger versions of the photos.

Book III

iMovie

The 5th Wave
By Rich Tennant
TROUBLE ON THE SET
©RICHTENNANT
All the software in the world won't make this a great film. Only you can, Rusty. Only you and the guts and determination to be the finest Frisbee catching dog in this dirty little town. Now come on Rusty–it's magic time.
We're losing the light, Dad.

Chapter 1: Digital Moviemaking

In This Chapter

- **Overview of moviemaking and what you can do with iMovie**
- **Using a digital camcorder and video shooting techniques**
- **A tour of iMovie and what you need to run it**

Video is so pervasive in our world that nearly everybody on the planet has seen it. Ordinary citizens have used camcorders to record violent weather, exchanges between police and suspects, home bloopers, weddings, and school plays. As the wise sage (and wisecracking baseball player) Yogi Berra once said, "You can observe a lot just by watching." We pay more attention to events and people that are the subjects of video clips.

Making home movies is nothing new. But even with the best analog camcorder, you can't edit a video. Before iMovie, you had to rent or buy thousands of dollars worth of video editing gear and use complicated software to edit videos. With iMovie, you can not only edit your video clips, you can improve them by adding transitions and special effects, matching the audio with the video or adding music, and creating a final movie with just the scenes you want. You can then copy the movie to your camcorder's tape cassette, watch the movie on TV, save the movie as a QuickTime file for use elsewhere, and even burn a DVD with it to use in DVD players.

Digital technology makes video editing easy and you can use the same editing techniques with video — making video cheaper and more fun to make, opening up entirely new possibilities. You'll find that with a Mac, iMovie, and a digital camcorder, creating video clips for the Web or producing DVDs or videotapes of weddings and other events is simple.

What You Can Do with iMovie

iMovie provides the basic, no-frills editing tools you need to put together a movie from a set of video clips. You can navigate freely from scene to scene in any manner, and save your edits and changes in digital format without the use of videotape. The result is a digital video movie you can save as a QuickTime file or dump back to digital videotape without any loss in quality.

If you aren't that familiar with video, you can do the following things to create and produce a movie, and you can do each step with iMovie. Although you may do these in sequence, you can go back and redo many of these steps over and over until your movie is exactly the way you want.

✦ **Shoot the video and transfer it to your computer.** Use a digital camcorder to record video, which of course includes audio (unless you are making a silent movie or adding sound later). Whatever you shoot becomes the basis for your movie.

  iMovie allows you to import your digital video footage with one click, and automatically separates the scenes for you into clips. You can then pick out the good parts, snip out the slow or boring parts, shuffle scenes around to your heart's content, and add sound.

✦ **Edit the video clips.** Use iMovie to organize and edit your clips, trim unwanted parts at the beginnings and endings, but make sure you don't lose any important sounds by trimming. You can edit the scenes in the timeline viewer using precise time code that synchronizes the audio to the video. Import photos from iPhoto and create still images from video scenes to mix in with your movie. Find out how to do tight editing, and how to establish a shot and create cutaways and cut-ins to make your movie more effective and interesting to watch.

✦ **Add special video effects and documentary-style effects for photos.** You can spiff up your video with visual effects like Lens Flare, Aged Film, Letterbox, and Electricity. Want to sprinkle a glittering trail of fairy dust over a festive scene? iMovie lets you to do that, and you can even decide at which point in the frame you want to use it. iMovie also enables you to add haunting visual effects such as fog and ghost trails to your movies in seconds. You can bring your photos from iPhoto to life with professional documentary-style impact, using pan and zoom effects.

✦ **Arrange the video clips in a sequence using a timeline, adding transitions between scenes.** Use iMovie to flow from scene to scene just right. iMovie offers smooth transitions to make your video look professional.

✦ **Edit the sound.** Video includes sound, and you can add even more sound to your movie three different ways:

  - Use one of the included sound effects to augment the sound from the video.
  - Add a musical track from a CD or your own iTunes library. You may want to fade music behind the sound from the video and use it for transitions.
  - Record your own voiceover. You can use iMovie to record directly into an audio track.

Why is video editing easier now?

Video editing conjures up images of darkened rooms with dedicated technicians tending to large tape machines surrounded by large consoles with thousands of levers, knobs, and buttons. To edit videotape professionally, at first technicians had to create a master tape by literally cutting and splicing together pieces of tape. Eventually machines were invented that synchronized two tape decks with time code so that editors could provide a list editing changes associated with time codes, and the machines would do the work of creating a master tape from other tapes. Any copy made of the master videotape was inferior in quality, and the quality degraded even further with copies of copies.

The improvements of digital technology took a while to reach the professional video editing room, but when it did, it transformed video editing completely. Professional video editing changed as digital video hardware replaced older, more expensive videotape controllers. The ability to edit the video changed dramatically with digital video compression technology, which allowed editors to store and edit video on hard disk without compromising quality.

iMovie is an even further improvement on digital editing, providing editing tools for people with no background in video editing. With iMovie you can navigate freely from scene to scene in any manner, and save your edits and changes in digital format on hard disk without the use of videotape. Digital copies are exact duplicates with no loss in quality. You can edit to your heart's content without ever sacrificing the original quality of the video.

- **Add titles and credits.** When done editing, you can add text as end credits, rolling commentary, or opening titles. You can choose from several styles, and decide on a text color and font.
- **Save the final version and make copies.** You can copy your movie to digital videotape (such as the cassette used in your camcorder), or save it as a QuickTime file for publishing on the Web and distributing by CD-ROM or other methods. You can send it over to iDVD to create a DVD with menus and everything that can play on any DVD player. You can even copy the movie to conventional videotape, all without any loss in quality, because the information is in digital form.

Don't let the reduced image quality of Web video keep you from publishing videos on the Web. Regardless of the fact that image quality suffers when you shrink movies in size to put them on the Internet — video still is the most effective medium for communicating.

What You Need for iMovie

Although iMovie makes video editing easy, you need a fairly robust Mac, and if you want to create your own DVDs, you need an Apple-supported DVD-R drive (such as the Apple SuperDrive).

If you don't have the right equipment, or the money to invest in new equipment (none of this is cheap), you can send your files to a service to be converted to DVD. Or you can use iMovie on one Mac and later transfer the project to another iMac with a DVD-R drive.

To use iMovie, you need the following requirements at a minimum:

- A digital video (DV) camcorder to record your footage, and to convert older footage and other video sources to the digital format.
- A Mac with a FireWire port to connect your camcorder and control it from iMovie.
- A FireWire cable to connect your camcorder to the Mac. FireWire is also known as IEEE 1394 DV terminal. The cable has a camcorder-style (very small) connector on one end, and a standard FireWire connector for the Mac on the other end.
- Lots of free space, measured in gigabytes, to store and edit video clips. We typically use a 60GB hard drive.
- At least 256MB of RAM and OS X version 10.1.5 or later, with QuickTime version 6 or later.
- DV cassette tapes (called mini-DV in camcorders) to store the digital video you capture with the camcorder.

With iMovie, you can record directly to hard disk without tape, but your camcorder must be connected to the Mac. Although this makes sense for interviews or other situations in which the camcorder is stationary, your ability to move freely is severely hampered (unless you have an assistant running after you, carrying a PowerBook running on batteries — don't laugh, this actually works). You'll find no qualitative difference in recording to disk or to the DV cassette in the camcorder, but the cassette is more convenient.

Why you need a digital video camcorder

If you buy a camcorder today, you should consider buying a digital camcorder. Digital video makes all former methods of recording video obsolete. You'll find many advantages for digital video over analog video:

- You can copy digital videotapes without any loss in quality.
- You can convert digital video on tape to digital video on hard disk with iMovie, which automatically detects scenes and creates individual clips for them. iMovie controls a digital camcorder for both recording directly to disk and transferring digital video from the camcorder's cassette.

Why digital? What's the difference?

Digital camcorders offer tremendous advantages over analog camcorders:

Camcorders are smaller and easier to use. Digital video (DV) camcorders are smaller because the size of the tape cartridge is smaller. The largest DV camcorder you can buy in an electronics store is about the same size as the smallest 8mm camcorder of yesteryear. Small size means more convenience, easier handling, and longer battery life (due to less equipment to power).

The quality is far better than ever before. Picture quality with video depends on the horizontal resolution, which is measured across the picture as if counting vertical lines. All video formats (except high-definition television, or HDTV) have the same vertical resolution, or number of lines going down the picture. The horizontal resolution, however, varies. VHS tape offers 240 lines of horizontal resolution, and a live TV broadcast offers 300 lines. A digital satellite broadcast offers 400 lines. Digital video in the mini-DV cassette format used by camcorders offers 500 lines of horizontal resolution, resulting in a much sharper, clearer picture.

You can edit digital video with a personal computer, a hard disk, and editing software. Digital video is data. Before you could edit video as digital data on a hard disk, you could only use a computer to control traditional videotape equipment that performed editing operations based on a list of instructions. You really didn't edit on the computer; your changes in an editing system translated into instructions for the analog machines. Digital video changed all that by providing a format for video that can record and play back as digital information. You can access the information — the video — at any point, without needing to rewind or fast-forward a tape.

You can make copies of copies with no loss in quality. Digital video lasts forever. You can make copies of copies of copies — the digital information is duplicated exactly. The quality of analog video, on the other hand, deteriorates when you copy a tape to another. You probably already see this with VHS tapes — a copy of a tape is not nearly as good as the original.

✦ You can combine digital video clips into a sequence without any seams between the clips — no weird fuzzy lines or flickers to cover up, and no need to mask the artifacts from the analog-to-digital conversion process that was necessary just a few years ago. The video you shoot is exactly the same quality after the editing process.

Don't throw out your old camcorder and forget about using analog videos. With the level of control iMovie has over a digital camcorder, you can use a digital camcorder for the importing of analog video by connecting your older camcorder or VCR to your digital camcorder. We describe how to do this in Chapter 2 of this book.

If you use a standard analog camcorder that uses 8 mm (millimeter) analog video cassettes, you can choose to buy a hybrid digital 8mm camcorder, such as the Sony Digital8, that plays standard 8mm cassettes and also stores digital video using that format.

Don't buy a more expensive camcorder in order to get features that you may not need. DV camcorders offer an impressive set of features, some of which you may never use. For example, in-camera editing is a feature that essentially allows you to do minimal clip editing and sequencing in the camcorder (such as the Sony camcorder that uses the Sony MiniDisc, instead of DV cassettes). But as an iMovie user, you will probably never do in-camera editing — moving your video clips to the iMac to edit them is much more convenient. And the iMovie editing software gives you far more flexible and powerful editing tools that are, paradoxically, easier to use than camcorder buttons.

Touring iMovie

iMovie allows you to bring multimedia elements together and place them in a sequence over time. iMovie keeps track of all these elements, capturing the video (including the video's audio portion) and storing a series of video clip files on your hard disk. You can then import other elements, such as photos from iPhoto, music from iTunes, and even other videos saved as QuickTime files.

Starting iMovie

On most Macs, you find the iMovie icon in the Dock, but in any case you can find it in the Applications folder. Double-click the icon to open iMovie, and a window appears, similar to the one in Figure 1-1.

If your display is not set to at least 1,024 x 768 or higher in the Displays preferences, you get a message from iMovie saying it can't run. Your display's resolution is set to a lower number than possible, either accidentally or intentionally. To change its resolution, follow these steps:

1. **Choose System Preferences from the Apple menu in the upper-left corner.**

   The System Preferences window appears.

2. **Click the Displays icon.**

   The icon appears in the Hardware row of icons (and also, typically, in the top row of most-used icons). The Displays pane appears.

3. **Click the highest pixel resolution setting in the Resolutions list.**

   Your display must be capable of at least 1,024 x 768 pixels to run iMovie; choose that setting or a higher one if available.

4. **Click the Millions option in the Colors pop-up menu.**

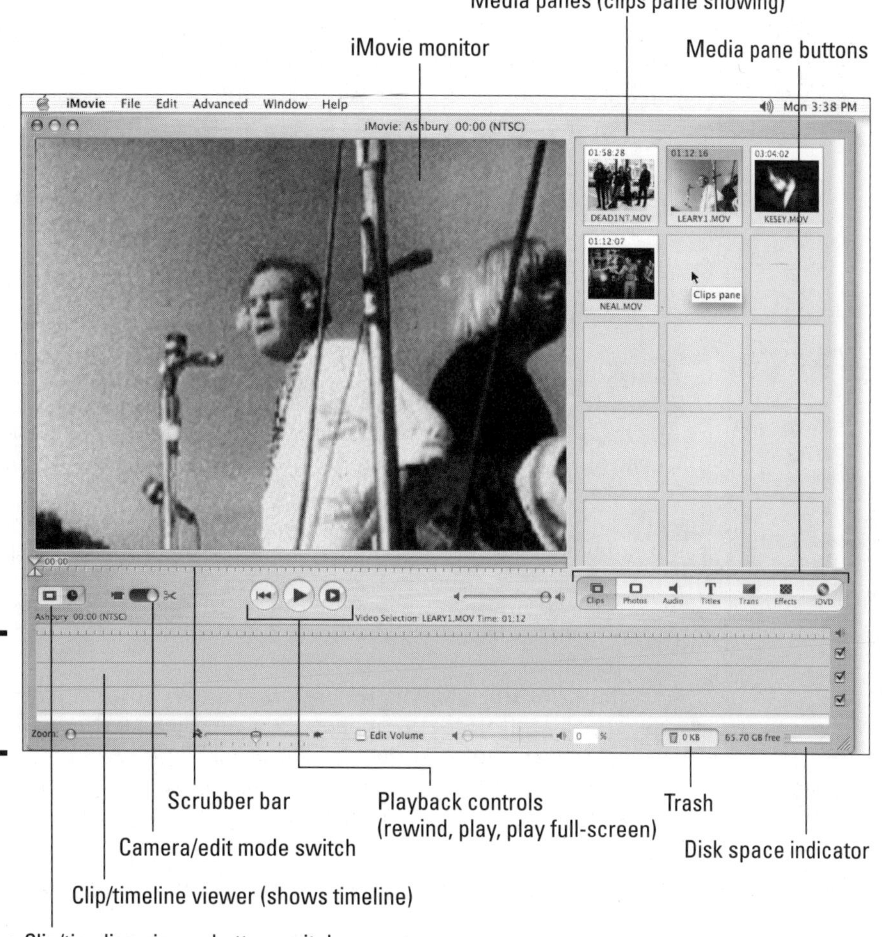

Figure 1-1: The iMovie window.

5. **Quit System Preferences by choosing System Preferences➪Quit System Preferences.**

   Now your display setting offers the best quality viewing for your movies. You can change your display settings at any time in OS X and your settings take effect immediately. However, if you lower the pixel resolution below 1,024 x 768 while iMovie is running, iMovie quits abruptly.

When you start iMovie for the first time, a Welcome to iMovie dialog box appears providing the following choices:

- **Quit:** Click to quit the program.
- **Open Existing Project:** Click this button to open a project already stored on your disk. The Mac OS X Open dialog box appears, which lets you browse folders to select a project file.
- **Create New Project:** Click this button to create a new project.

After clicking the Create New Project button, the Save dialog box appears. Type the name for your project in the Save As text field, and click the Where pop-up menu to locate a folder for storing the project. Click the down-arrow button to expand the dialog box into the full Mac OS X Save dialog box, which lets you browse folders easily.

After selecting a folder to save the project, click the Save button to save it. iMovie uses the project name as the name for both the project file, and for the folder that contains the project file and all the video clips associated with the project file. iMovie saves the project folder inside the folder you selected.

After creating a new project or selecting an existing project, the project appears in the iMovie window. If you are starting a new project, the iMovie window appears with the iMovie monitor set to all black and the clips pane empty.

The next time you start iMovie, the program opens automatically with this project — the last project you opened. You can then continue working in the project, or start a new project by choosing File⇨New Project, or open another project by choosing File⇨Open Project (or File⇨Open Recent, which displays a submenu of projects opened recently).

Understanding the iMovie window elements

The iMovie window elements you use most often are the following:

- **iMovie monitor:** Your video clip plays in the iMovie monitor, whether you select the clip in the clips pane or in the timeline or clips viewer.
- **Clips pane:** iMovie stores incoming clips in the clips pane until you use them in the timeline or clip viewer. The clips pane is one of the media panes — switch media panes with the media panes buttons.
- **Scrubber bar:** Drag the triangle along the scrubber bar to move through (or *scrub through*) a clip or sequence of clips frame by frame. The scrubber bar plays whatever displays in the iMovie monitor. You can select a single clip from the clips pane and scrub through it, or create a sequence in the timeline or clip viewer and scrub through that.

- **Camera/Edit mode switch:** Click this switch on the scissors side to switch to edit mode (edit video) or on the camera side to switch to camera mode (transfer video to and from your camcorder).
- **Clip viewer/timeline viewer switch:** The clip viewer/timeline viewer button switch on the far left switches the lower pane from clip viewer mode to timeline viewer mode and vice versa.
- **Playback controls:** Use the playback controls to skip to the beginning of a selected clip, play the clip in the iMovie monitor, or play the clip using the entire screen.
- **Media pane buttons:** Use these buttons to show different media panes, such as the clips pane (refer to Figure 1-1).
- **Timeline or clip viewer:** The timeline viewer displays the video clips over time (refer to Figure 1-1). When you click the clip viewer mode button, the timeline viewer switches to the clip viewer, which shows individual clips in the sequence.
- **Trash:** Drag unwanted video clips to the Trash to delete them and reclaim disk space. However, if you empty the Trash, you can no longer restore video clips to their original, unedited state. To empty the Trash, choose File➪Empty Trash.
- **Disk space indicator:** You can see how much disk space you use as you work. You need at least 2GB of free storage at any time while using iMovie. This bar turns yellow when you start running out of memory. When it turns red, you must free up some space (usually by emptying the Trash) in order to continue working in iMovie. To empty the Trash, choose File➪Empty Trash.

iMovie provides two modes of operation; you can switch from one mode to the other by clicking the Camera/Edit mode switch:

- **Camera mode:** Click the switch on the camera side for camera mode. Use only when connecting a camcorder and transferring video. You can control the camera with the playback controls. Read Chapter 2 of this book to find out about transferring video and using camera mode.
- **Edit mode:** Click the switch on the scissors side for edit mode. Use when editing the movie (when not in camera mode). All clip panes, editing tools, and views are available in edit mode.

The playback controls do the following:

- **Play button:** Plays the movie in the iMovie monitor.
- **Rewind button:** Moves back to the beginning of the movie.

- **Play full-screen button:** Plays the movie using the entire Mac display (full screen). Click your mouse to stop full-screen playback and return to the iMovie window.
- **Arrow keys on your keyboard:** Steps through the movie one frame at a time. The right arrow moves forward and the left arrow moves backward. Hold down the Shift key while pressing the arrow key, and the movie plays faster (ten frames at a time).

The media pane buttons give you access to media elements and effects by switching panes when you click them:

- **Clips:** Switches to the Clips pane, which holds transferred video clips and imported movies.
- **Photos:** Switches to the Photos pane, providing access to your iPhoto library and the Ken Burns photo effects.
- **Audio:** Switches to the Audio pane, providing iMovie sound effects and access to your iTunes library.
- **Titles:** Switches to the Titles pane, which offers a set of animation effects for creating frames with text, such as movie titles and credits.
- **Trans:** Switches to the Trans pane, which offers a set of transitions to use between video clips.
- **Effects:** Switches to the Effects pane, which offers a set of special effects for livening up video clips and images.
- **iDVD:** Switches to the iDVD pane, which lets you define chapter markers for a movie and create an iDVD project (see Book IV for iDVD).

Video Shooting Techniques

A professional video looks, well, *professional* for many reasons. But you *can* use iMovie to make a video look as professional as broadcast TV, if you have the skills required to set up shots properly. We can't teach that in this book — but a lot of books exist on the topic of shooting video properly and techniques haven't changed with the advent of digital video.

Keep these few tips in mind when shooting video:

- **Get the shot.** Quality matters, but nothing matters more than being at the right place at the right time with your lens cap off and your camcorder ready to record. Whether you cover important news events or document your baby's first steps, worry about quality later.

- **Shoot more than you need.** Before digital, shooting less and using the pause button often was the conventional wisdom. Editing the video was hard and expensive, if not impossible, and the audience ended up seeing everything, even the lousy footage. Digital video reverses this logic. Shoot more than you need and edit the video you don't need.
- **The sound is better with a carefully placed microphone.** Camcorders have microphones built into them, but because you're holding the camcorder, what you hear is mostly what is right around you (including your own heavy breathing if you're not careful). That faraway sound you hear in a home video interview sounds amateurish — and happens whenever the subject is too far away from the microphone. Use a separate microphone (even a clip-on Lavalier microphone works well with interview subjects) and place it appropriately to hear what you want to hear in the video. Many camcorders allow you to connect an external microphone for audio recording.
- **Don't pan or zoom too much while shooting.** Camcorders have wonderful pan and zoom features, but refrain from using them except before a shot. Zooming into a scene during a shot can make viewers uncomfortable, even nauseous (unless, of course, you are trying for that effect).
- **Keep the camcorder steady while shooting.** A steady image is probably the most distinguishing characteristic that separates home videos from professional ones. The trick is to keep the camcorder steady — using a tripod, if possible, helps this problem. Some camcorders offer image stabilization, which smoothes out the shakes and jiggles that show up when your camcorder is unsteady. If you can't use a tripod, use anything — a table, a window ledge, a tree stump, a body part — or at least lean against something to steady yourself.
- **Try for the best lighting conditions.** You've heard about directors canceling movie shots because the camera operator complained that the light wasn't right. Good lighting is extremely important, as with still-image photography. Video captures an even smaller range of light and darkness than film, and images sometimes lack depth (film, of course, is much higher in resolution). Videographers and cinematographers spend years developing lighting skills, but you can read books to find out the basics.

Chapter 2: Importing Video, Audio, and Photos

In This Chapter

- Importing video clips from a digital camcorder
- Importing video from other sources
- Importing photos from iPhoto and music from iTunes

When you start making a video, you may be thinking only about how to shoot the video clips. But you can add a lot more with iMovie. Your wedding video may be a bit more interesting and romantic with a sound track or perhaps even a voice-over narration. You may want to add embarrassing photos of your parents to spice it up. And what about putting in those *really* embarrassing photos, and adding sound effects to enhance them?

You can import video and other elements at any time in the process of making a movie. You can even import new shots to replace older ones that don't work out. You can also use one Mac to do all your video importing, and then copy the iMovie project folder to another Mac to do editing. Because the video is in digital format, you have the flexibility to copy the video files anywhere — to backup drives, CD-ROM, the camcorder's DV cassette, and even to removable media such as large-capacity Zip drives.

Using a DV Camcorder

Camcorders not only record video onto digital video (DV) tape; they also can play back the video you record. Recording and playing video are accomplished in two separate modes:

- ***Camera mode*** **records the video.** When your camcorder is in camera mode, its microphone and lens are ready to record when you press the record button.
- ***VTR*** **(video tape recorder) or** ***VCR mode*** **plays back the video you record.** When the camera is in VTR/VCR mode, the camcorder plays what is on the DV tape cassette when you press the Play button (you can also rewind and fast forward).

Just to confuse you (actually, not, but most people become confused), iMovie has its own camera and edit modes as described in Chapter 1 of this book.

Most DV camcorders also keep track of the time and date and store that information with the video. When you first use a new DV camcorder, be sure to set your camcorder's date and time in order for the date and time to be correct when the video transfers to iMovie.

Connecting a DV camcorder

To use your camcorder with iMovie and transfer video to your computer, connect the camcorder and let iMovie do the rest.

To connect your DV camcorder to your Mac:

1. **Locate the FireWire cable.**

   These cables are also available commercially. FireWire is known as IEEE 1394 DV terminal and has a camcorder-style (very small) square connector on one end, and a standard FireWire connector (also known as the six-pin connector) for the Mac on the other end.

2. **Connect the camcorder to the Mac by using the FireWire cable.**

   Locate the camcorder's IEEE 1394/DV terminal (also known as FireWire or i.Link) connection and plug the square connector into it. Locate the connection on your Mac marked by a radioactive-looking Y symbol, and plug the larger six-pin connector into it.

3. **Turn your camcorder to camera mode or VTR/VCR mode.**

   If you are recording video directly to disk, without using DV tape, choose camera mode and read the upcoming section, "Capturing video directly to disk."

   If you are importing prerecorded video from DV tape cassette, choose VTR/VCR mode and read the section, "Importing Clips from DV Tape," in this chapter.

If your camcorder has a sleep mode, make sure it's disabled or set to a time increment long enough to allow your video to play in full at normal speed. If possible, connect AC power to the camcorder during this process to save battery life.

After you connect and power on your camcorder, double-click the iMovie icon to start the program. Refer to Chapter 1 of this book for details.

You can transfer video into clips in a new project or an existing project. To open an existing project, choose File⇨Open Project. To start a new project, choose File⇨New Project.

Note: The hard disk you use to save the project folder is important. iMovie uses that folder to store copious quantities of video data, which occupies about 3.6MB of storage space per second — roughly 7GB for 30 minutes. If you have more than one hard drive, pick the fastest one — the internal Mac drive is usually faster than an external FireWire drive. *Don't* save your project file onto removable media, such as Zip or Jaz drives, which are not fast enough for digital video recording, and don't even think of using floppies or the network iDisk.

Capturing video directly to disk

You can use a DV camcorder with iMovie to record video directly from the camcorder's lens and microphone to your hard disk, without wasting DV tape. You can record directly to hard disk if your Mac is connected to the camcorder while recording. The benefit is that you can record scenes freely, delete clips you don't want as they appear in iMovie, and re-record scenes as you need to, up to the limit of your hard disk space, without using up DV tape. When recording directly to your hard disk, what you see on the iMovie monitor is automatically saved in a video clip.

With most DV camcorders, you put the camcorder in camera mode, but *don't* click the record button on the camcorder to record on tape — in fact, you don't need a tape cassette in the camcorder. Because you are recording directly to disk, you don't use the camcorder's record-to-tape mechanism — the video goes straight from the camcorder's circuitry to your computer. However, some camcorders don't pass the video through in this manner, and the opposite is true: You must insert a DV tape cassette and press the record button. If this is the case, you can still record directly to hard disk with the tape paused (or record to tape at the same time, and then rewind the tape for later use).

To control the DV camcorder from iMovie and capture directly to disk, follow these steps:

1. **Make sure your camcorder is powered up in its camera mode and iMovie is running.**

   Camera mode is the camcorder's mode for recording. However, don't press the record button unless the camcorder requires a cassette to record.

2. **Click the Camera/Edit mode switch on the camera side to switch to camera mode in iMovie (if it has not already switched automatically).**

   If iMovie already detects the camcorder, it may switch to camera mode automatically. The Import button appears under the iMovie monitor window in camera mode.

   You can now can see in the iMovie monitor what the camcorder is seeing. You may also hear an echo of every sound because you also hear everything the camcorder hears, played again through your Mac speakers. You can turn down the sound by clicking and dragging the volume slider underneath the iMovie monitor on the right side.

3. **Click the Import button.**

   iMovie stores the video information directly to disk and a new clip appears in the clip pane, as shown in Figure 2-1.

Figure 2-1: A clip captured directly to disk from a camcorder.

4. **Click the Import button again, or press the spacebar, to stop capturing video.**

   When you stop, iMovie automatically sets itself up to store another clip for the clip pane. You can repeatedly click the Import button to start, and then to stop recording; each time you create a new clip.

That's all there is to it. We describe how to play back these clips in the section, "Playing Your Clips." (Where else?)

Importing Clips from DV Tape

While you can record video directly to disk (as described in "Capturing video to disk" in this chapter), you will most likely want to record onto DV tape cassette so that you can take your camcorder everywhere and record anything. Recording onto tape also assures that you have another copy of the video you shot. You can take your camcorder anywhere, and then come back to your Mac and transfer the video to iMovie in one step.

To start controlling the DV camcorder and import already-shot video on the camcorder's cassette:

1. **Make sure your camcorder is powered up in its VTR/VCR play mode and iMovie is running.**
2. **Click the Camera/Edit mode switch on the camera side to switch to camera mode in iMovie (if it's not already switched automatically).**

   If iMovie already detects the camcorder, it may switch to camera mode automatically. The Import button appears under the iMovie monitor window in camera mode.
3. **Click the Rewind button on the camcorder to rewind the camcorder's cassette to start at the beginning of the cassette.**
4. **Click the Import button.**

   iMovie stores the video information directly to disk and a new clip appears in the clip pane for each new scene, as shown in Figure 2-2.
5. **Click the Import button again, or press the spacebar, to stop capturing video.**

   When iMovie reaches the end of the prerecorded video, it stops capturing to disk. However, the camcorder may continue playing blank tape. Stop the camera by pushing its Stop button.

Figure 2-2: Transferring taped video from the DV camcorder to create video clips in iMovie.

You can click the Rewind button to rewind the camcorder back to the beginning in order to set the camcorder up for recording again, over the older material just imported. Don't do this if you want to continue recording from the point in the tape where you left off, or if you want to keep a tape copy of your video.

Automatic scene detection

When you import video into iMovie, each scene you record automatically separates into video clips in the clips pane. How does iMovie know when one scene stops and another starts?

Actually, iMovie doesn't know; it simply checks the date and time stamp the DV camcorder puts into every frame of video. When iMovie detects a break in time — which happens when you stop recording with the camcorder, even for just a few seconds — the next piece of footage is a new clip. Automatic scene detection is one of the outstanding virtues that set iMovie apart from video editing systems costing thousands of dollars.

Separating scenes into clips is helpful in editing because you can:

- Transfer all the video automatically.
- Avoid doing edits to cut out scenes you don't want.
- Use clips in a different order.
- Trim clips to make them perfect before using them.
- Use clips in different movies.
- Make clips play back seamlessly.

If you are experienced at editing analog video, you may have to unlearn one practice: worrying about the seams between the clips. With digital video, no seams exist between clips, and using transitions, such as fade-outs, to mask seams is not needed (although you can certainly add transitions if you want). Simply stack the clips in order and play them; you won't see any seam between clips.

Automatic scene detection is, well, automatic. But you can also turn it off. Why would you want to turn off the automatic scene detection feature? When you want to have manual control over when each clip begins and ends. Choose iMovie⇨Preferences, click the Import button, and uncheck the Automatically Start New Clip at Scene Break option in the Import Preferences window.

You can still import video the same way after turning off the automatic scene detection feature. However, the video records as one clip until you press the spacebar or click the Import button a second time.

Pressing the spacebar is the same as clicking the Import button. If you press the spacebar when iMovie is not capturing video, iMovie starts to capture as if you click the Import button. When you press the spacebar again, the capturing process stops.

Don't try to use the iMovie capture feature for crude editing on the fly by capturing only some of the footage. Chances are you will miss something important. Instead use the iMovie frame-accurate clip trimming features, which we describe in the next chapter of this book.

Playing Your Clips

You can play video clips in the clips pane one at a time. The clip plays from beginning to end, and you can use the Rewind button to move back to the beginning. To see clips in a sequence, see Chapter 4 of this book.) To play a single clip, click the clip in the clips pane. The clip fills the iMovie monitor, and iMovie automatically switches to edit mode (see Chapter 1 of this book to read about iMovie modes). You can then click the iMovie Play button to play the clip.

As the clip plays, the scrubber bar moves forward, displaying the amount of time elapsed from the beginning of the clip. The time shows in minutes, seconds, and frames — in Figure 2-3 the video has reached the 22nd frame (00:22 means 00 seconds and 22 frames). You can drag the triangle, also known as the *playback head,* to jump to any part of the video clip. You can also click inside the scrubber bar at any point to start the video from that point.

Figure 2-3: Dragging the scrubber bar to jump to a section of the video clip.

Keeping time

Understanding the iMovie time measurements requires a bit of readjustment, unless you're used to video timing. iMovie displays the time code on the scrubber bar, and displays the total time for each clip in the clips pane. The frame counter and other time measurements use *mm:ss:ff,* where *mm* is the minutes, *ss* is the seconds, and *ff* is the number of frames. U. S. NTSC Video records at 30 frames per second, but this counting scheme starts at zero; the first second of video is from 00:00 to 00:29, and the next second is 01:00 to 01:29. If a clip is shorter than a minute, the minutes are left off.

To play back a section of the video clip over and over, click at the beginning of the section in the scrubber bar, and after it plays, click the same spot in the scrubber bar again.

You can use the playback controls, or the playback head in the scrubber bar, to play whatever shows in the iMovie monitor. The playback controls do the following:

- **Play button:** Plays the clip in the iMovie monitor.
- **Rewind button:** Moves back to the beginning of the clip.
- **Play full-screen button:** Plays the clip using the entire Mac display (full screen). Click your mouse to stop full-screen playback and return to the iMovie window.
- **Arrow keys on keyboard:** Steps through the clip one frame at a time. The right arrow moves forward and the left arrow moves backward. Hold down the Shift key while pressing the arrow key, and the clip moves forward or backward ten frames at a time, which is a bit less boring.

Importing Video from Other Sources

iMovie caters to your need to grab more and more stuff for your videos. You can import other digital movies saved as QuickTime movies, and you can transfer video from any source to your DV camcorder for importing. You can even include that old film footage Grandpa shot of your father as a baby. The video you import from other sources are most likely not the same quality, but your viewers may not even notice the difference.

Importing QuickTime movies

QuickTime is the Apple format for digital video. You can play a QuickTime movie on just about any PC or Mac. You can download the QuickTime player for free from the Apple Web site (`www.apple.com`), and also comes with software that requires it. As a Mac user, you most likely already have the standard QuickTime player (shipped with every Mac), or perhaps you upgraded to QuickTime Pro.

You can export QuickTime files from many programs. For example, you can create animation in a program, such as Macromedia Director, save it as a QuickTime file, and then transport the file into iMovie to use with your video.

What if the imported movie isn't full screen?

Many QuickTime movies are made to run in a small window, from the Web or from CD-ROM, at a time before computers were fast enough to run digital video at full screen. When you import a small-screen QuickTime movie, iMovie does its best to blow up it up to full-screen size when you play it in full-screen mode by enlarging the pixels, which produces a coarser video picture.

Of course, digital video technology has reached a point where DV camcorders are everywhere, and most computers are fast enough to play digital video full-screen, any QuickTime movies you make with iMovie can be full-screen, full-quality movies. You still have to create a smaller-picture movie in some situations, such as publishing video on the Web (described in Chapter 5 of this book), but you can still create full-screen versions to store on hard disk and DV tape.

To import a QuickTime movie, follow these steps:

1. **Switch to edit mode if iMovie is in camera mode.**

   Click the mode button that shows a camera on one end and a scissors on the other. Click the button so that it switches to scissors (edit) mode.

2. **Choose File⇨Import.**

   The Import dialog box appears.

3. **Select the QuickTime movie file and click the Open button.**

   QuickTime movies typically have a filename with .mov at the end (see Figure 2-4). The QuickTime movie appears in the clips pane of your project. You can then use it as any other video clip.

Figure 2-4: Locate a QuickTime movie to import.

Converting from film and video formats

You need a film projector or special film camera to play back film. Film also uses a wider screen aspect ratio than video, which is why films converted to video are offered in two formats: the standard video format and aspect ratio (in which the sides of the picture are cut off), and the wide-screen format (also known as "letterbox") that matches the aspect ratio of film. You can have film processed by a professional video service into either video format, but the standard format is best for matching computer displays and most televisions. Most services can dump film directly to digital videotape and some offer DVD.

Video recorded in a nondigital format can be converted to digital using a DV camcorder or a special converter, and then brought into iMovie where you can combine it with other video and save in a digital format. While you don't have to preserve commercial videos — nearly everything ever broadcast or released is re-released in DVD format — converting the videos you created is the best way to preserve them.

Video in other formats, such as VHS tape, smaller camcorder cassettes, or even locked into the commercial DVD format, can be brought into iMovie through your DV camcorder.

With the iMovie level of control over a DV camcorder, using a DV camcorder for the importing of analog video makes more sense than getting a costly A-D converter, which you can't control from iMovie.

DV camcorders typically have a video-in connection for S-video or RCA-type cables. Connect your older camcorder or VCR (or even a DVD player, cable or satellite receiver, or any device that outputs video with RCA or S-video connectors) to your DV camcorder, and use the camcorder as an A-D converter.

To use a DV camcorder to convert video and iMovie to import the video, follow these steps:

1. **Connect your video player's output to your DV camcorder's video/audio input connectors.**

   A video player (VCR, cable/satellite receiver, analog camcorder, DVD player) typically offers RCA-type connectors (one for video and two for audio), or better yet, an S-video connector for video along with two RCA-type audio connectors, for output to a television or video receiver. A DV camcorder typically offers either RCA-type or S-video or both, for recording (input) into the camcorder.

2. **Switch the DV camcorder to the proper mode to record from the input connectors rather than the lens. Instructions differ depending on the camcorder.**

   Follow the instructions with the DV camcorder to record from the input connectors. Some camcorders have a special record button for recording from analog sources in VTR/VCR mode (separate from the button for recording video in camera mode). We use a Canon ZR 60, which provides this function on a remote controller.

3. **Turn on the DV camcorder's record function to start recording from the input connectors, and start playing the video on the video player.**

   After you start the recording process, the video played on the analog device records in digital format on the DV camcorder's tape. This process preserves the video in digital format before bringing it into iMovie. You can watch the progress of the recording on your DV camcorder's monitor.

4. **After recording video in the DV camcorder onto DV tape cassette, start iMovie, and import from the DV tape to capture clips for your project.**

   See the section, "Importing Clips from DV Tape," earlier in this chapter.

Some DV camcorders allow you to pass the analog video straight through the camcorder to iMovie without saving it to DV tape, which saves the extra step of recording to tape before importing. To use this method, follow the camcorder's instructions to prepare the camcorder, and then read the section "Capturing video directly to disk," earlier in this chapter.

Importing Multimedia Elements

When compiling documentaries, many filmmakers use still photos for dramatic effect rather than re-enacting a scene with actors. Ken Burns is a documentary filmmaker well known for this technique, used extensively in his documentaries *Civil War* and *Jazz* — which is why Apple included the Ken Burns Effect in iMovie. Often music as well as the voice of the narrator accompanies the still photos.

You can create these effects with your photos and more with iMovie. Your photos in iPhoto are instantly ready for use, as are your songs in iTunes. We describe how to add narration and edit the audio in your movie in Chapter 4 of this book.

Using photos and graphics in iPhoto

Nothing captures the essential convenience of the iLife package than opening up iMovie and clicking the Photos button, which is one of the media pane buttons (as described in Chapter 1 of this book). Your entire iPhoto library appears automatically in the photos pane, replacing the clips pane, and ready for use in your movie, as shown in Figure 2-5. Nothing could be easier.

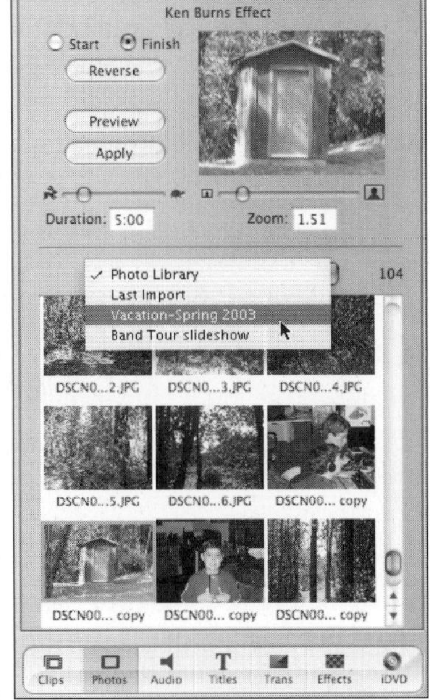

Figure 2-5: Clicking the Photos button automatically makes your iPhoto library available.

You can even use the pop-up menu in the photo pane to select a specific photo album and see only those photos (refer to Figure 2-5). We describe how to use still-image techniques in Chapter 3 of this book.

You can also use graphics created by chart and graph functions of spreadsheet applications, or created in applications such as Adobe Illustrator and Adobe Photoshop. The easiest way to do this is to import the graphics first into iPhoto, as we describe in Book II, Chapter 2.

After you import the file into iPhoto, the image in the file becomes part of your iPhoto library and automatically appears in the photos pane of iMovie.

While iMovie lets you use anything in your iPhoto library, including many different types of graphics files, not all of them look so good in digital video format.

Sizing photos for movies

For a variety of technical reasons, you can modify your photos in iPhoto to be the right size and aspect ratio for use in movies. Fortunately, digital cameras use the same 4:3 aspect ratio as video, but you may have enough resolution in your photos to focus in on the best part and use only that. In Book II, Chapter 3 we describe how to crop photos with the Constrain feature to create smaller photos, but in the right ratio so that you can use them in a movie that displays at 640 x 480 pixels.

If possible, save any graphics or still images exactly as you want them at a 640 x 480 pixel resolution. While digital video frames are actually 720 x 480, digital video uses rectangular pixels rather than square pixels. iMovie compensates for the discrepancy by converting the pixels for you. You can therefore plan to make your images fit the 4:3 aspect ratio for displaying at 640 x 480.

Using music and sounds in iTunes

With iLife, your music in iTunes is always, as Mick Jagger might say, just a click away. Click the Audio button, which is one of the media pane buttons. Your entire iTunes music library appears automatically in the audio pane, replacing the clips pane, and ready for use in your movie, as shown in Figure 2-6.

The music in the library appears in a list in the same order as you sort them in iTunes. Of course, that may not be the way you want to view the list in iMovie. You can sort the list alphabetically by artist by clicking the Artist heading, or by song by clicking the Song heading (see Figure 2-6). You can also select a playlist from the pop-up menu to see only the songs in the playlist, sorted in the playlist sequence. The playlist can also be re-sorted by clicking the Song or Artist heading. Sorting in the iMovie audio pane does not change your iTunes library.

You can also sort by the Time heading, which is useful if you create a playlist of movie theme music to use for scenes, and edited the music for time. A sort by time yields a list of songs sorted by duration. You can easily pick the song you need to match a particular duration in your movie.

While iMovie offers a nice set of sound effects that we describe in Chapter 4 of this book, you may have more that you want to add, such as sounds you create or record from other sources. You can use the following sounds:

✦ **Sounds from videos:** Import sounds simply as video clips. You can then use iMovie to split the sound from the nonexistent video picture and use only the sound. We describe how to do this in Chapter 4 of this book.

✦ **Sounds from the everyday world:** Record sounds right on your Mac through its microphone using iMovie. We describe how to do this, and how to record narration (same thing as outside sound, only different microphone techniques) in Chapter 4 of this book.

✦ **Sounds from CDs:** Rip music straight into iTunes, as we describe in Book I, Chapter 1.

✦ **Sounds from other sources:** Save sounds as digital audio files in the AIF, WAV, MP3, QuickTime, or other formats. Import sound files first into iTunes, as we describe in Book I, Chapter 3.

In addition, you can import digital audio files by choosing File➪Import. When importing a digital audio file, iMovie places it in the timeline viewer rather than the audio pane. We describe how to edit sound in the timeline viewer in Chapter 4 of this book.

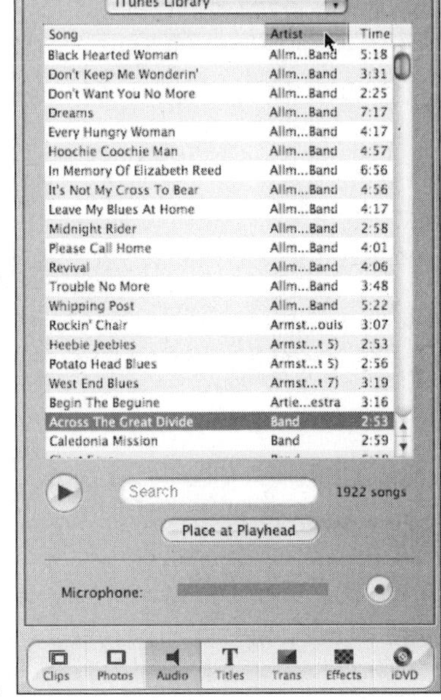

Figure 2-6: iMovie opens your iTunes library; sort the tunes by artist or song, or choose different playlists.

Chapter 3: Organizing and Improving Video Clips

In This Chapter

- **Managing video clips and copying projects**
- **Deleting and restoring video clips**
- **Cropping, trimming, and arranging video clips**
- **Adding documentary-style special effects to photos**
- **Adding special effects to video clips**

In moviemaking, the clapstick helps the sound editor synchronize sound with picture because in film, the picture and sound are recorded separately. With video, you can record both at the same time, so you may not need any sound synchronization except when adding more sound. But the most important function of the slate is to help the director and editor identify a particular *take* in the raw footage from the cameras. As director, you can then separate clips and rearrange them as you see fit.

Video production is similar. You can summarize the entire process of making a movie or a video as shooting scenes, organizing and selecting the video clips you want, trimming the clips, and arranging them in a sequence. The most important part of moviemaking is getting the shots; the second is working with your video clips.

This chapter explains how to organize video clips, select the ones you want to use, and edit those clips so that they show exactly what you want them to show. It also describes how to add motion and picture effects to clips that run the clip in reverse, adjust contrast and brightness, change colors or change the scene to black and white, or transform clips into visual eye candy with simulated flash bulbs, ghost trails, mirror images, rain, fog, earthquakes, and so on. With these effects, you can change something mundane into something visually interesting or convey feelings and emotions that you can't capture with a camera, or even prepare wildly vivid scenes for concert light shows and music videos.

Organizing a Project

An iMovie project is a file that defines a sequence using links to media files. The media files are photos from iPhoto, music from iTunes, and, of course, your video clips.

iMovie creates each video clip by checking the date and time stamp as it imports footage from your DV camcorder. With automatic scene detection, iMovie detects each break in time — which is what happens when you stop recording with the camcorder, even for just a few seconds — and separates each scene from the next, storing each scene in a separate video clip file. iMovie lets you work on separate clips and assemble them in any order.

Creating and saving a project

To create a project, choose File⇨New Project. You can choose where to store the project folder (we suggest in your Movies folder, inside your Home folder). You provide a name for the project, which iMovie uses as the project folder name. iMovie stores your imported video clips in a folder called Media, located within your project folder (see Figure 3-1).

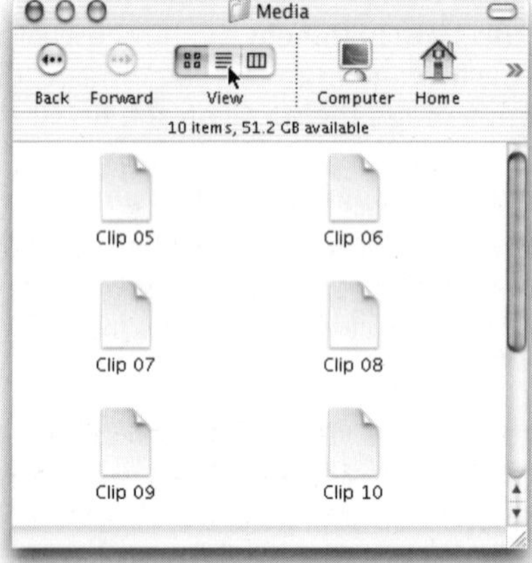

Figure 3-1: iMovie saves your video clips in a folder dedicated to your new project.

The project document contains information about clip edits, special effects, the sequence of clips that make the movie, and so on, while the clip files contain the actual video footage.

The project document file by itself is meaningless without the clip files, which is why iMovie puts them together in a single folder. If you copy only the project document file to a Zip drive or floppy disk, and bring it to another Mac, you'll be disappointed to find no video in your project. To copy a project, see the following section.

Copying a project

You may have a need to copy an entire movie project. Here are some reasons why:

- ✦ To create another version of a project in order to create a different movie using the same video clips. iMovie has no Save as command; the only way to create a new version is to copy the project folder.
- ✦ To save a version of a project halfway through editing the movie, or before adding special effects, so that you can go back to that version of the project if you don't like the results of editing and adding effects.
- ✦ To create a backup copy of the entire project for archive purposes.
- ✦ To move the project to another hard disk (such as another Mac).

Copying a project folder uses up lots of disk space — essentially doubling the space occupied by the clips, because you make a duplicate of everything. You may want to make this copy on another hard disk or removable media, such as a high capacity disk cartridge or save the clips to a DV tape (along with your original footage). We describe how to export to DV tape in Chapter 5 of this book.

To copy a project folder, follow these steps:

1. **Quit iMovie and locate the project folder using the Finder.**

   The project folder is inside your Movies folder, which is inside your Home folder. Using the Finder, open your Home folder to find the Movies folder, and open the Movies folder to find your project folder. (To find out how to use the Finder, see Mark L. Chambers' most excellent book, *Mac OS X All-in-One Desk Reference For Dummies* published by Wiley Publishing, Inc.)

   To copy the project folder to another storage device or folder, go to Step 2. To duplicate the folder on the same hard disk, skip Step 2 and go to Step 3.

2. **In the Finder, drag the project folder to another storage device or folder.**

   When you copy a folder to another storage device or a different folder, the folder name remains. You're done (you can skip the following steps).

3. **In the Finder, select the project folder and Choose File⇨Duplicate.**

   When you duplicate a folder on the same disk in the same folder, the Finder automatically adds "copy" to the end of the new folder's name.

4. **Optional: Rename the newly duplicated project document.**

   If you duplicate the project folder (and it now has "copy" at the end of its name), you should also rename the project file inside the new folder to have the same name, to differentiate it from the original.

Although you can rename the project folder and project file in the Finder, don't rename or delete any of the clip files in the Media folder using the Finder. You can use iMovie to rename clips (as we describe in the "Renaming a clip" section, later in this chapter), and to delete them, as we describe later in this chapter. iMovie controls the actual filenames for video clips. If you rename them in the Finder, iMovie no longer recognizes them. And don't take the Media folder out of the project folder.

When you start iMovie again, the last movie project you worked on opens automatically. You can open any movie project by choosing File⇨Open Project.

Organizing Clips

A video project with a lot of clips can quickly become hard to manage if you don't organize the clips in some way. The clips pane shows all your clips in the project, but you can use it as a makeshift storyboard for your project by rearranging them to suit your needs, and renaming them to identify them better. A *storyboard* is a set of thumbnails that tells the story in sequence, and it is typically used as a guide for editing as well as an organizational tool.

Arranging clips in the clips pane

Your iMovie clips pane can serve as a storyboard by rearranging the clips into a proper sequence and using descriptive titles for your clips.

To rearrange your clips, click each clip and drag it to a new location in the clips pane. You can drag a clip to any empty space, as shown in Figure 3-2.

You can also drag a clip to a location already occupied by a clip, and iMovie automatically shifts the other clips to the right and down, to accommodate the newly moved clip.

Figure 3-2: Drag clips to rearrange them in the clips pane.

You can move multiple clips at once by clicking the first clip, and either Shift-clicking the last clip for a consecutive range of clips, or ⌘-clicking each subsequent clip to add it to the selection. With the clips highlighted, click and hold down the mouse button to drag the selection to the new location.

Renaming a clip

Your imported clips appear in the clips pane with the default names "Clip 01," "Clip 02," and so on, and that may be okay for your project. But you can also change these names in iMovie to make them easier to recognize.

You may want to rename clips as you edit them to indicate that the clips have been edited. For example, you may rename "Clip 01" to "Clip 01 edited" or something equally innovative. Most likely you want to give your clips descriptive titles, such as "Uncle Monty does card tricks." You can use up to 127 letters and spaces.

To see clip information and rename a clip, double-click the clip in the clips pane or select the clip and choose File⇨Show Info.

The Clip Info window appears with information about the clip, including its real name in the Finder next to Media File and its size, capture date, and duration. You can edit the filename by clicking inside the Name box, highlighting the old name, and then typing the new one, as shown in Figure 3-3.

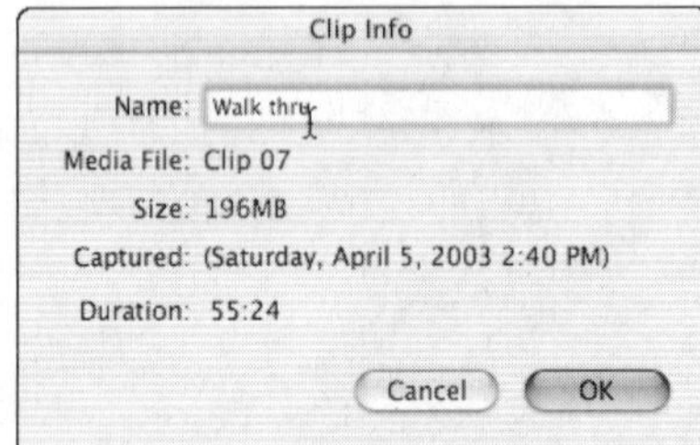

Figure 3-3: Rename a video clip in the Clip Info window.

The name you give the clip does not affect the clip's real name in the Finder, which must stay the same so that the project document can find it. Never rename a clip's real name in the Finder.

Importing clips from different projects

You can copy video clips from one project into another project to save yourself the time and trouble of connecting the DV camcorder and importing them again. The key piece of information you need to import a clip from another project is the real filename for the clip, which you can get from the Clip Info window.

Follow these steps to import a video clip from another project:

1. **Choose File⇨Open Project and open the project that has the video clip you want.**
2. **Select the video clip and choose File⇨Show Info or double-click the video clip.**

   The Clip Info window gives you the real filename for the clip next to the Media File entry (refer to Figure 3-3). Remember this filename. It's something like Clip 07.
3. **Click OK, and open the project into which you want to import the video clip by choosing File⇨Open Project.**
4. **Choose File⇨Import and use the Import dialog box to navigate to the other project folder's Media folder.**
5. **Find the clip by looking for its real name and click the clip for importing.**

Be sure to save the project after you import a video clip by choosing File➪Save Project.

Deleting and Restoring Clips

When you edit a video clip, you're performing a *destructive edit* — the video clip changes, perhaps irrevocably, by the edits. But iMovie is smart at digital editing and provides not only the ability to undo edits, but also the ability to restore the clip to its original state. As long as you don't empty the iMovie Trash, you can restore any clip.

Don't get too cozy with retrieving something from the Trash because at some point you have to empty the Trash to reclaim disk space.

The best techniques are those that allow you to recover gracefully, so we recommend that you copy the project folder to another drive, as we describe in the section, "Copying a project," earlier in this chapter. After the originals are safe, you can go ahead with all the editing you want with the secure feeling that you can always find the original version of the clip.

Restoring a clip to its previous form

You just made edits that you don't like. You could quit iMovie without saving the project. When you open the project again, the previous version opens (before you made the edits).

But what if you made some good edits and some bad edits? If you haven't yet saved the project and you just made some bad edits, you can undo each edit going backward by choosing Edit➪Undo for each edit. You can undo up to ten previous actions, or the actions up to the last time you saved (if fewer than ten).

You can only undo actions you've done since you saved the project last, or actions that occurred since you emptied the Trash.

You can restore specific clips if you also made some good edits to some clips but not others. Select the clip with the bad edits in the clips pane and choose Advanced➪Restore Clip. The clip is then restored to the last saved version.

If you need to go back to the original version before any edits, even saved ones, you need to import the original clip from the DV camcorder's tape or from a backup folder.

Deleting clips and emptying the Trash

Video clips can hang out in the clips pane forever, even if they're never used in the project. In fact, you may want to create a special project containing all your original clips, and then import those clips into new projects.

To delete a video clip, drag the clip to the Trash icon in the lower-right corner of the iMovie window, as shown in Figure 3-4. iMovie displays, right next to the icon, the amount of disk space occupied by the trashed items.

The iMovie Trash works in a different way than the Trash in the Finder. The iMovie Trash retains the clips in their original forms before editing. As long as you don't empty the Trash, you can undo actions and restore clips.

However, you probably will eventually need to free up some disk space. Granted, external hard disks cost less than $200, but that's not a permanent solution. Empty the Trash by choosing File⇨Empty Trash.

Figure 3-4: Delete a video clip with the iMovie Trash.

After you empty the iMovie Trash, you can't undo any action that occurred before emptying the Trash and you also can't restore clips to the forms they were in before emptying the Trash.

Editing Individual Clips

Most of the work of producing a video is editing the clips to make them more interesting or more effective at communicating. You may want to "tighten up" the video clips so that they start and stop at exactly the right moments, or remove unwanted sections of clips. You may also want to split a clip into two clips, so that you can use the two sections of the clip in different places in the sequence.

As with any editing changes to clips, you can always restore the clips to their original states as long as you don't empty the Trash (as described in "Restoring and Deleting Clips" in this chapter).

Trimming and cropping clips

As you play your video clip, you may notice that the clip starts too early or ends too late. *Trimming* removes the highlighted section of video from the clip. It is the opposite of *cropping*, which removes everything but the highlighted section.

Here's how to trim the beginning of a video clip:

1. **Click underneath the playback head in the scrubber bar and hold down the mouse button to see the two ghost triangles — the crop/trim markers.**
2. **Drag the right crop/trim marker to the last frame that you want to remove.**

   In Figure 3-5, we drag the right marker all the way to 05:00, highlighting the five second section at the beginning.

   The section you want to crop becomes highlighted.
3. **Choose Edit⇨Clear.**

   The highlighted section is removed.

You can use the arrow keys on your keyboard to make more accurate selections. Click a crop/trim marker and press the left or right arrow key to move the marker one frame at a time. To move the marker in 10-frame increments, hold down the Shift key while pressing the arrow key.

Figure 3-5: Drag the right crop/ trim marker, under the scrubber bar, to highlight a section from the beginning of the clip to trim off.

To trim off the end of a video clip, follow these steps:

1. **Drag the right crop/trim marker to the last frame that you want to remove.**
2. **Drag the left crop/trim marker to the first frame that you want to remove.**

   The selected portion is indicated by a yellow band in the scrubber bar.
3. **Choose Edit⇨Clear.**

   The highlighted section is removed.

When you remove a section of the video clip, the Trash icon at the bottom of the iMovie window indicates that the Trash contains some data — the amount (in megabytes or kilobytes) next to the Trash icon increases. (The five seconds we trim from the beginning puts 17MB in the Trash.) The removed sections accumulate in the Trash as you make edits.

Follow these steps to crop a video clip (select the portion to keep):

7. **Drag the right crop/trim marker to the last frame that you want to keep.**
2. **Drag the left crop/trim marker to the first frame that you want to keep.**

   The selected portion becomes highlighted.
3. **Choose Edit⇨Crop.**

   The video before and after the highlighted section is removed.

You can immediately play your video clip to see whether it's cropped or trimmed correctly. When your clips are edited the way you want, choose File⇨Save Project to save your editing changes. The project is saved in your Movies folder (or whatever folder you used when you created the project).

You don't have to drag both crop/trim markers to make a highlighted selection. You can also select portions of your video in the following ways:

- ✦ Drag one crop/trim marker to the beginning or end of a selection, and then click underneath the tick marks of the scrubber bar to establish the other end of the selection.
- ✦ Extend an existing selection by clicking under the tick marks to the right of the right marker, or to the left of the left marker. Clicking inside the selected area reduces the selection.
- ✦ Shift-click to highlight from one marker to the beginning or end of the clip.

Splitting a clip

Sometimes you need to split a clip into two clips. For example, you may have a clip that has two scenes shot one right after the other, without any pause in the recording, and you want to use them as two clips rather than one. You may want to insert a title in the middle of a scene.

To split a clip into two clips, select the clip and follow these steps:

1. **Move the playback head to the place in the clip where you want the split to occur.**
2. **Choose Edit⇨Split Video Clip at Playhead.**

   The video clip split into two clips at the point of the playback head.

After splitting the clip, iMovie saves the second clip with the same name, but with "/1" appended to it. You can rename the clip if you want.

Cutting out the middle of a clip

If a video clip has a great part at the beginning and a great part at the end, and nothing but junk in-between, you can cut out the middle part. You may find that many of your clips can use this treatment — especially those parts where you jiggled the camcorder.

To cut out a middle part, select the clip and follow these steps:

1. **Drag the right crop/trim marker to the last frame that you want to cut out.**
2. **Drag the left crop/trim marker to the first frame that you want to cut out.**

   The piece you want to cut out is highlighted, which is indicated by a yellow band in the scrubber bar.
3. **Choose Edit⇨Clear.**

   The highlighted video is removed.

Reversing the direction of a clip

Making video clips run backward may seem like a cheap gimmick, humorous when applied to skiers, high-divers, planes taking off, buildings in the process of being demolished, and so on. But it can also be a useful way to fix a problem or add a touch of professionalism to a video.

For example, if you zoomed into the subject with your camcorder without also zooming out, and later you discover that you wish you had zoomed out, you can split the clip (as we describe in the section, "Splitting a clip," earlier in this chapter). Make the zoom-in part a separate clip, copy it, and then reverse the direction of the copy. You end up with two clips: the zoom-in, and the reverse of the zoom-in, which looks just like a zoom-out. Put them together and the scene is complete.

You can combine the reversing and slow motion to achieve an overall effect that adds a sensitive feel to the video. Changing the speed of your video is described in Chapter 4 of this book.

To reverse the direction of the clip, follow these steps:

1. **Select the clip in the clips pane.**
2. **Choose Advanced⇨Reverse Clip Direction (or press ⌘+R).**

   The clip's thumbnail appears with a left-pointing arrow in the upper right corner indicating that it runs in reverse, as shown in Figure 3-6.

A reversed clip

Figure 3-6: Reverse the direction of a video clip.

An entire clip runs in reverse — including the sound. Recorded voices may now sound like the Beatles at the end of the song "Rain." Nature sounds, however, may sound fine backwards or forwards. If you don't like how it sounds, you can adjust the audio portion and even add a different soundtrack, as we describe in Chapter 4 of this book.

You can use the Reverse Clip Direction command on several clips at once, if you already dragged them to the clips viewer in sequence (we show how to do this in "Applying effects to video clips" in this chapter). The command not only reverses the direction of each clip, but also intelligently reverses the entire sequence.

Adding Motion and Picture Effects

Reality, as captured by your camcorder, may not be enough to convey what you want to convey. Perhaps the fireworks you recorded did not come out as well as you hoped, or you want to jazz up a sequence to make it look more like nightmare or a walk through the funhouse. You have at your disposal an arsenal of special effects and tricks that were previously available only to professional video editors and artists.

While the addition of special effects may be somewhat gratuitous if they're added for no reason, many of these tricks are used to fix real problems and make genuine enhancements. Maybe you didn't hold the camcorder steady enough in a particular shot, and you want to enhance the effect you caused accidentally. You can apply effects to lighten or darken a clip. You can also add motion effects to photos and still images.

Before performing any of these actions, you may want to make a copy of the clip in case the effect doesn't come out as you like. Select a clip in the clips pane, choose Edit➪Copy, and then Edit➪Paste. iMovie makes a copy of the clip and stores it next to the original. You can then work with either the original or the copy.

Adding the Ken Burns Effect to photos

After clicking the Photos button, your entire iPhoto library appears automatically in the photos pane, replacing the clips pane, and ready for use. You can select any photo or album in your iPhoto library.

Filmmaker Ken Burns may not be a household name, but his documentaries (such as *Ken Burns' Jazz*) have been watched by millions, and Apple pays him respect by naming the zooming and panning effect for photos after him — the Ken Burns Effect at the top of the photo pane. Ken Burns uses variations of this effect in his documentaries, with great success.

iMovie allows you to pan across, zoom in and out, and even combine panning and zooming to achieve interesting results that suggest movement, or the passing of time. The best way to use these effects is to experiment with the settings and watch the preview window.

Zooming in and out of photos

To experiment with the zoom effect, follow these steps:

1. **Select the photo in the photos pane.**

   The photo appears in the preview box of the photos pane.

2. **Click the Start button in the photos pane.**
3. **Adjust the Zoom slider to change the magnification for the starting point of the zoom effect.**

   The amount you choose appears in the Zoom box. In Figure 3-7, we chose a magnification of 1.48 for the zoom's starting point.

4. **Click the Finish button in the photos pane.**

5. **Adjust the Zoom slider to change the magnification for the ending point of the zoom effect.**

   The amount you choose appears in the Zoom box.

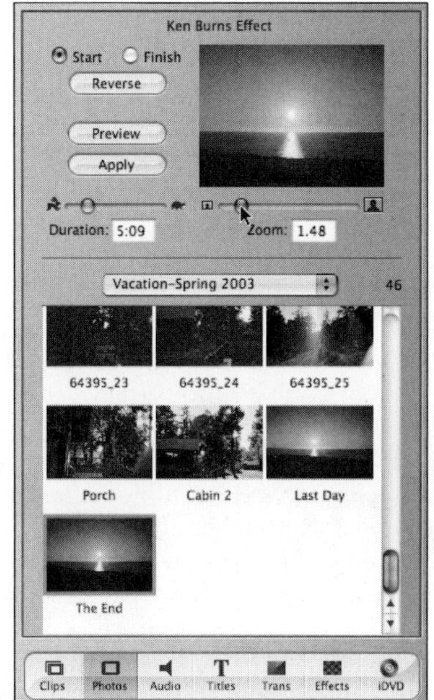

Figure 3-7: Set the start and finish magnification (zoom) levels.

6. **Click the Preview button.**

   A preview of the effect plays in the preview window.

7. **Adjust the Duration slider to change the duration of the zoom.**

8. **Click the Reverse button to change the direction of the zoom.**

   You can click the Reverse button again to change the direction back to the original setting.

9. **Click the Apply button to apply the effect.**

   iMovie creates a video clip of the zoom effect and places it in the clip viewer.

10. **Click the Clips button to display the clips pane.**

    Switch back to the clips pane from the photos pane while the clip you edited is still in the clip viewer.

11. **Drag the edited clip from the clip viewer to an empty spot in the clips pane (see Figure 3-8).**

    With the edited clip stored in the clips pane, you can use it anywhere in your video sequence. We describe building a sequence in Chapter 4 of this book.

Figure 3-8: You can add the video clip of the zoomed-in photo to the clips pane.

Panning across while zooming a photo

To experiment with the image panning effect, follow these steps:

1. **Select the photo in the photos pane.**
2. **Click the Start button in the photos pane.**
3. **Adjust the Zoom slider to set the magnification for the starting point of the panning effect.**

    The amount you choose appears in the Zoom box.

4. **Specify where to start the pan.**

    Hold your mouse pointer over the image in the preview window until a hand appears, and then click and drag the image to where you want the pan to begin.

5. **Click the Finish button in the photos pane.**
6. **Adjust the Zoom slider to change the magnification for the ending point of panning effect.**

   The amount you choose appears in the Zoom box.
7. **Specify where to end the pan.**

   Hold your mouse pointer over the image in the preview window until a hand appears, and then click and drag the image to where you want the pan to end.
8. **Click the Preview button.**

   A preview of the effect plays in the preview window.
9. **Adjust the Duration slider to change the duration of the zoom.**
10. **Click the Reverse button to change the direction of the pan.**

    Click it again to change the direction back to the original setting.
11. **Click the Apply button to apply the effect.**

    iMovie creates a video clip of the pan effect and places it in the clip viewer.
12. **Click the Clips button to display the clips pane.**

    Switch back to the clips pane from the photos pane while the clip you edited is still in the clip viewer.
13. **Drag the edited clip from the clip viewer to an empty spot in the clips pane.**

    With the edited clip stored in the clips pane, you can use it anywhere in your video sequence. We describe building a sequence in Chapter 4 of this book.

Creating an effect, called *rendering,* can take time. You'll notice the clip created by the photo has a red line slowly moving across it, showing the progress of the rendering. You can continue to do other things in iMovie while the effect is rendered. The rendering with the Ken Burns Effect usually takes a very short time, and before long, your clip is ready to play. Click the Play button to look at the effect in all its glory.

Applying effects to video clips

Video effects change the picture without changing the sound. iMovie provides a list of video effects ranging from Adjust Colors and Aged Film to Sepia Tone, Sharpen, and Soft Focus. The best way to use the Effects features of iMovie is to experiment.

To apply any effect, follow these steps:

1. **Pick a clip and drag it from the clips pane to the clip viewer.**
2. **Click the Effects button.**

   The effects pane replaces the clips pane, as shown in Figure 3-9.
3. **Click to reselect the clip in the clip viewer.**

   The clip now has a blue border.
4. **Choose an effect and adjust its settings.**

   When you pick an effect, the preview window shows what the effect looks like using the selected clip. The effect's specific settings appear at the bottom of the effects pane, and you can adjust them to your heart's content — with each adjustment you see a preview in the preview window.

Figure 3-9: The effects pane lists the special effects you can apply to a clip.

5. **Use the effect on the entire clip or just a portion of it.**

   To apply the effect to a portion of the clip, drag the crop/trim markers to highlight a section of the video (as we describe earlier in this chapter, in the section, "Trimming and cropping clips").

6. **Adjust the Effect In and Effect Out sliders if you want the effect to start and end gradually.**

   You can make the effect kick in more slowly by dragging the Effect In slider. Make it end more gradually by dragging the Effect Out slider. The time code, in seconds and frames, appears in the preview window.

7. **Click the Apply button to apply the effect.**

   If you apply the effect to only a portion of the clip, iMovie automatically splits the clip into two or more clips — one clip for the portion before the effect, one clip for after the section with the effect, and one clip just for the section with the effect. The clips are arranged in proper sequence in the clip viewer. In Figure 3-10, we end up with two clips, because we started the effect at the beginning of the clip.

   As the clip is being rendered, the clip's thumbnail shows a red line moving slowly across it, showing the progress. When the red line reaches the end, the rendering is done.

Figure 3-10: iMovie splits the clip.

You can then play the clip by itself, or you can Shift-click the clips in the clip viewer to play them in sequence.

8. **Click on Clips to display the clips pane.**

   Switch back to the clips pane from the photos pane while the clips you edited are still in the clip viewer.

9. **Drag the clips from the clip viewer to an empty spot in the clips pane.**

   With the clips stored in the clips pane, you can use them anywhere in your video sequence. We describe building a sequence in Chapter 4 of this book.

You can take advantage of an infinite number of possibilities with the iMovie Effects pane. You can combine multiple effects to a clip to get the look you want. Here are suggestions for various effects:

- **Adjust Colors:** Use this effect to change the colors in the picture or to make the color more or less vivid, or darker or brighter. You can use this effect to enhance a sunset view.
- **Aged Film:** Make your video look like newsreel footage with this effect, which creates a visual effect of scratched film, with a super grainy texture and lines and specks.
- **Black & White:** Turn your clip into black and white to simulate early television pictures, or to emulate the *Wizard of Oz* (everything's in black and white until Dorothy lands on Oz and opens the door). Sometimes a video shot on a gray day looks better in black and white.
- **Brightness & Contrast:** While the effect isn't a substitute for good lighting when recording video, it can help alleviate the problems associated with poor lighting and making the picture brighter, darker, and with less or more contrast.
- **Earthquake:** We use this effect to cover up an unsteady camcorder. It also works well if you happen to be videotaping in earthquake country. You can exaggerate some activity, such as a barroom brawl (staged, of course).
- **Electricity:** A bolt of lightning comes down out of the sky. Nice. You can control the animation of the lightning by dragging the Rotate slider to animate the lightning clockwise or counterclockwise around the picture.
- **Fairy Dust:** This effect sends an animated fairy wand's spark across the picture in an arc you can control with a Direction slider and with a trail you can control with the Trail slider. (Yes, Toto, we're not in Kansas anymore.)

- **Flash:** Use this effect to simulate flash bulbs going off. Perfect for weddings, graduations, simulated press conferences, and gala openings. You can control the number of flashes, the brightness of the flash, and the speed.
- **Fog:** Simulate a foggy night in London or San Francisco, or just crank up the fog machine for any purpose you want. You can control the amount of fog, the direction the fog is blowing, and the fog's shade of gray.
- **Ghost Trails:** Use this effect to show trails off moving objects and people, which is useful for portraying a runner at top speed, or a dancer using expansive gestures. Figure 3-11 shows the Ghost Trails effect on a walking youngster. You can control the length of the ghost images, how closely the ghost follows the image, and the transparency of the ghost images.
- **Lens Flare:** This effect produces a lens flaring effect that sweeps across the scene like sunlight in the lens. You can set the sweep angle and the intensity of the flare.
- **Letterbox:** To simulate the look of a film on DVD or VHS in letterbox format, shift the viewable area up or down, or resize the viewable area as you see fit.
- **Mirror:** This effect looks like a funhouse mirror. The clip splits in half. One half fills with a mirror image of the other half. You can reflect images horizontally and vertically.
- **N-Square:** Strictly for fans of the movie *The Fly,* this effect divides the picture into square panes, and you can control the number of squares.
- **Rain:** This effect looks quite convincing, and you can make it a light or heavy rainstorm using the Amount and Wind sliders. Combine this with the Black & White, Electricity, and Flash effects to simulate a thunderstorm.
- **Sepia Tone:** This effect gives you that brown-and-white look of a very old photo, which can help convey antiquity and nostalgia. You can follow up this effect with the Brightness & Contrast effect to adjust the picture further.
- **Sharpen:** Add a fine-grained look to your picture, giving it an unrealistic crispness, depending on how high you slide the Amount slider.
- **Soft Focus:** This effect gives everything a blurry, fuzzy-edged look for those hazy, dreamy, or romantic scenes; you also see this effect used in TV commercials with ancient stars because it hides facial wrinkles.

TIP

For that newsreel look of yesteryear, combine the effects of the Black & White and Flash effects set to a maximum count, minimum brightness, and fast speed.

Figure 3-11: The Ghost Trails effect.

Chapter 4: Editing Movies and Sound

In This Chapter

- **Arranging video clips**
- **Adding transitions, titles, and credits**
- **Editing the soundtrack**

You shot scenes, organized video clips, and selected the ones you want. You also trimmed the clips and added some effects. Now you're ready to perform perhaps the most creative task in all of moviemaking — you're ready to edit the movie into a sequence that tells the story with the emotional and intellectual impact you want the audience to have.

Movie directors are often lauded for creative efforts in the editing studio. Alfred Hitchcock, for example, is noted for raising editing to a new level of artistic success — he used tricks such as cutaways to show what an actor is reacting to, or very tight editing to show only the parts of a scene he wanted to show, leaving the audience to imagine the rest. Directors often create a rhythm for the movie established by the lengths of the edited clips, and use a chronological order to help advance the story line and introduce suspense.

This kind of editing requires a very strict timeline. The editing choices you make to arrange your video clips and audio tracks over time can be either wholly original or shamelessly imitative of the great directors of Hollywood. Good editing makes a movie; bad editing breaks it.

This chapter shows how to use the iMovie timeline and clip arrangement features to edit a movie. It walks you through the process of arranging clips and controlling their durations, and adding and controlling audio tracks. It describes various features of iMovie that can make your movies look professionally produced, and it describes the post-production process at the end to make the movie ready for distribution.

We suggest that you start the editing process with all the visual editing you need, such as clip adjustments and transitions, before tackling the audio portion of the movie. Visual edits can change the duration of the entire movie, and if you already synchronized other sounds in addition to the sound in the video clips, you may find these sounds out of sync. You can always move elements back into the positions you want to re-synchronize, but this is extra work you don't need to do if you start with visual editing.

Assembling an Oscar-Winning Sequence

Typically, you start movie editing by arranging video clips in a storyboard. If you already trimmed and cropped your video clips as we describe in Chapter 3 of this book, you most likely already know the sequence you want the clips to run, and arranging the clips is the fastest part of this process. iMovie also makes arranging the movie clips the easiest part of the process by providing a viewer that can show individual clip thumbnails arranged over time.

Arranging clips in the clip viewer

To arrange clips in a sequence, drag each clip to the clip viewer. As you drag clips to the clip viewer, you can play each clip by clicking the play button.

To place a clip after another clip, drag it to a position to the right of the first clip. You can also place a clip between two clips, and drag clips around as you wish, within the clip viewer, as shown in Figure 4-1. You can also drag clips back to the clips pane to remove them from the sequence.

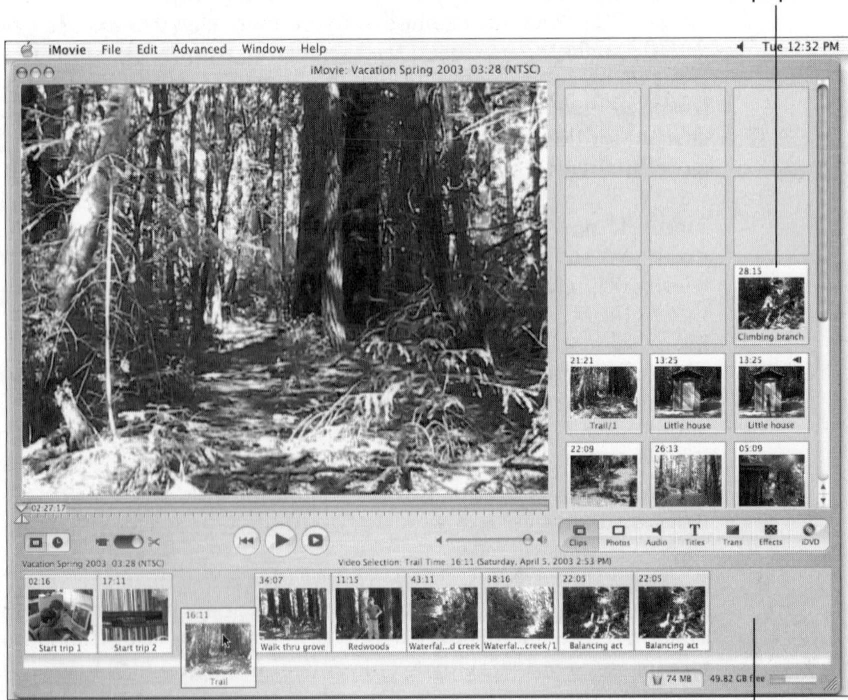

Figure 4-1: Rearrange clips in the clip viewer to change the sequence.

This one-clip-at-a-time dragging can be tedious. But if you already arranged clips in sequence in the clips pane, you can drag more than one clip at a time by selecting the first clip and holding down the Shift key while selecting more clips, and then dragging the entire set. iMovie places them into position in the same order as they were in the clips pane.

To play the sequence of clips in the clip viewer, you can use either of the following methods:

- Select the first one, and then hold down the Shift key and click the last one to highlight all the clips. Click the Play button. The entire sequence of clips plays.
- You can play the entire movie by first choosing Edit⇨Select None and then clicking the Play button.

While the sequence plays, the playback head in the scrubber bar moves forward as iMovie displays the time, in minutes, seconds, and frames.

Working in the timeline viewer

The timeline viewer gives you more control over the entire movie, enabling you to adjust the duration of any clip in the sequence and control audio tracks. The timeline viewer arranges the video clips along a timeline, with each clip clearly indicated by its thumbnail. You can select any clip and play only that clip by clicking the Play button, or you can click Rewind and Play to play the entire movie. You can also drag clips from the clips pane to the timeline viewer to add them at the end of the sequence or insert them between other clips.

The timeline viewer is simply a different view of the same arrangement of clips, and you can switch back and forth from the timeline viewer to the clip viewer using the mode buttons.

To show the timeline viewer, click the clock icon to the right of the clip icon in the clip viewer/timeline viewer switch.

Look in the timeline viewer to arrange clips and see how long they play. You can move to any point in the movie by dragging the playback head in the scrubber bar, or by dragging the playback head in the timeline, which appears like a ruler above the clips in the timeline viewer, as shown in Figure 4-2.

Besides using the Play button, you can play your movie from any point by pressing the space bar on your keyboard. Press the space bar again to stop playback.

Figure 4-2: Drag the playback head in the timeline viewer to move to any frame in the movie.

The timeline viewer displays the sequence horizontally and you scroll horizontally to see the entire sequence by dragging the horizontal scroll slider along the bottom of the timeline viewer to move from the beginning to the end and back. If you want a closer view of the frames so that you can move to an exact position, zoom in or out of the timeline viewer by dragging the Zoom slider at the bottom left of the iMovie window, as shown in Figure 4-3. Drag the slider to the right to zoom in, and to the left to zoom out.

You can perform clip editing operations, such as trimming and cropping (described in Chapter 3 of this book), from the timeline viewer. As you perform such operations, the timeline viewer automatically adjusts to reflect the editing changes.

Slowing down or speeding up video clips

Suppose you want to show your child's first swing of a baseball bat in slow motion for dramatic effect. Or perhaps you have a great video clip of your dog jumping and running around the yard that would crack everybody up if run much faster.

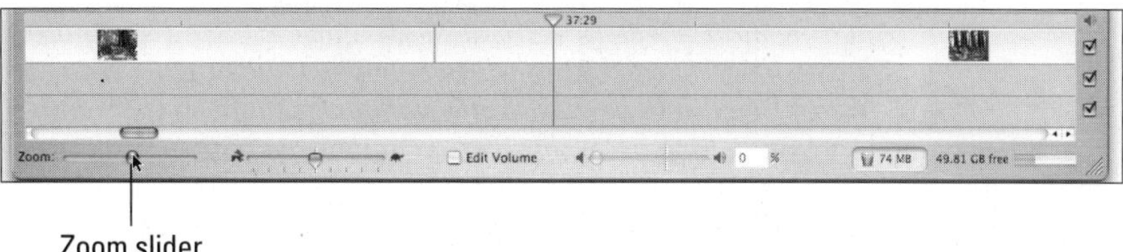

Figure 4-3: Zoom into the timeline viewer for more precise movements and adjustments.

To slow down or speed up a video clip, follow these steps:

1. **Select the clip in the timeline viewer.**

   The white space around the thumbnail image of the video becomes highlighted.

2. **Drag the Speed slider to the right (the tortoise) or left (the hare), as shown in Figure 4-4.**

   Each notch on the slider represents a multiple of its original speed — a single notch faster represents twice the original speed, two notches represents three times the speed, and so on.

When you change the speed of a clip, the timeline viewer automatically shrinks or stretches the clip to show its duration, and adjusts the movie accordingly.

When you change the duration of a video clip, the sound also changes. Faster or slower sound may seem humorous, but they can also be irritating. Fortunately iMovie allows you to edit the sound track, as we describe in the "Editing the Soundtrack" section, later in this chapter.

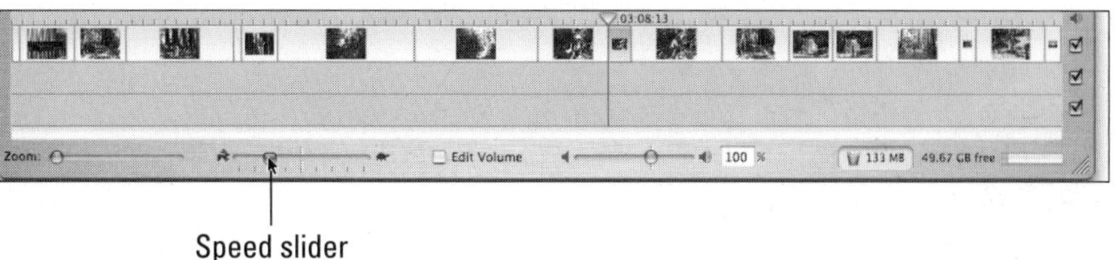

Figure 4-4: Change the speed of a video clip.

Transitioning between Scenes

One of the most visually interesting features of digital video editing software is the *transition effect* you can set between video clips. When one clip ends and other begins, the video plays seamlessly, but the scenes in the video clips may be so different that the sudden transition from one to another is jarring. You can smooth out these transitions with a transition effect.

Movies and professionally produced television shows typically use nothing but a simple cut from one clip to the next, even though professionals have an arsenal of transition effects they can use such as dissolves, wipes, overlaps, and so on. Transitional effects are usually kept simple because they can detract from the video and call attention to the video editing process.

But sometimes a transition makes sense artistically, or it can be useful for suggesting the passage of time, or to hide a flaw in the video itself. For example, the hit TV show *Six Feet Under* uses a cross-dissolve-to-white (or wash-out-to-white) transition between each major scene for artistic effect. The transition is not so obvious as to call attention to itself, and the transition is used consistently throughout the show and the series, providing a sense of unity in the work. Other popular transitions include fading in from black in the beginning of a movie, and fading out to black at the end (or fading into credits).

Adding transitions between clips

To add a transition between two clips in a sequence in the timeline (or clip) viewer, follow these steps:

1. **Select the second clip.**

   iMovie regards the selected clip as the clip to transition *into,* assuming the previous clip is the one to transition *from*. The only exception is if you select the very first clip in the movie — in which iMovie assumes, based on the transition you choose, that you want to place the transition between the first and second clips.

2. **Click the Trans button.**

   The clips pane switches to the transitions pane, which lists all the transitions and provides a preview window.

3. **Select a transition.**

   iMovie shows a preview in the small window, using the selected clip as the transition's ending.

4. **Adjust the duration of the transition with the Speed slider.**

   The Speed slider provides up to 4 seconds (04:00) of transition time. When you change this slider, iMovie plays another preview in the small window. You can continue to make adjustments and preview them until you have the duration you want.

5. **Adjust the direction of the transition.**

   With some transitions you can click the arrows to the left of the preview window to set the direction you want the transition to start from.

6. **Drag the transition to a position between the clips.**

   The transition appears as a special type of video clip between the two clips — a green bar with an icon indicating a transition (shown in Figure 4-5). If the transition needs time to finish rendering, a red progress bar creeps across the bottom of the green transition bar until the rendering finishes. Unlike many other video editing programs, iMovie allows you to continue working on the movie while rendering takes place.

Figure 4-5: Insert the transition between two video clips.

7. **Play the movie with the transition.**

   To see the transition in action after it finishes rendering, you can start the movie from the beginning, or drag the timeline viewer's playback head as shown in Figure 4-6.

Adding a transition between clips makes the entire movie shorter (with the exception of transitions, such as the Fade In transition that work its magic on only one clip). The transitions borrow portions of both clips to make the transition, which reduces the overall length of the movie. The transition may affect the sounds in the two clips as well, and we show you how to control the audio portion of a video clip in the section, "Editing the Soundtrack," later in this chapter.

Because the transition is itself a video clip, you can rename it to something you can recognize later. Double-click the transition's clip in the timeline to open the Clip Info window, and type a new name for the transition.

You can also edit the transition as a clip by selecting the transition in the timeline, and changing the Speed slider and using the direction arrows (if applicable) in the transitions pane. You can even change the type of transition. When you finish making adjustments, click the Update button to update the timeline viewer.

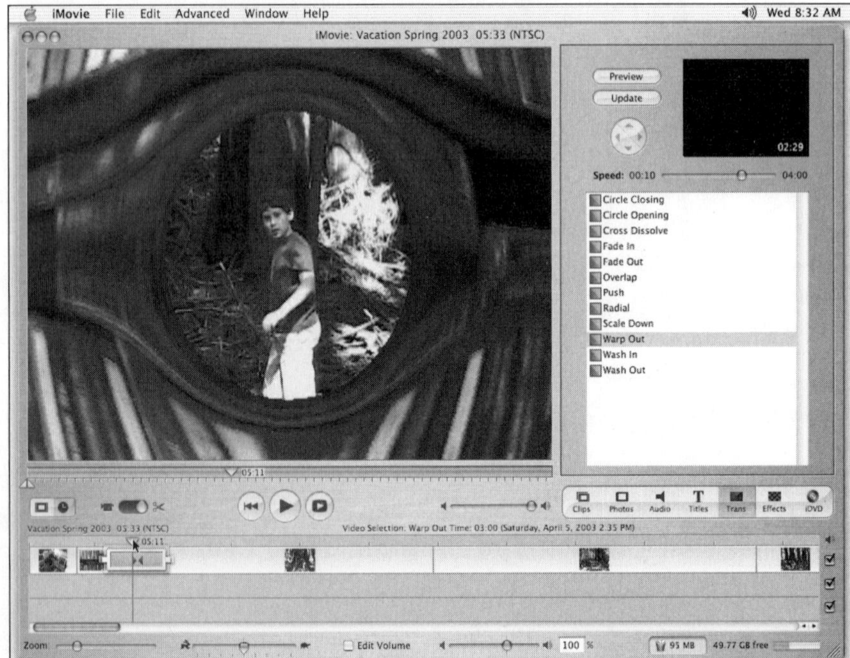

Figure 4-6: Play back the transition.

Fading in and out

Fading into the first clip is an excellent way to introduce the movie. Fading out of the last clip is a great way to end it. You may also want to use fading transitions in the middle of a movie between scenes.

To add a fade-in transition to the beginning of a movie, follow these steps:

1. **Select the first clip in the timeline viewer (or clip viewer).**
2. **Click the Trans button.**

   The clips pane switches to the transitions pane.
3. **Select the Fade In transition.**

   iMovie shows a preview in the small window, using the first clip as the transition's ending, so that the movie starts with a fade from black into the first frame of video.
4. **Adjust the duration of the transition with the Speed slider.**

   The Speed slider provides up to 4 seconds (04:00) of transition time. You can continue to make adjustments and preview them until you have the duration you want. If you specify a duration longer than the first clip, iMovie tells you that the clip is too short — you can specify a shorter duration for the transition, or slow down the first clip to make it longer.
5. **Drag the Fade In transition to the beginning of the movie.**

   You can use either the timeline viewer or the clip viewer. Drag the transition.
6. **Play the movie with the transition.**

   To see the transition in action after it finishes rendering, you can start the movie from the beginning, or drag the timeline viewer's playback head.

To add a Fade Out transition, follow the same steps, except that you select the last clip in the movie, and drag the Fade Out transition to the very end of the last clip.

Here are some suggestions for using various transitions:

- **Circle Closing:** Introduces the second clip by shrinking the first clip's ending in a circle that closes into nothing, leaving the second clip. This works best if the first clip's subject is in the center of the picture. Also known as *iris close* among video editors.

- **Circle Opening:** A neat reversal of the circle closing transition, a circle opens to reveal the second clip. This works best if the second clip's subject is in the center of the picture.
- **Cross Dissolve:** Fades the first clip seamlessly into the second clip with a superimposing effect. A short cross dissolve is very popular as a soft way of cutting from one scene to the next. Very short cross-dissolves often hide abrupt cuts in an interview in which a person is talking. The most popular transition, also known as the *crossfade*.
- **Fade In:** Fades in to the first clip from total blackness. This is most appropriate at the beginning of a movie. You may want to use a Fade In after a black clip. Find out how to add a black clip in the appropriately titled "Adding a black clip" section, later in this chapter.
- **Fade Out:** Fades out from the last clip into total blackness. This is most appropriate at the end of a movie. You may want to use a Fade Out before a black clip that you need at the very end of a movie. Skip ahead to the "Adding a black clip" section, later in this chapter for more info about black clips.
- **Overlap:** Freezes the last frame of the first clip while the new clip fades in superimposed over it. This is useful when the first clip is short and you want to draw more attention to the second clip. Similar to the Cross Dissolve transition.
- **Push:** One of the few transitions that you use to change the direction, the Push transition literally shoves the end of the first clip off the edge of the picture to play the second clip. With the direction buttons you can pick which side to push from. Rarely used professionally, this transition simulates the changing of a slide in an old-fashioned slide projector.
- **Radial:** Uses a sweeping clockwise wipe around the end of the first clip to reveal the second clip. Radial is sometimes used to indicate the passage of time because it reminds you of a clock.
- **Scale Down:** In this transition, the first clip gets smaller and smaller and disappears into the second clip. You may have seen this transition in documentaries and news programs — the first clip shrinks into the upper left part of the picture, not into the center. See this transition in Figure 4-7.
- **Warp Out:** In this transition, the second clip intrudes from the center, pushing the first clip's image out to the edges. The effect makes the first clip's ending scene look like it's opening up into the second clip. See Figure 4-6 for an example of the Warp Out transition.
- **Wash In:** Fades in to the second clip from total whiteness, in effect similar to the Fade In transition but from white rather than black. Because

the absence of an image is a black picture, you'll likely only use this to transition from a whitened-out scene, or from a Wash Out transition that washed the previous scene into white. You can use a Brightness & Contrast effect with a clip to gradually brighten it into nearly pure white. See Chapter 3 of this book for more on effects.

- **Wash Out:** Fades out from the second clip into total whiteness, in effect similar to the Fade Out transition but fades to white rather than black. Because the absence of an image is a black picture, you'll likely only use this to transition to a whitened-out scene, or to a Wash In transition that then washes the next scene in from white.

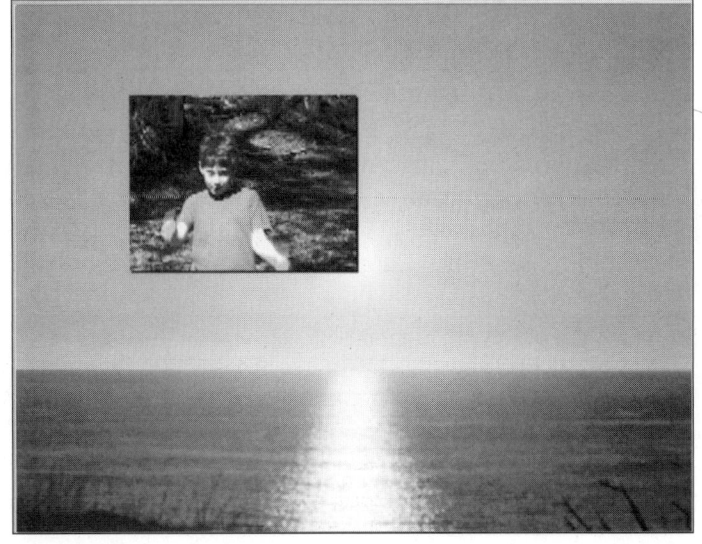

Figure 4-7: The Scale Down transition shrinks the first clip into the second clip.

Editing the Soundtrack

Editing the sound is as important, if not more important, than editing the picture. Viewers usually barely notice flaws in a moving picture compared to flaws in the sound, which linger in the mind and can be irritating. (For example, a scratchy newsreel is fine to watch as long as the sound isn't scratchy.)

If you add transitions, change the speed of any video clips, or perform a lot of clip trimming and cropping, chances are you have to edit the sound as well. Fortunately iMovie makes this as easy as editing video clips.

Controlling volume levels

By far the most common editing technique to do away with unwanted audio is to lower the volume. You can lower the volume of the sound on a clip-by-clip basis, and control the volume within each video clip.

To control the volume of the sound in a video clip, follow these steps:

1. **Click the video clip in the timeline viewer.**
2. **Click the Edit Volume check box at the bottom center of the timeline viewer.**

   The Edit Volume option should have a check mark next to it, as shown in Figure 4-8. A purple volume level bar appears across the middle of the clip.
3. **Drag the volume slider next to the Edit Volume option.**

   Drag the volume slider to the right for louder volume, or to the left for lower volume — or all the way to the left to mute the volume. As you drag this slider, the purple volume level bar rises or falls to reflect the volume level.

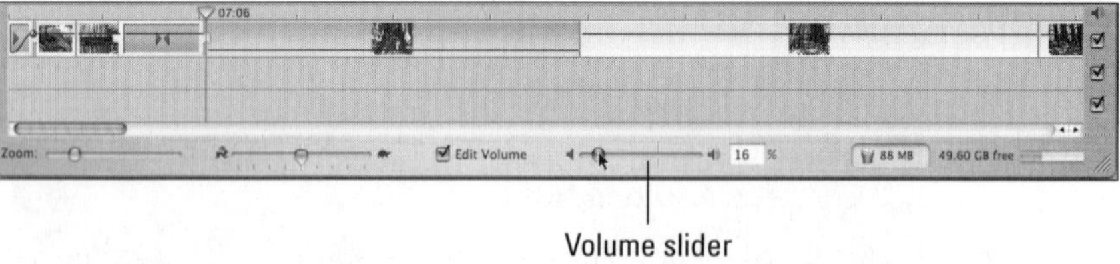

Figure 4-8: Change the volume of a video clip.

The volume changes, and you can lower it so that no one can hear it.

What if you want to lower only a portion of the sound in a video clip? For example, perhaps you want to fade the sound in at the beginning. To fade the sound from mute up to full volume at the beginning of a clip, follow these steps:

1. **Select the video clip in the timeline viewer, and click the Edit Volume check box.**
2. **Click a point in the volume level bar in the clip, and drag the marker that appears up for louder or down for softer.**

   The purple volume level bar allows you to adjust the volume directly.

You can select multiple video clips and adjust the volume all at once. To adjust the volume in multiple clips, click the first clip, and Shift-click the last clip, in the timeline viewer. Then, with the Edit Volume option selected, drag the volume slider next to the Edit Volume option.

Importing music from iTunes

Music can make your movies a lot more exciting and establish a mood. Imagine the opening scenes of *Apocalypse Now!* without the eerie music of the Doors and Jim Morrison singing "This is the end. . . " — it just wouldn't be the same.

You may want to synchronize actions in your video clips to musical moments or time videos to play at a certain rhythm with the beat supplied by a separate music track. iMovie helps you create music videos as well as videos with music, because you can edit videos to the music — using techniques such as slowing down and speeding up the video clips, using transitions, cropping and trimming clips, and so on. The music track can form the basis of the video.

iMovie gives you two tracks for adding extra sounds. However, you can overlay sounds in a single track, and iMovie automatically mixes all of the sound for playback, so the possibilities are endless.

To add music from your iTunes library to your movie, follow these steps:

1. **Click the clock icon to switch to the timeline viewer.**
2. **Click the Audio button.**

   The audio pane, shown in Figure 4-9, automatically opens your iTunes music library with a pop-up menu for selecting a playlist.
3. **Select a song.**

   To select a song, you can do one of the following:

   - Choose the iTunes library from the pop-up menu (if not already selected), and click a song (or scroll the song list if the song you want is not visible).
   - Choose a playlist from the pop-up menu and click a song in the playlist.
   - Sort by artist first, and then scroll down to find the song you want, and click it. The list of songs is initially sorted alphabetically by song, but you can sort the list by artist.

- Type a word or even just part of a word, as shown in Figure 4-10, into the text box below the song list. The songs with those characters anywhere in the title show up immediately as you type.

You can import songs directly from an audio CD into iMovie. Insert the audio CD, and after it loads into the Mac system, you can use the pop-up menu at the top of the audio pane to access it. Choose the CD from the pop-up menu, and then select the track.

4. **Drag the song to the timeline viewer, or click the Place at Playhead button.**

   The two lower tracks in the timeline viewer, as shown in Figure 4-11, are reserved for audio tracks. If you already moved the playback head to the exact spot where you want the music to begin, clicking the Place at Playhead button is easiest. The song becomes an audio clip in the audio track.

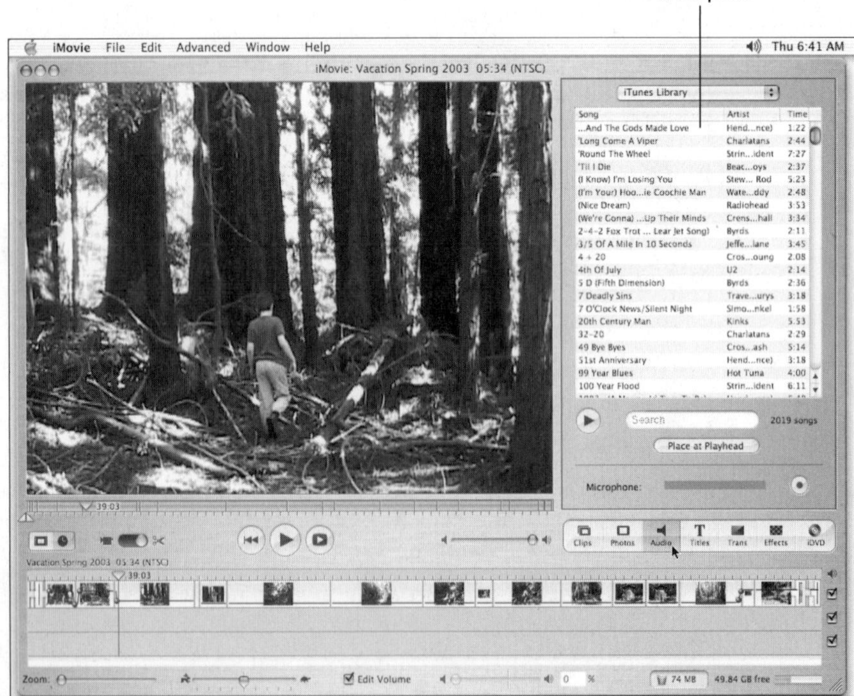

Figure 4-9: Select a tune from the iTunes library.

Figure 4-10: Type a few letters of the song's title to find a particular song.

Figure 4-11: Drag the song to the timeline viewer's lower audio track.

Whenever you select more than one clip in the timeline viewer, iMovie displays the total duration, which is helpful information if you want to measure the amount of time you have for the music, before importing the music. iMovie gives you control over how much of the song to play, and the volume level at different points in the song, but you can also prepare the movie for a full song by first noting how much time it takes, and preparing the movie for it. iMovie displays the total duration of the selected clips in the Video Selection note above the timeline and you can match the music to the length of the time frame.

Adjusting the audio track

The timeline viewer's audio tracks work the same way as the video clip track. You can drag horizontally to adjust the position of the audio track relative to the video. You can even adjust the volume of the audio track the same way. To change the volume of the music track, follow these steps:

1. **Select the song's clip in the audio track of the timeline viewer.**
2. **Click the Edit Volume check box.**

   A purple volume level bar appears across the middle of the audio track.
3. **Drag the volume slider next to the Edit Volume option.**

   Drag the volume slider to the right for louder volume, or to the left for lower volume. As you drag this slider, the purple volume level bar rises or falls to reflect the volume level.

Controlling volume

You can directly manipulate the volume level bar in the audio clip to control the sound volume at different places in the music. Follow these steps:

1. **Select the song's clip in the audio track and click the Edit Volume check box.**

   A purple volume level bar appears across the middle of the audio track.
2. **Click a point in the volume level bar in the clip, and drag the marker that appears up for louder or down for softer.**

Cropping audio clips

When the music is too long to fit the video clip sequence you need it for, and you don't want to extend the movie with blank space just because the music is that long (even if the music is muted, it's still there), you can crop the end of the music track to end at the proper place. You can also crop the beginning of the audio track to remove sound and start the track exactly where you want it to start.

To crop the beginning or end of a long music track, follow these steps:

1. **Select the sound clip in the audio track of the timeline viewer.**

   The sound clip has a triangular crop handle on either end, as shown in Figure 4-12.

2. **Drag the beginning or ending crop handle.**

   The crop handles cut off the beginning and ending, defining the enclosed portion as the sound you want to keep. You can also click a handle and use left or right arrow keys to move the handle one frame at a time in either direction. Using the crop handles, you can crop the music temporarily, without deleting the rest of the music — in case you want to use the rest of the music elsewhere, or you intend to edit the sequence to increase its duration and you may need to change the cropping.

3. **Optional: Choose Edit⇨Crop to delete the cropped-out portion of the clip.**

   This is an optional final step that you should not perform unless you are sure that you don't need the cropped-out music in your project. However, if you plan on extending the movie, perhaps with credits or other scenes, you may want to keep the music track available. The crop handles control what plays, so this is a drastic measure unless you really need to trim the disk space used by the movie project.

Figure 4-12: Crop a long audio clip to shorten it.

Splitting audio clips

Sometimes splitting an audio clip into two clips is useful. For example, you may want to use part of a song at the beginning of a movie, and another part at the end.

To split an audio clip into two clips, select the clip in the audio track of the timeline viewer and follow these steps:

1. **Move the playback head to the place in the clip where you want the split.**

2. **Choose Edit⇨Split Selected Audio Clip at Playhead.**

After splitting the audio clip, iMovie saves the second clip with the same name, but with "/1" appended to it. You can rename the clip if you want. You can also drag either audio clip somewhere else in the movie.

Separating audio from video

You can separate the audio portion of a video clip and use the audio as a separate clip — to use elsewhere if you want, or to preserve it in its entirety while you cut the video clip.

The audio is actually copied from the video clip — the video clip does not lose it. However, in the video clip, the audio volume is automatically muted.

You don't have to rejoin the audio to the video clip if you decide later that you want to use it. Because the audio is never deleted (only muted), you can bring it back by resetting the volume of the video clip.

To separate the audio from the video:

1. **Select a video clip in the timeline viewer.**
2. **Choose Advanced⇨Extract Audio.**

   The new audio clip appears as a separate clip in the top audio track of the timeline viewer.

While you may not think you need this feature, extracting the audio portion of a video clip offers a few new opportunities to experiment. For example, you can copy the audio clip, and position the copy to form an echo of the original audio clip. Select the audio clip in the timeline viewer, choose Edit⇨Copy to copy the clip and Edit⇨Paste. Then drag the new clip into position.

Adding sound effects

Sound effects can trigger excitement, surprise, and sometimes even humor. iMovie offers a long list of sound effects, ranging from the sounds of birds to the sound of a xylophone (our favorite is Suspense). Adding a sound effect is simplicity itself — follow these steps:

1. **Show the timeline viewer by clicking the clock icon.**
2. **Click the Audio button.**

   The audio pane automatically opens your iTunes music library, as shown in Figure 4-13.
3. **Choose the iMovie Sound Effects option from the pop-up menu.**

The sound effects appear. You can scroll the list of effects for the one you want — iMovie displays the duration for each effect.

4. **Select a sound effect and drag it to the timeline.**

You can control the volume of a sound effect clip just like any other audio clip, as shown in Figure 4-14, in which we fade the volume down at the end of the Jungle clip. You can also drag the triangular crop handles to define only a portion of the sound effect — especially for sound effects that are long, such as the Jungle effect.

You can insert as many sound effects as you like, or even use the same effect over and over — no rule says you can't annoy people (except the rule of good taste). You can achieve interesting effects by combining sounds effects. Simply drag them to the timeline and overlap the existing sound effect to combine effects.

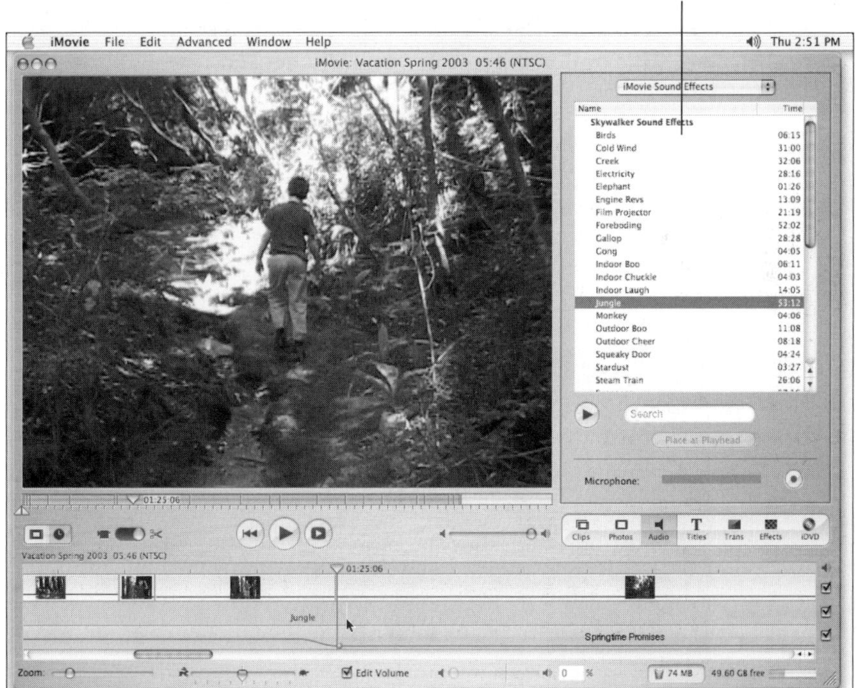

Figure 4-13: Select a sound effect to add to your movie.

Laying video over sound

Suppose that a video clip has a sound track that you want to use, but you want to paste some new, perhaps shorter, video clip (such as a still image jazzed up with a Ken Burns Effect, as described in Chapter 3 of this book) over a section of the first video clip without pasting over the sound.

You'll also want to overlay sound over video when you have a video clip of someone talking, but you want to replace portions of just the video image to show something else while the subject continues talking. In such cases, you replace the old video with the new video, but keep the old video's sound.

To paste a video clip over a portion of another video clip *without* replacing the audio, follow these steps:

1. **Choose iMovie⇨Preferences.**

   The iMovie Preferences window appears, as shown in Figure 4-15.

2. **Select the Extract Audio in Paste Over option and close the Preferences window.**

   This option is typically already checked.

Figure 4-14: Adjust the volume for a sound effect.

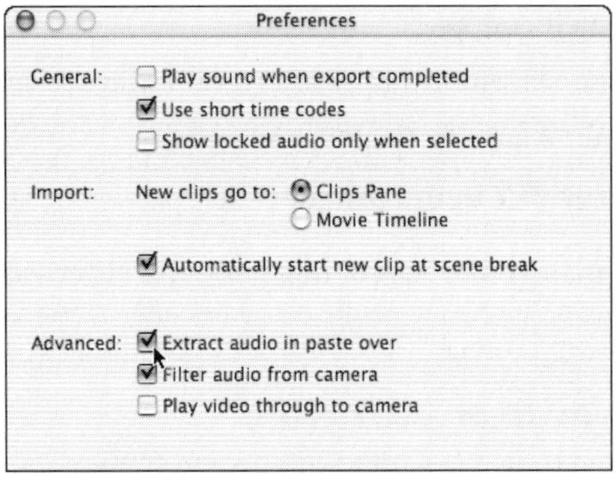

Figure 4-15: Paste a video over another video while retaining the other video's sound.

3. **Select the video clip or portion of a video clip**

   If you crop the video clip before copying, only the cropped video is copied. You can also select a portion of a video clip by dragging the crop markers in the iMovie monitor, as described in Chapter 3 of this book.

4. **Choose Edit⇨Copy to copy the selected video.**

   This is a new video clip, ready to be pasted onto a section of the first video clip.

5. **Drag the playback head to the first frame of the first movie.**

   The new video clip will replace this section.

6. **Optional: Drag crop markers to define the portion of the video you want replaced.**

7. **Choose Edit⇨Paste to paste the copied video.**

   The second video clip replaces only the defined portion of the first video clip (if the second video clip is longer, the excess video is not pasted; if shorter, iMovie fills the rest with a black clip). Otherwise the second video clip replaces the first video clip from the first frame forward until the end of the video.

The new video overlays the older video, but the older video's soundtrack is still heard.

On the other hand, suppose you have a new video clip that you want to use to replace a section of an older clip, and you want to use the new clip's sound as well. To paste a video clip over a portion of another video clip, replacing the audio as well, follow these steps:

1. **Choose iMovie⇨Preferences.**

   The iMovie Preferences window appears (refer to Figure 4-15).

2. **Unselect the Extract Audio in Paste Over option.**

3. **Follow Steps 3 through 7 in the previous list.**

The new video overlays the older video, replacing the older video's soundtrack.

Adding a voice-over or narration

One capability of iMovie that you won't find in even high-priced digital editing systems is the ability to record a voice-over or narration while you watch your movie. With this feature, adding narration is a snap — such as a storyteller or someone explaining the images in a documentary, or a voice-over, such as the voices you hear on commercials, announcers before shows, or even sportscasters. You can even record an optional extra voice-over track when played back on DVD. The possibilities are endless.

Every Mac has the built-in capability to record sound. Some Mac models offer built-in microphones, such as PowerBooks and iBooks and some iMac models. Some models allow you to connect an external microphone to a mini-plug jack, and you can connect a USB microphone to all Macs. Before recording sound directly into your Mac, you must first set the sound input in the Sound Preferences: Choose ⇨System Preferences, and click the Input tab, and then choose the type of microphone or input.

To record a voice-over or narration, follow these steps:

1. **Move the playback head to the position in the timeline viewer (or clip viewer) where you want the recorded audio to begin.**

   iMovie inserts the audio clip into the timeline or clip viewer at the position of the playback head.

2. **Click the Audio button.**

   The audio pane appears.

3. **Click the red record button and speak into the microphone (or make the sound you want to record).**

   The Record button is next to the input meter, as shown in Figure 4-16. While you speak, the input meter should be yellow — if it turns red, you're speaking too loudly or you are too close to the microphone. As you record, the movie also starts playing from the playback head, so you can watch the movie while recording the voice-over or sound.

4. **Click the red record button again to stop recording.**

The audio clip of the voice appears in the top audio track in the timeline viewer at the location of the playback head.

You can drag the clip to any position just like any other audio clip, and control its volume or crop it just like any other audio clip.

Figure 4-16: Record sound directly into an iMovie soundtrack.

Locking audio to video

If you have either music or a sound effect that must play at a certain frame of the video, you can lock the audio clip to that video clip.

Locking audio to video is especially useful if you done a lot of editing of sound to video, and you discover that you need to shorten or lengthen a video clip or add another clip. If you go ahead and edit the video clips without locking the audio, the audio clips will most likely be out of synchronization with the video. You would then have to drag all the audio clips back to the positions you want for them to be synchronized. A tedious job — and you're likely to forget something or drag something too far.

To lock an audio clip to a video clip:

1. **Move the playback head to where you want to lock the audio to the video.**
2. **Choose Advanced⇨Lock Audio Clip at Playhead.**

   Yellow pushpins appear to indicate that the audio clip is locked to the video.

Locking an audio clip freezes its position with regard to the video clip, so that if the video clip moves in any way on the timeline, the audio clip moves with it. Nothing you do to *other* video clips — including inserting, deleting, cropping, trimming, or changing their speed — changes the synchronized audio and video.

You can always unlock the audio clip by simply dragging it. But while the audio is locked to the video clip, if the video clip moves, the audio clip moves with it, so that they stay in sync.

Adding Post-Production Elements

Most movies start with a title and credits before the opening scene. It's not usual to see a movie start immediately with the opening scene, without some kind of title or credits at least appearing at some point. So why shouldn't your movies look professional? iMovie gives you lots of choices for titles and credits.

That may not be all that you need for your movie. If you're going to copy the movie to videotape or supply it to a television station, you need to add a blank section — a *black clip* — to the beginning of the movie. You may also want to add a black clip to the end. All these elements are typically created at the end of a project, in *post-production* phase or simply *post.* (So the next time someone asks you if your movie is ready to show, tell them it's still in post-production. They'll be impressed.)

Creating titles and credits

All movies should have titles. Even "Untitled" is a good title. This is your chance to be witty, even if it's a vacation video.

As for credits, who wouldn't want to take credit for a masterpiece? And if you don't want credit, you can resist making up names for all those strange job titles, such as gaffer, key grip, and associate executive producer.

iMovie simplifies the making of titles and credits. Everything is called a title in the titles pane. You can type whatever you want, including real titles and credits, and iMovie spins an interesting effect for you.

The title and credits can appear superimposed over the video, or against a plain black background — both look professional. If the goal is to make people read the text, using a black background is better because the text stands out and the viewer is not distracted by the video.

iMovie creates a clip in the timeline viewer to represent the title or credits section. To create a title or credit clip, follow these steps.

1. **In the timeline viewer, click the Titles button.**

   The titles pane appears, providing a list of effects, from Bounce Across to Zoom Multiple, with Speed and Pause controls, a font pop-up menu and character size slider, and boxes for typing text, as shown in Figure 4-17.

2. **Choose a title effect and type your text in the lower boxes.**

   The title effect you choose appears against a black clip in the small preview window. Experiment with different effects before choosing one.

3. **Set the Speed and Pause settings.**

   The Speed slider allows you to set the speed of the title effect, which is actually the speed of the animation. The Pause slider allows you to set the pause in the title effect, which is how long the title remains completely 100 percent visible and readable. The total duration of the title effect is the sum of these settings. iMovie conveniently sums these for you at the bottom of the small preview screen.

4. **Choose a font and set the size for the text.**

   The font pop-up menu allows you to select any font in your system, and you can make the characters larger or smaller with the size slider to the right of the pop-up menu.

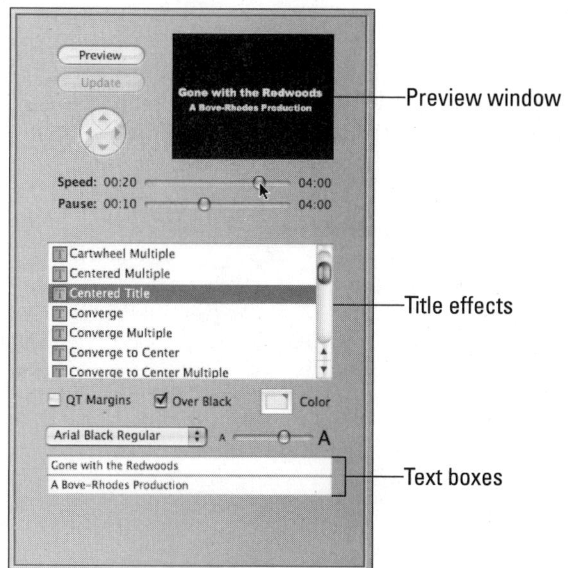

Figure 4-17: Type a movie title and preview the effect.

5. **Optional: Click the Color button (if you want a color other than black).**

   The Color window appears, as shown in Figure 4-18. You can select a color from the color wheel, or try the other color models, such as the spectrum or the crayons — available as buttons at the top of the Color window.

6. **Adjust the direction of the animation.**

   The arrow buttons to the left of the small preview window in the titles pane are grayed-out if not applicable, but with some title effects you can click these arrows to set the direction you want the animation to start from. For example, the Scroll with Pause title effect allows you to scroll the title from any of the four directions — bottom, top, left, or right.

7. **Select the Over Black check box.**

   iMovie creates a black clip with the title effect, adding seconds to your movie. If you leave this option unchecked, iMovie superimposes the title over video.

   For example, in Figure 4-19, we typed the title "THE END," chose the Centered Title effect, and unselected the Over Black option.

Be sure any separate audio clips are locked to video before adding a title effect over black. When iMovie adds a black clip, the additional seconds throw your audio clips out of sync with the video. We describe how to lock audio to video in the section, "Locking audio to video," earlier in this chapter.

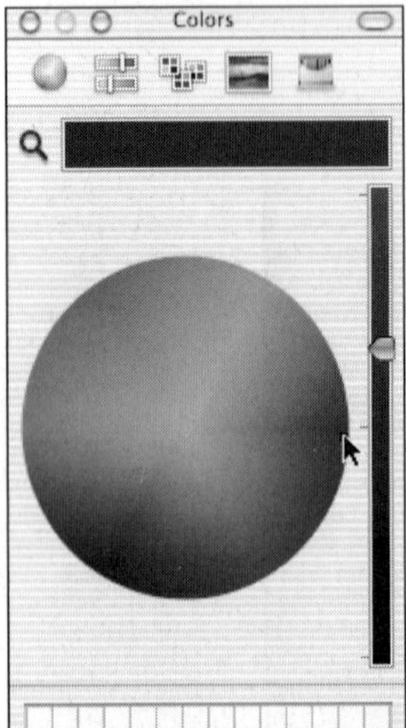

Figure 4-18: Change the color of the text in the title.

8. **Drag the title effect's name from the list to the timeline.**

   You may want to zoom into the timeline viewer to see the clips better, especially if you want to insert the title effect at the very beginning. The title appears in the viewer pane, as shown in Figure 4-20.

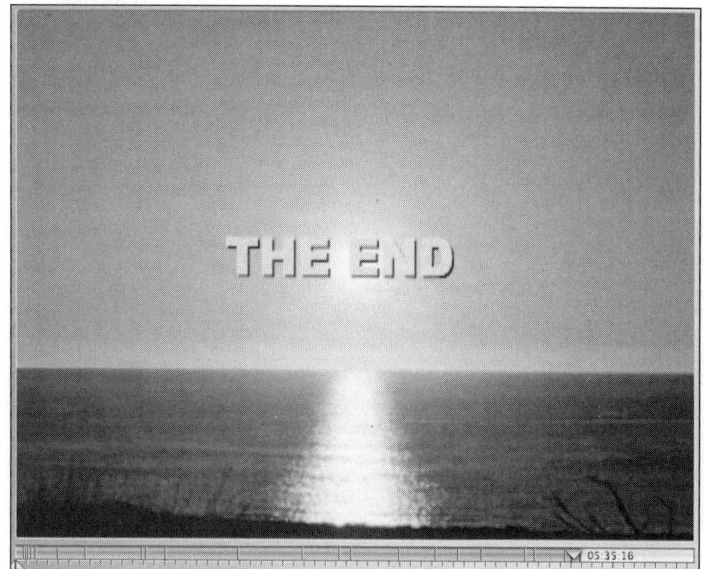

Figure 4-19: The title is superimposed over the video.

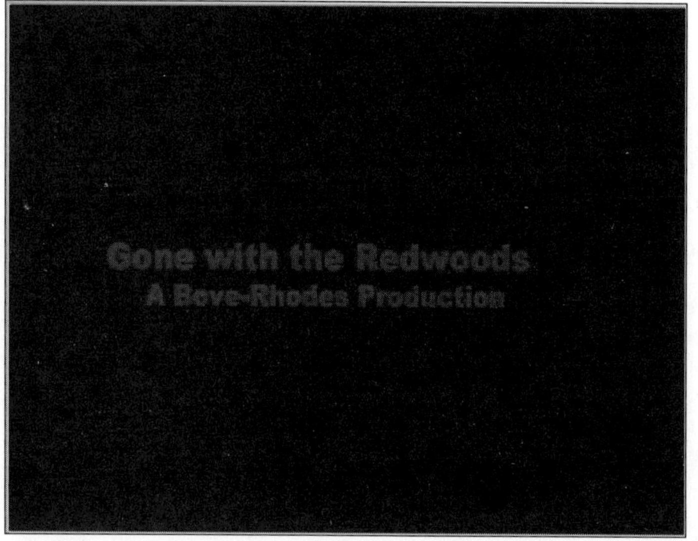

Figure 4-20: The title appears at the beginning of the movie.

Some title effects are set up for rolling or scrolling credits that you typically see at the end of a movie. These effects allow you to type many lines of text rather than one or two lines.

For example, the Rolling Credits effect, shown in Figure 4-21, offers the ability to add multiple lines of text. The effect displays two text boxes for each credit line. All you have to do is click the + button to add another pair of text boxes to create another credit line.

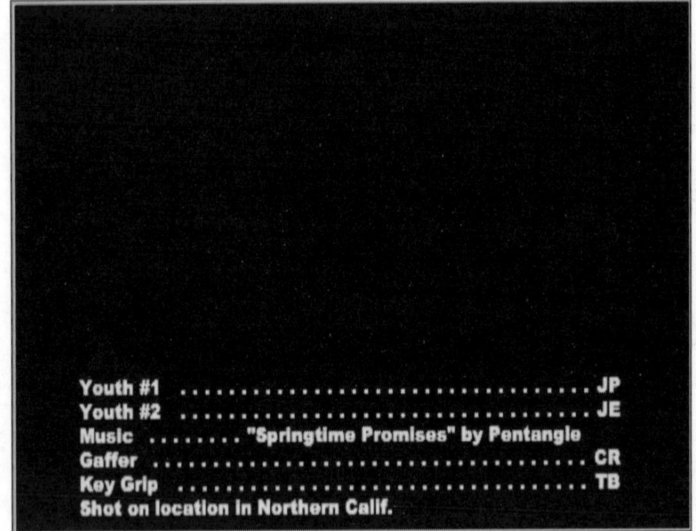

Youth #1 .... JP
Youth #2 .... JE
Music .... "Springtime Promises" by Pentangle
Gaffer .... CR
Key Grip .... TB
Shot on location in Northern Calif.

Figure 4-21: Add credit lines to your movie.

If you plan to export your movie in the QuickTime format only, at a smaller picture size, you can turn on the QT Margins option to increase the space in the picture to place titles. This increase in space means that iMovie can offer larger font sizes and wider lines of text. You want to use the largest font size available — when the picture shrinks to a smaller size useful for playing from Web sites, viewers can still read the text. However, this is *not* good for video played on normal televisions.

Leave the QT Margins option turned off if you want to play your movie on different types of devices, including normal televisions. The QT Margins option widens the margins for title effects, but televisions cut off the edges of the picture, as we describe in the "Staying inside the safe area" sidebar and your titles may have their edges cut off.

Staying inside the safe area

The picture size is also important when developing a movie for television. You need to keep the best part of your video away from the edges of the picture. Most people still have televisions that *overscan* the screen — the cathode-ray guns overshoot the margins of the screen to make sure that the screen is "painted" edge-to-edge. As a result, you lose about 10 percent of the picture on each edge (sometimes less on top and bottom, depending on the TV). If you place something on the very edge of the picture, such as the beginning of a title, it may get cut off when viewed on a television. Television producers work around this limitation by defining the *TV-safe area* where all the action takes place. The safe area is, essentially, inside the edges of the picture, leaving at least a 10 percent margin around all sides.

Adding a black clip

You may have already done this by accident — we certainly did, a number of times. If you drag a video clip away from another clip, you end up with a gap in the video between the two clips, which is all black (the absence of color).

Known as a black clip, these gaps can be useful in a number of ways:

- **Separate one video segment from another:** If you want to show two different short movies, but keep them together in one digital video file, you can separate them with a black clip.
- **Create a tape lead-in:** If you need to provide enough blank video so that older VCRs can get up to speed before playing the movie, create a black clip at the beginning of your movie.
- **Create longer transitions between scenes with black clips:** You can use precisely timed black clips to serve as transitions, especially between a Fade Out transition and a Fade In transition.
- **Add comic relief at the end of a movie:** You see movies that have comic outtakes playing behind the credits or at the very end, separated first by a black clip. Black clips are also effective transitions between the outtakes.

If you plan to send your video on tape or in digital format to a television station or production house, you need to leave more than 60 seconds of black clip at the beginning, so that they can add color bars and other images before the start of your movie. You may want to do this by exporting the movie to DV tape, and start the recording with one minute of blank tape, which is another way of adding a black clip, but without making it a part of your movie file.

To create a black clip, simply drag a video clip to the right on the timeline, creating a gap. iMovie turns that gap into a black clip. Switch to the clip viewer to see it, as shown in Figure 4-22.

Creating chapter markers for DVD

If you plan to create a DVD of your movie, you can create chapter markers in advance, so that viewers can jump directly to their favorite scenes. When you use the movie with iDVD, the DVD-authoring portion of iLife, your chapter markers are automatically assigned to the DVD menu of scenes in the movie.

Follow these steps for each chapter marker you want to add:

1. **Select a clip in the timeline viewer, and if necessary, also move the playback head to the beginning of the clip.**

   When you select a clip in the clip viewer, and then switch to the timeline viewer, the playback head is already at the beginning of the clip you selected.

2. **Click the iDVD button.**

   The iDVD pane opens.

3. **Click the Add Chapter button and type a chapter title.**

   Type the chapter title next to the thumbnail that appears in the iDVD pane. The chapter markers appear in the timeline viewer as diamonds.

4. **Move the playback head to a new position and repeat Step 3.**

   You can continue to move the playback head and add chapter markers with the iDVD pane open, as shown in Figure 4-23.

After you create these chapter markers, you can use them to jump around the movie and start playing from any chapter.

With post-production finishes, you are ready to share your movie with others. We describe a variety of ways to share your movies in the next chapter.

Figure 4-22: Create a black clip.

Figure 4-23: Create multiple chapter titles in the iDVD pane.

Chapter 5: Viewing and Sharing Movies

In This Chapter

- Switching to full-screen playback
- Exporting to QuickTime
- Exporting to a camcorder
- Copying a movie
- Publishing with HomePage

Finally, a distribution deal! Call your agent! Suddenly everyone wants to see your movie.

And you are in a great position to distribute that movie. The movies you make with iMovie can be played full-screen on any computer or TV set. Read that sentence again. *Any* computer or TV set.

You can play your movies even in the wilderness villages on the Burma-Thailand border, where we hear television sets with VCRs are powered by battery. You can play them in campers, boats, recreational vehicles, airplanes, and even submarines. Wherever there's a VCR, or better yet, a DVD player, you can play your movies.

Computer users have even more choices: They can view DVDs, download videos from the Internet, or watch a video streaming from a Web site. They can even receive small movies by e-mail. This chapter shows how to make your movies available to just about anyone with a hankering to watch it.

Playing Your Movie in Full-Screen Playback

Murphy's Law states that if something can go wrong, it will go wrong. Although iMovie doesn't play your movie in full-screen mode in the best possible quality, playing back your movie in full-screen mode during the editing and post-production process and before you copy it to any other medium is useful. That way if you need to make any changes at the last minute, you can make them before wasting any time with exporting and copying.

To play a movie in full-screen mode, click the enclosed Play button next to the larger Play button in the iMovie monitor. The movie starts playing from the position of the playback head. Click the Rewind button first to start at the beginning of the movie. If you select a clip first, only that clip plays. To deselect all clips, choose Edit⇨Select None, and then click the Play full-screen button.

To interrupt the movie in full-screen mode, click your mouse or press any key on your keyboard.

In full-screen mode the quality of the picture is not as crisp as it appears in the camcorder's viewer, the computer's monitor with the QuickTime Player, or television monitors. To see the best quality on your computer screen, export the movie in the QuickTime format, as described in the section, "Exporting to QuickTime," in this chapter. To copy your movie to a DV camcorder or videotape, see the section, "Exporting to a Camera," in this chapter.

Exporting Your Movie

You can play your movie in iMovie, but you need to export the movie into some format for others to use. iMovie can export movies to QuickTime files, to your camcorder, or to iDVD. Follow these steps:

1. **Choose File⇨Export.**

   The Export window appears as shown in Figure 5-1.

2. **Choose the appropriate option from the Export pop-up menu.**

   To Camera: Export to your DV camcorder's digital videocassette for archive or use with other projects. See the section, "Exporting to a Camera," later in this chapter.

   To QuickTime: QuickTime files play on almost any computer (and certainly every Mac). See the "Exporting to QuickTime" section, later in this chapter.

   To iDVD: Export the movie to iDVD to create a DVD that plays with any DVD player. See the section, "Exporting to iDVD," later in this chapter.

   The Format menu appears.

3. **Choose the appropriate format from the Format pop-up menu.**

4. **Click the Export button, and choose a destination folder for the movie if you are exporting a QuickTime movie.**

Figure 5-1: Exporting your movie.

Exporting to QuickTime

QuickTime is your friend and ally when it comes to video distribution. Like a Hollywood agent that can get you any deal you want, QuickTime provides the settings you need to export your movie into a format that you can widely distribute.

QuickTime provides the key to Internet distribution, which opens your audience to millions of potential viewers. You can distribute QuickTime files by e-mail, publish them on Web pages in downloadable form, or in a streaming format.

QuickTime is a digital video file format that offers many choices for quality, compression, picture size, and playback format. Saving a high-quality QuickTime version of the movie as a backup and for playing on your computer is a good idea.

You can play the movie by double-clicking the file — your QuickTime player automatically starts up and provides controls for playing the movie, as shown in Figure 5-2.

The QuickTime file also takes up *a lot* of disk space in this format, because no compression is involved. You may want to copy the resulting QuickTime file to another hard disk, removable hard disk, or backup device (such as CD or cartridge). To give you an idea of how large the file can get, we saved a movie that is 6:11 (six minutes and 11 seconds) and the file size is 1.24GB.

Figure 5-2: Playing the QuickTime movie with the QuickTime Player.

QuickTime files for e-mail

QuickTime, which shrinks the movie down with video and audio compression, reduces the picture size as well, to create a file you can attach to an e-mail.

To export a movie you want to distribute by e-mail, choose the E-mail option from the Export pop-up menu in the Export window.

Check the size of your movie before e-mailing it. Movie files are large and e-mail is not meant for large files. The Internet Service Provider (ISP) that provides your e-mail server may have limitations on the size of e-mails — ours has a limit of about 4.5MB. Anything larger gets bounced back.

The e-mail format may create a blurry movie that is too small to have an impact. It may also create a movie file that's still too large to attach to an e-mail — our 6-minute video became a 14.7MB file. However, reducing the picture size or increasing the compression factors renders the movie even harder to watch. ***Remember:*** The return is not always worth the effort.

QuickTime files for the Web

Publishing a movie on the Internet is an exercise in compromise. While many people have high-speed connections to the Internet that make downloading a large file quickly possible, most people suffer with a lower-speed connection. You can create multiple versions of your movie for the different types of access.

You can save a QuickTime movie for the Web in three ways by choosing these options in the Export dialog box, which are suitable for Web distribution:

✦ **Web:** The standard Web setting creates a QuickTime movie that has, at 240 x 180 pixels, a slightly larger picture than the e-mail setting for QuickTime, but the larger size is much more viewable. Files are still quite large — our 6-minute movie came out to 32.3MG. Web viewers must download the entire movie before starting to play it.

✦ **Web Streaming:** Streaming video starts playing as soon as the Web viewer clicks the Play button, no matter how long the video is. The video streams into the computer from the Internet in short bursts, which is enough to start the movie playing while the computer receives more streaming data. The streaming format is the most useful QuickTime format for large-scale movies, because it provides instant gratification for the Web viewer. Otherwise, the Streaming Web setting is the same as the Web setting.

✦ **Expert Settings:** This option provides several windows of options for specifying picture size, frame rate, compression methods, and various quality settings for streaming and other features. In short, it gives you access to the entire menu of QuickTime settings. We don't have space in this book to provide in-depth coverage of the expert settings. Pick up a copy of *iMovie 2 For Dummies,* by Todd Stauffer (published by Wiley Publishing, Inc.).

See the section, "Publishing Movies on the Web," to find out what to do once you have the QuickTime files on your hard drive.

Exporting to a Camera

To copy your movie to DV tape, you need a digital video (DV) camcorder and a DV cassette (also called *mini-DV*) to store the digital video.

Camcorders not only record video in *camera mode;* they also play back the video recorded in *VTR* (video tape recorder) or *VCR mode.* In VTR/VCR mode the camcorder can record to its tape from an external source, which is what you do when you export your movie to the camcorder. Copying the movie to the camcorder and playing the movie takes the same amount of time.

Connect your camcorder to your Mac (see Chapter 1 of this book). Then from the Export window, follow these steps:

1. **Choose the To Camera option from the Export pop-up menu.**

   The Export window expands, as shown in Figure 5-3.

2. **Set at least 5 seconds for the camera to get ready, and add as many seconds of black as you like.**

   Most camcorders do not start recording instantly, but take a few seconds to get the tape rolling properly. In addition, you may want to add a few seconds of black to the beginning, so that viewers can settle down and be ready to watch the movie.

   If you plan on sending this DV tape to a professional video studio or tele-vision station, leave at least a minute of black before the video starts.

3. **Click the Export button.**

   iMovie controls the copying of the movie from your Mac to the DV camcorder. With most DV camcorders, you can watch the recording happen on the camcorder's display.

When copying completes, iMovie automatically stops the camcorder's recording operation. Your finished movie is now safely stored on DV cassette, and you can play it on your DV camcorder, which you can connect easily to a TV or to VCR.

iMovie: Export

Export: To Camera

Wait 5 seconds for camera to get ready.

Add 20 seconds of black before movie.

Add 13 seconds of black to end of movie.

Please make sure your camera is in VTR mode and has a writable tape in it.

Cancel Export

Figure 5-3: Export the movie to a DV camcorder's cassette.

After exporting to the DV camcorder, you can switch iMovie to camera mode by clicking the camera icon (moving the blue ball away from the scissors icon). You can then control the camcorder with the Rewind and Play buttons.

If you have trouble recording to your DV camcorder, check to see if your DV cassette is write-protected. Some PAL camcorders are set with FireWire input disabled — check the documentation that came with your camcorder.

Exporting Still Images

You may capture a rare shot of someone or something that you want to preserve as a still photo — for example, the last shot of someone looking at a sunset, or a winner at the finish line. You can then use the image as a photo or a graphic for a printed piece.

To export an image from your movie, follow these steps:

1. **Select the clip and position the playback head in the timeline viewer to show the image you want to save.**
2. **Choose File⇨Save Frame As, and choose a format from the Format menu.**

   iMovie gives you two choices for the file format: JPEG or PICT.

Use the JPEG format for images that you intend to use on Web pages or as attachments to e-mails. Use the PICT format for images you intend to use with other applications, such as Adobe Photoshop. You can import either type of image into iPhoto, as we describe in Book II, Chapter 2.

You may want to use a single image, or frame, of the movie as a *freeze frame* — the movie holds that image for dramatic effect or just to show the image longer than usual. iMovie takes the image in a single frame and creates a video clip with it. To save an image as a freeze frame video clip, follow these steps:

1. **Select the clip and position the playback head in the timeline viewer to show the image you want to save.**
2. **Choose Edit⇨Create Still Frame.**

   iMovie creates a video clip with the image with a default duration of 5 seconds.
3. **Choose File⇨Show Info.**

   The Clip Info window opens.
4. **Type a new duration in the Duration box.**

Copying Movies to VHS Tape

While you lose a lot of picture and sound quality when copying a movie to the type of VHS tape used in VCRs and nondigital camcorders, you also gain a much larger audience.

You need a DV camcorder to copy movies to a VCR — a DV camcorder acts like a digital-to-VHS converter, and is much cheaper and easier to use than converters used in the past. Follow these steps to copy the movie to a VCR:

1. **Copy the movie to a DV cassette in a DV camcorder**

   Copy the movie to your DV camcorder, which iMovie controls. See the "Exporting to a Camera" section, earlier in this chapter.

2. **Connect your video recorder (VCR) to your DV camcorder's video/audio output connectors.**

   A video recorder such as a VCR typically offers RCA-type connectors (one for video and two for audio), or an S-video connector for video along with two RCA-type audio connectors, for input to the VCR for recording onto tape. A DV camcorder typically offers either RCA-type or S-video or both, for output from the camcorder. Connect the input of the VCR to the output of the DV camcorder.

3. **Press the Record button on the video recorder (VCR), and press the Play button on the DV camcorder.**

That's all there is to it. The VCR records the movie from the DV camcorder, and you can go back to work on your Mac. Remember to press the Stop button on the VCR when the movie finishes copying.

If, on the other hand, you want to copy the movie directly to the VHS-format VCR without saving it to DV cassette first, you can use the DV camcorder to pass the video directly through to the VCR. Follow these steps:

1. **Connect your video recorder (VCR) to your DV camcorder's video/audio output connectors.**

2. **Choose iMovie⇨Preferences.**

   The iMovie Preferences window appears.

3. **Select the Video Play Through to Camera option and click OK.**

4. **Choose File⇨Export.**

   The Export window appears.

5. **Select the Camera option from the Export pop-up menu.**

6. **Switch the DV camcorder into VCR/VTR mode.**

   Do not insert a blank tape into your camcorder.

7. **Press the Record button on your VCR.**

8. **Click the Export button in the Export window.**

   iMovie plays the movie through the DV camcorder and records the movie to the VCR.

9. **Press the Stop button on the VCR when the movie finishes copying.**

The art of compression

If you want to dabble with the expert setting Export dialog box, you can choose how to compress your movie. We have the best success with the following choices for QuickTime exporting:

- **Web:** The standard Web setting in the Export dialog box does not offer streaming — the quality of playback is 12 frames per second, which offers smoother motion than 10, but not the highest quality (30). The sound is compressed by resampling at a sample rate of 22.05 kHz (16-bit sample size), which is good but not the best quality. We instead use the Web Streaming setting. MPEG-4 is the compressor most PCs can play, and you find that choice in the expert settings. For audio compression, we use Qdesign Music or uLaw 2:1, which are optimized for the QuickTime Streaming Server.
- **CD-ROM:** We recommend the CD-ROM choice in the Export dialog box.
- **DVD:** We export directly to iDVD. iDVD handles all DVD compression. If you can't afford a DVD-R to burn your DVDs, you can use any number of services that can do it for you, for a small fee.
- **Professional studios and services:** We provide the movie on DV cassette, or as a QuickTime DV file, or use the DV Stream export option, which produces a pure video file that we use with professional digital editing equipment and applications, such as Final Cut Pro.
- **Converting between PAL and NTSC:** You can use iMovie to capture video clips using either format, and then export the movie as a DV stream; you can then import the movie and copy it to either type of camcorder (PAL or NTSC). You can also export the movie as a QuickTime movie file with the DV-PAL or DVCPRO-PAL compression codec used in Europe.

If you want to find out more about compression and codecs when converting movies to QuickTime, pick up a copy of *iMovie 2 For Dummies,* by Todd Stauffer (published by Wiley Publishing, Inc.).

Exporting to iDVD

The newest way to save your movie is to burn a DVD, which can be shown with any type of DVD player. If you have an Apple-supported CD-RW or DVD-R drive (such as the Apple SuperDrive), you can create your own DVDs. You can transfer your entire movie directly from iMovie to iDVD in two steps:

1. **Click the iDVD button in iMovie.**

   The iDVD pane displays, as shown in Figure 5-4.

2. **Click the Create iDVD Project button.**

   iMovie automatically transfers your movie to iDVD, which opens immediately.

Creating DVDs is a much bigger topic than we can cover here — look for the iDVD story in Book IV.

Figure 5-4: Export the movie to iDVD.

Publishing Movies on the Web

To publish your QuickTime movie on the Web, you can use the HomePage feature of the .Mac service, or export your movie to the Site folder on your hard disk, where you can use Web publishing software to post it.

Apple offers the .Mac service for all Mac users, which provides an easy way to create and publish a Web page with your movies. With HomePage on the .Mac service, viewers can download your movie from your home Web page.

To use the .Mac service you must first have a .Mac account, which is simple to set up at www.apple.com — all you need is a credit card.

Follow these steps to publish your movie with the .Mac HomePage service:

1. **Log into .Mac, open your iDisk, and copy your movie to the Movies folder on iDisk.**
2. **Browse to the HomePage in your .Mac account.**

   The HomePage window appears, as shown in Figure 5-5, with any sites you already created. The HomePage editing page provides several choices for the movie page layout.

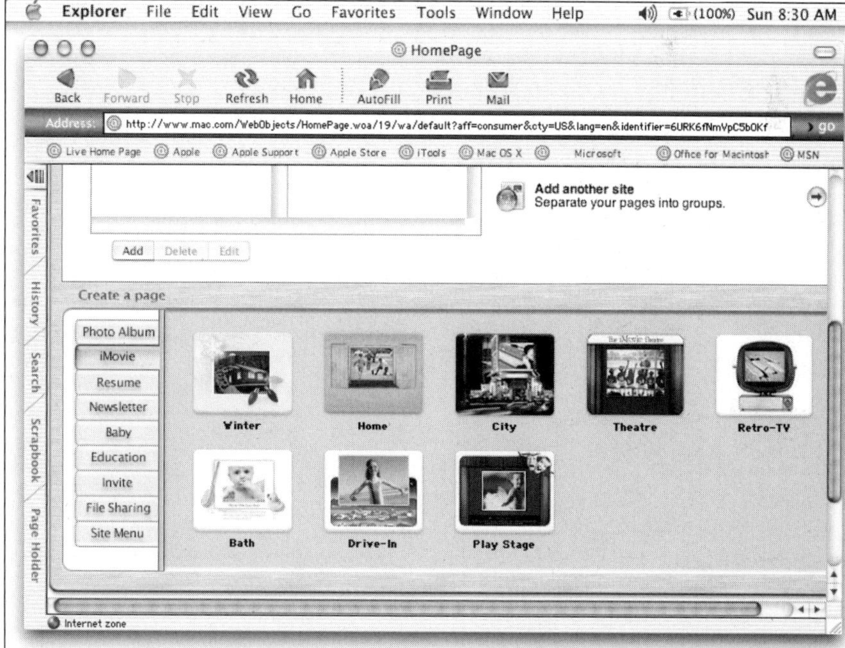

Figure 5-5: You can choose a layout for your Web movie page using the HomePage feature of the .Mac service.

3. **Edit the title and caption for the Web page.**

   Click inside the text area, select the text, and then type your own.

4. **Choose a QuickTime movie file from your iDisk.**

   Click the button in the layout you chose to select a QuickTime movie. Your iDisk appears; you can navigate to the Movies folder and select the movie file you copied in Step 1.

That's it. Your movie is now up on the Web, viewable by anyone, anywhere. All they need to do is find it, click it.

Book IV

iDVD

The 5th Wave
By Rich Tennant
©RICHTENNANT
ROOM 101
"I failed her in Algebra but was impressed with the way she animated her equations to dance across the screen, scream like hyenas and then dissolve into a clip art image of the La Brea Tar Pits."

Chapter 1: Instant iDVD Authoring

In This Chapter

- **Touring iDVD**
- **Importing movies from iMovie**
- **Importing QuickTime files**
- **Adding slideshows**

DVD is the medium of choice for movies, having replaced VHS in the last few years. DVD stands for *Digital Versatile Disc,* not digital videodisc (which is an older medium that has since bought the farm, along with the short-lived Betamax format for video, and music 8-track cartridges). The name reinforces the concept that DVD holds anything from video to music to photos and is a versatile medium to use — it is, in fact, the first consumer medium that allows the viewer to interact with the content by using menus to navigate the disc's movies, excerpts, photos, and multiple soundtracks.

DVD authoring is the process of assembling the contents of a DVD and designing the interface — the menus and buttons that allow you to navigate the contents. Authoring used to require expensive digital video and DVD mastering hardware and software and authoring expertise. But with iDVD and a SuperDrive-equipped Mac, you can easily create DVDs to distribute your own videos and presentations.

iDVD is an application that offers tools for creating DVD discs with menus and buttons to navigate the contents of the disc. It requires a Mac with an Apple SuperDrive, which is a DVD-R (recordable DVD) burner. Besides offering professionally designed menu themes with spectacular special effects, iDVD allows you to grab your photos from iPhoto, import your QuickTime movies from iMovie, and use music from iTunes. Like the page layout programs that ushered in the era of desktop publishing, iDVD is helping to launch the new era of desktop interactive video.

What You Can Do with iDVD

With iDVD you can put movies on DVD, of course. But you can add several features to the DVD beside a menu with a button to play a movie:

- Mark sections of your movie as chapters, as described in Book III, Chapter 4, so that viewers can jump to specific sections. Those chapter titles can be automatically turned into a scene menu to access the specific sections of the movie. See Chapter 2 of this book to add menus to your DVD.
- Add nifty movie menus animated with scenes from the movie. You can define up to 30 menus in one iDVD project, and define up to 6 buttons in a menu, linking to submenus, slideshows, or movies. See Chapter 2 of this book to add menus to your DVD.
- You can add photos to your movie as well, accompanied by music in a slideshow format. Each slideshow can contain up to 99 images, and a DVD can contain up to 99 slideshows or movies in any combination. Read the section, "Assembling Photo Slideshows," later in this chapter.

Saying that you can fit a lot of information on a DVD is an understatement, but video takes up a lot of disc space. You can fit up to 90 minutes of video on a DVD-R disc using iDVD, including all still images, backgrounds, and movies. However, if you put more than 60 minutes of video on a DVD-R disc, the picture quality may suffer because iDVD uses stronger compression with a slower bit rate to fit more than 60 minutes, and both factors reduce overall picture quality. The best approach is to limit each DVD-R to 60 minutes.

DVD is a mass-produced medium, like audio CDs. The discs are *read-only* — they can't be modified in any way; only viewed. To create even a mass-produced DVD, you have to burn a recordable DVD (DVD-R) with the content. The DVD-R serves as a master to mass-produce the type of DVDs you see in stores. With iDVD you can burn a DVD-R disc that you can then use in normal DVD players, and you can also use the DVD-R disc as a master to provide a service that mass-produces DVDs.

Follow these steps to make a DVD:

1. **Import all the content into iDVD.**

   iDVD allows you to import movies from iMovie projects, QuickTime movies, and iPhoto slideshows. This chapter describes the importing process — see "Importing Digital Video into iDVD" and "Assembling Photo Slideshows."

2. **Choose a theme for your DVD menus, buttons, and background.**

   iDVD is supplied with professional themes you can use to create your own menus and submenus. Themes provide a design that integrates menu elements in a consistent way and makes navigation easier. iDVD allows you to customize these themes into unique menus for your DVDs. Chapter 2 of this book describes themes and how to use them.

Where you can play your DVD-R disc

The discs are called DVD-R discs because they are a recordable format. DVD-R discs should play in all new DVD players.

We say *should* with some trepidation. If you purchased your DVD player in 2003, it's likely compatible with DVD-R discs. But some older players and some inexpensive models can't play DVD-R media, or can play them only marginally well, with picture artifacts, sound problems, or navigation problems.

In addition, most commercial DVDs have a *region code* that ties the DVD to specific regions of the world, as a measure of copy protection. Fortunately you can play DVD-R discs created by iDVD in all regions and you don't have to specify a region code. But keep in mind that you must burn a different DVD-R disc for some countries — you must use the proper format (NTSC for the United States, PAL for Europe), and your DVD can't hold more than one format. iDVD is already set to use the proper format for your region (depending on where you bought your Mac), but you can also change the format used by iDVD.

The Apple SuperDrive burns standard 4.7GB 2.0 General DVD-R media. These discs are playable in most standard DVD players and computer DVD-ROM drives. Apple provides a list of consumer DVD players that Apple specifically tested for playability — you can find it at `www.apple.com/dvd/compatibility/`.

3. **Customize the theme with your specific menus, buttons, backgrounds, and content.**

   After choosing a theme, you assign media elements, such as movies and sounds to menus, buttons, and backgrounds, to make your DVD project look as professional as a commercial DVD. iDVD gives you a great deal of control over theme elements, including resizing the buttons and arranging them on-screen any way you like. Read Chapter 2 of this book to find out how to customize themes and add your own menu elements.

4. **Preview and then burn your DVD-R disc.**

   iDVD makes previewing the interactive experience of your DVD-R disc before you waste a blank disc on a flawed presentation easy. You can make changes and adjustments, and preview it again. When ready, you can burn a DVD-R quickly and easily with your SuperDrive-equipped Mac. Chapter 3 of this book describes the process of previewing and then burning a DVD-R.

REMEMBER

You get one chance with a DVD-R disc — once you burn video to it, you can't rewrite it. Gather everything you want to put on the disc beforehand, so you don't waste a disc.

Touring iDVD

Double-click the iDVD icon on the Dock to open iDVD, and a window appears, similar to the one in Figure 1-1. iDVD starts with only its theme window on display with buttons underneath.

To see an iDVD project, click the Customize button. A drawer slides out to the left of the theme window, displaying the iMedia browser. The iDVD window consists of the following elements:

- **Main window:** iDVD shows the DVD project in the main window and allows you to arrange buttons and edit slideshows. This window changes to a preview window when you click the Preview button.
- **Customize:** Click the Customize button, which offers the following, shown in Figure 1-2:
  - **Themes:** Browse and select themes.
  - **Settings:** Customize the buttons, titles, and backgrounds of a theme — see Chapter 2 of this book.
  - **Audio:** Browse your iTunes library and add music to slideshows (see the section, "Adding sound to a slideshow," later in this chapter), as well as add music to enhance a theme (see Chapter 2 of this book).
  - **Photos:** Browse your iPhoto library and create slideshows (as we describe in the section, "Assembling Photo Slideshows," later in this chapter).
  - **Movies:** Displays thumbnails of movies imported into the iDVD project. To discover how to import movies, see the section, "Importing Digital Video into iDVD," later in this chapter.
  - **Status:** Check the status of the imported movie's encoding process. See the "Importing Digital Video into iDVD" section in this chapter.
- **Folder:** Click the Folder button to create a submenu for your DVD project. See Chapter 2 of this book to find out about submenus.
- **Slideshow:** Click the Slideshow button to create a slideshow using photos from iPhoto. See the section, "Assembling Photo Slideshows," later in this chapter.
- **Motion:** Click the Motion button to turn off the motion in menus and buttons; click it again to turn motion back on. Motion slows down the performance of iDVD and you may want to turn it off until you are ready to preview and burn your DVD project.
- **Preview:** Click the Preview button to preview the DVD project in the main window. See Chapter 3 of this book for more details.
- **Burn:** Click the Burn button to burn a DVD-R disc. See Chapter 3 of this book for more details on burning.

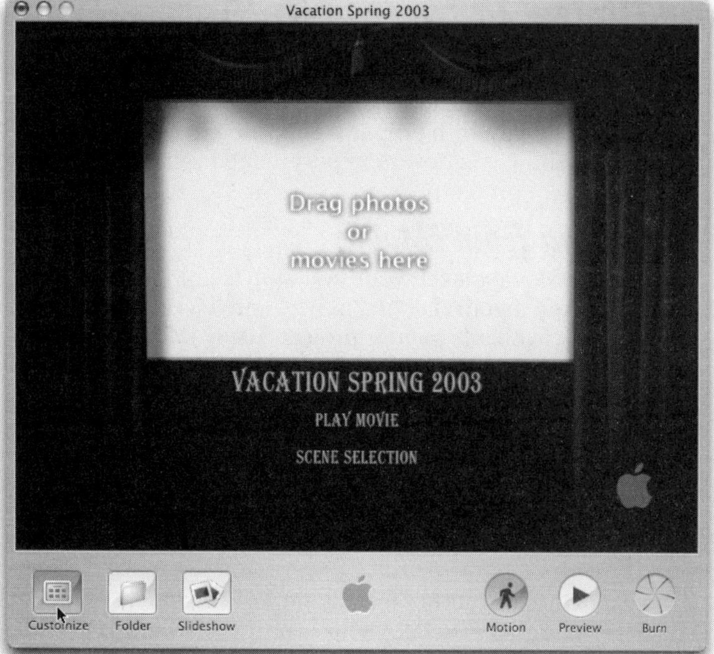

Figure 1-1: The iDVD main window.

Figure 1-2: An iDVD project with the customize drawer open.

Importing Digital Video into iDVD

Before you burn your movie to a DVD disc, you have to import the video into iDVD. When you import digital video, iDVD automatically *encodes* and *compresses* the video — prepares the video to be burned to a DVD. In this section, we show you how to import video from iMovie and QuickTime.

Importing from iMovie

If you're an iMovie-maker, your first step is not with iDVD at all — you use iMovie to export your finished movie, and iDVD automatically compresses it and makes it available in your project. Using iMovie to export your movie greatly reduces the possibility of error in making high-quality DVDs. The compression is performed automatically with the appropriate settings.

You can also import QuickTime movies directly into iDVD (see the "Importing QuickTime movies" section, later in this chapter). You can't use QuickTime VR, MPEG, Flash, or streaming movies — they must be in the standard QuickTime format with linear video tracks.

If your movie is in another format, import the movie into iMovie first (Book III), and then use iMovie to export the movie to iDVD.

To import your movie to iDVD from iMovie, follow these steps:

1. **Open iMovie and export your movie.**

   See Book III, Chapter 5 if you're not sure how to export.

   iMovie automatically transfers your movie to iDVD. iMovie links the movie to iDVD.

   If you use slow motion, reverse clips, or other special effects, you may get a message reminding you to render them before exporting your movie. Click the Render and Proceed button to export to iDVD with a high-quality movie; otherwise, the movie may not be as good as expected. The rendering process may take some time.

2. **Optional: In iDVD, click the Motion button to turn off animation and sound temporarily.**

   Turning off motion and sound improves the iDVD performance during the authoring phase. You can turn enable motion before previewing and burning the disc.

3. **Click the Customize button.**

   A drawer slides out to the left of the main window, displaying the iMedia browser.

4. **Click the Status button to see the status of the imported movie's encoding process.**

   iDVD takes some time to compress and encode your movie to the DVD format, and the Status pane shows a progress bar. You can continue working in iDVD doing other things while the encoding process continues. When the status shows `Done`, the movie is ready.

5. **Click the Movies button to see the icon for the movie.**

   The iMedia browser opens with your movie files imported, as shown in Figure 1-3.

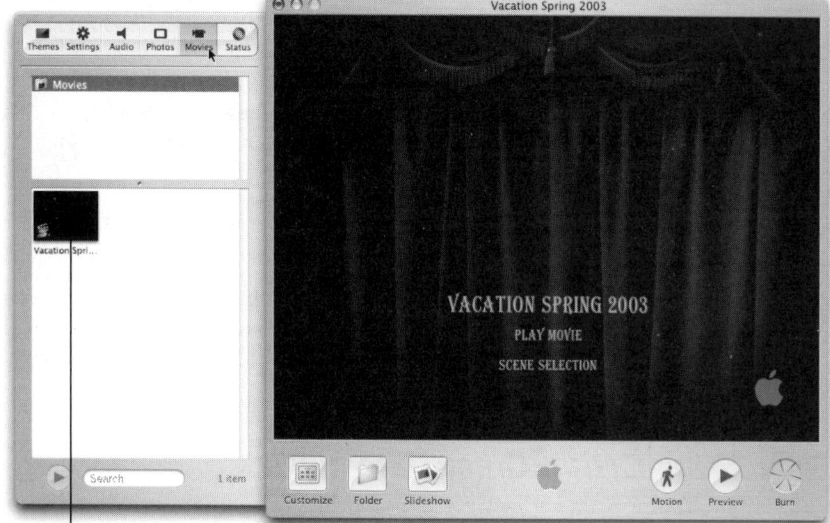

Figure 1-3: Your movie files import to the iMedia browser.

If you see other movies in the iMedia browser, they are most likely movie files saved in the Movies folder. iDVD looks in the Movies folder in your Documents folder on your hard drive for any QuickTime movie files. If you created other QuickTime files, you may want to move them into a subfolder within the Movies folder (or out of the Movies folder altogether), so that iDVD does not import them.

Don't delete your source files for any movie or picture imported into iDVD. When you add a movie to your iDVD project, the project contains only a reference to the location of the file on your hard disk. When you import from iMovie, that file is stored in the Movies folder of your Documents folder. If you move your iDVD project to another computer, you must also move the source files.

Changing the format from NTSC or PAL

You may never have to do this, but if you need to create a DVD-R for a different country that uses a format other than the one iDVD is set up for, you can change the format. You're not being unpatriotic — spreading your culture abroad is a good thing.

NTSC is used in North America, Japan, and various non-European countries, while PAL is used in most European countries and in Brazil. Your Mac comes configured with iDVD set to the appropriate format for your region. But if, for example, you live in North America and you want to create a DVD-R for Europe, you can do this. You can't, however, mix formats on the same disc using iDVD.

After creating a new project, but before adding any media files, choose iDVD➪Preferences and select the format — either NTSC or PAL.

You can't use iDVD to convert a movie from one format to another. You must first use iMovie to export the movie as a QuickTime file, using the DV (Digital Video) format for PAL or NTSC. For example, to convert movies from NTSC to PAL, you export the NTSC-format movies as QuickTime files using the DV-PAL or DVCPRO-PAL setting. Then you can import the QuickTime files into iDVD.

After you import your movie into iDVD from iMovie, you're ready to choose a theme for your menus, buttons, and backgrounds. You can skip the rest of this chapter unless you want to assemble a slideshow with photos from your iPhoto library.

Importing QuickTime movies

To import a QuickTime movie to iDVD that isn't in iMovie, you can simply drag it from the Finder to the background of an iDVD menu, or to the iMovie browser. Or, if you prefer, choose File➪Import➪Video. Click the Movies button at the top of the customize drawer to open the iMovie browser.

You can always check the status of the compressing and encoding by clicking the Status button.

You can't import uncompressed QuickTime files or QuickTime files with only thousands of colors (rather than millions, which is the normal setting). The QuickTime files also can't contain 48-bit color images. You also can't use movies saved with the Fast Start option for Web Streaming format (described in Book III, Chapter 5).

After you import your QuickTime movie into iDVD, you're ready to choose a theme for your menus, buttons, and backgrounds. You can skip the rest of this chapter unless you want to assemble a slideshow with photos from your iPhoto library.

Assembling Photo Slideshows

Photo slideshows are reason enough to burn DVDs. You can show your photos on your home TV, or bring a DVD over to your friends or relatives to show on their televisions. All they need is a DVD player.

Photos look better when played from DVD than from any other video medium except the Mac itself, and they look nearly as good on DVD as they look on the Mac. You can offer a complete slideshow on DVD with buttons for navigating among the photos.

You can use any photo in your iPhoto library in slideshows or as part of your project's DVD menus.

You can create slideshows three different ways:

- Create the slideshow first in iPhoto, as described in Book II, Chapter 4. You can then export it to iDVD to start a DVD project with the slideshow already arranged and ready for burning to disc, as we describe in the "Importing slideshows from iPhoto into iDVD" section, later in this chapter. You can also change the slideshow's arrangement in iDVD.
- Create the slideshow in iDVD by dragging any image from your iPhoto library to a new iDVD project in the order you want.
- Create a slideshow in iMovie with music synchronized to specific points in the show, and then export the movie to iDVD. See Book III, Chapter 4, to synchronize music to a sequence of clips in iMovie.

iDVD stretches or compresses photos to fit in the standard DVD window for slideshows, which is 640 x 480 pixels (720 x 480 pixels for video). If your photos are larger, the iDVD compression makes them look fine. But if the photos are smaller, iDVD stretches them to fill the display, often with undesirable results (jagged lines and visible pixels, to name a few). For best results, make sure your photos are taken by a digital camera with a resolution of at least 640 x 480 pixels or higher. Photos that have a different aspect ratio than 4:3 may appear with black bands to fill the screen.

Importing slideshows from iPhoto into iDVD

To import a slideshow from iPhoto to iDVD and automatically create a new iDVD project with the slideshow, follow these steps:

1. **With iPhoto open, click the Organize mode button and select a photo album prepared as a slideshow.**

   See Book II, Chapter 5 to create a slideshow in iPhoto.

2. **Click the iDVD icon in the iPhoto tools pane.**

   iDVD opens with a new iDVD project with a link to the slideshow in iPhoto. The title is the name of the slideshow photo album in your iPhoto library. In Figure 1-4, our slideshow is named Band Tour Slideshow.

3. **Click the Preview button to see the slideshow.**

   The slideshow plays as it would if burned on a DVD. The DVD remote control appears for selecting menu items and advancing through the slideshow manually.

   To stop the preview, click the Preview button again.

If you are satisfied with the preview, the slideshow is ready for burning onto DVD. See Chapter 3 of this book to find out how to burn a DVD. If you think the slideshow can use some work, you can edit the slide order and add other photos and images, as we describe in the section, "Rearranging the photo order," later in this chapter.

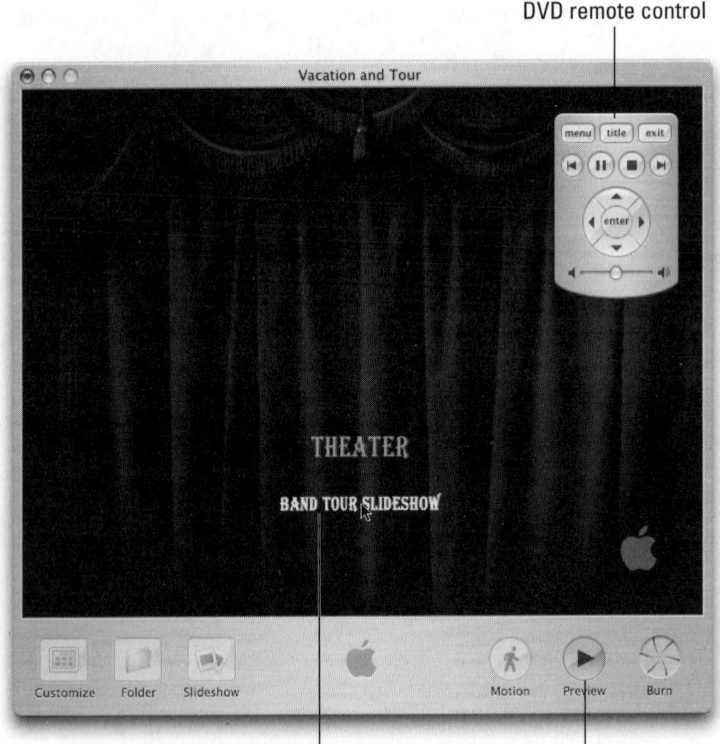

Figure 1-4: Preview a slideshow.

Creating a slideshow in iDVD

If you don't have slideshows ready to go in your iPhoto library, you can still use iDVD to create a slideshow with photos from iPhoto. Follow these steps to access your photos in the iPhoto library:

1. **In iDVD, click the Customize button, or choose Project⇨Show Customize Panel.**

   The customize drawer slides out providing access to the iMedia browser buttons.

2. **Click the Photos button in the customize drawer.**

   The iMedia browser displays your entire iPhoto library, along with albums and slideshows.

3. **Click the Slideshow button in the iDVD window.**

   iDVD creates a link to the slideshow, as shown in Figure 1-5. The text button is named "My Slideshow" until you rename it.

4. **Double-click the "My Slideshow link.**

   The slideshow editing window appears, as shown in Figure 1-6.

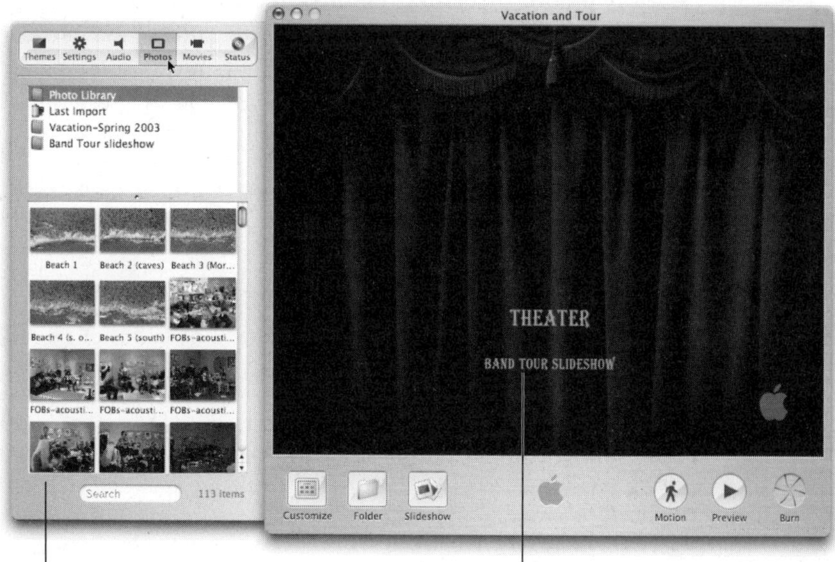

Figure 1-5: Create a slideshow with your iPhoto photos.

Figure 1-6: Drag photos into iDVD.

5. **Drag photos directly from the iMedia browser into the slideshow editing window in the order you want for your slideshow.**

   Each photo appears in a list of thumbnails, numbered consecutively to represent the slideshow order, and you can drag the thumbnail images into a different order.

When you want to return to the iDVD main window, click the Return button at the bottom of the slideshow window.

Rearranging the photo order

You can rearrange and fine-tune any slideshow, whether created in iDVD or exported from iPhoto.

Arranging and rearranging is as easy as dragging the images in the slideshow editing window. Double-click the slideshow link to open the slideshow editing window.

Select the image in the list and drag it to the new location, as shown in Figure 1-7. As you drag the image, the list opens up to make room for it. You can change the size of the thumbnail images with the Thumbnail pop-up menu at the bottom of the window.

Figure 1-7: Rearrange and fine-tune a slideshow.

Playing the slideshow manually or automatically

One of the most important decisions that you must make about your slideshow is how you want it to play — either manually, so that the viewer has to click the next button to move to the next slide, or automatically, so that the slideshow advances according to a specified slide duration.

You set this with the Slide Duration pop-up menu in the slideshow editing window. The slideshow is automatically set to the Manual setting, unless you add sound — in which case it is automatically set to the Fit to Audio setting.

The Fit to Audio setting in the Slide Duration menu matches the duration to the length of the audio clip. See the section, "Adding sound to a slideshow," later in this chapter.

Given the vast amount of space on a DVD, you may want to create multiple versions of the slideshow — one that advances manually, and one that advances timed to fit the audio.

The slideshow editing window also provides the Display During Slideshow option that automatically adds left and right arrows to the slideshow. The arrows don't actually work as buttons: They simply indicate that slides precede or follow the current slide, much like slideshows provided with commercial DVD titles.

Importing images and graphics files into slideshows

You may want to include other graphics and image files in your DVD slideshow. You can drag these files directly from the Finder into the slideshow window.

You can drag the image directly to a position in the slideshow list in the slideshow edit window. As an alternative, you can choose File➪Import➪Image and select an image or graphics file. iDVD places the imported image at the end of the list.

Adding sound to a slideshow

You probably think you already have enough audio, with the sound effects, narration, and music incorporated into the movies for your DVD. But you can also add an audio clip to a slideshow in iDVD to make your slideshow interesting to the ear as well as the eye. Most commercial DVD titles have these nice audio perks, and you can provide them with your DVD.

You can use any song stored in your iTunes library as part of your DVD.

You can add the music in your iTunes library to menu backgrounds and buttons, as we show in Chapter 2 of this book. You can also add music to a slideshow by following these steps:

1. **Click the slideshow link for your slideshow to open the slideshow editing window.**

   The slideshow link is automatically created when you export the slideshow from iPhoto, or click the Slideshow icon to create a slideshow from scratch.

2. **Click the Audio button in the customize drawer.**

   The iTunes library opens in the iMedia browser, as shown in Figure 1-8.

3. **Drag a song from the iTunes library to the Audio icon in the slideshow editing window.**

   The Audio icon in the slideshow editing window changes to show an icon for the type of sound file — for example, an MP3 icon for an MP3 file or an AIFF icon for an AIFF sound file.

   You can also import a sound file by dragging it directly from the Finder over the Audio icon. iDVD imports the sound file and changes the icon to show the type of sound file.

4. **In the slideshow editing window, select a duration setting in the Slide Duration pop-up menu.**

   The Fit to Audio setting in the Slide Duration pop-up menu matches the duration to the length of the song. Alternatively, if your song is short and you have a lot of slides, try a timed duration for each slide by picking a duration in the Slide Duration pop-up menu (such as 5 seconds). The sound loops back and plays again if there are more slides to show than music to play. On the other hand, if you want a very quick slideshow, you can set the duration as low as one second.

5. **Preview your slideshow by clicking the Preview button.**

   To stop the preview, click the Preview button again.

The next step is to choose a theme for your menus, buttons, and backgrounds, as described in Chapter 2 of this book. You can then move on to burning your DVD — see Chapter 3 of this book.

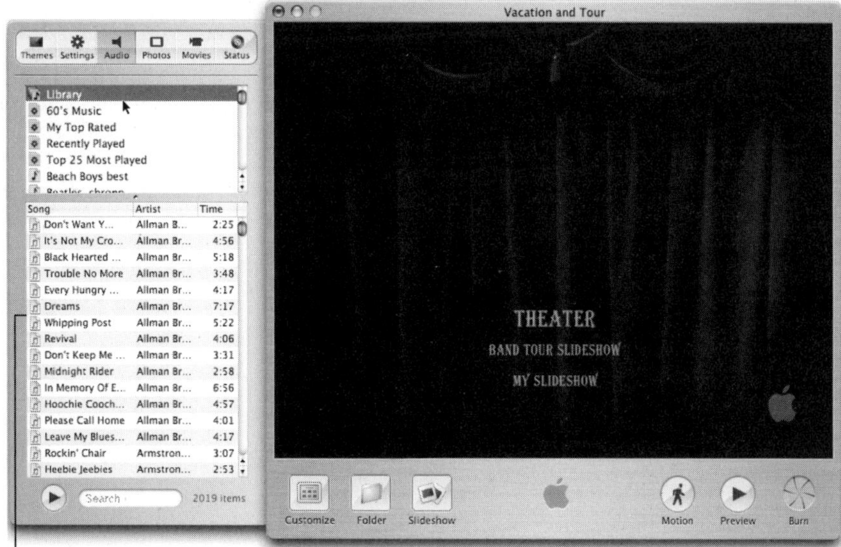

Figure 1-8: Browse the iTunes library to add music.

Chapter 2: Making Menus and Buttons

In This Chapter

- **Selecting and customizing menus**
- **Adding buttons**
- **Fine-tuning motion and other button features**
- **Adding and customizing scene selection submenus**

In order to present all the bonus material you expect on a DVD, you must create a menu for your DVDs to allow users to navigate it.

With iDVD, you can create menus and backgrounds for your DVD project that are similar to the ones you see in commercial DVDs. iDVD gives you a great deal of control over menus, buttons, and backgrounds, with properly-designed themes ready to use, and the ability to customize these elements for a unique presentation.

Creating DVD Menus

The menus in a DVD don't just provide choices: They also help set up the entire experience. Commercial DVDs need to offer menus so that you can find all the content stored on them. But you want to use menus, backgrounds, and buttons for your DVDs as well, not just to provide ways to select the content, but also to set up a mood or capture the attention of the viewer. Many DVD menus resemble touch-screen kiosks. Sound and video are staples of these menus, with buttons that play little movies and backgrounds that show animation and video clips. Movies that run from start to finish are also broken up into *chapters,* or scenes, that viewers can select independently.

iDVD is excellent for creating these menus. You can have a lot of fun with menus, buttons, and backgrounds. Introduce your children's videos using the Book theme, or use a wilder theme like Gen Y. The Sport, Western, and Passport themes are naturals for vacation videos. Or add your own video clip as a background, repeating in a loop with the menu selections set apart and easy to click.

The themes in iDVD do the work of supplying motion buttons and backgrounds, and iDVD allows you to customize these themes into unique menus for your DVDs.

Selecting menu themes

In iDVD, a *theme* consists of a professionally designed combination of background elements, a music clip, and a button style that comprises a menu. Typically the menu is designed with typefaces and images to match the theme, and the text selections are set to readable font sizes and placed in areas on the page that attract attention.

Start with a theme and then customize it — you can change the music for musical themes, change the background picture and text, change the buttons, and add your own movies and slideshows to areas in the background and to buttons, which we cover in the section, "Adding drop zones to the menu," in this chapter. You can then save your customized theme and burn a DVD with it.

To see the themes, click the Customize button. A drawer slides out to the left of the theme window, as shown in Figure 2-1. If the Themes browser is not already open, click the Themes button to open it.

Figure 2-1: The Themes browser displays all the themes supplied with iDVD.

The browser offers a pop-up menu to select themes. Thumbnails of the themes appear in the Themes browser. Thumbnails that show a silhouette of a walking man in the lower-right corner offer motion. To select a theme, click its name. The theme replaces whatever theme was displayed before in the main window, as shown in Figure 2-2. Click the Motion button to view motion on the themes that offer sound and motion.

What's cool is that if you already created some buttons for a menu, the new theme has the same buttons. With all themes, buttons automatically appear where they should, in the proper text font, button shape, and size, when you add a button. We describe buttons in the "Creating Buttons" section, later in this chapter.

Themes come in several types, including

- **Picture-only:** These themes offer a background style with a static image you can change. Examples include Your Photo Here, Brushed Metal One, and Parchment.
- **Picture with audio:** These themes offer a picture-only style and image you can change, accompanied by music or sound that you can change. One example is Claim Check. You can customize most themes to include your own audio clip.

Figure 2-2: When we select the Projector theme, it displays in the main window.

- **Motion:** These themes offer short video clips in the background that repeat in a loop (with or without audio). Motion themes sport an icon of a running man within a circle. Examples include Global, Sky, and Baby Blue.
- **Drop zone:** These themes offer sections of the main background for running movies and slideshows. Drop zones are not links to movies — they show only part of the movie in your menu. Examples include Postcard, Projector, and Theater.

Themes have titles you can edit to make the menu your own. Click the title to select it and type your own title.

iDVD is very forgiving if you do things you don't like. You can undo just about every operation you perform, going backwards. Just choose Edit⇨Undo for each consecutive operation to undo them.

Adding a photo or movie to the theme

You can change the background of any theme. Some themes, such as the Picture in Picture theme, are designed specifically for you to add your own photo as a background. Others, such as the Global theme, are designed to play a movie in the background, and you can replace this movie with your own.

However, the vast majority of the themes offer sections of the background for movies and slideshows, called *drop zones*. Drop zone themes, which we cover in the section, "Adding drop zones to the menu," later in this chapter, are designed so that movies or slideshows play within frames. You probably don't want to play video as the entire background of a theme that also has a drop zone — the two movies would clash.

To replace the background of a theme with either a photo from your iPhoto library or a movie from iMovie, follow these steps:

1. **Select the theme and click the Photos button to open the iPhoto browser, or the Movies button to open the iMovie browser.**

   The Photos button in the customize drawer provides access to your iPhoto library and the Movies button provides access to any exported movies from iMovie.

2. **Select a photo or movie and drag it over the Settings button until the Settings pane appears, and then drop your photo or movie into the Background Image/Movie well.**

   The Background Image/Movie well fills with the photo or movie you selected, shown in Figure 2-3.

   The image now appears as the background of your menu, as shown in Figure 2-4.

Figure 2-3: Drag a photo from the iPhoto library to a theme's background.

If you drag a movie into the background of a theme that offers a drop zone, the drop zone is also replaced along with the rest of the background — unless you also hold down the Option key as you drag, which retains the drop zone. We describe drop zones in the section, "Adding drop zones to the menu," later in this chapter.

You can also drag an image file or QuickTime movie file from the Finder directly into the Background Image/Movie well in the Settings pane. With the Settings pane open, choose File➪Import➪Image to import an image file, or File➪Import➪Video to import a movie. iDVD imports the file directly into the Background Image/Movie well.

The Settings pane provides options for the background, including pop-up menus that control the position of the title and its font, size, and color. For movies used in the background, you can also control the duration of the movie's loop with the Motion Duration slider. This sets how long the movie plays before repeating in a loop. A movie in a background can play up to 30 seconds before looping.

Figure 2-4: The background photo is now set for this menu.

Changing the music of a theme

All of the themes allow you to add music to your menu background (or replace music already there). To add a song from your iTunes library, follow these steps:

1. **Select the theme and click the Audio button to open the iTunes browser.**

   The iTunes library opens.

2. **Select a song and drag it over the Settings button until the Settings pane appears, and then drop your song into the Audio well.**

The song appears in the Audio well, as shown in Figure 2-5. The music plays in the background and repeats in a loop until the viewer clicks a button in the menu.

You can't add audio to a drop zone or a button — that would be a bit too cacophonous, with audio already playing in the drop zone and possibly also in the background.

Figure 2-5: The theme's background audio setting is set to a song from the iTunes library.

Adding drop zones to the menu

Drop zones sound like places where military helicopters land, but in iDVD, *drop zones* are sections of the menu background that can play movies and slideshows. You can also place a still image in a drop zone.

Drop zones are not buttons — you won't get anywhere by clicking them. They are essentially cool ways to frame a movie or slideshow loop. Only a portion of the movie or slideshow plays in the drop zone, and that portion repeats in a loop. It starts with the first frame of the movie — unlike buttons, you can't change the starting frame in a drop zone.

To add a movie, slideshow, or image to a drop zone, follow these steps:

1. **Select a theme that has a drop zone.**

   Themes with drop zones have a section of the background that says `Drag photos or movies here` or something similar.

2. **Click the Movies button to open the iMovie browser, or the Photos button to open the iPhoto browser.**

   You can use any movie or photo, or an entire slideshow. The Photos button opens the iPhoto browser.

3. **Drag a movie, photo, or slideshow to the drop zone.**

   As you drag, the drop zone highlights, which makes dropping the element in the zone easy.

   The movie or photo drops into the drop zone, as shown in Figure 2-6.

Click the Motion button in the main window to see the drop zone motion. Click the Motion button again to stop the motion. Movies and slideshows play within the drop zone, showing part of the picture (depending on the size of the drop zone). If not enough of the picture appears, drag the picture around with the mouse within the drop zone until more of the picture shows.

The Settings pane in the customize drawer gives you control over the duration of the drop zone's movie or slideshow loop with the Motion Duration slider. This sets how long the movie plays before repeating in a loop. A movie in a drop zone can play up to 30 seconds before looping.

If you drag movies of different durations to drop zones in a menu that also has a background movie, the Motion Duration slider overrules them all, and they all play with the same duration set by the slider. If you want to get wilder than that, consider using iMovie to create a single movie with all moving background elements.

Figure 2-6: Add a movie or photo to the background of a menu.

To remove something from a drop zone, hold down the Control key and click the image, slideshow, or movie in the drop zone, and then select the Clear option from the shortcut menu that appears. You can also drag the element from the drop zone to a place outside the iDVD window. The element is not deleted — you simply remove it from the drop zone.

Creating Buttons

Menus offer buttons that you click to play movies and slideshows, and to access submenus. Without buttons, viewers can't select anything. Find out how to add submenus in the "Adding Submenus" section, later in this chapter.

Some themes offer text buttons and some offer motion buttons that can play miniature movies. You can customize any button in any theme and create truly wacky combinations if you want, but remember professionals designed the themes and probably would be insulted by your creations. No matter — they'll never know. Customize away!

Adding buttons

When you export a movie from iMovie or a slideshow from iPhoto, iDVD automatically creates a button for your menu in whatever theme you used the last time you used iDVD. If this is the first time you opened iDVD, the theme is usually the Theater theme.

To create a button, you can do any of the following:

- **Button for a movie:** Drag a movie from the iMovie browser in the customize drawer, or drag a QuickTime file in the Finder, to any area of the background that is not a drop zone. When the menu appears on the DVD (and also when you use the Preview button to preview the DVD), clicking the button plays the movie.
- **Button for a slideshow:** Drag an existing slideshow from the iPhoto browser in the customize drawer to any area of the background that is not a drop zone. If you don't have a slideshow already prepared, click the Slideshow button to create the button, and then double-click the button to open the slideshow editing window (see Chapter 1 of this book).

Some themes provide text buttons. You can change the text label of the text button by clicking its label to select it, and then typing a new label.

Fine-tuning motion buttons

Motion buttons play a movie or slideshow inside the button. Unlike a drop zone, which only plays motion, a motion button also acts as a menu selection you can click.

When you add a button for a movie, iDVD uses the first frame of the movie as the button's preview image. If the theme you're using offers motion buttons (indicated by the running man icon in the theme's thumbnail), the button automatically plays the first 30 seconds of the movie. You can also change the starting and ending frame of the looping video that plays within the button.

To fine-tune a motion button, follow these steps:

1. **Drag a movie or slideshow to the menu to add a button.**

   If the movie has chapter markers already set for individual scenes, indicated by a folder icon for the button, double-click the folder icon to open the individual scenes menu, which offers individual movies to play.

2. **Click the button in the menu.**

   A slider appears above the movie button, as shown in Figure 2-7.

3. **Drag the slider to the frame of the movie you want to appear first.**

   The slider defines the first frame to appear when the movie plays inside the button. The Movie check box that appears above a movie button indicates that motion is turned on; if you turn it off, the single frame appears in the button as a single image, without motion.

4. **Set the duration by adjusting the Motion Duration slider in the Settings pane of the customize drawer.**

   This sets how long the movie plays inside the button before repeating in a loop. A movie in a button can play up to 30 seconds before looping. The Motion Duration slider controls all the movies in the menu — they all play for the number of seconds set by the slider.

To see the movie play inside the button, click the Motion button. Click the Motion button again to stop the movie because motion in a menu can slow down the performance of iDVD.

Customizing buttons

You can customize buttons, like just about everything else in iDVD, to your liking. You can change the text of the button's label by clicking its label to select it, and then typing a new label. The Settings pane of the customize drawer, shown in Figure 2-8, has an entire Button section for changing the style of the button along with the button label's position, font, color, and size.

Don't want text labels on your buttons? You can choose the No Text option from the Button Position pop-up menu in the Settings pane.

Set the movie duration.

Figure 2-7: Drag a movie button's slider to set the first frame.

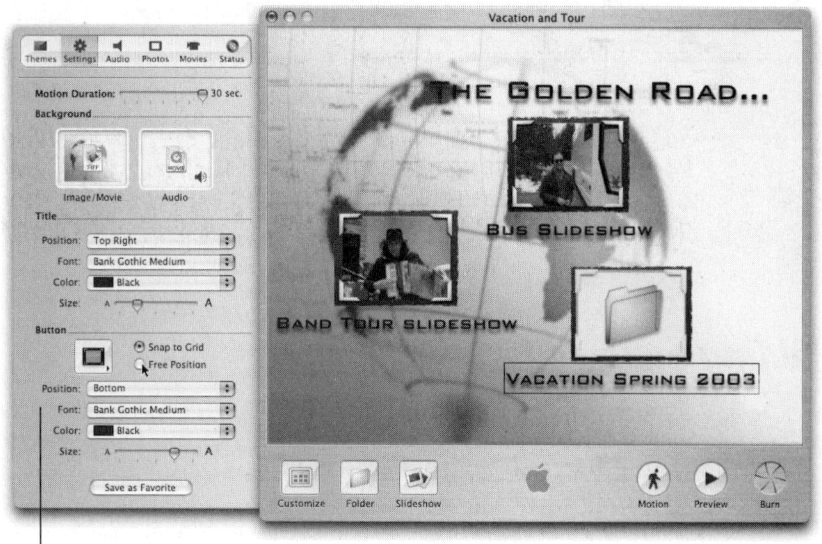

Figure 2-8: Change the button's style.

Change the button's properties.

Checking the TV safe area

When you arrange buttons within a theme, keep in mind that buttons should not be close to the edges of the picture area. Most DVDs are made to play on televisions connected to DVD players, even though a growing segment of the population uses computers to show their DVDs. But TV is the common denominator, and when it comes to DVD menus and buttons, you should keep all the relevant information away from the edges of the picture.

Most televisions *overscan* the screen — the cathode-ray guns overshoot the margins of the screen to make sure that the screen is edge to edge. As a result, you lose about ten percent of the picture on each edge (sometimes less on top and bottom, depending on the TV). If you place something on the very edge of the picture, such as the button's label, it may get cut off when viewed on a television. iDVD works around this limitation by defining the *TV-safe area* where all the action takes place. The safe area is, essentially, inside the edges of the picture, leaving at least a ten percent margin around all sides.

The themes provided with iDVD follow the rules — all buttons and drop zones are within the TV safe area. But it doesn't hurt to check, and if you move buttons around or otherwise customize your menu, you really should check the TV safe area.

Choose Advanced⇨Show TV Safe Area. The gray-shaded border of the iDVD movie window is outside the safe area, and everything inside the border is inside the safe area. You can move buttons, or reduce the font size of labels, to bring these things safely inside the safe area. To turn off the safe area display, choose Advanced⇨Hide TV Safe Area.

You can move the buttons around the menu freely if you click the Free Position option, or move them to positions on an invisible grid set by the theme's designer by selecting the Snap to Grid option. Be careful not to get buttons too close to the edges of the menu — remember to check the TV safe area.

Adding Submenus

A menu can have up to six buttons, and with most commercial DVDs, the menus typically offer fewer than six. This makes menu selection easy for the viewer. Too many choices only confuse people.

Where do you put all the good stuff — the individual scenes from the movie, the alternative version of the slideshow, the outtakes? You put them behind a single button that opens a submenu. And if you have lots of choices, your submenus can have buttons that open more submenus.

Submenus are similar to Mac folders, which is why iDVD uses a folder icon to distinguish a folder button. You can click the Folder icon in the control panel below the iDVD preview window to add a folder button. But if you export your movie from iMovie with chapter markers to indicate individual scenes, iDVD automatically creates a folder button for you.

Turning chapter markers into submenus

With iMovie, you can create chapter markers in advance to divide a movie into scenes. When you add a movie button for a movie you import from iMovie with chapter markers, iDVD creates a submenu for the chapters of the movie. (To add chapter markers in iMovie, see Book III, Chapter 4. You can add the chapter markers and go back to iDVD, and re-import the movie.)

To add a movie with chapter markers, follow these steps:

1. **Drag the movie to the menu to add a button.**

   If the menu has no other buttons, iDVD puts two buttons on the menu: one to play the entire movie, and a Scene Selection button with a folder icon that links to the submenu. If the menu already has buttons, iDVD creates one button with a folder icon and the title of the movie, which links to the submenu, as shown in Figure 2-9.

2. **Double-click the Scene Selection button to see the submenu.**

   The button names in the submenu are the ones set for the chapter markers in iMovie.

Each submenu has a back button to go back to the previous menu, and a forward button if your submenu needs to offer more than six selections. The Global theme puts these nifty arrow buttons on either side of the menu for going backward or forward in the submenu.

Customizing submenus

You can customize the buttons in the subfolders as you need, such as setting the first frame and duration of motion buttons, and dragging custom images to individual buttons. You can even change the button style in a submenu without affecting the other menus.

You may want to change the folder icon used for submenu links to something more interesting. For example, to change the Scene Selection button in Figure 2-10, click the button and drag the Folder slider to a frame in the movie. The button uses the chosen frame as its image, rather than the image of a folder.

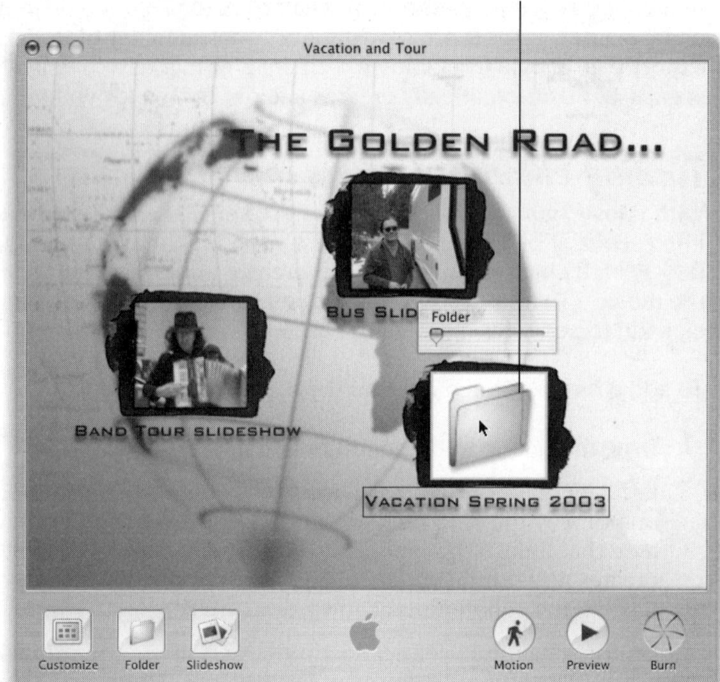

Figure 2-9: Opening the scene selection submenus for a movie with chapter markers.

Figure 2-10: Change the Scene Selection button.

You can use a different theme for each submenu. While you can pick contrasting themes that boggle the mind and confuse everyone, using different themes to differentiate submenus is helpful for viewers to know they're in a different place on the DVD.

When iDVD shows the submenu in the window, choose a different theme from the Themes browser, and iDVD complies.

You can arrange and rearrange your menus to your heart's content, but don't forget to save the project before quitting iDVD. Choose File⇨Save Project to save a project. You can also make another version of a project by choosing File⇨Save As, typing a new name for the project, and choosing a destination folder for the project.

Chapter 3: Burning DVDs

In This Chapter

- Using the simulated remote control
- Adding photos and files to the DVD
- Burning the DVD-R disc

The discs you can create with the Apple SuperDrive are called DVD-R because they are a recordable format. DVD-R discs should play in all new DVD players purchased in 2003. Some older players and some inexpensive models can't play DVD-R media, or can play them only marginally well, with picture artifacts, sound problems, or navigation problems. The Apple SuperDrive burns standard 4.7 gigabyte 2.0 General DVD-R discs, and Apple provides a list of consumer DVD players that can play SuperDrive-created DVD-R discs at `www.apple.com/dvd/compatibility/`. If your player is not on the list, that does not mean it is not compatible, only that Apple hasn't tested it yet.

You can technically fit up to 90 minutes of video on a DVD-R including still images, backgrounds, and movies. However, if you put more than 60 minutes of video on a DVD-R, the picture quality may suffer because iDVD uses stronger compression with a slower bit rate. The best approach is to limit each DVD-R to 60 minutes.

Previewing the DVD

You don't want to burn a disc with mistakes because most DVD-R discs cost about five dollars each, and you can't redo or fix a disc after you've burned it. To be on the safe side, use iDVD preview mode to preview the DVD menus and movie playback before you burn.

Using the Motion and Preview buttons

Make sure your motion video menus, drop zones, and buttons are moving — click the Motion button in the iDVD window to turn on motion, click it again to turn motion off.

Make sure you click the Motion button before previewing and certainly before burning, or you will get a warning from iDVD informing you that your project contains motion menus that are currently turned off.

To see a preview of your DVD presentation, click the Preview button at any time. iDVD provides a cute remote control panel on the display, shown in Figure 3-1, to simulate a physical remote control for a DVD player. When you're done, you can click either the Exit button on the remote control, or the Preview button again.

Using the remote control

Like remote control units for DVD players, the preview remote control in iDVD provides navigation, selection, and movie-playing buttons:

- **Arrow buttons:** Select a button in a menu. Use left and right arrows to advance through slides in a slideshow.
- **Enter button:** Activate a selected button.
- **Movie buttons:** Play or pause, stop, fast-forward, and rewind the movie.
- **Volume control:** Drag this slider to control the audio volume.
- **Menu button:** Return to the menu or submenu you just used.
- **Title button:** Return to the title menu (first menu).
- **Exit button:** Exit preview mode and return to iDVD.

Testing your DVD menus with the remote control is best because viewers will view the movie on a commercial DVD player with a remote. However, you can also click the menus with your mouse.

The last thing you should do is go back and preview it again. Make sure there are no typos or mistakes. Make sure your slideshow runs the way you want it to run. Also make sure the movies are the correct ones. You'd be surprised how often it happens that people forget to include something, and a typo on a DVD will haunt you forever.

Adding Project Files to the DVD

Besides using iDVD to create movies, you can also use it to back up your photo and image archives, and to put just about any digital file on the DVD-ROM portion (the part not accessible with a DVD player) of the DVD-R.

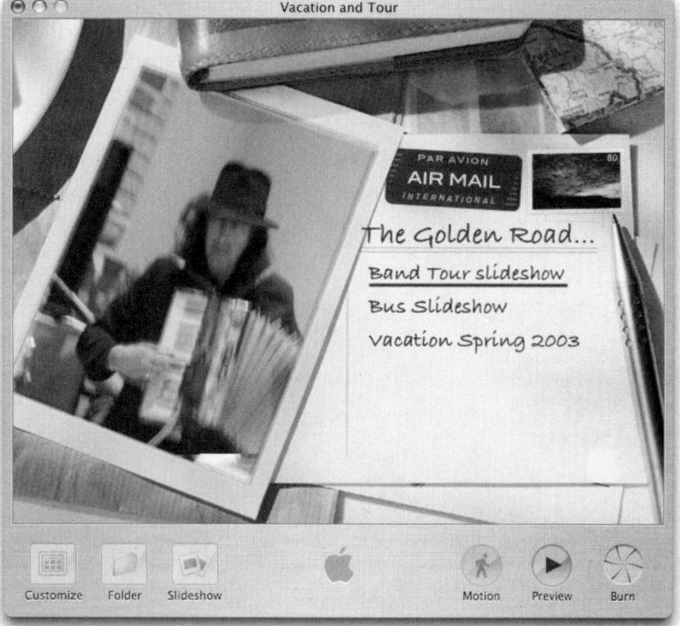

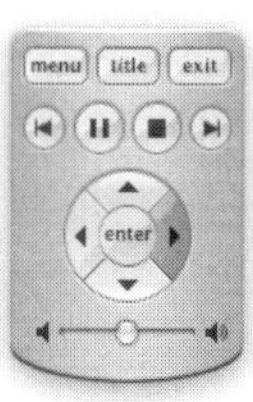

Figure 3-1: The DVD preview includes a simulated DVD player remote control.

You can check the disc space available with the Project size meter shaped like a disc at the top of the Status pane. Open the Status pane by clicking the Status button in the customize drawer. The video portion of the disc is in green, the DVD-ROM portion is in blue, and the rest is blank.

You may not want the recipients of your DVD-R (or DVD created from it, if you plan on making multiple copies) to be able to access these files — which they can, if you put the files on the disc. But if you want to archive the photos and possibly other files associated with a DVD-R project, you can add them to the disc.

Putting photos on DVD-ROM

You can add all the photos in a slideshow to the DVD-ROM portion of your DVD-R. Viewers using computers can open the DVD-ROM portion of the disc and copy the photo files to their systems. Commercial DVD players can't access the DVD-ROM section.

To add the photos of a slideshow to DVD-ROM, double-click the slideshow's text button to open the slideshow editing window as described in Chapter 1 of this book, and select the Add Original Photos on DVD-ROM option.

To see the list of files to be placed in the DVD-ROM portion of the disc, click the Customize button to open the customize drawer, and then click the Status button. From the pop-up menu, choose the DVD-ROM Contents option as shown in Figure 3-2. The DVD contents appear in the browser. Click the Slideshows folder to open it and see its contents.

Figure 3-2: Check the list of photos to be burned to the DVD-ROM portion of the DVD-R.

Putting any digital files on DVD-ROM

You can put any type of digital file in the DVD-ROM portion of the disc, making the file accessible from a computer with a DVD-ROM drive. This is a nice way to make a backup of some of the source files of a project.

We don't recommend copying movie files this way because you can't play a movie file from the DVD-ROM portion of the disc if it is larger than 1GB. Also, if you try to save more than a few thousand files, you may run into problems, according to Apple (what kind of problems Apple doesn't say, but we take the company's word for it). Apple suggests that if you want to back up your entire hard disk onto DVD-R, don't use iDVD. Instead, use the Burn Disc feature of the Finder, which makes sense to us.

On the other hand, if you have some files you want to save in the DVD-ROM portion of the disc, you can copy them directly into iDVD. Follow these steps:

7. **Click the Customize button to open the customize drawer, and then click the Status button.**

2. **Choose the DVD-ROM Contents option from the pop-up menu.**

3. **Click the New Folder button to create a new folder.**

   You can add as many folders as you like, and type a name for each folder, as shown in Figure 3-3.

4. **Drag files or folders to the new folder in the Status pane.**

   Dragging the files does not actually copy them, but establishes links to them so that when the DVD-R is burned, the files are copied. When you burn the disc, these files appear in the DVD-ROM portion of the disc.

Figure 3-3: Create folders for your project files.

Burning a DVD

As part of your Mac system, your SuperDrive laser is always ready to burn media.

Before you start burning a disc, close all other projects you may have open. Burning a DVD takes a lot of processing power, and may also tie up your computer for a while. Let the computer do its thing with the SuperDrive.

Don't press the Eject button on your keyboard while a burn is in process because you will ruin a five-dollar disc.

Here's a checklist of things to do before burning:

✦ **Add photos and files to DVD-ROM portion of the disc.**

  See the section "Adding the Project Files to the DVD," earlier in this chapter.

✦ **Make sure Motion is turned on.**

✦ **Change the name of the DVD if you wish by choosing Project➪Project Info and typing a new name in the Project Info window, as shown in Figure 3-4.**

  By default, iDVD uses the name of your iDVD project as the name for the DVD.

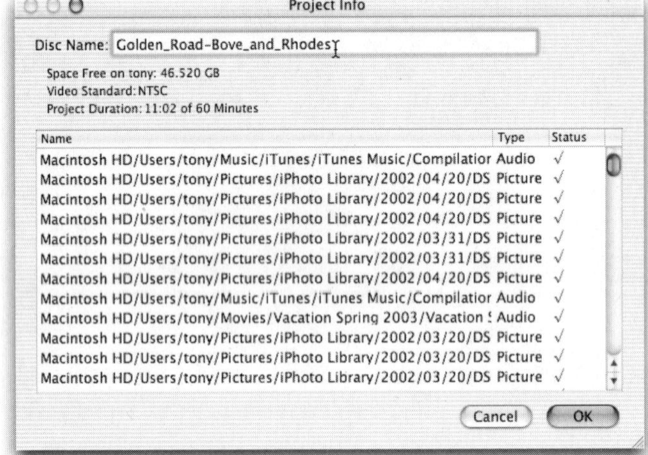

Figure 3-4: Changing the name of the DVD-R in the Project Info window.

Follow these steps to burn your DVD:

1. **Click the Burn button once.**

   The Burn button starts pulsating, its icon replaced with the symbol for radioactivity (Apple at least has a sense of humor). This is your fail-safe point.

2. **Click the Burn button a second time to start the burn process.**

   When prompted, insert a blank DVD-R disc, as shown in Figure 3-5. iDVD then burns the new DVD-R, rendering and encoding the menu and the movie files if necessary. You may want to take a break now — the progress bar tells you the number of minutes it takes for the burning process.

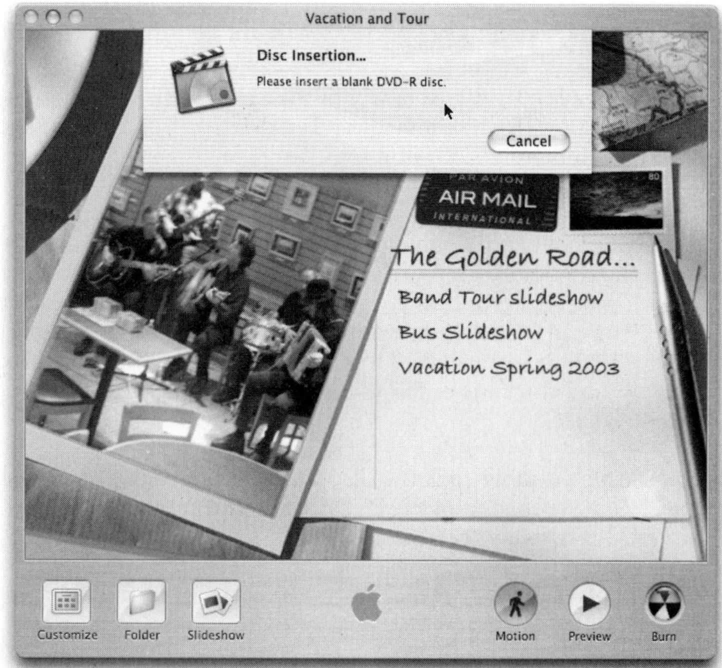

Figure 3-5: The DVD-R burn process renders, encodes, and burns the DVD-R.

If you see a `Your project contains motion menus that are currently turned off` warning, immediately cancel the operation and click the Motion button to turn on motion in the menus (unless you don't want motion in your menus for some reason). Then repeat the process.

The burn process may take some time, and you may see `Multiplexing and burning` message in the progress window. Don't worry; everything is fine. If you want to know what some of these messages mean, we heartily recommend *CD and DVD Recording For Dummies* by Mark Chambers, published by Wiley Publishing, Inc.

3. **At the end of the process, iDVD spits out your newly burned DVD-R disc and displays a message asking if you want to burn another one just like it. Click OK to burn another disc, or Cancel.**

Although you may be tempted to fire off a dozen more for your friends, we recommend testing the first disc first, before making duplicates. You can always open iDVD and burn another one later.

Testing Your DVD-R Disc

The best way to test your newly burned DVD-R disc is to pop it right back into your SuperDrive or similar DVD-R drive on your Mac. It should play just like any commercial DVD title.

The DVD Player application, supplied with every Mac that has a DVD drive, provides a simulated remote control for controlling playback. DVD Player also offers the capability to play the DVD in half-screen, normal size, or maximum size window depending on your display by choosing options from the Video menu. You can resize the viewer to take over the entire screen by choosing Window➪Viewer, or use ⌘+0 to toggle between full-screen and a viewer window. And you can control the sound volume by dragging the slider in the remote control.

You can also double-click the disc's icon in the Finder to see the contents of the DVD-ROM portion of the DVD-R disc. You can copy the folders and files to a hard disk using the Finder.

After you test the DVD-R disc on a Mac, test the DVD with a commercial DVD player. If it works on the Mac but not on the commercial player, there may be a compatibility problem with the commercial player and DVD-R discs.

That's it! You can now call yourself a DVD author, and DVD is now an important part of your iLife.

Troubleshooting DVD Problems

We created our first DVD-R with movies, music, sounds, with lots of files copied to the DVD-ROM portion. It worked perfectly the first time. How often does that happen with new technology? If you're not so lucky, check out the following solutions.

✦ ***Problem:*** The disc won't burn.

  Solution: Perhaps it's a bum disc (it happens). Try another one, and get a refund if the other one works.

✦ ***Problem:*** iDVD can't find all the media files.

  Solution: This happens often, especially if you use media from audio CDs without first copying the audio to your hard disk (via iTunes or some other method). This also happens if you move or delete the source files for the media you are burning to the DVD-R disc or the DVD-ROM portion. Copy the files back into the hard disk in their proper places, and re-import the media into the project.

✦ ***Problem:*** The DVD-R won't play on my DVD player.

  Solution: If this happens, try the DVD-R disc in your Mac. If it works fine in your Mac, the disc is burned properly. Your DVD player probably doesn't play DVD-R discs. If it doesn't work, try another blank DVD-R, and make sure you have turned off any virus protection, automatic updating or automated backup software and are disconnected from the Internet, and quit all applications. Then start iDVD again to burn the disc.

✦ ***Problem:*** My eMac went to sleep while burning and never woke up.

  Solution: You have found one strange glitch that fortunately applies to eMacs set to go into sleep mode. As a safety precaution, turn off sleep mode in the Energy Saver preferences (in System Preferences) before starting a burn. If these troubleshooting steps don't help, you might want to try the Apple iDVD support site at `www.info.apple.com/usen/idvd`.

Book V

iPod

"I could tell you more about myself, but I think the playlist on my iPod says more about me than mere words can."

Chapter 1: Have iPod, Will Travel

In This Chapter

- Connecting the iPod
- Playing music with the iPod
- Updating the iPod automatically
- Copying songs manually to the iPod

In his trademark style, Apple CEO Steve Jobs introduced the 30GB iPod with a remark about the Apple competitors: "We're into our third generation and the rest of them haven't caught up with the first."

The iPod is indeed different from any portable music device that came before. The iPod is, essentially, a hard disk and a digital music player in one device. The hard disk enables the device to hold far more music than MP3 players. The 30GB iPod model available as of this writing can hold around 7,500 songs, which is about 7,400 more songs than can fit on a typical MP3 player.

The design of the iPod is superb. At 5.6 ounces, it weighs less than two CDs. With an LCD screen, touch wheel, and buttons that feature a backlighting for clear visibility in low-light conditions, the iPod is designed for easy one-handed operation. And with a thickness of only 0.62 inches, the iPod fits comfortably in the palm of your hand.

This chapter shows you how to get your iPod connected, synchronized with iTunes, and ready to play music anywhere. You also gain a working knowledge of how to use the iPod to browse music.

Getting Started with Your iPod

The iPod is a music *player,* not a recorder (not yet anyway), but what makes the iPod great is the way it helps you manage your music. It updates itself automatically to copy your entire iTunes music library, if you want. With automatic updating, any changes, additions, or deletions you make in your iTunes library reflect in your iPod. You also have the option to copy music directly to your iPod, delete music on your iPod, and manage updating by playlist.

You'll spend only about ten seconds copying a CD's worth of music from iTunes on your Mac to your iPod. The iPod supports the most popular digital audio formats, including MP3 (including MP3 Variable Bit Rate), AIFF, WAV, and the new AAC format, which features CD-quality audio in smaller file sizes than MP3. It also supports the Audible AA spoken word file format.

The iPod is also a *data player,* perhaps the first of its kind. As a hard disk, the iPod serves as a portable backup device for important data files. You can transfer your calendar and address book to help manage your affairs on the road. Although the iPod is not as fully functional as a PDA — for example, you can't add information directly to the device — you can view the information. You can keep your calendar and address book automatically synchronized to your computer, where you normally add and edit information. We cover using the iPod as a data player in detail in Chapter 3 of this book.

The iPod is a convenient information-viewing device on the road (while listening to music, of course). It offers a sleep timer that shuts off the iPod after an amount of time that you specify, so that you can fall asleep to your music. You can even use the iPod as an alarm clock: You can choose either an alarm tone or your favorite music to wake you up.

Thinking inside the box

As you open the elegantly designed box (which reminds us of the awe we felt at opening the Beatles' *White Album* in 1968), try not to get too excited. First make sure you receive everything you were supposed to get inside the box.

The box includes a CD-ROM with the iTunes software for the Mac, MusicMatch for the PC, and the cables you need to connect to a Mac:

- Current models offer a dock and a special cable to connect the dock to the Mac's FireWire connection.
- Older models offer a FireWire cable for connecting the iPod FireWire connection to the Mac's FireWire connection.

All models come with a FireWire-compatible power adapter for connecting either the older iPod or the newer iPod-in-dock to an AC power source.

You also get a set of portable earphones and a remote controller that connects to the iPod by wire. The accessories don't stop there — you may also have a carrying case and some other goodies. A long list of optional accessories, many of which we describe in this book, is available.

You also need a few things that don't come with the iPod:

- A Mac with a built-in FireWire port, running Mac OS X version 10.1.4 or newer. You can also use the iPod with a 300 MHz or faster PC with at least 96MB of RAM running Windows ME, 2000, or XP (with at least 128MB of RAM), and a built-in or Windows-certified IEEE 1394 (FireWire) or a USB connection.
- You need to install iTunes 4.0 or newer (provided on CD-ROM with the iPod, or downloaded directly from Apple through the Software Update feature in System Preferences). Double-click the installer on the CD-ROM (or on your desktop if downloaded) to install iTunes. For PCs, you can install MusicMatch Jukebox 7.5, also included on the CD-ROM that comes with your iPod.
- ***Optional:*** Mac users can install iSync, a free utility program from Apple for synchronizing your iPod with your address book and calendar, and iCal for creating and editing your calendar. Both are available for free downloading from `www.apple.com`.

Powering up your iPod

You can take a six-hour flight from Philadelphia to Oakland, California, and listen to your iPod the entire time. The iPod includes a built-in rechargeable lithium polymer battery that provides up to eight hours of continuous music playtime on three hours of charge (playback battery time varies, however, with the type of encoder you use for the music files in iTunes — Book I, Chapter 3 has more info).

You can also fast-charge the battery to 80-percent capacity in one hour. The iPod battery recharges automatically when you connect the iPod to a power source. That power source can be either the power adapter supplied with the iPod, or a Mac connected by FireWire cable.

Older iPod models offer a Mac-like FireWire connection on the top of the iPod, but newer models use a dock that connects to the iPod and offers FireWire and USB to various devices. The dock can also connect to your home stereo through a line out connection. The dock includes a cable with a dock connector on one end and a FireWire (or optional USB) connector on the other, as shown in Figure 1-1. You can connect the FireWire end of the cable to either the Mac (to synchronize with iTunes and play iPod music in iTunes), or to the power adapter, to charge the iPod battery. The FireWire connection to the Mac provides power to the iPod as long as the Mac is not in sleep mode.

You can't remove or replace the iPod internal battery. When it goes, you need a new iPod. Don't fry the thing with some generic power adapter — use *only* the power adapter supplied with the iPod from Apple. Charging the battery to about 80 percent takes about an hour, and four hours to charge it fully, which is fast enough for most people. If your iPod is inactive for more than 14 days, you must recharge its battery — and you may as well send your iPod to us; we can find a use for it!

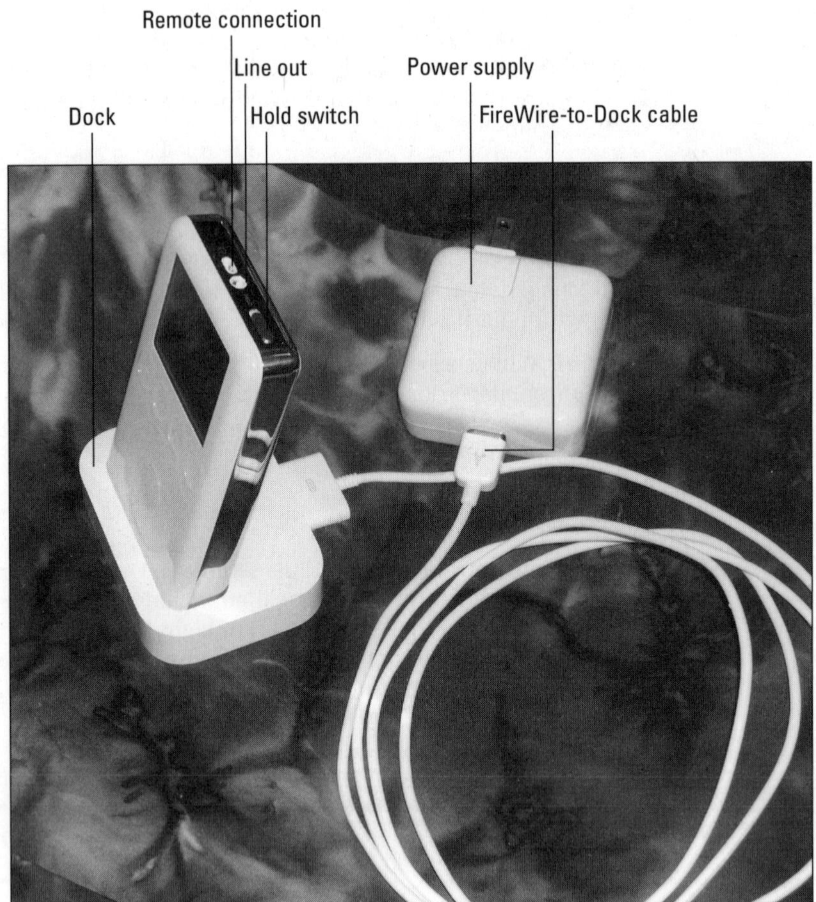

Figure 1-1: The iPod in its dock, connected to the Apple power adapter.

Keeping the iPod encased in its carrying case when charging is tempting, but also foolish — the iPod needs to dissipate its heat, and you could damage the unit. The bottom of the iPod warms up when it is powered on — the bottom functions as a cooling surface that transfers heat from inside the unit to the cooler air outside. Be sure to remove the iPod from its carrying case before you recharge it.

A battery icon in the top right corner of the iPod display indicates with a progress bar how much power is left. When you charge the battery, the icon turns into a lightning bolt inside a battery. If the icon does not animate, it means the battery is fully charged. You can disconnect the iPod and use it before the battery is fully charged.

Setting the language

Wiedergabelisten? Übersicht? (Playlists? Browse?) If your iPod is speaking in a foreign tongue, don't panic — you're not in the wrong country. You may have purchased an iPod that's set to a language you don't understand. More likely, someone set it to a different language either accidentally or on purpose (as a practical joke). Fortunately you can change the setting without having to know the language it's set to.

To set the language, no matter what language the menu is using, follow these steps (iPod software version 2.0):

1. **Press the Menu button repeatedly until pressing it does not change the words on the display.**

   When the Menu button no longer changes the display, you are at the main menu.

2. **Select the fourth item from the top (it should be the Settings item in English).**

   Use your finger or thumb to scroll clockwise on the scrolling pad until the fourth item is highlighted, and then press the button at the center of the scrolling pad (the Select button) to select the item. The Settings menu appears.

3. **Select the sixth item from the top (it should be Language).**

   The Language menu appears.

4. **Select the language you want to use. (English is at the top of the list.)**

If these steps don't do the trick, the iPod main menu may have been customized (something you can find out how to do in Chapter 3 of this book). To get around this, you can reset all of the iPod settings back to the defaults. (Unfortunately, resetting your iPod settings back to the defaults wipes out any customizations you may have made, so you will have to redo any repeat/shuffle settings, alarms, backlight timer settings, and so on.)

Follow these steps to reset all your settings, no matter what language is displayed:

1. **Press the Menu button repeatedly until pressing it does not change the words on the display.**

   When the Menu button no longer changes the display, you are at the main menu.

2. **Select the fourth item from the top (it should be the Settings item in English).**

Use your finger or thumb to scroll clockwise on the scrolling pad until the fourth item is highlighted, and then press the button at the center of the scrolling pad (the Select button) to select the item. The Settings menu appears.

3. **Select the item at the bottom of the menu (it should be the Reset All Settings item).**

   The Reset All Settings menu appears.

4. **Select the second menu item (it should be the Reset item).**

   The Language menu appears.

5. **Select the language you want to use. (English is at the top of the list).**

The language you choose is now used for all the iPod menus. Now don't go pulling that joke on someone else!

Connecting to the Mac

Your Mac should have a FireWire connection marked by a radioactive-looking Y symbol. The cable supplied with your iPod has a six-pin connector that inserts into your Mac's FireWire connection.

Depending on your iPod model, that cable either connects directly to your iPod (older models) or to a dock. If you already use the cable to charge up the iPod, you can disconnect the cable from the power adapter and connect that same end to the Mac. In fact, you can leave your dock connected to your Mac in this fashion and use the Mac to also charge up the iPod battery.

When you first connect the iPod to the Mac, the iTunes Setup Assistant appears, as shown in Figure 1-2. In this dialog box, you can name your iPod, which is a good idea if you plan on sharing several iPods among several computers.

Figure 1-2: Set up the iPod for use with a Mac with the Setup Assistant.

In the Setup Assistant, you can also turn on or off the option to automatically update your iPod. If this is your first time using an iPod, you probably want to fill it up right away, so leave this option checked. If you want to copy only a portion of your library to the iPod, uncheck this option and skip to the section, "Copying music directly to the iPod," later in this chapter.

The Setup Assistant allows you to register your iPod with Apple to take advantage of Apple support. When you reach the last dialog box of the Setup Assistant, click the Done button.

After you click the Done button in the Setup Assistant, the iPod name appears in the iTunes Source list near the top. If you selected the automatic update feature in the iTunes Setup Assistant, the iPod name appears grayed out in the Source list, and you can't open it. If you have the automatic update feature turned off, the iPod name appears just like any other source in the Source list, and you can open it and play songs on the iPod through iTunes and your Mac speakers. See Book I for more about the Source list in iTunes.

After finishing setup, the iPod icon also appears on the Finder desktop. If you leave your iPod connected to the Mac, the iPod appears on the desktop and in iTunes whenever you start iTunes.

To see how much free space is left on the iPod, click the iPod icon on the desktop and choose File⇨Get Info. The Finder displays the Get Info window with information about capacity, amount used, and available space. You can also use the About command in the iPod Settings menu: Settings⇨About from the main menu. The iPod information screen appears with capacity and available space.

Playing in the Hand

Apple designed the iPod to be held in one hand with simple operations performed by thumb (see Figure 1-3). A unique circular scrolling pad makes scrolling through an entire music collection quick and easy. As you scroll, items on the menu are highlighted. The button at the center of the scrolling pad (the Select button) selects whatever is highlighted in the menu display. The buttons above the scrolling pad perform simple functions when you press them.

Thumbing through the menus

The iPod menu starts out with five selections, as follows:

- **Playlists:** Select a playlist to play.
- **Browse:** Select by artist, album, song, genre, or composer.

- **Extras:** View and set the clock and alarm clock, view contacts, view your calendar, view notes, and play games. See Chapter 3 of this book for more information on these features.
- **Settings:** Set display settings, menu settings, the backlight timer, the date and time, the language, shuffle and repeat modes, the clicker, and the method of sorting your contacts. We describe these functions in Chapter 3 of this book. You can also use the equalizer (covered in Chapter 2 of this book),
- **Backlight:** Turns on or off the backlighting for the iPod display.

Using the buttons

The buttons above the scroll pad do obvious things for song playback:

- **Previous/Rewind:** Press once to start a song over. Press twice to skip to the previous song. Press and hold to rewind through a song.
- **Menu:** Press once to go back to the previous menu. Each time you press, you go back to a previous menu until you reach the main menu. Press and hold the button to turn on the backlight.
- **Play/Pause:** Press to play the selected song, album, or playlist. Press Play/Pause when a song is playing to pause the playback.
- **Next/Fast-forward:** Press once to skip to the next song. Press and hold Next/Fast-forward to fast-forward through the song.

The scroll pad and buttons can do more complex functions when used in combination:

- **Turn iPod on:** Press any button.
- **Turn iPod off:** Press and hold the Play/Pause button.
- **Disable the iPod buttons:** Push the Hold switch to the other side, so that an orange bar appears (the Hold position). Do this to keep from accidentally pressing the buttons. To reactivate the iPod buttons, push the Hold switch back to the other side so that the orange bar disappears (the normal position).
- **Reset the iPod:** Set the Hold switch to the Hold position, and then back to normal. Then press the Menu and Play/Pause buttons simultaneously for about five seconds, until the Apple logo appears in the iPod display. See Chapter 3 of this book for more about resetting.
- **Turn Backlight on and off:** Press and hold the Menu button (or select the Backlight option from the main menu).

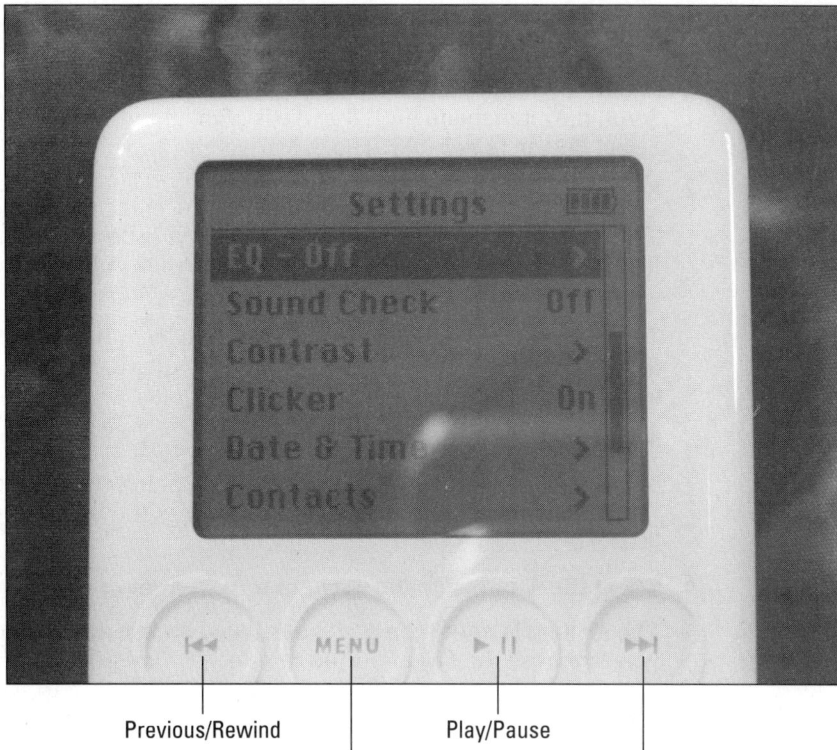

Figure 1-3: The iPod scrolling pad and buttons.

- **Change the volume:** While playing a song (the display says `Now Playing`), use the scroll pad to adjust the volume. A volume slider appears in the iPod display indicating the volume level as you scroll. See the section, "Adjusting the sound volume," later in this chapter.
- **Skip to any point in a song:** While playing a song (the display says `Now Playing`), press and hold the Select button until the progress bar appears indicating where you are in the song, and then use the scroll pad to scroll to any point in the song.

Locating and Playing Songs

To play a song, you can select a song by artist, by album, or by playlist. You create playlists in iTunes, which we describe in Book I, Chapter 2.

Follow these steps to locate a song by artist and then album:

1. **Select the Browse item from the iPod main menu.**

   Scroll the main menu until Browse is highlighted, and then press the Select button to select it. The Browse menu appears.

2. **Select the Artists item.**

   The Artists item is at the top of the menu and should already be highlighted; and then press the Select button to select it. The Artists menu appears.

   To browse by genre, select the Genres item, and then select a genre from the Genres menu to get a reduced list of artists that have songs in that genre (in alphabetical order).

3. **Select an artist from the Artists menu.**

   The artists are listed in alphabetical order. Scroll the Artists menu until the artist name is highlighted, and then press the Select button to select it. The artist name's menu appears.

4. **Select the All item or the name of an album from artist name's menu.**

   The All item is at the top of the menu and should already be highlighted; you can press the Select button to select it. Or scroll until an album name is highlighted, and then press the Select button to select it. A song list appears.

5. **Select the song from the list.**

   The songs in the album list are in album order (the order they appear on the album); in the All list, they are in album order for each album. Scroll the list until the song name is highlighted, and then press the Select button to select it. The artist name and song name appear.

Follow these steps to locate a song by album directly:

1. **Select the Browse item from the iPod main menu.**

   Scroll the main menu until Browse is highlighted, and then press the Select button to select it. The Browse menu appears.

2. **Select the Albums item.**

   Scroll the Browse menu until Albums is highlighted, and then press the Select button to select it. The Albums menu appears.

   Select the Composers item to choose a composer, and then select a composer from the Composers menu to get a list of songs for that composer.

3. **Select an album from the Albums menu.**

   The albums are listed in alphabetical order (without any reference to artist, which may make identification difficult). Scroll the Albums menu until the album name is highlighted, and then press the Select button to select it. A song list appears.

4. **Select the song from the list.**

   The songs in the album list are in album order (the order they appear on the album). Scroll the list until the song name is highlighted, and then press the Select button to select it. The artist name and song name appear.

Follow these steps to locate a song by playlist:

1. **Select the Playlists item from the iPod main menu.**

   The Playlists item is at the top of the main menu and may already be highlighted; if not, scroll the main menu until Playlists is highlighted, and then press the Select button to select it. The Playlists menu appears.

2. **Select a playlist.**

   The playlists are listed in alphabetical order. Scroll the Playlists menu until the playlist name is highlighted, and then press the Select button to select it. A list of songs in the playlist appears.

3. **Select the song from the list.**

   The songs in the playlist are in playlist order (the order defined for the playlist in iTunes). Scroll the list until the song name is highlighted, and then press the Select button to select it. The artist name and song name appear.

Repeating and shuffling songs

If you want to drive yourself crazy repeating the same song over and over, the iPod is happy to oblige. More likely you will want to repeat a sequence of songs, and you can easily do that too.

You can also shuffle songs within an album, playlist, or the entire library. By *shuffle,* we mean play in random order. You can even set the iPod to repeat an album or playlist, but still shuffle the playing order.

While simply pressing the Previous/Rewind button to repeat a song is easier, you can set the iPod to repeat a single song automatically by following these steps:

1. **Locate and play a song.**

   Locate and play a song as described in "Locating and Playing Songs." The song starts playing.

2. **Press the Menu button repeatedly to return to the main menu, and then select the Settings item.**

   The Settings menu appears.

3. **Scroll the Settings menu until Repeat is highlighted.**

   The Repeat setting displays `Off` next to it.

4. **Press the Select button once (`Off` changes to `One`) to repeat one song. If you press the button more than once, keep pressing until `One` appears.**

To repeat all the songs in the selected album or playlist:

1. **Locate and play a song in the album or playlist.**

   Locate and play a song, described earlier in this chapter, in the "Locating and Playing Songs" section. The song starts playing.

2. **Press the Menu button repeatedly to return to the main menu, and then select the Settings item.**

   The Settings menu appears.

3. **Scroll the Settings menu until the Repeat item is highlighted.**

   The Repeat setting displays `Off` next to it.

4. **Press the Select button twice (`Off` changes to `All`) to repeat all the songs in the album or playlist.**

To shuffle songs in an album or playlist:

1. **Locate and play a song in the album or playlist.**

   Locate and play a song, described in the section, "Locating and Playing Songs," earlier in this chapter. The song starts playing.

2. **Press the Menu button repeatedly to return to the main menu, and then select the Settings item.**

   The Settings menu appears.

3. **Scroll the Settings menu until the Shuffle item is highlighted.**

   The Shuffle setting displays `Off` next to it.

4. **Press the Select button once (`Off` changes to `Songs`) to shuffle the songs in the selected album or playlist.**

To shuffle all the albums in your iPod while still playing the songs in each album in normal album order:

1. **Press the Menu button repeatedly to return to the main menu, and then select the Settings item.**

   The Settings menu appears.

2. **Scroll the Settings menu until the Shuffle item is highlighted.**

   The Shuffle setting displays `Off` next to it.

3. **Press the Select button twice (`Off` changes to `Albums`) to shuffle the albums without shuffling the songs within each album.**

When the iPod is set to shuffle, it won't repeat a song until it has played through the entire album, playlist, or library.

Creating on-the-go playlists

If you don't have playlists from iTunes (or you don't want to hear those playlists), you can create a temporary on-the-go playlist (not available in older iPod models). You can select a list of songs or entire albums to play in a certain order, queuing up the songs or albums on the iPod. Queued songs appear automatically in a playlist called "On-The-Go" in the Playlists menu (to use the Playlists menu, see the section, "Locating and Playing Songs," earlier in this chapter).

To select songs or entire albums for the on-the-go playlist:

1. **Locate and highlight a song or album title.**
2. **Press and hold the Select button on the scroll pad until the title flashes.**
3. **Repeat Steps 1 and 2 in the order you want the songs or albums played.**

To play the on-the-go playlist, scroll to the On-The-Go item, which is always at the very end of the list in the Playlists menu. To find the Playlists menu, see the section, "Locating and Playing Songs," earlier in this chapter.

To clear the list of queued songs:

1. **Press the Menu button repeatedly to return to the main menu, and then select the Playlists item.**

   The Playlists menu appears.

2. **Select the On-The-Go item.**

   The song list in the on-the-go playlist appears.

3. **Scroll to the very end of the song list, and select the Clear Playlist item.**

   The Clear menu appears.

4. **Select the Clear Playlist item.**

   The songs disappear from the playlist

Adjusting the sound volume

The iPod is quite loud when set to its highest volume. To adjust the volume:

1. **Select and play a song on the iPod.**
2. **Change the volume with the scroll pad.**

   A volume bar appears in the iPod display to guide you. Scroll with your thumb or finger clockwise to increase the volume, and counter-clockwise to decrease the volume.

If you have the Apple iPod Remote that attaches to the iPod connections on the top, you can control the volume using the volume button on the remote. Use the remote to adjust the volume, play or pause a song, fast-forward or rewind, and skip to the next or previous song. You can also disable the buttons on the remote by setting the remote's Hold switch (similar to the iPod Hold switch). To find out about the iPod Remote, see Chapter 2 of this book.

Updating Automatically

If you're too busy to copy specific songs to your iPod and your entire iTunes music library fits on your iPod, why not just copy everything? Copying your library is just as fast as copying individual songs, if not faster, and you don't have to do anything except connect the iPod to the Mac.

Out of the box, the iPod updates itself automatically, *synchronizing* itself — the iPod matches your library exactly, song for song, playlist for playlist — with your music library. iTunes automatically copies everything in your iTunes music library to the iPod. If you made changes in iTunes after the last time you synchronized, those changes are automatically made in the iPod when you synchronize again. If you added or deleted songs in your library, those songs are added or deleted in the iPod library.

Songs stored remotely (such as songs shared from other iTunes libraries on a network) are not synchronized because they are not physically on your computer. See Book I for more info on how to share music over a network with iTunes.

If you share an iPod with someone else, chances are you want to update the playlist rather than the entire library. That way, you automatically erase all the music on the iPod associated with the other guy's playlists, and copy the music in your library associated with *your* playlists. All this happens automatically so that you don't have to think about it after setting it up. Of course, because the music for your iPod is on your computer, someone erasing your music from the iPod isn't a big deal — you can update the iPod quickly with your music when it's your turn.

You can prevent the iPod from automatically updating by holding down the ⌘ and Option keys as you connect the iPod, and keeping them held down until the iPod name appears in the iTunes Source list. This works even if you choose to automatically update the iPod in the Setup Assistant, as we describe earlier in this chapter, in the "Connecting to the Mac" section.

Updating from the library automatically

The iPod is set up by default to automatically update itself from your iTunes library. Just follow these simple steps to set the updating process in motion:

1. **Connect the iPod to your Mac through the Mac's FireWire connection.**

   When you connect the iPod to the Mac, your iPod first automatically synchronizes with your iTunes music library, unless you turned off the Automatic Update option in the Setup Assistant, or hold down the ⌘ and Option keys while connecting the iPod. (See the section, "Connecting to the Mac," earlier in this chapter, for more information about connecting.)

2. **Click the iPod eject button, which appears in the bottom right side of the iTunes window.**

   You can also eject (or *unmount*) the iPod by dragging the iPod icon on the desktop to the Trash. After you drag it to the Trash, the iPod displays an `OK to disconnect` message. You can then disconnect the iPod from its dock, or disconnect the dock from the computer.

While the updating is in progress, do not disconnect your iPod. The iPod displays a `Do not disconnect` warning. The iPod is a hard disk, after all, and hard disks need to be closed down properly in order for you not to loose any critical data.

If you change your iPod preferences to update manually or automatically by playlist, as we describe later in this chapter, in the "Updating Manually" section, you can change the setting back to automatic update at any time. After changing the setting to automatic update, updating occurs automatically unless you change the setting back to manual, or hold down the ⌘ and Option keys while connecting the iPod.

Change your iPod preferences to automatic update by following these steps:

1. **Connect the iPod to your Mac through the Mac's FireWire connection.**
2. **Select the iPod name in the iTunes Source list.**
3. **Click the iPod options button on the bottom right side of the iTunes window, to the left of the equalizer button, as shown in Figure 1-4.**

   The iPod Preferences window appears, as shown in Figure 1-5.
4. **Select the Automatically Update All Songs and Playlists option.**

   iTunes displays a confirmation message (see Figure 1-6).

Figure 1-4: Open the iPod options to set preferences.

Figure 1-5: Setting preferences.

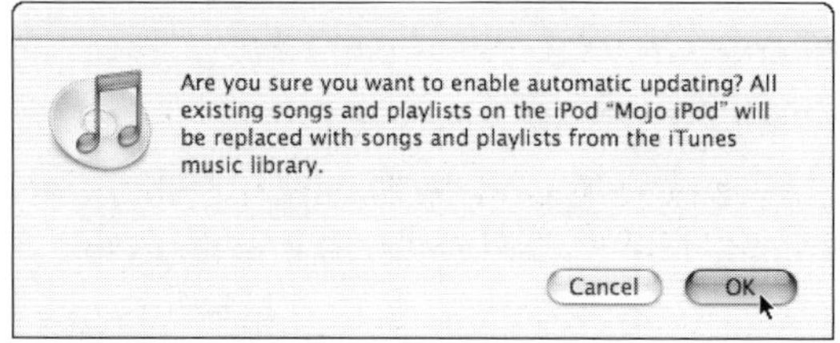

Figure 1-6: Confirm you want to update your music library automatically.

5. **Click OK to go ahead.**
6. **Click the iPod eject button which appears in the bottom-right side of the iTunes window.**

   You can also eject (or *unmount*) the iPod by dragging the iPod icon on the desktop to the Trash. After you drag it to the Trash, the iPod displays an `OK to disconnect` message. You can then disconnect the iPod from its dock, or disconnect the dock from the computer.

If you connect your iPod to another Mac, you may be in for a surprise. When you connect an iPod previously linked to another Mac, iTunes displays the message `This iPod is linked to another iTunes music library. Do you want to change the link to this iTunes music library and replace all existing songs and playlists on this iPod with those from this library?` If you don't want to change the iPod to have this other music library, click the No button. Otherwise, the contents of the iPod erase and iTunes starts to update the iPod with its library. By clicking the No button, you change that computer's iTunes setting to manually update.

You can prevent the iPod from automatically updating by holding down the ⌘ and Option keys as you connect the iPod, and keeping them held down until the iPod name appears in the iTunes Source list.

Updating automatically by playlist

You can set up the iPod to update only selected playlists automatically. If you want to copy playlists manually, see the section, "Updating Manually," later in this chapter.

Before using this update option, create the playlists in iTunes (see Book I, Chapter 2) that you want to copy to the iPod. Then follow these steps:

1. **Connect the iPod to your Mac through the Mac's FireWire connection.**
2. **Select the iPod name in the iTunes Source list.**
3. **Click the iPod options button.**

   The iPod Preferences window appears (refer to Figure 1-5).
4. **Select the Automatically Update Selected Playlists Only option.**
5. **In the list box, select the check box next to each playlist that you want to copy in the update, as shown in Figure 1-7.**

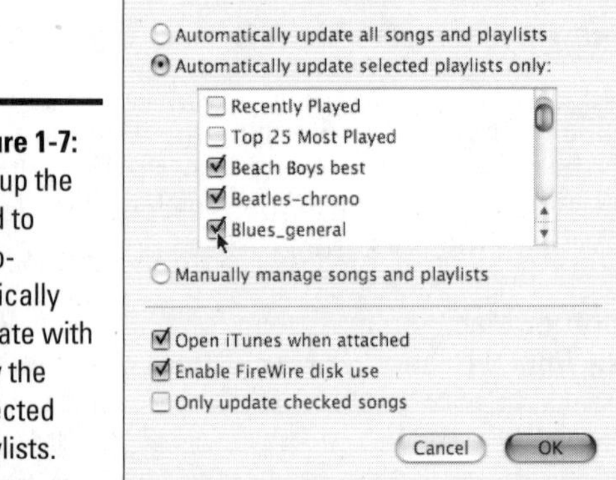

Figure 1-7: Set up the iPod to automatically update with only the selected playlists.

6. **Click OK.**

   iTunes automatically updates the iPod by erasing its contents and copying only the playlists you selected in Step 5.
7. **Click the iPod eject button which appears in the bottom-right side of the iTunes window.**

Updating selected songs automatically

You may want to update the iPod automatically, but only with selected songs. To use this method, you must first select the songs you want to transfer to the iPod in the iTunes library and unselecting the songs you don't want to transfer.

You can quickly select or unselect an entire album by selecting an album in Browse view, and holding down the ⌘ key.

After selecting the songs to transfer, follow these steps:

1. **Connect the iPod to your Mac through the Mac's FireWire connection.**
2. **Select the iPod name in the iTunes Source list.**
3. **Click the iPod options button.**

   The iPod Preferences window appears (refer to Figure 1-5).
4. **Select the Automatically Update All Songs and Playlists option and click OK for the** `Are you sure you want to enable automatic updating` **message that appears.**
5. **Select the Only Update Checked Songs check box and click OK.**

   iTunes automatically updates the iPod by erasing its contents and copying only the songs in the iTunes library that you selected.
6. **Click the iPod eject button which appears in the bottom-right side of the iTunes window.**

Updating Manually

When your iPod is set to update automatically (the entire library, by playlist, or by selected song, as described in the "Updating Automatically" section, earlier in this chapter), the iPod contents are grayed out in the iTunes window. Because you manage the contents automatically, you don't have direct access to the songs in the iPod using iTunes.

However, if you set your iPod to update manually, the entire contents of the iPod is active and available in iTunes. You can copy music directly to your iPod, delete songs on the iPod, and edit the iPod playlists directly.

You may have one or more reasons for updating manually, but some obvious ones are the following:

✦ Your entire music library may be too big for your iPod, and therefore, you want to copy individual albums, songs, or playlists to the iPod directly rather.

✦ You want to share a single music library with several iPods, and you have different playlists that you want to copy to each iPod directly.

- You want to copy some music from another computer's music library, without deleting any music from your iPod.
- You want to play the songs on your iPod using iTunes on the Mac, playing through the Mac's speakers.

With manual updating, you can add or delete music from your iPod using iTunes. The iPod name appears in the iTunes Source list, and you can double click to open it, displaying the iPod playlists.

Setting the iPod to update manually

To set your iPod to update manually, follow these steps:

1. **Connect the iPod to your Mac, holding down the ⌘ and Option keys to prevent automatic updating.**

   Continue holding them down until the iPod name appears in the iTunes Source list.

2. **Select the iPod name in the iTunes Source list.**
3. **Click the iPod options button.**

   The iPod Preferences window appears (refer to Figure 1-5).

4. **Check the Manually Manage Songs and Playlists option.**

   iTunes displays the `Disabling automatic update requires manually unmounting the iPod before each disconnect` message.

5. **Click OK to accept the new iPod preferences.**

   The iPod contents now appear active in iTunes, and not grayed out.

Copying music directly to the iPod

To copy music to your iPod directly, follow these steps:

1. **Select the iTunes music library in the iTunes Source list.**

   The library's songs appear in a list view or in Browse view, as described in Book I, Chapter 1.

2. **Drag items directly from your iTunes music library over the iPod name in the Source list, as shown in Figure 1-8.**

   When you copy a playlist, all the songs associated with the playlist copy along with the playlist itself. When you copy an album, all the song in the album are copied.

3. **Click the iPod eject button which appears in the bottom-right side of the iTunes window.**

Figure 1-8: Copy an album of songs directly from the iTunes library to the iPod.

Deleting music from the iPod only

With manual updating, you can delete songs from the iPod directly. While an automatic update adds and deletes songs, manual deletion is a nice feature if you just want to go in and delete a song or an album.

To delete any song in the song list with your iPod set to manual updating, follow these steps:

1. **Select the iPod in the iTunes Source list.**
2. **Open the iPod's contents in iTunes.**
3. **Select a song or album on the iPod in iTunes, and press the Delete key, or choose Edit⇨Clear.**

   iTunes displays a warning to make sure you want to do this; click OK to go ahead or Cancel to stop. If you want to delete a playlist, select the playlist and press the Delete key or choose Edit⇨Clear. As in the iTunes library, if you delete a playlist, the songs themselves are not deleted.

Editing Songs on the iPod

With manual updating, you have the option to edit song information and playlists directly in the iPod using iTunes. While information edited in the iTunes library is automatically copied, with automatic update, you may want to edit playlists and song information manually, just on your iPod.

Editing playlists

You can also create playlists just on the iPod itself, by following these steps:

1. **Select the iPod in the iTunes Source list and open the iPod contents.**
2. **Create a new playlist by clicking the + button in the bottom left corner of iTunes under the Source list, or choose File⇨New Playlist.**

   An "untitled playlist" appears in the Source list.
3. **Type a name for the untitled playlist.**

   The new playlist appears in the Source list under the iPod. After you type a new name, iTunes automatically sorts it into alphabetical order in the list.
4. **Click the name of the iPod in the Source list and drag songs from the iPod song list to the playlist.**

   You can also turn click the Browse button to find songs more easily.

The order of songs in the playlist is based on the order in which you drag them to the list. You can rearrange the list by dragging songs within the playlist. For more information about creating playlists in iTunes and arranging songs in playlists, see Book I, Chapter 2.

You can create smart playlists in exactly the same way as in the iTunes music library — read all about it in Book I, Chapter 2.

Editing song information

With the iPod contents open in iTunes, you can edit song information just like you do in the iTunes library by scrolling down the song list and selecting songs.

After selecting the iPod in the Source list and opening its contents, click the Browse button. In Browse view, you can browse the iPod contents, and find the songs by artist and album. See Book I, Chapter 2 to find out how to browse in iTunes.

You can edit the Song Name, Artist, Album, Genre, and My Ratings information for the iPod songs directly in the columns in the song list. To edit song information, locate the song, and click inside the text field of a column to type new text.

Editing this information by choosing File⇨Get Info and typing the text into the Song Information window may be easier. Book I, Chapter 2 describes how to edit song information in detail.

Although the track information iTunes grabs from the Internet is usually enough, it is by no means complete. Some facts, such as composer credits, may not be included in the information grabbed from the Internet. However, composer information is important for iPod users because the iPod lets you scroll music by composer as well as by artist, album, and song. If you have the time and inclination to add composer credits, it is worth your while because you can then search, sort, and create playlists based on this information. Book I, Chapter 2 describes how to edit song information and add information such as composer credits to songs in your library. When you copy these songs from iTunes to your iPod, his information also copies.

Chapter 2: Getting Wired for Sound

In This Chapter

- **Playing the iPod through the Mac**
- **Connecting the iPod to home stereos, headphones, and speakers**
- **Playing the iPod while traveling**
- **Enhancing the sound quality**

Sound studio engineers who make recordings can tell you that to produce music for listening environments, you have to listen in that environment. Studios typically have home stereo speakers as monitors so that the engineers can hear what the music sounds like on a home stereo. When tape cassettes and car decks became available, pop music artists started to routinely take mixes of their music on cassette and go on long drives.

The point is that the quality of the sound is no better than the weakest link in the audio system. Music mixed to a mono channel for car radios is not going to sound as good on a home stereo, and vice-versa.

The audio CD bridges the gap between home stereos and car stereos and opens up the use of high-quality music anywhere, with a decent pair of headphones. Music production changed considerably over the last few decades as more people listened to higher-quality FM radio, bought massive home stereos, and eventually bought CD players for their cars and boats and portable players to use while flying and jogging.

The iPod represents a major leap forward in bridging the gap between home stereos, car stereos, and portable players. Picking up where CDs left off, the iPod offers all of the features of high-quality music not just for home stereos, but for all listening environments.

This chapter explains how to connect the iPod to a variety of different speaker systems and use the iPod in different listening environments. We also offer a summary of accessories, such as headphones, power cables, and connection cables and devices, which together enable you to use the iPod just about anywhere.

Making Connections

The sleek iPod has only two connections (well, two and a half on the newer models), but those two are enough to make the iPod a versatile music player. The connections, shown in Figure 2-1 (current models) and Figure 2-2 (older models), are as follows:

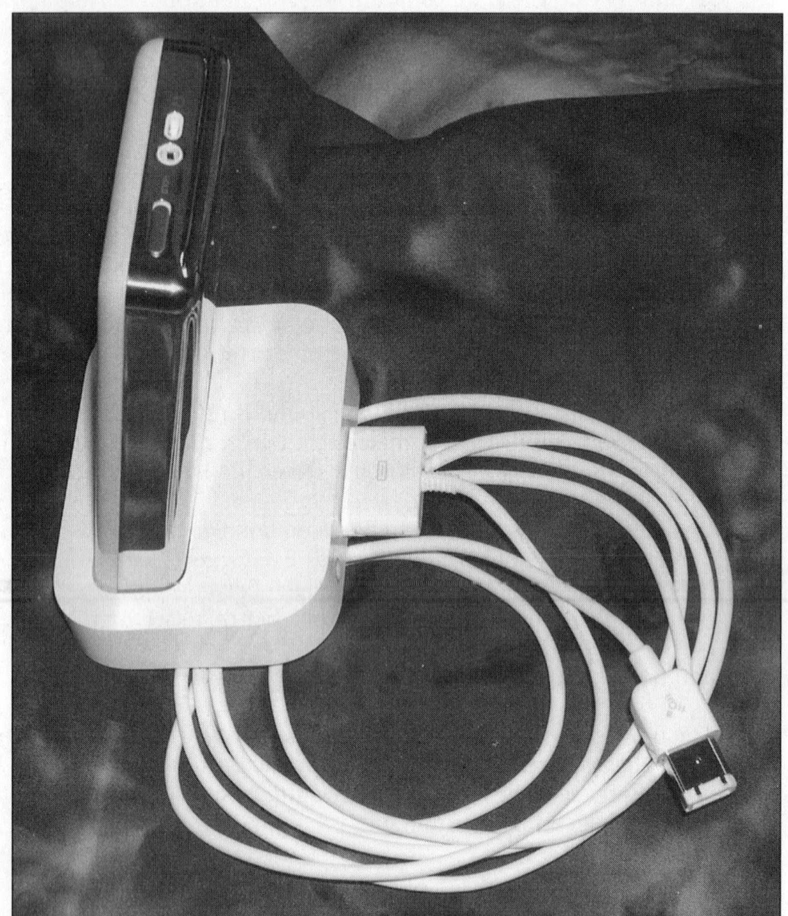

Figure 2-1: A current model 30GB iPod with its dock.

Figure 2-2: An older model 20GB iPod with connections on top.

- **FireWire:** New models have a dock connection on the bottom. The dock includes a cable with a dock connector on one end and a FireWire (or optional USB) connector on the other. Older iPods have a Mac-style FireWire connection on the top that works with any standard Mac FireWire cable.
- **Headphone out (with control socket):** The headphone and control socket combination connection allows you to plug in the Apple iPod Remote controller, which in turn offers a headphone out connection. The remote offers playback and volume control buttons. You can also connect headphones, or a 3.5-millimeter stereo mini-plug cable, to the headphone out connection.
- **The dock connections:** The iPod dock offers two connections — one for the special cable to connect to a FireWire (or USB) connection, and a line-out connection for a stereo mini-plug cable (or headphones).

You can connect the FireWire end to either the Mac (for synchronizing with iTunes and playing the iPod with the Mac), or to the power adapter to charge the iPod battery. The FireWire connection to the Mac provides power to the iPod as long as the Mac is not in sleep mode.

Playing through the Mac

You can play your iPod music on your Mac, through your Mac's speakers. Depending on your Mac model, you may already have excellent speakers. If you're short on disk space, use the iPod to hold all your music. Your music library doesn't have to be on your Mac's hard disk. You can use an iPod music library with iTunes on your Mac or on another Mac running iTunes. You hear the music from the Mac's speakers and through the headphone connection to the Mac.

Apple designed Macs to have connections for adding your own speakers. When you play music in iTunes, it plays through those speakers.

With an iPod set to manual updating, as we describe in Chapter 1 of this book, its contents are available in the iTunes window. You can play the songs on your iPod in iTunes.

To play music on your iPod in iTunes, follow these steps:

1. **Connect the iPod to your Mac, holding down the ⌘ and Option keys to prevent automatic updating.**
2. **Set your iPod to update manually.**

   To set your iPod to update manually, refer to Chapter 1 of this book.
3. **Select the iPod name in the iTunes Source list.**
4. **Open the iPod contents in iTunes.**

   After selecting the iPod in the iTunes Source list you can click the triangle next to its name to open the iPod, so that you can scroll or browse the iPod songs. You can open the iPod lists just like any other iTunes source in the list, as shown in Figure 2-3.
5. **Scroll or browse the iPod song lists in iTunes to locate a song.**

   To find out how to browse in iTunes, see Book I, Chapter 2.
6. **Click the song in iTunes and click the iTunes play button.**

   To find out how to play music tracks in iTunes, see Book I, Chapter 1.

Figure 2-3: Play the iPod songs and playlists, and browse the iPod using iTunes on your Mac.

To connect to a different Mac than your own, and play your iPod music, follow the steps. However, after connecting your iPod to the other Mac, iTunes starts up and displays the `This iPod is linked to another iTunes music library. Do you want to change the link to this iTunes music library and replace all existing songs and playlists on this iPod with those from this library?` message. Click the No button.

By clicking the No button, you change that computer's iTunes setting to manually update. You can then add songs from that computer to your iPod, or edit your iPod playlists and song list on that computer (as we describe in Chapter 1 of this book).

Unless you want to change the contents of your iPod to reflect this computer's music library, don't click the Yes button, If you click the Yes button, the contents of the iPod erase and iTunes updates the iPod with the library on this computer. If you're using a public computer with no music in its library, you are erasing the iPod without any music to add. If you're using a friend's computer, your friend's library copies to the iPod, erasing whatever was in your iPod.

Connecting to a home stereo

Home stereo systems come in many shapes and sizes, from the monster component racks of audiophiles to the itty-bitty boom boxes for kids. We're not talking about alarm-clock radios, but stereos with speakers that allow you to add another input device, such as a portable CD player. You need to be able to connect a device to the component of the stereo system that accepts input.

In more expensive stereo systems, the component is typically the preamp/amplifier/tuner. Less expensive stereos and boom boxes are all one piece, but connections should be somewhere on the device for audio input.

Most stereos allow you to connect an input device using RCA-type cables — one (typically marked red) for the right channel, and one for the left channel. All you need is a cable with a stereo mini-plug on one end, and RCA-type connectors on the other, as shown in Figure 2-4. Stereo mini-plugs have two black bands on the plug, while a mono mini-plug has only one black band.

We recommend the Monster high performance dual "balanced" iCable for iPod, available in the Apple Store, for audiophiles with excellent stereo equipment; any cables you can get at a consumer electronics store are fine for anyone else.

Connect the stereo mini-plug to the iPod dock's line-out connection, or to the headphone connection at the top of the iPod (use the headphone connection on iPods without docks). Connect the left and right RCA-type connectors to the stereo system's audio input — whatever's available, such as AUX IN, for auxiliary input, or TAPE IN, for tape deck input, or CD IN for CD player input.

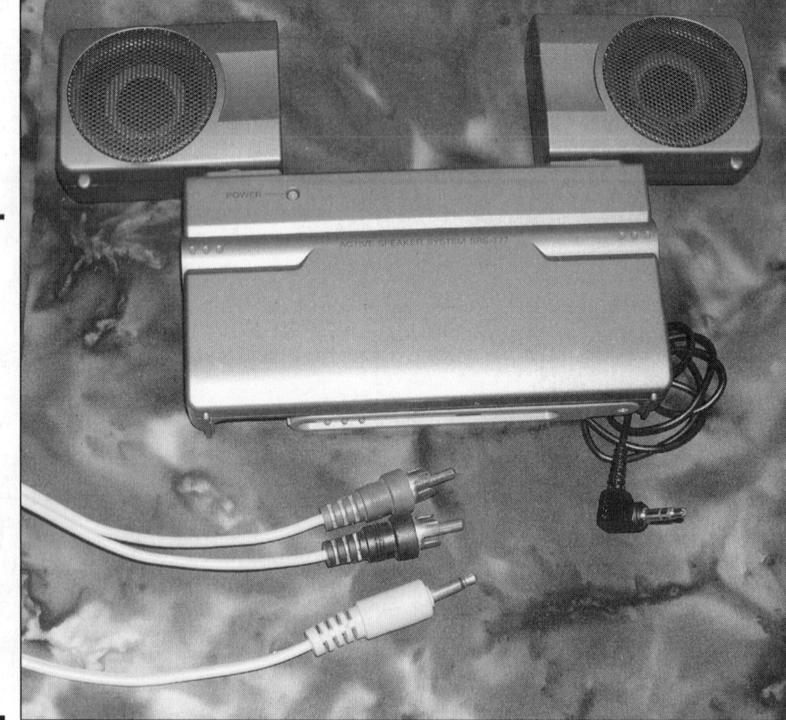

Figure 2-4: RCA left and right connectors are on top, and the stereo mini-plug on the bottom, along with a hard-wired portable speaker system and its stereo mini-plug.

Don't use the PHONO IN (for phonograph input) on most stereos. These connections are for phonographs (turntables) and are not properly matched for other kinds of input devices. You may get a loud buzzing sound if you do this, which could damage your speakers.

You can control the volume from the iPod using the scroll pad, which we describe in Chapter 1 of this book. This controls the volume of the signal from the iPod. Stereo systems typically have their own volume control to raise or lower the volume of the amplified speakers. For optimal sound quality when using a home stereo, set the iPod volume at less than half the maximum output and adjust your listening volume through your stereo controls (using the volume knob or equivalent). You prevent over-amplification, which can cause distortion and reduce audio quality.

Connecting headphones and portable speakers

Apple designed the iPod to provide excellent sound through headphones, and through the headphone connection the iPod can also serve music to hard-wired portable speaker systems. The speaker systems must be self-powered and allow audio to be input through a 3.5 mm stereo connection.

The iPod has a powerful 60 mW amplifier to deliver audio through the headphone connection. It has a frequency response of 20 Hz to 20 kHz, which provides distortion-free music at the lowest or highest pitches.

Hard-wired speaker systems typically offers a stereo mini-plug you can attach directly to the iPod headphone connection or the dock line-out connection. To place the speakers farther away from the iPod, you can use a stereo mini-plug extension cable available at most consumer electronics stores, which has a stereo mini-plug on one end and a stereo mini-socket on the other.

Hard-wired portable speaker systems typically have volume controls to raise or lower the volume. For optimal sound quality when using a hard-wired speaker system, set the iPod volume at less than half the maximum output and adjust your listening volume through your speaker system controls.

Listening aboard Planes, Trains, and Automobiles

When you travel, take an extra pair of headphones or earbuds, and a splitter cable, such as the one in Figure 2-5, available in any consumer electronics store, or the Monster iSplitter available in the Apple Store. You can plug both headphones into the iPod and share the music with someone on the road.

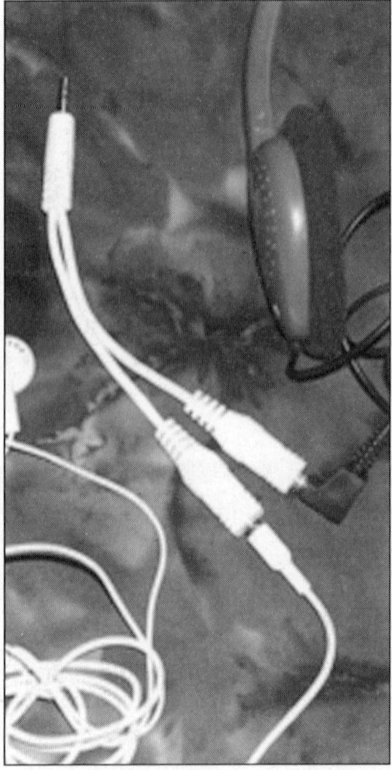

Figure 2-5: A headphone cable that splits into two, allowing two sets of headphones.

You can truly go anywhere with an iPod. If you can't plug it into a power source while playing, you can use the battery for up to ten hours of playing time before having to charge. You can find all the accessories needed to travel with an iPod in the Apple Store at `www.apple.com`.

Put on "Eight Miles High" by the Byrds while cruising at 40,000 ft. Ride the rails listening to "All Aboard" by Muddy Waters, followed by "Peavine" by John Lee Hooker. Or cruise on the Autobahn with Kraftwerk. Whatever. You have an entire music library in your shirt pocket.

The iPod is designed to provide high-quality music no matter what the environment — even in an earthquake. With skip protection, you don't have to worry about turbulence, potholes, or strenuous exercise causing the music to skip. In addition to the hard drive, iPod has a 32MB memory cache. The cache is made up of solid-state memory, with no mechanical or moving parts, so movement doesn't affect playback. Skip protection works by preloading up to 20 minutes of music to the cache at a time. The iPod plays music from the memory cache rather than the hard drive.

Playing car tunes

We always wanted a car you can fill up with music just as easily as filling it up with gasoline, without having to carry cassettes or CDs. With an iPod, an auto-charger to save on battery power, and a way to connect to your car's stereo system, you're ready to pump music.

Be careful to pick the right type of auto-charger — the auto-chargers for older iPods provide a FireWire connector, while the auto-charger for the new dockable iPods use a dock connector cable. You can find an auto-charger from Belkin with the appropriate FireWire-to-dock connector cable, shown in Figure 2-6, in the Apple Store. It offers a convenient socket for a stereo mini-plug cable, which can connect directly to a car stereo if you have a mini-socket in the car for audio input.

Unfortunately, not many car stereos offer a mini-socket for audio input. And as of this writing, no car or car accessory will allow you to plug in an iPod the same way as its dock. That would be totally cool because the iPod is clearly designed for plugging into a "car dock" that offers both power and a connection to the car's stereo system.

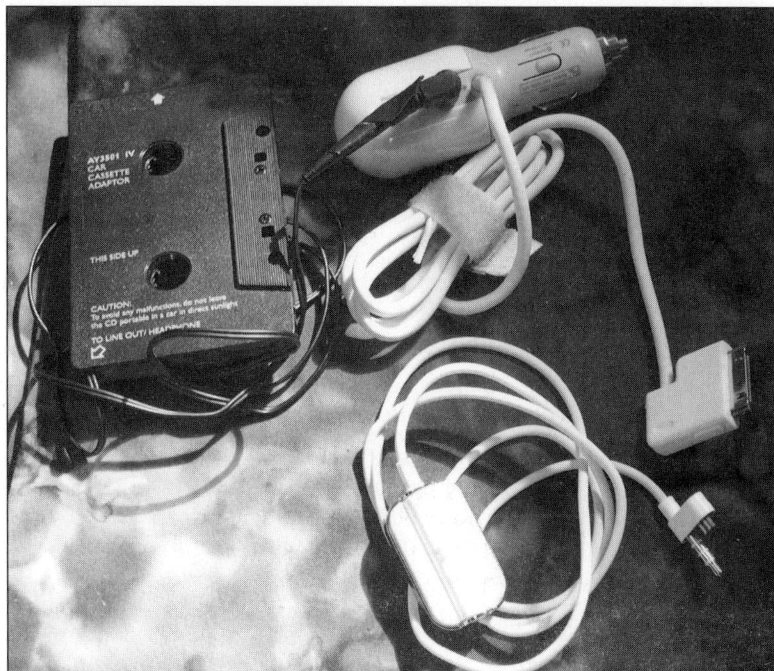

Figure 2-6: Car accessories — cassette-player adapter, auto-charger, and iPod Remote switch.

Until then, you can use either a cassette player-adapter to connect with your car stereo, or a wireless device we describe in the next section, "Achieving wireless playback."

Most car stereos have a cassette player, and you can buy a cassette-player adapter from most consumer electronics stores or from the Apple Store. Adapters look like a tape cassette, with a wire mini-plug cable that sticks out through the slot, as shown in Figure 2-6.

You can connect the mini-plug cable directly to the iPod, or to the auto-charger if a mini-socket is offered, or to the iPod Remote switch that in turn is connected to the iPod. Then insert the adapter into the cassette player, being careful not to get the cable tangled up inside the player.

One inherent problem with this approach is the cable that dangles from your cassette player, which looks unsightly. You may have some trouble ejecting the adapter if the cable gets wedged in the door. But overall, this method is the best for most cars because it provides the best sound quality.

Connecting by wireless radio

A wireless music adapter allows you to play music from your iPod on an FM radio, with no connection or cable, although the sound quality may suffer a bit due to interference. You can use a wireless adapter in a car, on a boat, on the beach with a portable radio, or even in your home with a stereo system and tuner. We even use it in hotel rooms with a clock radio.

To use a wireless adapter, follow these steps:

1. **Set the wireless adapter to an FM radio frequency.**

   The adapter offers you a choice of several frequencies — typically 88.1, 88.3, 88.5, and 88.7 MHz. You choose the frequency, and set the adapter according to its instructions.

2. **Connect the wireless adapter to the iPod headphone connector or the line-out connector on the iPod dock.**

   The wireless adapter (see Figure 2-7), such as the iRock, available in the Apple Store or the popular Belkin Tunecast Mobile FM Transmitter, acts like a miniature radio station, broadcasting to a nearby FM radio. (Sorry, you can't go much farther than a few feet, so no one else can hear your Wolfman Jack impersonation.)

3. **Tune to the appropriate frequency on the FM dial.**

   Tune any nearby radio to the same FM frequency you chose in Step 1.

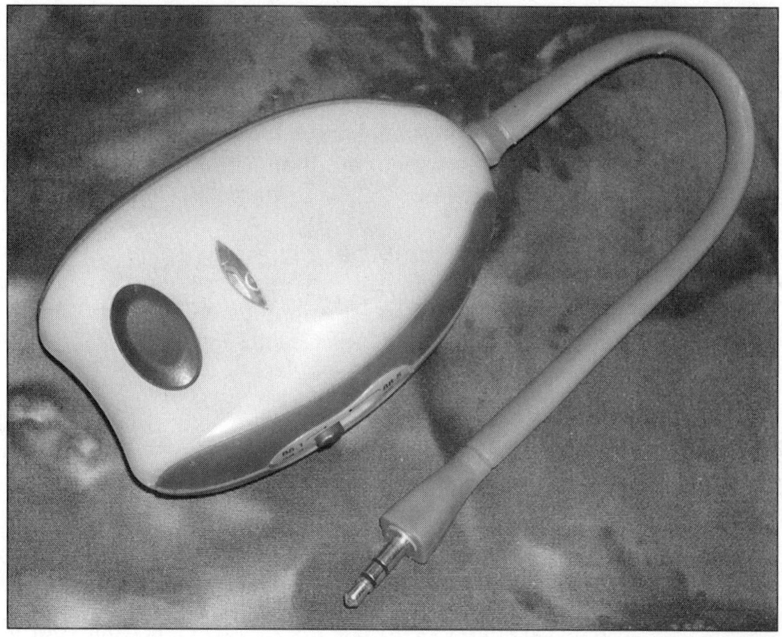

Figure 2-7: An example of a wireless adapter.

Most adapters use two standard AAA alkaline batteries. You can use it with an iPod running on a battery or connected to power, but you eventually need to replace the adapter's batteries — the wireless adapter lacks any connection for AC power. You also need to set the adapter close enough to the radio's antenna to work, making it impractical for home stereos — you can get better quality sound by connecting to a home stereo with a cable.

Taking music abroad

If you want to charge your iPod battery wherever you are, don't count on finding the same voltage as in the United States. You need to plug your Apple power adapter into something. Fortunately power adapters are available in most airports, but the worldly traveler may want to consider saving time and money by getting a travel kit of power accessories.

The Apple Store offers the World Travel Adapter Kit, which includes a set of six AC plugs with prongs that fit different electrical outlets around the world. The kit works with the white portable power adapter that ships with the iPod. The AC plugs included in the kit directly support outlets in North America, Japan, China, United Kingdom, Continental Europe, Korea, Australia, and Hong Kong.

One way to solve the power problem is to use rechargeable batteries found in any convenience store. The Belkin Battery Pack, available in the Apple Store, allows you to power your iPod with replaceable batteries — even when your internal battery is drained. It uses four standard AA alkaline batteries that you can replace when the charge is gone. Discreet suction cups secure the unit to the back of your iPod, without marring your iPod finish, and a charge-level indicator tells you when your batteries are running low.

Another way is to use your iBook or PowerBook laptop to supply the power, and then use a power adapter with your laptop. You can use, for example, the Kensington Universal Car/Air Adapter from Apple to plug your PowerBook or iBook into any car cigarette lighter or Empower-equipped airline seat. Then use your FireWire-dock cable and dock to power your iPod (or just FireWire cable with older iPods).

The Sound of Music

The Beach Boys were right when they sang "Good Vibrations" because that's what music is — the sensation of hearing audible vibrations conveyed to the ear by a medium such as air. The frequency of vibrations per second is how we measure sound.

When you turn up the bass or treble on a stereo system, you are actually increasing the volume, or intensity, of certain frequencies while the music is playing. You are not actually changing the sound itself, just the way it is being amplified and produced through speakers.

The iTunes equalizer (EQ), described in Book I, Chapter 3, allows you to fine-tune the specific sound spectrum frequencies in a more precise way than with bass and treble controls. You might pick, for example, entirely different equalizer settings for car speakers, home speakers, and headphones, or for different genres of music.

The iPod also has a built-in equalizer, but you can't directly change the frequencies — it offers presets for musical genres and listening environments. You can use the iPod equalizer for on-the-fly adjustments of the sound by picking a preset on the iPod. You can also use the iTunes equalizer to improve or enhance the sound, assigning built-in or your own custom equalizer settings to each song, and then you can use these settings with the iPod.

Using the iPod equalizer

You leave the back-road bliss of the country to get on the freeway, and now the music in your car doesn't have enough bass to give you that thumping rhythm you need to dodge other cars. What can you do? Without endangering anybody, you can pull over and select one of the iPod equalizer presets, such as Bass Booster.

The iPod built-in equalizer modifies the volume of the frequencies of the sound, and while you don't have sliders for faders like the iTunes equalizer, you get the same long list of presets to suit the type of music, or the type of environment.

To select an iPod equalizer preset, choose Settings⇨EQ from the main menu, and select one of the presets as shown in Figure 2-8.

Each EQ preset offers a different balance of frequencies designed to enhance the sound in certain ways. For example, Bass Booster increases the volume of the low (bass) frequencies, while Treble Booster does the same to the high (treble) frequencies.

To see what a preset actually does to the frequencies, open the iTunes equalizer and select the same preset. The faders in the equalizer display show you exactly what the preset does.

The Off setting turns off the iPod equalizer — no presets are used, not even one you may have assigned in iTunes. You have to choose an EQ setting to turn on the iPod equalizer.

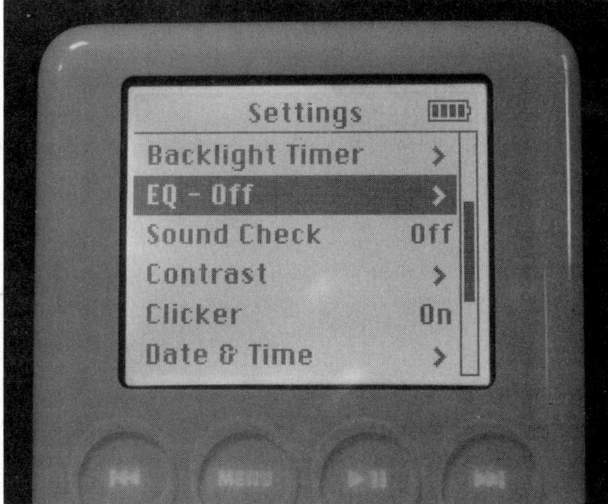

Figure 2-8: Choosing an equalizer preset for the iPod output.

Using the iTunes custom EQ presets

If you assign a preset to the song using iTunes, iPod uses the assigned EQ preset from iTunes when you choose an EQ preset on the iPod. In other words, the assigned EQ preset from iTunes takes precedence over the preset in the iPod.

If you know in advance that certain songs need specific presets assigned to them, use iTunes to assign the preset to the song before copying the song to the iPod. On the other hand, if you don't want your songs preordained with a certain preset, and you want to experiment with the presets in the iPod to get better playback in different listening environments, don't assign a preset in iTunes — wait until you have the song in your iPod, and then you can use different EQ presets on the song.

To assign built-in or custom presets to songs using the iTunes equalizer, see Book I, Chapter 3.

After assigning a preset to a song in iTunes, you turn on the iPod equalizer by choosing any EQ setting (other than Off), and the iPod uses the song's preset for playback. To find out more about the iTunes equalizer, see Book I, Chapter 3.

Using sound check

Because music CDs are mastered differently, songs on different albums can have large discrepancies in volume. With the Sound Check feature in iTunes and your iPod for the Mac, you can standardize the volume of all the songs in your music library.

First, in iTunes, select the Sound Check feature as we describe in Book I, Chapter 1. This sets all the songs to the current volume controlled by the iTunes volume slider.

Then, on the iPod, to have all the songs play at the same volume level all the time, choose Settings⇨Sound Check⇨On from the main menu to turn on the sound check feature. To turn it off, choose Settings⇨Sound Check⇨Off.

Chapter 3: Managing Life on the Road

In This Chapter

- **Setting time, date, alarm, and sleep functions**
- **Customizing and resetting the iPod**
- **Synchronizing information**
- **Adding calendars, to-do lists, and text notes**
- **Using the iPod as an external hard disk and backup device**
- **Installing a custom Mac system on the iPod**

The iPod is capable of helping you manage your activities on the road to the point where it competes on some level with PDAs (personal digital assistants). We chose the iPod for music, but we also find it useful for viewing information we need when traveling, using it as a *data player.*

For sure, the iPod keeps time and can awaken you to your favorite music. But it can do far more. This chapter shows you how to use the contacts and calendar functions and keep your information synchronized with your laptop, just like a PDA. You can get the most from your iPod with bookmarks, customizing the iPod menu, and playing games. It also describes how the iPod can function as an external and portable hard disk, holding files you can transfer to other computers or keep as a secure backup while on the road (try *that* with your PDA). Last but not least, it describes how to solve the most common problems you might have with an iPod, and how to reset the iPod.

Getting the Most from Your iPod

You may have purchased an iPod simply to listen to music, but those thoughtful engineers at Apple who get to travel a lot with *their* iPods put a lot more into this device. In particular, you can alleviate the boredom of airplane travel with games, bookmark your reading material, and check the time, date, and month (in case you're stranded for a long time).

Setting date, time, and sleep functions

Some iPods have a digital clock that doubles as an alarm clock and a sleep timer. To access the clock, choose Extras⇨Clock from the main menu.

To set the date and time, follow these steps:

1. **Press the Menu button.**
2. **Choose Extras⇨Clock.**

   The clock appears with menu selections underneath, shown in Figure 3-1.

   You can also set the date and time by choosing Settings⇨Date & Time from the main menu.
3. **Select the Date & Time option.**

   The Date & Time menu appears.
4. **Select the Set Time Zone option.**

   A list of time zones appears in alphabetical order.

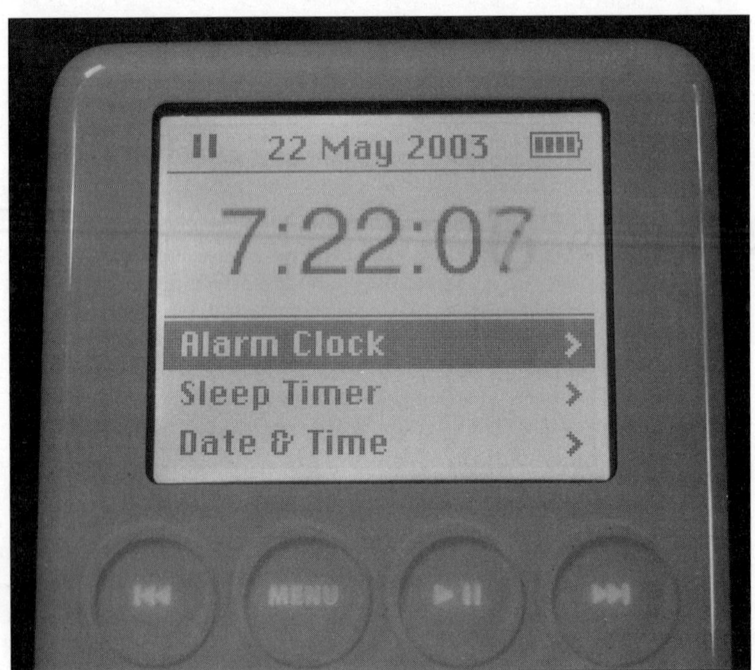

Figure 3-1: View the clock.

5. **Scroll the Time Zone list and select a time zone.**

   The Date & Time menu appears again.

6. **Select Set Date & Time.**

   The Date & Time display appears with up and down arrow indicators over the hour field, which is highlighted.

7. **Change the hour using the scroll pad.**

   Scroll clockwise to go forward in time and counterclockwise to go backward.

8. **Press the Select button after scrolling to the appropriate hour.**

   The up and down arrow indicators move over to the minutes field, which is now highlighted.

9. **Repeat Steps 7 and 8 for each field of the date and time: minutes, AM/PM, the calendar date, calendar month, and year.**

When you finish setting the year by pressing the Select button, the Date & Time menu appears again. You can select the Time option and click the Select button to show hours as 24-hour increments (military style). You can also select the Time option, and click the Select button to show the time in the menu title of your iPod menus.

Just like a clock radio, you can set the iPod to play music for a while before going to sleep. To set the sleep timer, select the Sleep Timer option from the Clock menu. A list of time amounts appears, from 15 minutes to 120 minutes in 15-minute intervals. You can select a time amount or the Off setting (at the top of the list) to turn off the sleep timer.

Setting the alarm clock

Time is on your side with the iPod Alarm Clock function, which is available in the iPod Clock menu, as shown in Figure 3-2. To set the Alarm Clock, follow these steps:

1. **Choose Extras⇨Clock⇨Alarm Clock from the main menu.**

   The Alarm Clock menu appears.

2. **Highlight the Alarm option and click the Select button (`Off` changes to `On`).**

3. **Select the Time option.**

   The Alarm Time menu appears with up and down arrow indicators.

Figure 3-2: Set the time for the alarm in the Alarm Clock menu.

4. **Change the time using the scroll pad.**

   Scroll clockwise to go forward in time and counterclockwise to go backward.

5. **Click the Select button after scrolling to the appropriate alarm time.**

   The Alarm Clock menu appears again.

6. **Select the Sound option in the Alarm Clock menu.**

   A list appears, with the Beep option at the top of the list, followed by playlists on your iPod in alphabetical order.

7. **Select an option as the alarm sound.**

   When the alarm goes off, the playlist goes until you stop it by pressing the Play/Pause button.

Bookmarking Audible audio books

When you use Audible books, articles, and spoken-word titles in iTunes (obtained from `www.audible.com`), you can automatically bookmark your place in the text with the iPod. Bookmarks only work with certain formats of Audible files. If you have an audio book or spoken word file in any other format, such as MP3, bookmarks are not available.

To find out how to download Audible audio files into iTunes, see Book I, Chapter 1.

When you use the Pause/Play button to pause an Audible file, the iPod automatically bookmarks that spot. When you hit the Play button again, the Audible file starts playing from that spot.

Bookmarks synchronize when you copy an Audible title to your iPod — whichever bookmark is farther along in iPod or iTunes becomes the effective bookmark.

Customizing the menus and display

The Settings menu in the iPod main menu offers ways to customize the iPod experience. You can change the main menu to have more choices, set the timer for the backlight, and so on. Choose the Settings menu from the main menu. Some of these options include:

- **About:** Displays information about the iPod, including number of songs, how much space is used, how much is available, the version of the software in use, the serial number, and the model number.
- **Main Menu:** Allows you to customize the main menu. For example, you can add items from other menus, such as Artists or Songs from the Browse menu, to the main menu. You can turn each menu item on (to appear in the main menu) or off.
- **Backlight Timer:** You can set the backlight to remain on for a certain amount of time by pressing a button or using the scroll pad. Specify two seconds, five seconds, and so on. You can also set it to always be on.
- **Contrast:** You can set the contrast of the iPod display by using the scroll pad to increase or decrease the slider in the Contrast screen. If you accidentally set the contrast too dark, you can reset it by holding down the Menu button for at least four seconds.
- **Clicker:** When on, you hear a click when you press a button; when off, you don't hear a click.
- **Language:** Set the language used in all the menus. See Chapter 1 in this book for how to set the language.
- **Legal:** Display the legal message that accompanies Apple products.
- **Reset All Settings:** Reset all the settings in your iPod, returning the settings to the state they were in originally. However, your music and data files on the iPod are not disturbed. See Chapter 1 of this book for how to reset your iPod.

Playing games with your iPod

The games that come with the iPod — Brick, Parachute, and Solitaire — are a bit dorky for the information age, but hey, they're extras, added just because it was possible to add them. To reach the games, choose Extras⇨Games.

Brick reminds us of the original version of Pong, a kind of solitary ping-pong. Parachute is a crude shoot-em-up with cute helicopters that explode and paratroopers that drop like ants to engulf you. We can't get the hang of either of them, but we return to the Solitaire card game often enough. And, of course, you can play music while you play.

Adding Personal Information

You can manage your address book, calendar, and to-do list for the road all on your Mac, and synchronize your iPod to have all the information you need for viewing and playback. As a result, you may not ever need a PDA.

To input, or not to input: There is no question

We could never get used to tiny portable computers and PDAs. We use computers for all our information needs, but have never really gone smaller than a laptop because the keyboards on smaller devices are too small for touch-typists.

People who use the "one-finger-plunk" method of typing can quickly adapt to using forefingers and thumbs, and type reasonably well on a PDA and even a cell phone. But PDAs can be hard for people who are trained to hold their hands a certain way and touch-type with all fingers to adapt to.

There's true irony in this. The original reason for the QWERTY arrangement of keys on the keyboard, standard to this day, was to *slow down* the human typist and place commonly used letter combinations on opposite sides of the keyboard, so that the mechanical arms of the typewriter wouldn't jam. Efforts to change this during the computer age were ignored, even if they did allow for increased typing speed and higher productivity. People assimilated the original arrangement and learned to type fast with it, and simply wouldn't change.

Small keyboards and clumsy human interfaces hamper the use of PDAs for input, and raise the question for the laptop users, why bother? Laptops (and possibly the new tablet computers) are excellent for this purpose, and all your information is centralized on that machine. If you add new information using two different devices, you run the risk of being out-of-sync (most often you end up accidentally overwriting the new stuff put into the PDA with the stuff from your laptop).

The Apple PowerBook and iPod combo is one reasonable answer to this dilemma. You input and edit all your information using the PowerBook, and update the iPod as necessary. Then take the iPod into situations when you need to view the information but don't need to change it. As a portable external hard disk, the iPod is ideal for temporary secure data storage, *because* you can't change it.

Using iCal for custom calendars

Your iPod has a standard calendar you can view by choosing Extras⇨Calendars⇨All. This function is far more useful after you update your iPod with your calendars and to-do lists using iCal.

Imagine a musician going backstage after a performance and meeting his booking agent who says he can get him ten more gigs if he can confirm the dates *right now.* This musician happens to carry around an iPod, and amid the backstage craziness, he scrolls through his calendar for the entire year, finding all the details he needs about gigs and recording sessions, right down to the minute, including travel directions to each gig. "No problem," he says.

iCal, the free desktop calendar application from Apple, creates calendars you can copy to your iPod. You can create calendars for different activities, such as home, office, road tours, exercise/diet schedules, mileage logs, and so on, and view them separately or all together. After editing your calendars on the Mac, you can synchronize your iPod to have the same calendars.

To create a custom calendar, open iCal on the Mac by double-clicking the iCal application or clicking its icon in the Mac OS X dock. iCal displays a calendar as shown in Figure 3-3. Choose File⇨New Event to add an event to a particular day. You can specify the date and time for the event and add a description. Give the calendar a new name by clicking its name in the Calendars list, and click the plus (+) button (or choose File⇨New Calendar) to create separate calendars.

Figure 3-3: Use iCal to manage separate calendars.

To see the information for any event, select the event and choose Window➪Inspector. iCal also keeps track of your to-do list: Choose File➪New to Do to add an item to the list. You can import calendars from other applications that support the iCal or vCal format.

With your calendar information in iCal, transfer your calendars automatically to the iPod and keep them always up-to-date with iSync, which is available for downloading free from `www.apple.com`. To find out more about iCal, pick up a copy of *Mac OS X All-in-One Desk Reference For Dummies*, by Mark Chambers (published by Wiley Publishing, Inc.).

Using Address Book

The most likely bit of information you may need on the road is someone's phone number or address (or both). While a cell phone can keep phone numbers handy, cheap cell phones aren't useful for extended addresses, comments, and other info. The iPod stores up to a thousand contacts right alongside your music.

If you use Mac Mail as your e-mail program, you already have an address book, managed by the Address Book application that comes with every Mac. If you use some other e-mail program, chances are your e-mail addresses are stored in the appropriate vCard format or your e-mail program allows you to export them as vCards, as we describe in the "Adding addresses from other sources" section, later in this chapter.

If you use Address Book on your Mac, keeping your iPod synchronized with your newest addresses and phone numbers is simple and automatic. Launch Address Book by double-clicking the Address Book application or clicking its icon in the Mac OS X dock. Address Book displays a card as shown in Figure 3-4, and you can add address cards for people. Choose File➪New Card to add a new card or click the plus (+) button at the bottom of the Name column.

To edit a card, select the person in the Name column and click the Edit button. You can add multiple addresses, phone numbers, e-mail addresses, and so on — just click the tiny plus (+) icon next to each type of information to add more. To save your changes, click the Edit button again, and Address Book saves the edits.

If you receive a vCard from someone as an e-mail attachment (with the .vcf extension), you can simply drag the attachment to your Address Book window — if that person filled out the vCard with phone numbers and address information, you don't have to type anything. Wouldn't it be nice if all your friends sent you vCards to keep you up-to-date, and you never had to retype the information?

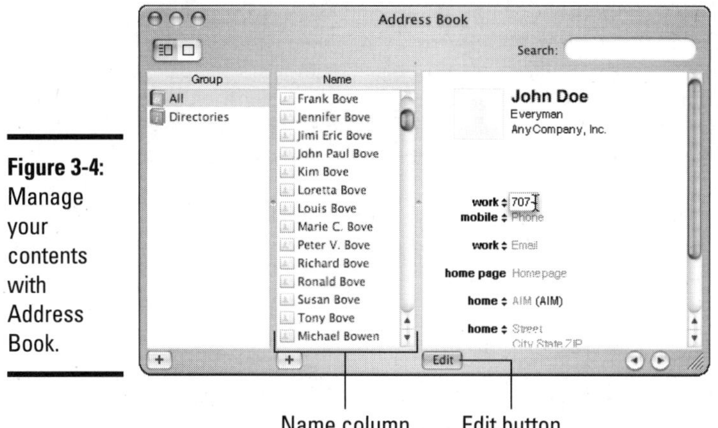

Figure 3-4: Manage your contents with Address Book.

To put your addresses on the iPod, you can either export a vCard file to the iPod Contacts folder (as we describe in the "Adding addresses from other sources" section, later in this chapter) or use the iSync application, which is automatic and keeps your iPod synchronized with changes you make on your Mac.

Not N'Sync? Try iSync

Chances are you make a lot of changes to addresses, phone numbers, calendar events, and to-do lists on your Mac. Information changes often and new information accumulates quickly. Even though you can update your iPod with this information manually, remembering to copy each file you need is hard. iSync performs this function automatically and keeps all your information updated.

iSync is available free from Apple (`www.apple.com`) for downloading. After installing iSync, connect your iPod to the Mac, open iSync, and choose Devices➪Add Device. iSync searches for all your devices. Select the iPod from the list of devices, and the iPod icon appears in the iSync bar. Click the iPod icon and the iPod synchronization settings window appears, as shown in Figure 3-5.

You can synchronize all contacts and calendars, or just the ones you select. Select the Automatically Synchronize When iPod Is Connected option and every time you connect your iPod, iSync goes to work. If you don't want that level of automation, you can launch iSync anytime and click the Sync Now button. iSync performs its magic, pausing twice to inform you that you are changing your iPod contacts and calendars, as shown in Figure 3-6.

Figure 3-5: The iPod synchronization window.

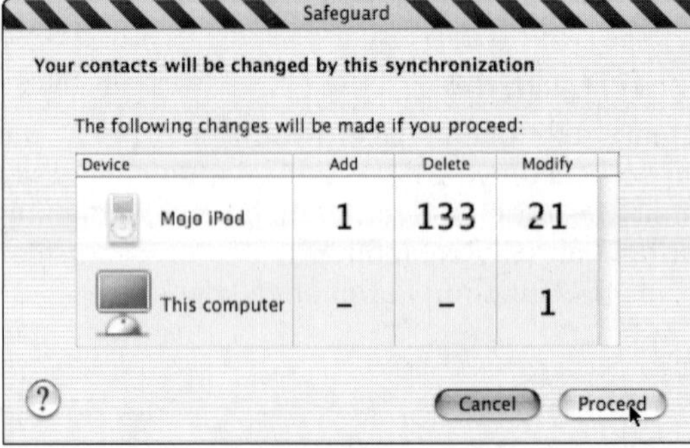

Figure 3-6: Use iSync to keep the iPod calendar and contacts updated.

After you finish synchronizing, be sure to drag the iPod icon to the Trash before disconnecting it. After updating and ejecting the iPod, you can view your addresses and phone numbers by choosing Extras➪Contacts, and then choosing a name.

You can look at your calendars by choosing Extras➪Calendar➪All. Select a calendar, and then use the scroll wheel to scroll through the days of the calendar. Select an event to see the event's details. Use the Next and Previous buttons to skip to the next or previous month. To see your to-do list, choose Extras⇨Calendar⇨To Do.

Sorting your contacts

The iPod contact list, updated by iSync from your Address Book, is sorted automatically, and the iPod displays contact names in alphabetical order when you choose Extras⇨Contacts. You can choose whether to display them by last or first name. Choose Settings⇨Contacts⇨Display. Then press the Select button in the scrolling pad for each option:

- **First Last:** Displays the contact list first name and then last name, as in "Ringo Starr."
- **Last, First:** Displays the contact list last name followed by a comma and first name, as in "McCartney, Paul."

You can also change the way the contacts sort, so that you don't have to look up people by their first names (which can be time-consuming with so many people named Elvis). The sort operation uses the entire name, but you decide whether to use the first or the last name first. Choose Settings⇨Contacts⇨Sort. Press the Select button in the scrolling pad for each option:

- **First Last:** Sorts the contact list by first name, followed by the last name, so that "Mick Jagger" sorts under "Mick" (after Mick Abrahams but before Mick Taylor).
- **Last, First:** Sorts the contacts by last name, followed by the first name, so that "Brian Jones" sorts under "Jones" ("Jones, Brian" appears after "Jones, Alice" but before "Jones, Mick").

Using the iPod as a Disk

You have a device in your pocket that can play weeks of music, sort your contacts, remind you of events, wake you up in the morning, and tuck you in at night. Did you also know that you can keep a safe backup of your most important files, and even help restore your computer to life if the system won't work?

You read that right. You can keep a safe backup of files, and you can put a version of the Mac system on the iPod to use in case of emergencies. Apple doesn't support the last item, but you can do it. You can also copy applications and utility programs you may need on the road, or even copy your entire User folder to the iPod if you have room after putting music on it.

The key to these capabilities is the fact that the iPod serves as an external hard disk. After you mount the iPod on your Mac desktop, you can use it as a hard disk.

We don't recommend using the iPod regularly as a hard disk to launch applications. Because the iPod is designed more for sustained playback of music, you could eventually burn out the device by frequently using it to launch applications. Instead, use it as an external disk for backing up and copying files and, in emergency situations, for starting up the system (as described in the section, "Taking your system on the road," later in this chapter).

Mounting the iPod as a hard disk

The iPod can double as an external hard disk for your Mac. And like any hard disk, you can transfer files and applications from your computer to the iPod and take them with you wherever you go. The iPod is smart enough to keep your files separate from your music collection so that they are not accidentally erased when you update your music. And because the iPod is with you, it's as safe as you are.

To use the iPod as an external drive, follow these steps:

1. **Connect the iPod to your Mac.**
2. **Open iTunes.**

   To prevent iPod from automatically updating itself, hold down the ⌘ and Option keys.
3. **Select the iPod name in the iTunes Source list.**
4. **Click the iPod options button.**

   The iPod Preferences window opens.
5. **Select the Enable FireWire Disk Use option and click OK.**
6. **Open the iPod icon in the Finder to see its contents.**

   The iPod hard disk opens up to show three folders — Calendars, Contacts, and Notes, as shown in Figure 3-7. You can add new folders, rename your custom folders, and generally use the iPod as a hard disk, but don't rename these three folders, because they link directly to the Calendar, Contacts, and Notes functions on the iPod.

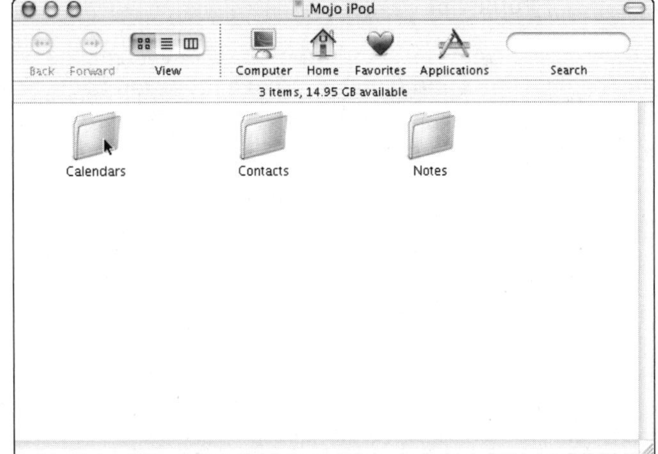

Figure 3-7: The iPod hard disk mounted on the Mac.

7. **Drag files or folders to the iPod.**

   To keep data organized, create new folders on the iPod, as shown in Figure 3-7, and then drag files and folders to the newly created folders.

8. **When finished, drag the iPod icon to the Trash.**

After unmounting the iPod, its display shows the message `OK to disconnect`. You can then disconnect the iPod from its dock, or disconnect the dock from the computer. Don't ever disconnect an iPod before unmounting it. You may have to reset your iPod if you do, as described in the section, "Resetting Your iPod," later in this chapter.

To delete files and folders from the iPod, drag them to the Trash just as you would with an external hard disk.

Don't use a disk utility program, such as Disk Utility or Drive Setup, to erase the iPod. If you erase the iPod disk this way, it may be unable to play music.

To see how much free space is left on the iPod, you can use the Finder. Select the iPod icon on the Finder desktop, and choose File⇨Show Info. You can also use the About command in the iPod Settings menu: Choose Settings⇨About from the main menu.

Adding addresses from other sources

A vCard, or *virtual card*, is a standard method of exchanging personal information. The iPod sorts and displays up to a thousand contacts in the vCard format. The iPod is compatible with popular applications such as Microsoft Entourage, Microsoft Outlook, and Palm Desktop.

After mounting the iPod as a hard disk, simply export your contacts as vCards directly into the Contacts folder of your iPod. In most cases, you can simply drag vCard-formatted contacts from the application's address book to the iPod Contacts folder.

You can export one card, or a group of cards, or even the entire list as a vCard file (with a .vcf extension), by dragging the vCard file into the Contacts folder, as shown in Figure 3-8. Contacts must be in the vCard format to use with the iPod.

As of this writing, the iPod supports only a portion of what you can put into a vCard. For example, you can include photos and sounds in vCards used by other applications, but you can't open up those portions of the vCard using the iPod.

After updating and ejecting the iPod, you can view your addresses and phone numbers by choosing Extras⇨Contacts, and then choosing a name.

Figure 3-8: Add a vCard file to the iPod.

Adding calendars from other sources

iPod supports industry-standard iCalendar and vCalendar files, which can be exported by many applications including Microsoft Entourage, Microsoft Outlook, and Palm Desktop.

In most cases you can drag an iCalendar file (with the filename extension .ics) or a vCalendar file (with the filename extension .vcs) to your iPod Calendar folder, as shown in Figure 3-9.

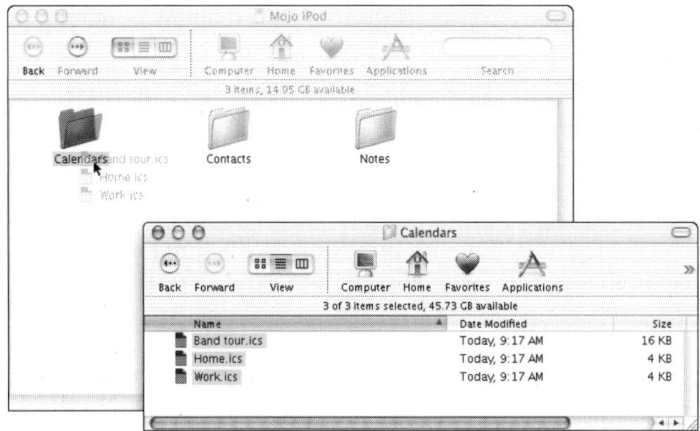

Figure 3-9: Add exported calendars in the iCalendar format to the Calendars folder on the iPod.

If you deleted the Calendars folder on the iPod, you can create a Calenders folder, and then drag the calendar event files into the folder.

You can look at your calendars by choosing Extras➪Calendar➪All. Select a calendar, and then use the scroll wheel to scroll through the days of the calendar. Select an event to see the event's details. Use the Next and Previous buttons to skip to the next or previous month. To see your to-do list, choose Extras➪Calendar➪To Do.

Adding notes and text documents

In a perfect world you could rip audio CDs and also capture all the information in the liner notes — the descriptions of who played which instruments, where the CD was produced, and other minute detail. Then, while sharing your iPod music with others, you could view the liner notes on the iPod screen whenever a question arises about the music.

You can almost achieve the same result by typing some of the liner notes, or any text you want, into a word processing program (such as TextEdit, provided free with the Mac), save the document as an ordinary text file (with the filename extension .txt), and drag it to the Notes folder of the iPod, as shown in Figure 3-10. You can copy song information from your iTunes music library, which we cover in Book I, Chapter 2.

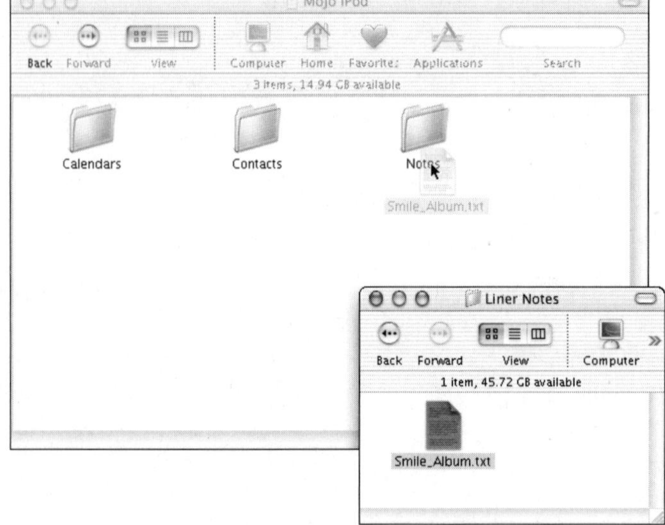

Figure 3-10: Drag a text file with liner notes for an album to the Notes folder on the iPod.

Text files in the Notes folder are organized by filename. You can view these notes files by choosing Extras➪Notes. By using descriptive filenames (such as the album name), you can easily scroll the list of notes files to find the liner notes for the album you are listening to.

Taking your system on the road

While not officially supported by Apple, you can save your Mac in a system crisis. You can load the iPod with system software and used to start up your Mac.

Life on the road can be hazardous to your computer's hard disk, and if any portion of the hard disk containing system files is damaged, your system may not start up. When this happens, you ordinarily use the installation CDs to start the computer, scan and fix the hard disk trouble spots, and reinstall the system. With an iPod, you can at least start the computer and scan and fix the hard disk trouble spots, and also use any other files or applications you previously put on the iPod hard disk.

For example, you may want to take an important presentation in the form of a QuickTime movie on the road, to use with the QuickTime Player. You can copy the movie file, the QuickTime Player, and a custom version of Mac OS X to the iPod for emergency use. If your laptop fails, you can start the laptop from the iPod, and run the QuickTime Player and its movie from the iPod, using the iPod as a hard disk.

To copy files and applications to the iPod, mount the iPod as a hard disk, as we describe in the section, "Mounting the iPod as a hard disk," earlier in this chapter. To install a custom version of OS X on your iPod, follow these steps:

1. **Insert your Mac OS X installation CD into your Mac, and follow the directions to start up the installation process.**

   You have to restart the Mac with the installation CD while holding down the C key to start the computer from the CD.

2. **When you are asked to select a destination, choose the iPod hard disk.**

   Do not use the option to erase and format the hard disk, because the hard disk is your iPod.

3. **Specify a custom installation rather than a standard installation.**

   To make sure that you don't use up too much disk space on your iPod, choose a custom installation of OS X. In the custom installation section, choose only the languages you need. These language options take up a lot of space and you probably don't need them in emergencies.

4. **After installation finishes and the computer restarts from the iPod, continue through the setup procedure, and then use Software Update in System Preferences to update the system on your iPod.**

   Most likely a lot of system updates are waiting for you — updates released after the date of your installation CDs. Spend the time to update your system because these updates may make a difference in how your computer performs with certain applications.

To get the most functionality from your iPod, make sure you have the latest version of iPod software. To find out which version of software your iPod uses, select the About command from the iPod Settings menu. To update your iPod software to the latest version, go to `www.apple.com/ipod` and download the iPod Software Updater application.

While iPod is the road warrior's dream weapon for combating road fatigue and boredom, if you update and maintain its hard-disk contents wisely, you will find that it is also invaluable as a tool for providing quick information and for saving your computer from disaster. Don't let hard disk space go to waste: Fill up your iPod and let the iPod be your road manager.

Resetting Your iPod

If your iPod doesn't turn on, don't panic — at least not yet. First check the Hold switch's position on top of the iPod. The Hold switch locks the iPod buttons so that you don't accidentally activate them. Slide the Hold switch away from the headphone connection, hiding the orange layer, to unlock the buttons. (If you see the orange layer underneath one end of the Hold switch, the switch is still in the locked position.)

Check to see if the iPod has enough juice. Is the battery charged up? Connect the iPod to a power source and see if it works.

If it still doesn't turn on, follow this reset sequence:

1. **Toggle the Hold switch.**

   Set the Hold switch to hold (lock), and then set it back to unlock. This is like the beginning of a secret handshake.

2. **Press the Menu and Play/Pause buttons simultaneously and hold for at least five seconds until the Apple logo appears.**

3. **Release the buttons when you see the Apple logo.**

   Releasing the Menu and Play/Pause buttons after the Apple logo appears is important. If you continue to hold down the buttons after the logo appears, the iPod displays the low battery icon and you must connect it to a power source before using your iPod again.

After resetting, everything is back to normal, including your music, data files, and customized settings. If you want to also reset your customized settings, choose Settings➪ Reset All Settings➪ Reset from the main menu.

Book VI

iLife Extras

The 5th Wave
By Rich Tennant
JERRY AND LYLE ATTEMPT TO LOAD THE NEWEST VERSION OF "TOAST," CD-BURNING SOFTWARE
©RICHTENNANT
OK, I got the Sunbeam firewired to the iMac. Try putting the CD in the slot again.

Chapter 1: Understanding Your iEnvironment

In This Chapter

- Knowing what you need
- Backing up iMovies and iDVDs
- Cruising and using the Apple Web site
- Summoning help when needed
- Troubleshooting your configuration

John Donne wrote, "No man is an island entire of itself. . . ," and what he observed as true of man (or woman) is also true of software. All your applications depend to some extent on their environment: the operating system and other services available to them (fonts, graphics routines, and hardware, to name just a few). These environmental dependencies are even more obvious and pronounced when separate applications (like your iLife applications or the applications comprising a suite such as Microsoft Office) communicate and interconnect.

Science fiction author Robert Heinlein (or economist Milton Friedman) popularized the expression, "There ain't no such thing as a free lunch." The acronym, TANSTAAFL, arises from this quote and is one of the great truisms of modern times. Everything has its price. And although the iLife application integration isn't free, you get it at a significantly reduced price when compared to working with all the pieces separately. For example, accessing your iPhoto Library through the Photos pane in iMovie increases the iMovie requirements for RAM, but that increase is not as great as the RAM requirement for running copies of iPhoto and iMovie simultaneously. Besides, selecting from the Photos pane is easier than dragging an image from an iPhoto window into iMovie.

This chapter shows you how to take maximum advantage of the integration and what it costs you to do so. I discuss the costs in terms of effort, memory, and disk space; the dollar costs fluctuate with component pricing.

Knowing What You Need

When Apple or any other software developer lists system requirements for software, you should take those requirements as being the minimum environment in which the developer affirms the software can function. That's not necessarily the same thing as saying that it is an environment where you'll be happy with the software's performance. In fact, even the "recommended" environment might be insufficient to please you.

These caveats are particularly germane when discussing graphics- or processor-intensive applications like iPhoto, iMovie, and iDVD. iTunes generally functions well at or near the minimum recommended configuration, but (trust us on this one) you'll want more memory even for iTunes if you run it in the background while doing real work in more demanding applications.

Helping iPhoto run smoothly

The first way to smooth iPhoto's path is to upgrade to the most recent versions of iPhoto and Mac OS X, which (at the time of this writing) are iPhoto 2.0 and Mac OS X 10.3.x, respectively. iPhoto's performance is better in Panther (OS X 10.3.x) than in Jaguar (OS X 10.2.x) and is better in Jaguar than in Cheetah (OS X 10.1.x) because Apple is continually optimizing for performance, within both iPhoto and the system routines that applications (like iPhoto) use.

Though it isn't immediately obvious, iPhoto gobbles memory. The larger your Photo Library or the more photos you have in an album, the more memory iPhoto requires to image the photos in your viewing pane.

You can do two things to deal with the iPhoto appetite — make more memory available or reduce the number of photos that need imaging. Making more memory available is, generally, a hardware solution — simply add more (or larger capacity) RAM modules to your Mac.

Reducing the number of photos that require imaging is a solution that you can manage in the following ways:

- **By archiving older or less important photos to CD or DVD and then removing them from your Library.** If you need to retrieve photos stored this way, just insert the archive disc. iPhoto makes the disc's contents available as a subordinate library, as described in Book II, Chapter 3, and as shown in Figure 1-1.
- **By choosing View⇨Arrange Photos⇨by Film Roll and collapsing the disclosure triangles.** Doing this hides the photos you're not currently interested in and makes scrolling much faster. Figure 1-2 shows a Photo Library with lots of collapsed film rolls and only one open roll.

Figure 1-1: CDs and DVDs burned in iPhoto show up in iPhoto as sublibraries.

✦ **By using a third-party utility such as iPhoto Buddy, iPhoto Library Manager, or iPhoto Librarian.** Each of these utilities (available for download from `www.versiontracker.com/macosx/`) helps you break your Photo Library into multiple, smaller libraries, and switches between them.

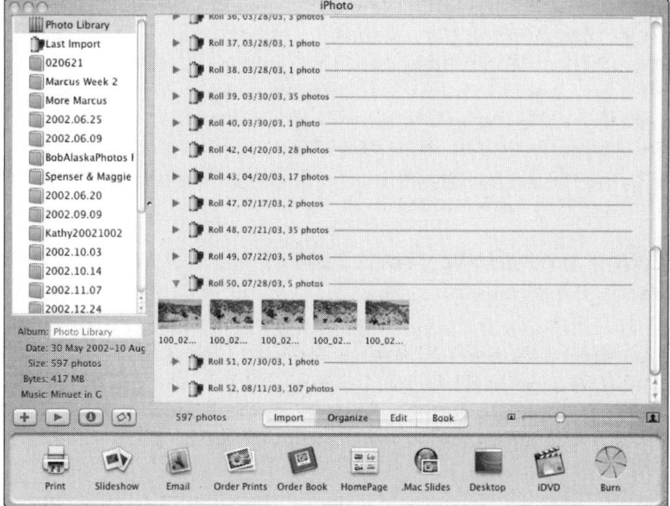

Figure 1-2: Collapsing film rolls that you aren't using speeds performance.

Of course, you can also combine the techniques outlined in this bullet list, and that will probably give you the best results of all.

To optimize iPhoto's performance, you need to take note of other memory-gobbling applications that may be running. For example, if you have iDVD encoding a movie in the background while you're working in iPhoto, less of your Mac's memory is available to iPhoto. And iPhoto gets a smaller percentage of the available processor time when other applications are running, which also slows performance.

Optimizing iMovie performance

Other than purchasing a faster Mac, you really have two main ways to wring the best possible performance from iMovie. And they are

- **To (surprise!) make more memory available.** Having a lot of RAM makes rendering of effects and transitions faster and improves encoding performance (exporting to QuickTime).
- **To optimize your hard disk.** A fast hard disk with a lot of contiguous free space greatly improves iMovie import and preview performance. Many (maybe most) serious iMovie users keep a separate hard drive for their projects and reformat it before starting a project.

These two items, of course, are general performance enhancers. iMovie also offers you some keyboard shortcuts that can make your editing faster, more accurate, and easier.

Although dragging the playhead (or a crop marker) to the approximate frame you want is easy and convenient, dragging a slider isn't the easiest way to position on a specific frame. Use the arrow keys to move the playhead (or crop marker) one frame at a time — the left-arrow key moves back a frame, and the right-arrow key moves forward a frame. If you press the Shift key while using the arrow keys, the playhead moves 10 frames at a time.

Getting the most from iDVD

Like iMovie, iDVD benefits from copious RAM and fast, unfragmented hard disks. Encoding your movies into the MPEG-2 format used on DVDs is a memory- and processor-intensive operation. Because the default procedure is to encode your movies, slideshows, menus, and buttons in the background while you continue to work in iDVD, having a lot of RAM available cuts down on editing sluggishness.

If you find your authoring tasks becoming sluggish while iDVD encodes in the background, you have two choices:

- **You can turn off background encoding in your iDVD Preferences** (iDVD⇨Preferences, on the General pane). Turning off background encoding smoothes the actual editing and authoring process, but you pay the price when you're ready to burn your DVD. That is, you'll have to wait longer at this point while iDVD encodes everything that isn't already encoded.
- **Alternatively, you can find something else to do while iDVD does its encoding** (not a very satisfactory option, but if your computer is lacking in memory, it could be your least obnoxious choice).

Another iDVD General Preferences setting that can impact your authoring performance is the Delete Rendered Files After Closing a Project check box. Selecting this check box minimizes the disk space used while you're not running iDVD. But this setting has a downside: If you haven't finished and burned your iDVD project during the session, then all the background rendering iDVD did is gone and will have to be redone the next time you open this iDVD project.

Finally, if you can keep your iDVD projects on a separate, unfragmented disk (maybe the same one where the related iMovie projects reside), you can minimize problems with disk *latency* (the time required to move the heads from one disk sector to another) and *contention* (conflicting read or write operations). A hard disk can read from or write to only one place at a time, so if you have multiple disk operations going concurrently, the head has to move from one area to another — often hundreds or thousands of times. All this movement results in a slowing down of the whole disk access process.

Leveraging iMovie and iDVD

Both iMovie and iDVD are based around the concept of a *project*. iMovie stores this project in a folder that contains a document and a Media subfolder of the clips, images, and audio files that make up your movie. Figure 1-3 shows an example iMovie project. iDVD hides more from you by making your project appear as a single icon. This icon is really a special kind of folder called a *package*, just as most of your OS X applications are packages masquerading as single items. As shown in Figure 1-4, you can Control-click on an iDVD package and choose Show Package Contents from the contextual menu that appears to see what's inside.

As discussed in the two preceding sections, both iMovie and iDVD see performance benefits when you use a large, fast, unfragmented, and dedicated hard disk. Although iMovie has a larger appetite for disk space (about 210MB per minute of video) than iDVD (about 70MB per minute at high quality or just under 50MB per minute at the 90-minute setting), neither can be accused of being light eaters.

Name	Date Modified	Size
Example	Wed, Mar 26, 2003, 4:42 PM	8 KB
Example.mov	Wed, Mar 26, 2003, 4:42 PM	140 KB
Media	Mon, May 26, 2003, 7:45 PM	--
2-02 God Bless America.mp3 02	Sat, Feb 1, 2003, 3:55 PM	28 MB
Allie&Michelle.jpg	Mon, Feb 3, 2003, 9:30 AM	764 KB
Bess-Xmas.jpg	Mon, Feb 3, 2003, 9:30 AM	520 KB
Circle Opening 01	Mon, Feb 3, 2003, 8:22 AM	7.3 MB
Clip 01	Sat, Feb 1, 2003, 12:43 PM	17.2 MB
Clip 02	Sat, Feb 1, 2003, 1:53 PM	17.2 MB
Clip 03	Sat, Feb 1, 2003, 2:06 PM	136 KB
Clip 04	Mon, Feb 3, 2003, 12:17 PM	231.8 MB
Clip 05	Mon, Feb 3, 2003, 9:32 AM	17.2 MB
Clip 06	Sun, Feb 2, 2003, 6:40 PM	17.2 MB
Clip 07	Mon, Feb 3, 2003, 9:32 AM	17.2 MB
Clip 08	Mon, Feb 3, 2003, 12:18 PM	17.3 MB
Clip 09	Mon, Feb 3, 2003, 9:32 AM	17.2 MB
Clip 10	Mon, Feb 3, 2003, 12:17 PM	17.1 MB
Clip 11	Mon, Feb 3, 2003, 12:18 PM	136 KB
Clip 12	Mon, Mar 24, 2003, 3:33 PM	16.8 MB
DCP_0005.jpg	Mon, Feb 3, 2003, 9:30 AM	844 KB
DCP_0061.jpg	Sat, Feb 1, 2003, 4:19 PM	376 KB
Marcus2.jpg	Sat, Feb 1, 2003, 12:41 PM	720 KB
MarcusNap.jpg	Sat, Feb 1, 2003, 1:53 PM	236 KB
Spread from Center 01	Sat, Feb 1, 2003, 1:56 PM	17.1 MB
Voice 02	Sat, Feb 1, 2003, 3:09 PM	5 MB

Figure 1-3: iMovie keeps all your project files visible in a folder and its Media folder.

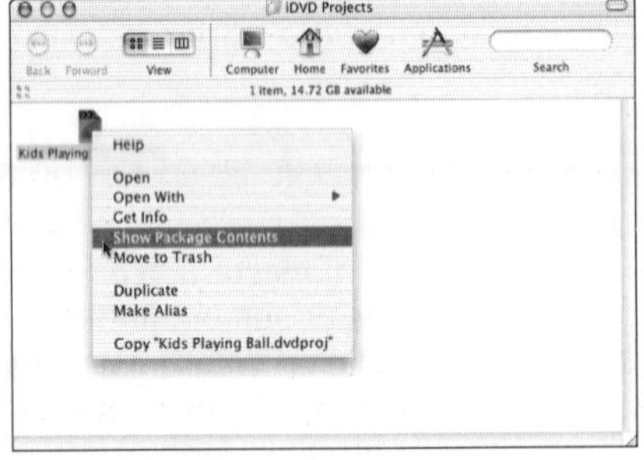

Figure 1-4: Choose Show Package Contents (left) to open a window where you can navigate your project's parts (right).

Backing up an iMovie Project

When you complete the work on your project and want to free up your hard disk space, you can archive (back up) the entire project to tape or CD/DVD. Doing this requires backup software — such as the Apple Backup utility that comes with a .Mac subscription or Dantz Software's Retrospect — but this is the route to go if you think you might want to make modifications later or to repurpose portions of the project.

Unless your project is fairly small, backing up to CD is going to be a painful process. After all, you can fit less than 30 seconds of digital video (DV) on an iDisk, a little over 3 minutes on a single CD-R (or -RW), or about 20 minutes on a DVD-R (or -RW). Given these limitations, we recommend one of the following choices:

- ✦ Backing up to DAT (tape) or DVD-R/RW by using a commercial backup solution like Retrospect.
- ✦ Backing up to another hard disk by using a tool like Mike Bombich's Carbon Copy Cloner (`http://software.bombich.com/software/ccc.html`).

Carbon Copy Cloner is a great donation-ware tool. It is free to educational institutions and comes as totally uncrippled shareware (with a request for a donation from the rest of us). Pay what you think it's worth. If you're honest with yourself, you'll make a nice donation — we did.

As an alternative to backing up, you can export the completed movie back to your DV camera. The downside to this solution is that you get a DV Stream with all your edits, transitions, effects, and so forth cast in concrete and none of the supporting or original files present. Multiple audio tracks are now merged into a single track and, if you re-import the footage, you don't have access to the original clips or to any of the edited clips that were still in the Clips pane when you exported. The upside is that you can fit a full 60 (or 90) minutes on a single small tape that can be purchased for under $6.

We found a shareware utility named DV Backup (around $25 at `www.coolatoola.com`) that backs up a hard disk folder structure to a camcorder's miniDV or Digital8 tape through your FireWire connection. We've tried it out and it seems to work, but our experience with DV Backup is not extensive enough to put in an unequivocal recommendation. This utility does offer a nice compromise, though, by keeping all your project's pieces intact while still providing the relatively inexpensive 10GB to 15GB storage of a tape.

Backing up an iDVD project

Preserving your iDVD project includes some hidden gotchas. The largest of the gotchas is that iDVD doesn't include the original media (movies) in the project package but instead includes just the rendered MPEG-2 files and pointers to the original movie files. Further, if you choose to delete rendered files when you close the project, even the rendered data won't be available.

Our recommendation is to archive your iDVD project with any iMovie projects it uses if you think you might want to modify it at a later time. If all you need to do is burn more copies of your DVDs, you can do that fairly easily as described in Apple's Knowledge Base article 42724 (`http://docs.info.apple.com/article.html?artnum=42724`).

Surfing the Apple Web Site

The Apple Web site provides a wealth of information on the various iLife applications and the iPod. You can go to the individual product pages, which are found at `www.apple.com/`*`productname`*. (Replace *productname* in this URL with iTunes, iPhoto, iMovie, iDVD, or iPod, as the case may be.) These product pages are actually mini-Web sites on their own, with links to pages that

- ✦ Show off the technology in QuickTime tutorials and demos
- ✦ Offer (frequently free) downloads for extras and add-ons
- ✦ Link to Apple Feedback pages where you can report bugs or tell what you like and don't like about a particular program

More importantly, you can go to `http://kbase.info.apple.com/index.jsp` to search the extensive Knowledge Base to satisfy your curiosity or to find answers to questions about issues that frustrate you — like bugs. The Knowledge Base articles frequently acknowledge anomalous program behavior and, more importantly, detail any known workarounds for the problem.

Another area to check, especially if you want to extend your iLife application's functionality, is the AppleScript section. Other than iMovie, the iLife applications (iTunes, iPhoto, and iDVD) each have their own pages within the `www.apple.com/applescript` hierarchy (just add *`/productname`* to the URL). *AppleScript* is a powerful, easy-to-use programming language to control scriptable applications. Even if you don't want to learn how to program, you can take advantage of hundreds of freely available scripts and enhance your iLife experience.

Calling for Help

Apple doesn't include manuals for its iLife applications (or OS X, or other consumer applications such as AppleWorks), but that doesn't mean the company doesn't document how to use the products. The Apple Help Viewer is really a specialized Web browser, and the help you find there comes from HTML pages. These pages aren't only on your hard disk. If you have a live Internet connection, Help Viewer is set up to search the Apple

Web site where it can download the latest help information and update the pages stored on your hard disk. Figure 1-5 shows you the Help Viewer, ready to search iDVD's Help pages.

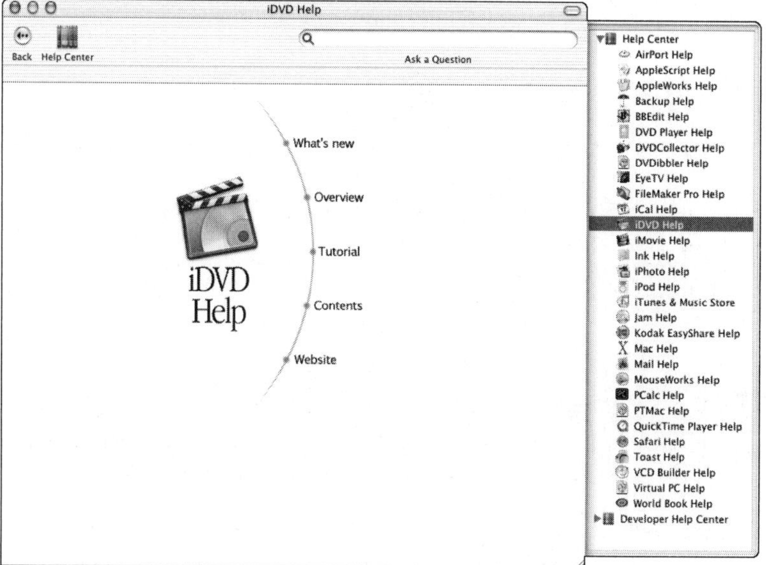

Figure 1-5: Help Viewer is a browser where you can search for help on most applications.

The little round Back button on the left end of the toolbar behaves just like the Back button in a Web browser, taking you to the previously viewed page. This button even has the same keyboard shortcut (⌘+[ ) as the Back button in Safari or Internet Explorer.

The toolbar's Help Center button shows and hides the drawer (visible at the right of the main window in Figure 1-5). Each entry in the Help Center drawer is a link to the Help pages on the named application or technology. Click one, and you briefly see a progress indicator (below the Ask a Question text box) which tells you that Help Viewer is retrieving information.

That Ask a Question text box, though, is the heart of Help Viewer. To get to the heart of the matter and find the help you need, follow these steps:

1. **Type a question or keywords into the Ask a Question text box, and press Return.**

   Help Viewer searches the Help databases for matches and displays all the matches it finds — along with an indicator of how relevant its algorithms determine the match to be. Figure 1-6 shows example search results.

When you search the Help databases, *relevance* is, primarily, how closely together and how frequently the keywords in your query appear in the topic found. As you can see from the list of topics in Figure 1-6, the search is exhaustive but far from perfect. The lower the Relevance, the more likely it is that you got a "hit" from just one of the keywords and that the topic probably isn't germane to your query.

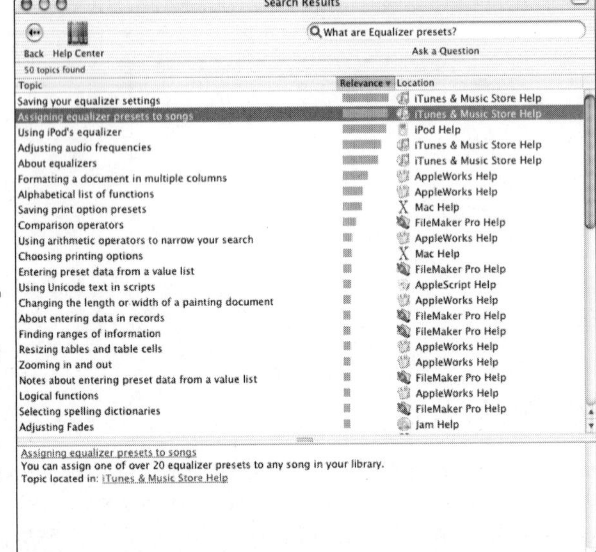

Figure 1-6: When asked about Equalizer presets, this is what Help Viewer found.

2. **Select a topic from the matches listed.**

   In the window's (resizable) bottom pane, Help Viewer shows you the topic name, the first few words or sentence from the topic, and where the topic is located.

3. **Click the link in the bottom pane, and you're transported to the topic's full page, as shown in Figure 1-7.**

   Many pages include a Tell Me More link which, when clicked, refines the search, giving you yet another list of topics and their computed relevance.

To increase or decrease the font size used by Help Viewer, choose Edit⇨Increase Font Size (⌘++) or Edit⇨Decrease Font Size (⌘+-). If you think that you're going to need to refer to a page frequently and don't want to have to go through Help Viewer to find it again, choose File⇨Print and either print the page or save it as a PDF for future reference.

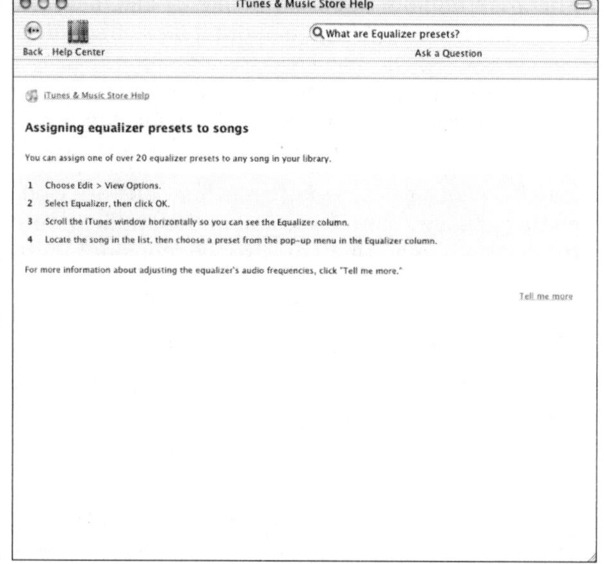

Figure 1-7: Check out the information on the topic you selected.

Troubleshooting Problems

If anyone ever tells you that a piece of software is bug-free, you can assume that either they're blowing smoke or the program is very constrained in what it can and will do. The more complex an application, the more (minor) bugs it is going to contain. Fortunately, the iLife applications are used so often by so many people — and Apple is so responsive in releasing updates to fix bugs as they're encountered — that the bugs that do exist tend to be quite minor and, even then, only rear their ugly little heads in unusual circumstances.

The most frequent problem encountered, and not just with the iLife applications, can appear as a *program crash* or *application freeze* (where the program stops responding to input from the mouse or keyboard).

If the program crashed, attempt to relaunch it. If the program froze, you should Force Quit (⌘+Option+Escape to display the Force Quit dialog box) and attempt to relaunch. If the program relaunches okay, the problem may be the result of some strange, not easily reproducible interaction (or maybe even sunspot activity). However, if the problem persists and you can narrow down the sequence of steps that causes the misbehavior, you can check the Apple Knowledge Base to see whether the problem is known. And, if not, report the situation via the Feedback pages mentioned in the "Surfing the Apple Web Site" section, earlier in this chapter.

Running at or near minimum system requirements can make bugs more obvious (and, thereby, the need for troubleshooting more frequent), as follows:

- Using an older release of your OS X can make you more likely to encounter System-related bugs (those involving an interaction between the application and core System routines and libraries).

  You should also check to see whether either Software Update or the Apple Web pages have a newer version of the application you're running. If so, we recommend that you strongly consider updating your version to the current version.
- Running with minimal RAM or free hard disk space, particularly on your startup volume, is also begging for trouble. OS X makes extensive use of *virtual memory* (hard disk space used to simulate RAM) and not having sufficient free (and preferably contiguous) hard disk space to allocate as virtual memory can grind things to a halt.
- We recommend keeping at least 10% (we run closer to 20%) of your startup disk space available for OS X to use as needed. Remember, iPhoto, iMovie, and iDVD use lots of memory *and* temporary disk space to perform their magic.

Corrupted preference files seem to be at the root of so many application problems that removing the preference file(s) and then relaunching the application should be one of the first remedial actions you attempt. You can usually find the preference file(s) in the Preference folder within your Home directory's Library folder. The iLife applications' preference files are

- **iTunes:** `com.apple.iTunes.plist`
- **iPhoto:** `com.apple.iPhoto.plist`
- **iPod:** `com.apple.iPod.plist`
- **iMovie:** `com.apple.iMovie3.plist`
- **iDVD:** `com.apple.iDVD.plist`
- **Other related preference files:** `com.apple.iApps.plist`, which is used by iTunes to track databases used (like the iTunes Music Store) and `com.apple.iTunes.eq.plist` for equalizer preferences.

Chapter 2: Enhancing Your iLife Environment with Other Tools

In This Chapter

- **Adding plug-ins**
- **Scripting your iLife applications**
- **Getting freeware and shareware assistance/assistants**
- **Enhancing iLife with commercial tools**

Since the early days of personal computing, popular software packages have provided ways for users to get more out of the product than was originally envisioned. From the Peek and Poke commands in BASIC, external commands in dBASE, and the XCMDs and XFCNs in HyperCard, through today's Web browser and Photoshop plug-ins, whole industries have grown to fill niche markets.

This modular approach to function availability is (mostly) a win-win situation for software developers and users. By providing the hooks for third parties to add functionality rather than trying to provide every function that an imaginative marketing person can conceive, software developers can ship a working product in less time, at lower cost, and with a smaller disk and memory footprint. Users benefit because you pay for the additional functions only if you want them and because a smaller product can be more thoroughly tested and is usually more reliable. If a plug-in is buggy, you can just remove the plug-in without affecting the stability of the rest of the program. The one downside is that you have more files to keep track of. You need to make sure that you have the plug-in installed in the right directory and that you keep up to date with the most recent version.

The enhancements made available via AppleScript to communicate between programs, automate repetitive tasks in an application, or just add functionality are yet another the way the Apple iLife applications (except for the currently unscriptable iMovie) enable you and others to extend the iLife domain.

You can use other programs to work with the output from your iLife applications. If QuickTime doesn't provide you with the export encoder you seek, you can use another tool to work with iMovie's reference file. Similarly, if iPhoto doesn't provide sufficient editing tools or print formats for your needs, you can use an external editor for that task as well.

In this chapter, we cover all these ways to expand your iReach, delving into examples of each along the way.

Plugging In

All four iLife applications support one or more types of *plug-ins* — external code or graphics modules that expand upon the application as shipped by Apple.

As a general rule, plug-ins are installed in a special folder within one of the following folders:

- ✦ The Library folder at the root level of your startup disk.
- ✦ Your Home folder's Library folder, if you don't want the plug-ins available to other accounts on your Mac.

iTunes plug-ins

The iTunes visualizer isn't your only choice for adding a visual effect to your music. At the time of this writing, 17 visual effects plug-ins (also known as visualizers) for iTunes are available for download via VersionTracker (`www.versiontracker.com/macosx/`). They're all freeware or inexpensive shareware. They range from variations on the iTunes visualizer, such as Fountain Music from Binary Minded Software (`www.binaryminded.com`) to a plug-in that plays QuickTime movies based upon the selected song — Satoshi Kanmo's ShortCut74 plug-in, available at `homepage.mac.com/smalltalker/english.html`. Figure 2-1 shows EasyViewX from Trinity Software (`www.trinfinitysoftware.com/easyview.shtml`) in use.

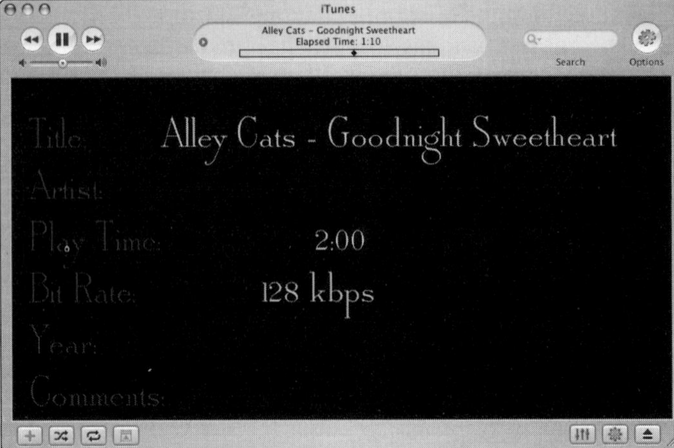

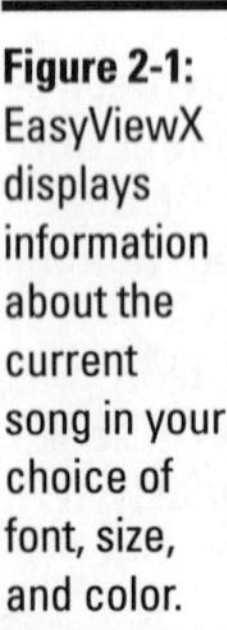

Figure 2-1: EasyViewX displays information about the current song in your choice of font, size, and color.

The button-of-many-personalities in the iTunes upper-right corner bears the label Options when a visual effect is running. Not all visual effects include a preference dialog box, but if they do, the Options button is enabled (not dimmed). If enabled, click the Options button to set preferences for that visual effect. Figure 2-2 shows the Options dialog box for the EasyViewX plug-in.

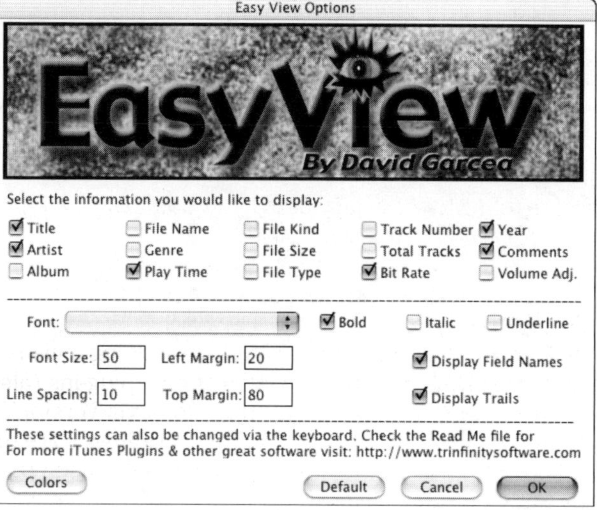

Figure 2-2: Some visualizers offer an Options dialog box, accessible through iTunes' Options button.

If you're interested in writing your own visualizers, you can download the iTunes visual plug-ins SDK for free from `developer.apple.com/sdk`. All it requires is that you sign up for a free membership in ADC, the Apple Developer Connection.

iMovie plug-ins

If you thought that iMovie came with a lot of transitions, titles, and effects, a quick check of the offerings from such companies as GeeThree (`www.geethree.com`), Virtix (`www.virtix.com`), eZedia (`www.ezedia.com/products/eZedia_plug-ins/`), and CSB Digital (`www.csbdigital.com`) will boggle your mind. You can find even more iMovie effects packages via a VersionTracker search for iMovie plug-ins.

Whereas most of the iTunes plug-ins are free, iMovie plug-ins are almost exclusively commercial offerings. Most of the plug-in developers offer free samplers, and Apple includes download links to these samplers on the iMovie Web pages (`www.apple.com/imovie/visual_effects.html`).

Figure 2-3 shows a preview of GeeThree's Picture-in-Picture Frame visual effect, part of its Slick Transitions & Effects suite. Just a few of the other effects in this package include a camcorder effect, where the white framing rectangles you see in a camcorder's viewfinder are added, a lens flare, and an effect that turns your clip (or a portion of a clip) into black and white, with a white outline around the edges of distinct objects.

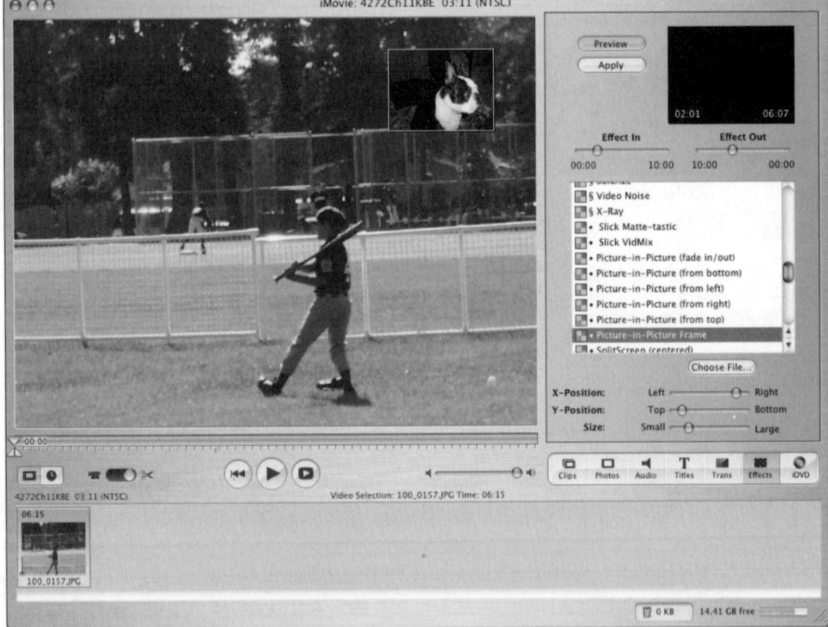

Figure 2-3: Picture-in-Picture is just one of the dozens of effects available from GeeThree.

Additional title styles are also in the GeeThree package, such as the Marquee title effect shown in Figure 2-4. Marquee comes in two flavors, solid semitransparent letters or letters that display a gradient effect. One of our favorites is News Flash, which takes the text you provide and scrolls it across the bottom of the screen, just like the news ticker messages that television networks use.

The bulk of the plug-ins available for iMovie fall into the Transitions category. Like the transitions included with iMovie, most of these are eye-catching but could easily distract your viewer from your movie's content. Therefore, use them sparingly and only when you want to call attention to a scene change.

iPhoto plug-ins

You can really expand the iPhoto Export Photos (File⇨Export) capabilities via plug-ins. Each plug-in adds another tab to the iPhoto Export dialog box, as shown in Figure 2-5. The standard iPhoto 2 installation offers only three tabs: File Export, Web Page, and QuickTime. These three tabs are also implemented as plug-ins.

Figure 2-4: New title styles, such as GeeThree's Marquee, are also available via plug-ins.

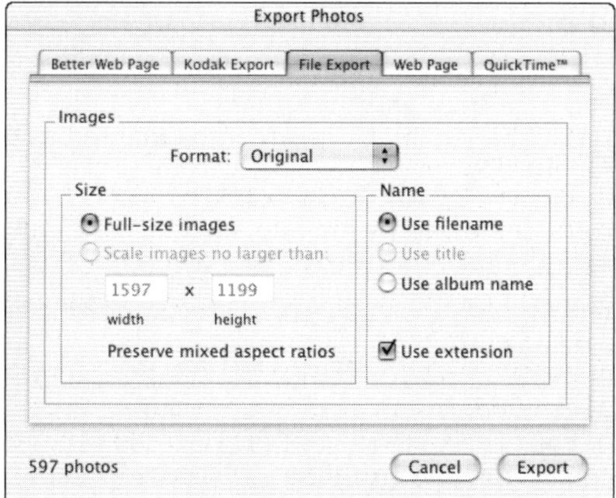

Figure 2-5: The Export Photos dialog box.

Unlike iTunes or iMovie, where the plug-ins remain in a Library folder visible to the user, iPhoto plug-ins are installed into a PlugIns folder inside the iPhoto application package. If you select the iPhoto application and choose File⇨Get Info (⌘+I), you see a Plug-ins panel in the iPhoto Info window. Click the disclosure triangle next to Plug-ins to see a list of your installed plug-ins, as shown in Figure 2-6. In this pane, you can disable (uncheck) and enable (check) your installed plug-ins; add new plug-ins by clicking the Add button and navigating to the plug-in you want to install; or remove an installed plug-in by selecting it and clicking the Remove button.

You must quit iPhoto to make changes to the Plug-ins list. The changes show up when you relaunch iPhoto.

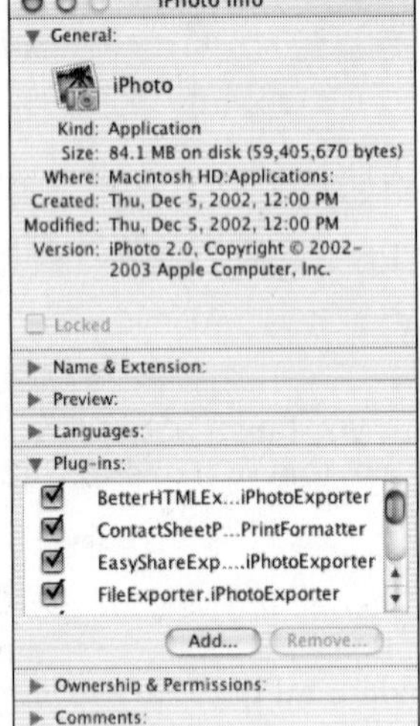

Figure 2-6: You can add, remove, disable, and enable iPhoto plug-ins in the iPhoto Info window.

Although we have yet to see any third-party printing plug-ins, iPhoto plug-in architecture also supports custom print formats. In fact, the various Print formats, such as Contact Sheet and N-Up, are implemented as plug-ins and are visible in the Plug-ins list.

iDVD plug-ins

In the case of iDVD, the plug-ins we discuss are installed in a Favorites folder within either of the following:

- ✦ The iDVD folder of your startup disk's Library folder
- ✦ The iDVD folder of your Home directory's Library folder

These themes show up in the Customize drawer's Themes pane. Just click the Customize button and, if necessary, click the Themes button to display the Themes pane. Click the pop-up menu, and if you installed third-party themes, an entry for that theme collection appears in the menu — see ThemePAK in Figure 2-7.

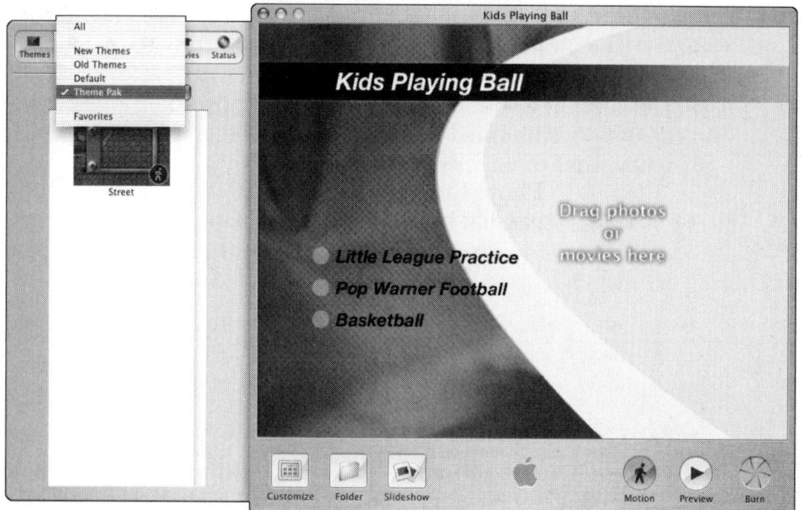

Figure 2-7: Custom theme collections, like ThemePAK from `www.iDVDThemePAK.com`, show up in the Themes pane's pop-up menu.

At `www.apple.com/idvd/themes.html`, you find a link to iDVDThemePAK, as well as two free sample themes (at least, that's what's available at this moment).

Interestingly enough, a number of actual code plug-ins are available within the iDVD 3 application package. These include such code as the encoder that turns your movie into a DVD-compliant MPEG-2 file. So far, though, Apple hasn't publicized how to write iDVD code plug-ins. If it ever does, you can look forward to additional encoding, importing, and exporting capabilities becoming available.

Enhancing iLife with AppleScript

With the exception of iMovie, the iLife applications are scriptable. That means that you can write AppleScript code to automate repetitive tasks, communicate data from one program to another, and perform operations that are inaccessible via the program's menus and buttons.

Just because you don't want to have to learn how to program doesn't mean that you should skip this material. Untold numbers of useful AppleScripts are ready for you to use. Just because you don't want to learn C++, Objective-C, Pascal, Java, or some other language doesn't mean you can't use programs written by others in these languages (iMovie, iTunes, iPhoto, iDVD, Photoshop, and so on).

Of course, if you're a little curious and willing to put in some time and effort learning AppleScript programming, you'll have an even richer experience because most of the AppleScripts you can download are easily modifiable, allowing you to customize them to do exactly what you want.

We mention the product-specific pages of Apple's AppleScript Web minisites in the previous chapter, but those pages are just the tip of the iceberg. You also may want to check out these sites:

- `www.scriptbuilders.net`, a large script repository for `MacScripter.net`, a great learning place if you want to enhance your AppleScript knowledge
- `cocoaobjects.com/applescript/index.php`, another site for finding AppleScripts

Scripting iTunes

Of all the iLife applications, iTunes has the longest, richest AppleScript history and the greatest AppleScript support. iTunes even includes a Scripts menu (the little scroll icon between Window and Help) to provide easy access to your iTunes scripts. These scripts live in one of two locations:

- A Scripts folder contained in your Home Library's iTunes folder
- A Scripts folder in the iTunes folder of your startup disk's Library folder

The scripts in your startup disk's Library folder are accessible to any user on your Mac running iTunes. The scripts in your Home Library's iTunes folder are accessible only by you.

Smart playlists are cool, but have you ever noticed that you can't mix the tests to get all your five-star songs in the Musical and Soundtrack genres? AppleScript can easily create this playlist, but it doesn't have a live update option like a smart playlist. The script shown in Figure 2-8 creates the described playlist.

Don't be intimidated by the number of lines of code here. The guts of this script are the eight lines starting with making a new playlist and ending with the second "end tell" following the duplicate command. The rest of the script is just boilerplate error-checking to make sure that the version of iTunes supports AppleScript, to offer those users with an old version the chance to download a current version, and to display progress dialog boxes telling you what's going on.

This isn't to say that the boilerplate is unimportant, just that it doesn't differ much from one script to the next. Mainly, it just makes your scripts a little friendlier and more robust. We'd like to thank Apple for its sample scripts, from which we shamelessly borrowed the version checking and `access_website` code.

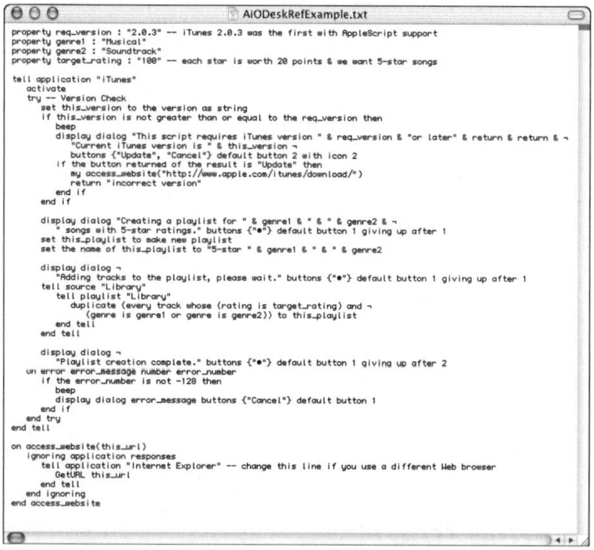

AiODeskRefExample.txt

```
property req_version : "2.0.3" -- iTunes 2.0.3 was the first with AppleScript support
property genre1 : "Musical"
property genre2 : "Soundtrack"
property target_rating : "100" -- each star is worth 20 points & we want 5-star songs

tell application "iTunes"
   activate
   try -- Version Check
      set this_version to the version as string
      if this_version is not greater than or equal to the req_version then
         beep
         display dialog "This script requires iTunes version " & req_version & "or later" & return & return & ¬
            "Current iTunes version is " & this_version ¬
            buttons {"Update", "Cancel"} default button 2 with icon 2
         if the button returned of the result is "Update" then
            my access_website("http://www.apple.com/itunes/download/")
            return "incorrect version"
         end if
      end if

      display dialog "Creating a playlist for " & genre1 & " & " & genre2 & ¬
         " songs with 5-star ratings." buttons {"•"} default button 1 giving up after 1
      set this_playlist to make new playlist
      set the name of this_playlist to "5-star " & genre1 & " & " & genre2

      display dialog ¬
         "Adding tracks to the playlist, please wait." buttons {"•"} default button 1 giving up after 1
      tell source "Library"
         tell playlist "Library"
            duplicate (every track whose (rating is target_rating) and ¬
               (genre is genre1 or genre is genre2)) to this_playlist
         end tell
      end tell

      display dialog ¬
         "Playlist creation complete." buttons {"•"} default button 1 giving up after 2
   on error error_message number error_number
      if the error_number is not -128 then
         beep
         display dialog error_message buttons {"Cancel"} default button 1
      end if
   end try
end tell

on access_website(this_url)
   ignoring application responses
      tell application "Internet Explorer" -- change this line if you use a different Web browser
         GetURL this_url
      end tell
   end ignoring
end access_website
```

Figure 2-8: This AppleScript creates a playlist with all your five-star Musical and Soundtrack songs.

For those of you who also have AppleWorks, Apple provides some scripts that create CD case covers in AppleWorks for your iTunes playlists. These scripts come in handy when you burn a CD and want to remind yourself what's on the disc.

AppleScripting iPhoto

Although iPhoto doesn't offer a Scripts menu of its own, you can get the same effect by using the system-wide Scripts menu. Inside the AppleScript folder within your Applications folder is a file that bears a folder icon named Script Menu.menu. Double-click this menu extra to add a system-wide Scripts menu to the right side of your menu bar, as shown in Figure 2-9.

Apple makes a nice assortment of example scripts available at `www.apple.com/applescript/iphoto/`. Not only are these great examples from which you can learn scripting techniques, but most of them are also extremely useful in their own right. One example, Find Unassigned Images, creates an album for you consisting only of images from your photo library that aren't already in at least one album. Not only is that script useful, but you can also easily modify the script to create a list of albums to which an individual photo belongs. As authors, we maintain separate user accounts where the only items in our photo library are the screenshots used in our projects. Using the Photo Summary script, we can easily produce an HTML (or RTF) file showing all the images and listing where they are and any other information about them. This summary is useful to us, and to our editors, in tracking the artwork for a project.

Figure 2-9: The Scripts Menu menu extra provides a home for the scripts used with applications that don't provide Scripts menus of their own.

AppleScripting iDVD

As with iPhoto, you can most easily access iDVD's scripts via the system-wide Scripts menu. A good starter set is available at `www.apple.com/applescript/idvd/`.

One nice feature in iDVD is that you can position your menu buttons wherever you want on the menu if iDVD's default arrangement is not to your liking. Unfortunately, no alignment commands, visible grid, or rulers are available to assist you in precisely positioning your buttons. Don't give up, though. AppleScript makes distributing your buttons where you want them easy, as shown in Figure 2-10.

But, even as handy as those scripts are, a full-blown application named iDVD Companion is available via the AppleScript iDVD Web page. iDVD Companion is written in AppleScript Studio, a pure OS X development environment where you use AppleScripts to do your work and Apple's development tools (they're part of your OS X distribution but aren't installed by default) to create the user interface.

Figure 2-11 shows the iDVD window with the iDVD Companion window displaying its Nudge tab. Using the Nudge tab, you can move selected buttons in 1-, 6-, 36-, or 72-pixel increments to the left, right, up, or down. Click the Include Title check box, and the menu's title also moves.

If you've ever wanted to reposition the Back button on an iDVD menu, but were frustrated because you couldn't, iDVD Companion provides a solution. Choose Edit⇨Select Back Button and use the Nudge tab to move it where you want.

Figure 2-10: The result of running a script that tells the user to select exactly three buttons.

Figure 2-11: iDVD Companion lets you nudge buttons exact distances.

iDVD Companion's other two tabs are the Align and Title tabs. Using the Align tab, you can line up the left, right, top, or bottom edges of two or more selected buttons. Use the Title tab to set the location for the menu's title.

The iDVD Companion menu bar includes other helpful shortcuts. In addition to the Select Back Button choice, the Edit menu also includes commands allowing you to Select All buttons, Deselect All buttons, and Delete All buttons. Be careful, though, with the Delete All buttons command; no Undo is available.

Navigating your menu structure in iDVD to make changes to subordinate menus can be time-consuming and annoying. iDVD Companion provides a Go menu that lets you select your destination menu from a list and then tells iDVD to display that menu, eliminating the need to navigate a possibly complex menu structure. The Themes menu sports a handy little Layouts submenu with four predefined button layouts. The menu named Menu was more useful with iDVD 2.1 than it is with iDVD 3, because iTunes and iPhoto are now accessible in iDVD's Customize drawer. Nevertheless, the first item, Name Current Menu is handy because it allows you to use the previously cited Go To Menu command conveniently. Similarly, the Button menu lets you name buttons, specify exact positions for buttons, and swap the positions of two selected buttons.

One of the best features of iDVD Companion is that all of these palette and menu operations take place by calling AppleScripts, and the source code for all those scripts is present for you to learn from and modify as you desire.

Supplementing iLife with Other Programs

The four iLife applications are a wonderful collection of multimedia products, enabling you to collect, organize, present, and repurpose your music, photos, and video. In many cases, they are all you need to fulfill your needs or desires. But (isn't there always a "but") sometimes you want to do more or just something a little different.

We, the users of Mac OS X, are blessed with some wonderful supplementary programs, most of which are free or relatively inexpensive. The fact that OS X is built upon a Unix framework has opened the doors to a wide collection of Unix utilities, and to make things even better, the OS X development tools made putting a Mac interface onto these command-line tools a simple task.

Freeware and shareware

In the next few sections, we cover some of the free and shareware tools that are available and invaluable additions to the iLife user's tool chest.

iTunes enhancements

One of the most popular MP3 encoders on many platforms (Mac, Windows, and various implementations of Unix and Linux) is LAME, which stands for LAME Ain't an Mp3 Encoder (because, in the beginning, it wasn't). Implemented for iTunes users as an AppleScript around the Unix command-line tool, you install the script, which is a free download from VersionTracker; then you select the songs you want encoded with LAME and choose Import with LAME from iTunes' Scripts menu. The iTunes-LAME window appears, and you just click the Import button when you're ready to start the encoding (as shown in Figure 2-12).

Another handy utility, this one shareware ($5), is Josh Aas's iTunes Publisher. iTunes Publisher is the iTunes File⇨Export Song List command on steroids. You can save your playlists as HTML files, which iTunes Publisher links back to your iTunes Library. iTunes Publisher also provides a simple interface to producing QTSS (QuickTime Streaming Server) playlists, as well as generating the m3u playlists used by many MP3 players (such as WinAmp), or text- or tab-delimited text files.

Though not really an enhancement to iTunes, MacMP3CD (`www.mireth.com`) is a useful adjunct to iTunes. To switch from burning audio CDs to MP3 CDs in iTunes requires that you change your Burning preferences (and then, probably, switch them back when you're done). With MacMP3CD, you can build your MP3 playlist and burn it directly. Additionally, iTunes doesn't recognize MP3 CDs when they're inserted as it does with audio CDs. MacMP3CD also plays back your MP3 CDs.

Figure 2-12: The LAME encoder even converts AC3 files to MP3.

iPhoto enhancements

If you want more control over the Web pages you export from iPhoto, check out BetterHTMLExport (shareware, $20, from Simeon Leifer's Drooling Cat Software, www.droolingcat.com). BetterHTMLExport is an iPhoto plug-in that adds a Better Web Page tab to the iPhoto Export Photos dialog box. Choosing the Better Web Page tab displays another row of tabs:

- **Pages** (shown in Figure 2-13) controls the overall look of your Web pages.
- **Thumbnails** is where you control the small image links and how they look.
- **Images** controls the size and organization of the exported images.
- **Custom** is where you add additional text in a table form (such as author, date, and venue).
- **Info** tells you your registration information, accesses the documentation, and checks for updates.

Additionally, you can build and save your own page templates. (A template exchange service is even set up at Drooling Cat.)

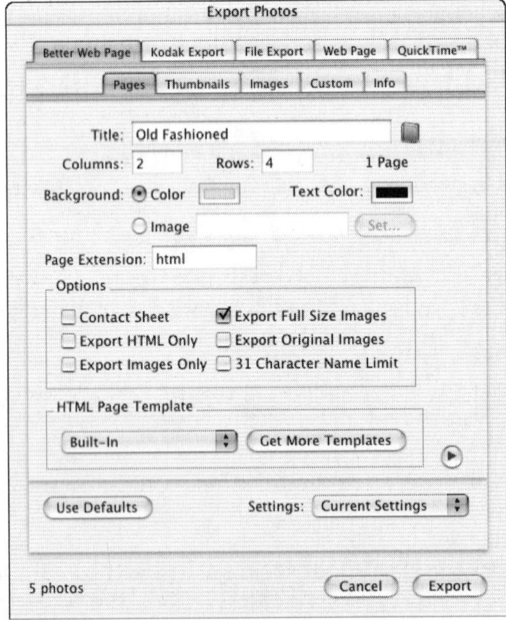

Figure 2-13: The Pages tab of the Export Photos dialog box.

iPhoto slows down as the iPhoto Library gets larger. One way to circumvent this slowdown is to have multiple libraries, but iPhoto doesn't support multiple libraries as shipped. At least three handy utilities work around this barrier: iPhoto Buddy (donationware), iPhoto Library Manager (freeware), and iPhoto Librarian (freeware). Each utility approaches the problem a little differently, but all have large followings among iPhoto users. You can find all of them at www.versiontracker.com/macosx/.

iPhoto Mailer Patcher is a free but handy hack that adds Mail support for e-mail clients other than the four (AOL, Eudora, Entourage, and Mail) Apple built into iPhoto 2. In fact, it even extends support to such classic mail clients as Claris Emailer and Outlook Express. Check it out at perso.mycable.ch/jacksim/software/.

If you have Roxio's Toast Titanium software (either version 5 or version 6), you'll find iPhoto Toast Export Plugin (free from www.elgato.com) a handy way to write photos or albums to disk, especially if you want them in a format usable by friends who don't have iPhoto. We talk more about Toast in the section, "Toast goes well with iLife," later in this chapter.

iPhoto's slideshows are nice, but they're pretty staid and traditional. One picture follows the next, filling your display area. David Ahmed's ExhibitionX ($15, www.davidahmed.com) offers another way to view your iPhoto albums. It offers six viewing styles and provides direct access to your iPhoto Library and albums via a pop-up menu:

- **Gallery** (shown in Figure 2-14) emulates your photos hanging on the walls of an art gallery, which you traverse with the keyboard arrow keys (left and right rotate; up and down zoom in and out).
- **Carousel** rotates a virtual carousel consisting of your photos.
- **Book** flips the pages of a book, each containing one photo.
- **Cube** is actually four rotating cubes (similar to the old Rubik's Cube puzzle), with your photos coming into view on any of the four cubes.
- **Flat** is a traditional slideshow.
- **Circle** displays the circular centers of your photos, rotating around a vertical axis.

Another option is switching back and forth between full-screen viewing and viewing in a window.

So, you want to create panoramas of scenes that are too expansive for a single frame? Check out REALVIZ's Stitcher EZ ($33, www.realviz.com).

Just take a sequence of overlapping photos (REALVIZ recommends about a 30-degree rotation for the typical 35mm camera or digital equivalent) and let Stitcher EZ combine them into a beautiful panorama with just a single click of the mouse. It even performs color equalization for you as the lighting changes from frame to frame.

Figure 2-14: ExhibitionX offers six views, including Gallery.

iMovie enhancements

iMovie is a great tool for creating QuickTime movies and creating finished productions to use on videotape or DVD via its interaction with iDVD. But, what if you want to create a DivX file to share with your Windows-using friends, or a Video CD or Super Video CD? Or what if you want to create a DVD and your DVD burner is not a SuperDrive? Free and shareware software, originating in the Unix community, is available to help you out.

These programs are relatively easy to use, but generally do not sport the interactive smoothness or pleasant appearance of the iLife tools. The first tool in our arsenal of enhancements is ffmpegX (`homepage.mac.com/major4/`), the main window of which appears in Figure 2-15.

The secret to making ffmpegX easy to use is the Quick Presets pop-up menu at the bottom of the window. Choose your destination format, and ffmpegX sets appropriate parameters for you in all the tabs. Now, you can just click the Open button to choose your source file (such as the reference iMovie in an iMovie project's folder) and the Save As button to specify a name and location for your encoded movie.

Figure 2-15: ffmpegX lets you encode to and transcode among various MPEG varieties.

If encoding movies was all that ffmpegX did, the $15 shareware fee would be more than covered; however, ffmpegX offers even more tools, including the following:

- A demuxer to let you split multiplexed MPEG files into their component audio and video streams.
- A split tool that lets you properly segment a movie into multiple files so that they will fit on a CD.
- Authoring tools that allow you to create IMG files or CUE/BIN pairs, ready for burning to disc.

Best of all, it can encode to DVD-compatible MPEG-2 files, even on a G3 or some other Mac that doesn't run iDVD.

Just so you can't accuse us of not telling you ahead of time, downloading ffmpegX does not give you the complete tool. Due to licensing restrictions on MPEG-2, the encoders and decoders must be downloaded separately and installed in ffmpegX. Fortunately, Major has built a small "run me first" application that tells you where to download the pieces and, after you point the application at the downloaded items, performs the installation for you.

Sizzle (`thegoods.ath.cx/~hmason/sizzle/`) is a simple, free DVD authoring application. Unlike iDVD, it won't encode your movies to MPEG-2; you have to supply it with MPEG-2 video and compatible audio streams, but that is easily taken care of by ffmpegX, which we just discussed. The main Sizzle window, shown in Figure 2-16, is pretty straightforward. You build your menus in the large pane on the left. You can change the background image for a menu, as well as its audio, by dropping an image or sound file into the appropriate well on the right.

Although Sizzle doesn't offer such iDVD niceties as Themes, drop zones, and motion menus, it does offer something that iDVD doesn't — support for subtitle tracks. Buttons are text-only, but you can overlay them against a background graphic that has images in the places you want buttons. Sizzle builds a DMG file that you can burn to DVD with any DVD-burning software that supports your DVD burner, even if it isn't a SuperDrive.

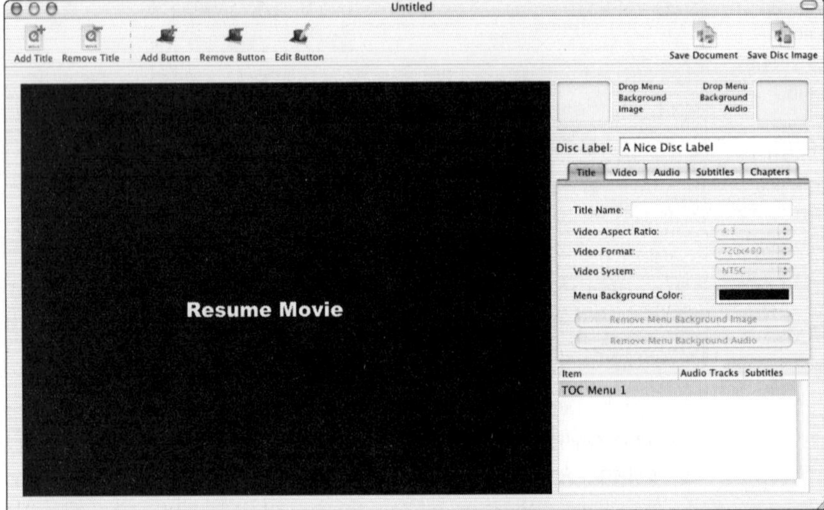

Figure 2-16: Sizzle is a pretty simple DVD-authoring program that doesn't rely on your having a SuperDrive or a G4.

If QuickTime Player doesn't play all the various movies you find — for example, the DivX files with `.avi` extensions common in the Windows world — two free video players are available that handle a lot more: VideoLAN Client (known as vlc) and MPlayer OS X. You can find both via VersionTracker. VideoLAN Client also plays VCDs and DVDs.

Mireth Technologies (`www.mireth.com`) has a couple of handy offerings to augment your iMovie creation and MPEG viewing. Its iVCD program ($29.95) encodes and burns Video CD and SuperVideo CD discs from the movies you give it. Figure 2-17 shows the iVCD interface.

One known limitation of iVCD applies only to users with the Pioneer 104 SuperDrive, which is the "2x" model. iVCD's bundled burning tool (a Unix program called cdrdao) is not compatible with that specific SuperDrive model, so you need to use another burning solution, such as Roxio's Toast Titanium.

MacVCD X, also from Mireth ($19.95) is a player for Video CDs and Super Video CDs.

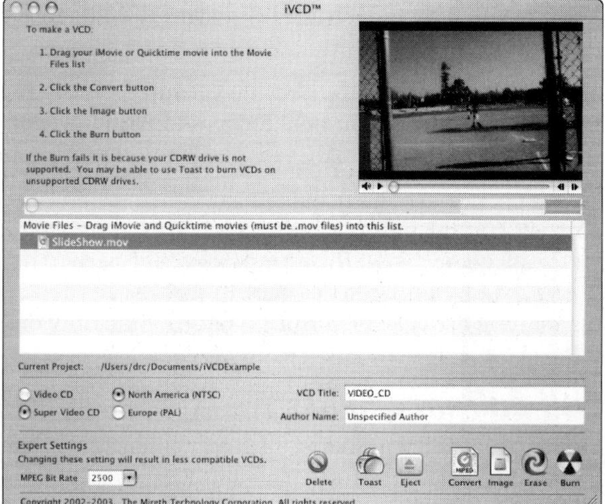

Figure 2-17: iVCD's straightforward interface lets you encode and burn Video CDs and SVCDs.

VCD Builder (donationware from Johan Lindström) lets you create Video CD and Super Video CD disc images ready for burning with (optional) still or motion menus. You also have control over what various buttons on your DVD remote does, including going to specific chapters within a movie (which you can also define in VCD Builder).

iDVD enhancements

Not many free or shareware enhancements to iDVD have been developed so far. The best one, though, in our opinions is the 3.0.1 update to iDVD. For the first time, you can use iDVD to encode your projects even if you don't have a SuperDrive (it just won't burn them). You still have to copy the files to a Mac with a SuperDrive to burn your DVD.

Once again, we recommend checking out iDVDThemePAK for additional themes to augment the ones that come with iDVD 3.

Here are some Internet references that can help answer compatibility questions as well as provide the nitty-gritty, low-level details of DVD, SVCD, and VCD:

- www.dvdrhelp.com: This is one of the most extensive sites about digital video in existence. Most of the material is slanted toward Windows users, but Mac- and Unix-related discussions are available as well. Mostly, the DVD Players compatibility and user feedback pages are a great reference when trying to determine whether a set-top player meets your needs.
- rec.video.desktop: This Internet newsgroup covers the history, current state, and future trends in desktop video. You find coverage of cameras, techniques, burners, players, and much more related to creating your own DVDs and Video CDs.
- **The Macintosh Digital Video Mailing List:** This e-mail list is available in individual message or digest form from www.themacintoshguy.com/lists/MacDV.html. Similar in concept to the rec.video.desktop newsgroup, this mailing list is a subscription-based, Mac-only discussion.

Commercial enhancements

Many commercial programs and add-ons are available to enhance your iLife. We touch on a few of the best here.

Toast goes well with iLife

The number one commercial enhancement, in our opinions, adjunct to iLife is Roxio's Toast 6 Titanium. The number one CD and DVD burning solution on the Mac just keeps getting better with every version. Toast 6 brings numerous new features to the product, ones tying into iLife very well (particularly in the video realm). Figure 2-18 shows the main Toast 6 window, and Figure 2-19 shows the Audio and Video drawers, displaying their Advanced tabs.

We just hit the high points here. Toast does so much, so well that it merits a book in its own right.

You discovered that you can include a data portion on an iDVD disc, containing material accessible via a Mac (or Windows) computer. Toast includes similar capabilities for audio CDs, with the Enhanced Audio CD option. You can include photos or even QuickTime movies that supplement the audio tracks. Some older computers don't support this multisession format, so you also have the option of creating Mixed Mode CDs, which contain separate audio and data tracks recorded as a single session.

Figure 2-18: Just click the button for the type of disc you want Toast to burn.

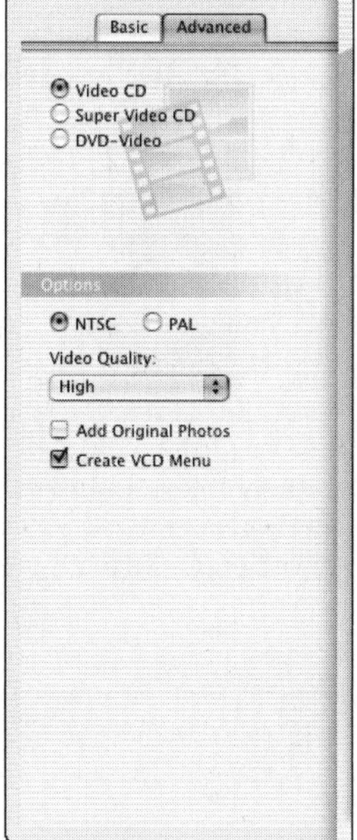

Figure 2-19: Toast 6 gives you lots of options for audio discs (left) and video discs (right).

The Video pane is a little deceptive because it supports far more than you might think at first glance. For example, if you drag a bunch of image files (say from iPhoto) into the pane, Toast creates a slideshow for you from those pictures, waiting to be encoded to your choice of Video CD, Super Video CD, or DVD-Video. Select the slideshow entry in the window and click its Edit button to display a sheet where you can customize the slideshow:

- The Text tab is where you specify what will appear beside the resulting movie's menu button.
- The Slideshow tab lets you specify the picture to be used for the button, add or remove slides, reorder the slides, and set independent durations for each slide (if you want), as shown in Figure 2-20.

Even better is Toast's Plug & Burn capability. If you have a digital camcorder attached, turned on, and cued to where you want to start importing, the Video pane displays a camera icon. Just click the Import button, and Toast starts importing and encoding the video. You even have a thumbnail view of what's coming in and remote-control buttons to control the import process, such as pausing, rewinding, and fast-forwarding the tape.

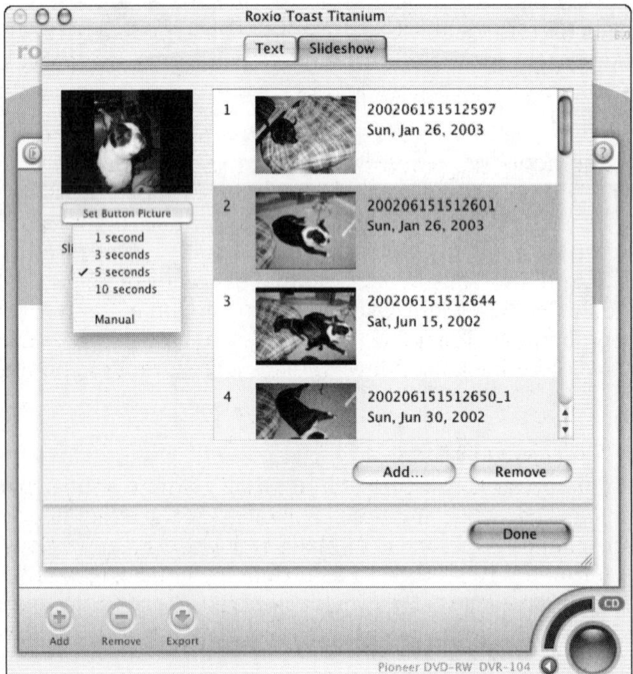

Figure 2-20: Toast lets you specify independent durations for each slide.

For Video CDs, Super Video CDs, and DVDs, Toast also (optionally) creates an on-screen menu for the disc. Toast allows three buttons per menu but creates additional menus and links between them as needed.

The new ToastAnywhere feature is great for those of you with networked Macs, only some of which have burners. ToastAnywhere lets you share burners with other Toast 6 users on your network or across the Internet.

Toast It is a contextual menu plug-in allowing you to Control+click a Finder icon and choose Toast It from the shortcut menu to burn your files without having to manually add them to the Toast window.

The features included within the Toast application are just the tip of the iceberg. The Toast package includes these supplementary programs:

- **Déjà Vu** is a backup program that allows for automatic or manual backups of your important data.
- **CD Spin Doctor 2** lets you digitize vinyl records, cassette or other tapes, or even live recordings. CD Spin Doctor includes a number of filters to reduce clicks, pops, and other noises, but you can also add VST filters for even more control.
- **Discus RE** (stands for Roxio Edition) is a version of the Discus label-making software to assist you in creating your own labels, case covers, and inserts. Using iTunes Artwork feature, you can emulate professional covers.
- **Motion Pictures** is a new tool added to the Toast 6 package. It's similar to the iMovie 3 Ken Burns Effect, but in addition to the Pan & Zoom effects, crossfades and soundtrack support are included directly.

One piece from the Toast 5 package that's missing in Toast 6 is the handy iView Media utility, a slightly scaled-down version of iView Media Pro. If you're upgrading to Toast 6 from Toast 5, you may want to make sure not to delete this folder because iView Media is a great tool to complement iPhoto.

Elements of Photoshop

When it comes to touching up digital images, iPhoto's tools can best be described as "good but minimal." The only special effect offered is to drain the color and convert photos to black and white. Fortunately, iPhoto supports external photo editors. In fact, right from the original iPhoto introduction, Apple points out that you can use external editors to touch up and otherwise process your photos without losing the organizational advantages of iPhoto.

The undisputed King of the Mountain when it comes to image editing is Adobe Photoshop, which comes with a princely price tag at $650. You lose very few features by choosing Adobe's personal image-editing application, Photoshop Elements 2, with a list price under $100. Elements enables you to enhance your artwork, embellishing it with special effects and dozens of filters. Figure 2-21 shows a simple case cover design produced for a Super Video CD about Spenser the Boston terrier. Simply cropping a photo and adding some text using Layer Styles adds a three-dimensional effect to the caption and improves the cover's appearance.

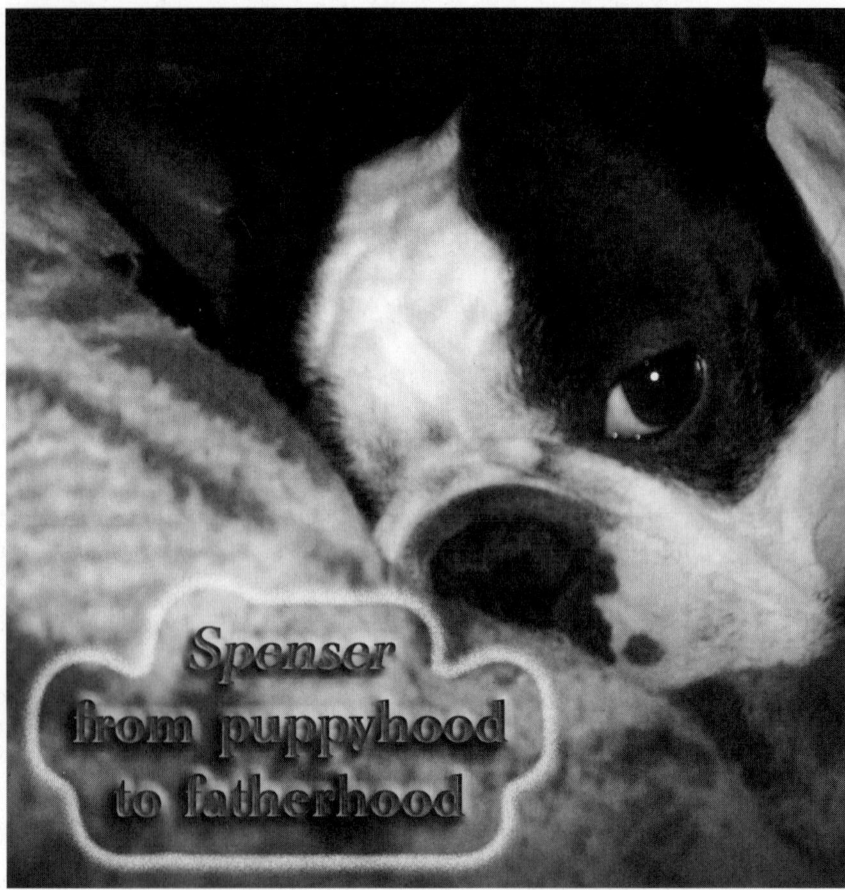

Figure 2-21: Using Photoshop Elements' tools, you can repurpose your photos to great effect.

Filters, transitions, and titles, oh my!

We touch on the various iMovie filters, effects, and transitions available from third-parties like GeeThree, Virtix, and eZedia in the previous chapter. We mention them again here because they offer you so many options for enhancing your video:

- The **QuickTime Pro** upgrade ($29.95) unlocks a large number of editing and display capabilities not present in the standard QuickTime Player application. From adding text tracks to your QuickTime movies to providing alternate audio tracks and iMovie-like trimming, QuickTime Pro is a virtual must for the serious iLife videographer. The Pro upgrade also provides more capabilities when editing your audio files, although it doesn't provide filters such as the VST filters used in CD Spin Doctor.
- **Totally Hip Software's LiveSlideShow** (`www.liveslideshow.com`) is yet another slideshow tool for converting your photo collections into compelling video presentations. It has an iMovie-like interface, but with features dedicated to slideshow creation. You have control over the transitions from one slide or group of slides to the next, as well as extensive control over the accompanying soundtrack.

LiveSlideShow creates QuickTime movies that you can then import into iDVD, iVCD, or Toast 6 to burn. Or you can just make the QuickTime files available to other Mac- or Windows-using friends (make sure the Windows friends have QuickTime).

It's not just software

The iPod is the most obvious hardware enhancement to your iLife, giving you the best portable MP3 player available today. Similarly, CD and DVD burners are obvious hardware accessories to improve your iLife. Here are some of the (slightly) less obvious possibilities:

- **Headphones:** The ear buds that come with an iPod provide excellent quality for their size, but what if you want something more or if you find sticking the bud in your ear less than comfortable? A vast array of headphones, including infrared wireless ones, produce higher fidelity and are more comfortable.
- **Speakers:** The built-in and external speakers that come with most Macs are okay, actually better than most standard-issue computer speakers. However, they'll never be the equal to some of the external speakers from JBL, Harmon-Kardon, and others.

- **Scanners:** Digital cameras are great, but many of us have old photographs that we would like to preserve. You can find excellent scanners in the $100 to $300 range from companies such as Hewlett-Packard, Epson, and Umax. Many of these scanners even come with slide attachments so that you can scan slides as well as photos.
- **Media converters:** Just like old photographs, old VHS, VHS-C, Super-8, and even Beta tapes beg to be digitized. You can copy them onto a miniDV or Digital8 tape and then import that to iMovie, or you can use a media converter to go directly from the VCR to iMovie. The Dazzle Hollywood, Formac Studio DV/TV, and Canopus ADVC are all well-regarded and generally available for under $300. If you know that you're going to be going directly to Video CD, though, you can cut out the iMovie step altogether with Elgato's EyeTV (`www. elgato.com`). EyeTV takes your video input, converts it to Video CD–compatible MPEG-1, and stores that through a USB connection onto your hard disk. The accompanying software even lets you do some editing (cutting out footage, for example) before burning to Video CD with Toast.
- **Tripods:** Tripods are an invaluable tool for both the still and motion photographer. Using a tripod improves your focus, removes jitter, smooths any panning operations, and generally improves your photos and movie footage.

Chapter 3: Taking a Cue from the Media Pros

In This Chapter

- Shooting tips from digital photo and movie gurus
- Recording strategies and techniques for audio
- Planning the shoot and shooting the plan
- Authoring the DVD

First things first. All we can do in this chapter is show you some of the techniques used by expert photographers, videographers, and scorers. How you apply those techniques and your artistic sense are left to experience and genetics, respectively. Like Commander Data of Star Trek fame, you can create a technically perfect composition and still have it lack "soul."

Many subjects in this chapter can easily fill a book (or more) of their own, and we mention some additional references along the way if you're curious enough to explore a topic further.

Taking Better Photos and Movies

The guidelines to create more visually appealing photos and video are so similar that discussing them separately is redundant. Being static entities, photos lend themselves to more after-the-fact fixes and repairs. This section is geared toward photographs; however, the general composition rules apply equally well to movies.

You rarely see a photo that doesn't have a subject and a background. The closest exception we can think of is a field of stars in the night sky or an expanse of terrain or a water shot from above. Even in these cases, though, you have a subject. Positioning your subject against the background and taking advantage of that positioning to highlight your subject is the gist of photo composition.

If you have a camera with a high enough resolution, you can work around many composition problems by cropping appropriately. We show examples throughout this chapter of how you can fix less-than-optimal compositions. See Book II to find out more about cropping photos with iPhoto.

Some excellent references on taking better photos and fixing the ones that aren't quite right include *50 Fast Digital Photo Techniques* (by Gregory Georges) and *Digital Photography: Top 100 Simplified Tips & Tricks* (by maranGraphics) both published by Wiley Publishing, Inc.

Obeying the rule of thirds

Going back to ancient (or Renaissance) times, artists have applied the rule of thirds to focus attention on their subject or a specific aspect of their subject. The rule states that the focal points in a picture tend to fall along the lines that divide the picture into thirds, both horizontally and vertically. Check out portraits, and you find that the principle feature is almost precisely one-third of the way from the top of the picture, as shown in Figure 3-1. The famous and enigmatic smile of Mona Lisa rests on that line.

Figure 3-1: Mona Lisa's famous smile rests atop the one-third dividing line.

You can focus attention on your subject by positioning it within a cropped image if you have enough pixels to spare. This is one of the great advantages in having a camera that can take shots at a higher resolution than you actually require for your normal printing needs. Check out Figure 3-2, where we cropped a 1600×1200 resolution photo to 1024×768, repositioning Maggie to the upper-right intersection described by the rule of thirds.

Figure 3-2: Position your subject within a subset of the frame and crop.

Simplifying the background

The more distinctive objects (and people) in your photo, the more likely your subject will get lost in the clutter. A few things you can try to simplify your background are

- **Avoid busy backgrounds.** When possible, have a neutral background behind your subject. A wall or a plain backdrop works much better than a busy street or a store window.
- **Zoom in or move closer to your subject.** The more your subject fills the frame, the less the background intrudes. Figure 3-3 shows an example of how you can zoom in to make your subject stand out.
- **Try a different angle.** Sometimes, by rotating your scene, you can avoid or minimize the distractions. Similarly, you can lower the camera and shoot slightly upward to avoid many intrusions at eye level.

Figure 3-3: Zooming in (left) eliminates most of the distractions present (right).

- **Change the orientation.** If your subject is a person (pretty common situation), portrait orientation puts more of your subject in the picture and avoids a lot of background. On the other hand, if your subject is a horse, a landscape shot usually works better.
- **Mute the background with an image-editing program's filters.** The selection techniques in a graphics program, such as Photoshop Elements 2, can allow you to isolate your subject from the background and then apply a filter to tone down the background, making your subject stand out, as shown in Figure 3-4.

Figure 3-4: The Photoshop Elements Magic Lasso selects and excludes the subject, and then applying a Gaussian Blur to the background makes Spenser stand out.

If your camera takes pictures of a high enough resolution, you can still get a good print after cropping the image to eliminate background distractions.

Sometimes, you have just one little element disrupting your background, such as a light switch or electrical socket on the wall. In such situations, Photoshop Elements or a similar tool works wonders by letting you clone good portions of the background to cover the intrusion.

Adjusting the altitude

When you want to emphasize a person or object, shooting the picture from below the subject can help. Conversely, shooting down on a subject tends to minimize them. Check out Figures 3-5 and 3-6 to see what we mean.

Figure 3-5: Shooting up can make even a toddler seem larger.

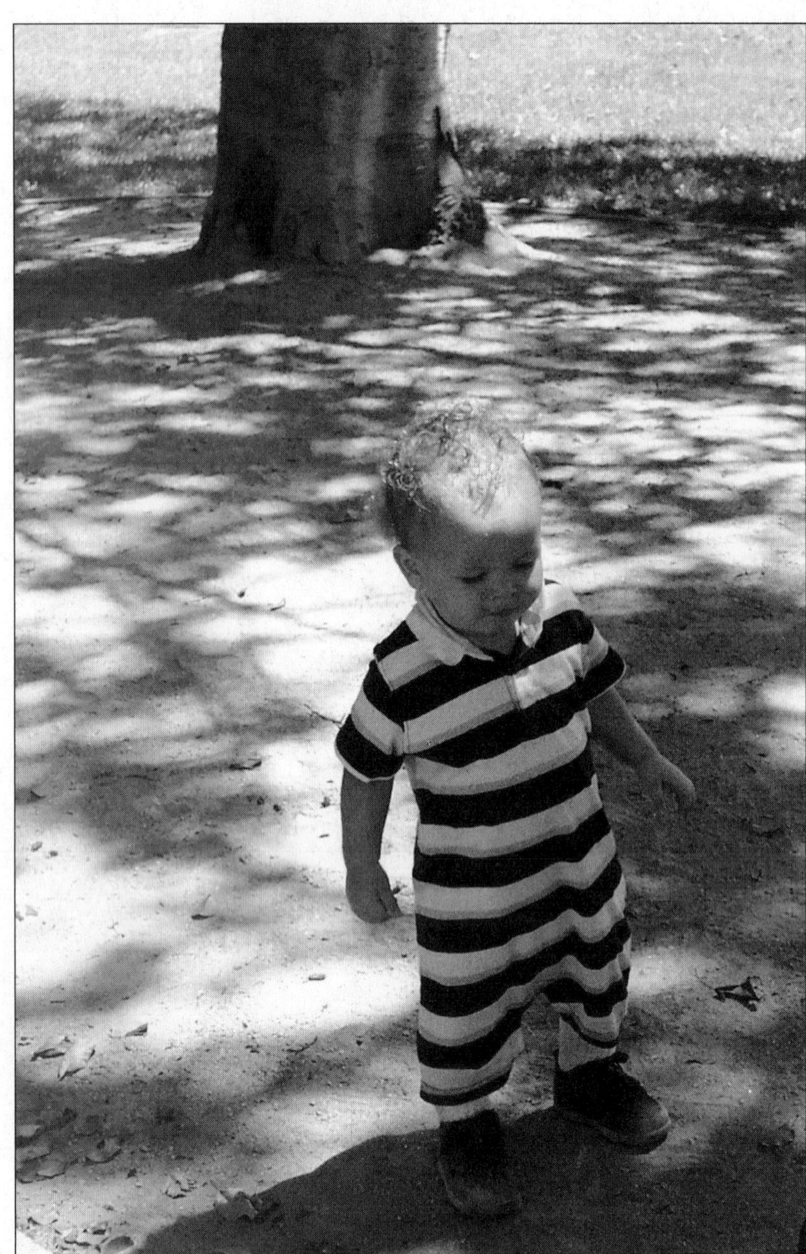

Figure 3-6: Taking a picture from above diminishes the subject.

Stabilizing the camera

Your camera captures an image during a very short interval while the shutter is open. Tripods are inexpensive accessories that help greatly to avoid the following problems:

- ✦ If your camera moves during or just before that interval, you end up with a blurred image or the subject may not be framed the way you intended.
- ✦ When taking panoramic shots that you want to stitch together at a later time, a lack of stability translates into a panorama requiring a lot of cropping to avoid white gaps at the top and bottom.
- ✦ When filming a scene, you want a stable frame of reference to avoid an amateurish effect of the scene bouncing around.

The darker it is when you shoot, the longer the shutter stays open to capture a clear image. Tripods are even more important in low-light shots.

Throwing some light on the subject

Keep in mind that your camera is an electronic device and that it doesn't perceive color in quite the same way as the human eye. In fact, not all people see color the same way — many men suffer from some degree of color-blindness (yes, that's a sex-linked characteristic).

Your pupils dilate in low-light conditions and can lead you to believe sufficient light exists for your shots. Use reflectors or fill lights to increase the lighting on your scene and subject, not a flash. Think of your flash as the lighting of last resort.

One time when a flash comes in really handy: If you're in virtually total darkness, you can take a picture of someone (or something) and get a great shot with almost no background involvement.

The human eye compensates for the color casts inherent in light. A camera faithfully renders the color of light. Incandescent lights tend toward a yellow cast, sunlight tends to blue, and fluorescent lights tend toward green. Many digital camcorders and still cameras have specific settings you can apply for differing lighting conditions. Check your camera's user manual to see what adjustments you have available.

Shooting more than you need

Just as professional photographers shoot multiple images (often staccato fashion) and filmmakers shoot multiple takes of a scene, you should take a lot of shots with your camera and extra footage with your camcorder. You never know exactly which one is going to be best, and having a variety to choose from enhances the likelihood you'll produce a better product.

If you can arrange for a second camcorder, try to film the same scene from two angles, even if they differ only slightly. Sometimes, you get better audio fidelity from one than the other. Generally, though, you can swap angles during your iMovie editing, resulting in a livelier, more realistic scene.

Watching the zoom

Both digital cameras and camcorders advertise two zoom settings: optical and digital. We recommend using optical zoom (digital zoom is almost useless).

Digital zoom selects a portion of the captured image and blows it up, similar to the way you resize an image in a graphics program (such as Photoshop or Photoshop Elements), discarding the remainder of the captured image. But you don't get a detailed magnification of the image, just larger pixels. Figure 3-7 shows an unzoomed scene; Figure 3-8 shows the same scene, digitally zoomed.

Figure 3-7: We shot this scene without a zoom.

Figure 3-8: The same scene shown in Figure 3-7, shot with a digital zoom.

Optical zoom, shown in Figure 3-9, functions like a telescope or magnifying glass. It captures the detail by changing your camera's focal length. Two types of lenses offer an optical zoom:

- Telephoto lenses attach to the camera and provide a fixed magnification. The advantages to telephoto lenses are that they don't put a strain on your camera's batteries and you can obtain a wide range of magnifications if your wallet can handle the expense of multiple lenses.
- Zoom lenses are built into the camera and adjust the magnification incrementally. Zoom lenses, on the other hand, make your camera setup more portable and allow you to change the zoom more quickly and conveniently.

The more you zoom, the more likely you are to need a tripod as even tiny motions are magnified. Additionally, your camera's *depth of field* decreases as zoom increases — the objects around your subject are less likely to be in focus (just as items at the periphery of a telescope image are less sharp).

Reading the fine manual

New camera models appear constantly. Each has different features and capabilities. More than that, some of them have the same feature called by different names (such as *shutter priority mode* and *time value,* which allow you to specify a shutter speed and the camera adjusts the lens aperture to compensate). To make things even more difficult, you may find the same feature on a menu, a dial, or even a switch, depending upon the camera make and model.

Figure 3-9: The scene shown in Figure 3-7, shot with an optical zoom.

All this means is that you need to read the manual, even with its usually egregious English. Carry it with you whenever you plan to take a lot of pictures until you know your camera inside and out.

Carrying the manual with you becomes more important when you own more than one type of digital camera, lest you start confusing their feature sets.

Enhancing the sound with an extra mic

Your camcorder's microphone won't cut the mustard for most serious efforts. For one thing, it's inside your camera where it picks up ambient mechanical noises and has a limited range, which means that you won't pick up dialog more than a few yards (or meters) away.

Don't rely on your camera's built-in mic. Use an external microphone whenever possible, attached to your camera's Mic jack, and positioned as close as practical to your subject. Additionally, use a set of headphones (even the ear buds that come with your iPod do the job) plugged into the camera's headphone jack. This lets you hear what the camera is recording. You may be surprised at some of the sounds it picks up that you don't even notice without the headphones.

Many microphones come with foam covers. Keep the foam cover on when recording as, contrary to what you may think, their purpose isn't to protect the mic — they're windguards that filter sibilant sounds, such as wind, as well as mitigating the presence of some *popping* sounds, such as the sound of a *b* or *p*.

Finding out more on the Internet

While most everyone is at least a little bit familiar with the Web, a bulletin-board-like system, called Usenet, predates the Web and is still very active. With tens of thousands of newsgroups (topic areas) available, newsgroups are an excellent vehicle for interactive learning. Two newsgroups, in particular, are especially useful to photographers or videographers: `rec.photo.digital` and `rec.video.desktop`.

If you are unfamiliar with Usenet newsgroups and the software to access them, check out what's available at `www.newsreaders.com/mac/clients.html` or `www.macorchard.com/usenet.html`. These sites also contain links that tell you more about Usenet newsgroup organization and operations.

Figure 3-10 gives you an idea of the discussion topics available on a random day in `rec.video.desktop`. The news client being employed is Brian Clark's popular Thoth newsreader (`www.thothsw.com`).

Depending on your ISP, the shelf-life of Usenet messages can be very short. Some high-volume groups (particularly those with large binary postings in addition to text messages) can have messages being purged in under one day. The established discussion groups, such as `rec.photo.digital`, do not fall in that category. In most cases, messages are still be there after a week or more, so you can trace through the related messages as well (these are called *threads*).

A superb digital camera and camcorder Web site with an enormous collection of information, reviews, and links is Steve's DigiCams (`http://steves-digicams.com`). You even find discussion forums for specific brands of cameras as well as general question and answer (Q&A) forums.

Many (and we're tempted to say most) camera manuals are very poorly written. If, as is likely, your manual falls into that rather large niche, you can seek out a better one at `www.shortcourses.com`. The books are all written on heavy stock and spiral bound. In addition to the available manuals for most major brands, you can also find tutorials, camera pocket guides, and digital photography and video references.

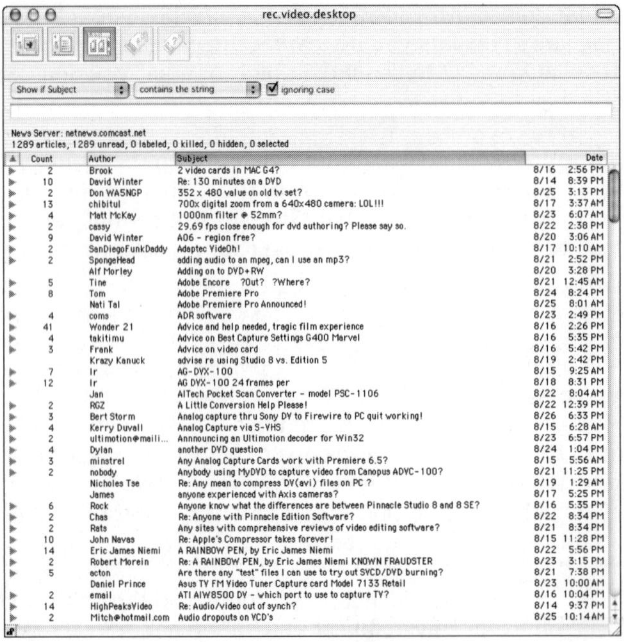

Figure 3-10: The `rec.video.desktop` newsgroup is an active discussion board with a wide range of desktop video topics.

Although Kodak tends to push its own brand, you can also find a lot of useful general information at the Kodak Web site (`www.kodak.com`). Just click the Consumer Photography tab and then the Taking Great Pictures icon.

When you want the latest reviews of camera models, probably the best site to check is the Digital Camera Resource page (`www.dcresource.com`).

Capturing Better Audio

"Garbage in, garbage out" is every bit as true of audio as it is video or any other kind of data you process. Whether you're making a QuickTime movie, ripping music for your iPod, or making a DVD doesn't matter — you need the best audio you can get as a starting point. Given a choice, you should start with AIFF or WAV (the PC world's equivalent of AIFF) files rather than already-compressed formats, such as MP2, MP3, or AAC. If you must work with compressed formats, find the highest bit rate that you can.

Using the right hardware and software

As built-in microphones go, the ones built into iMacs, PowerBooks, and so on are near the top of the heap; however, *built-in* is a huge qualifier. Compared to traditional mics, they aren't all that great. In fact, the PlainTalk mics that came with many older Macs were appreciably better, and professional mics and USB microphones, such as the iVoice (Macally Peripherals, `www.macally.com`) or the Verse-704 (Labtec, `www.labtec.com`) are better yet. The Griffin Technology iMic (`www.griffintechnology.com`) is a USB device allowing you to plug in almost any kind of microphone. In fact, with a simple cable connection, you can plug a stereo tape deck or turntable into the iMic microphone port to capture your audio.

Roxio Toast 6 Titanium comes with a support program, CD Spin Doctor 2, built specifically to capture audio input from tape players and stereos. The program then helps you clean up the hisses, whistles, and pops that are so common in analog media, divide the capture into tracks, and store your tracks on disk. Figure 3-11 shows the CD Spin Doctor 2 window, with the Filter drawer open.

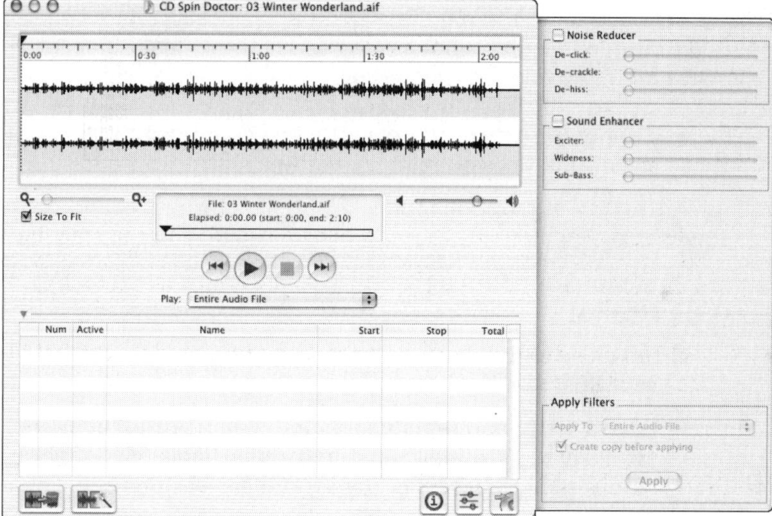

Figure 3-11: CD Spin Doctor 2 imports and helps you clean up your audio.

The version of CD Spin Doctor that Roxio included with Toast 5 was accompanied by a cable with RCA miniplugs at one end and a line-in plug at the other to facilitate attaching an audio device to your Mac. This cable is not included in the Toast 6 box.

Another way of capturing high-quality audio is to record it on your digital camcorder. Use the analog input jack to capture the audio from your original source and then import it into iMovie, where you extract the audio track, discard the video, and export the AIFF file to your audio editor of choice, such as CD Spin Doctor or Amadeus II ($25 shareware from HairerSoft, `www.hairersoft.com/Amadeus.html`).

When recording a movie on your digital camcorder, make certain that the camcorder is set to record 16-bit sound rather than 12-bit audio. Not only is 16-bit sound higher quality, but synchronization problems occur when you export an iMovie with 12-bit audio. If you do have 12-bit audio and want to avoid the synchronization problem, use QuickTime Pro to convert the 12-bit audio back to 16-bit audio before you encode your QuickTime movie or use iDVD.

DVDs not only use 16-bit audio, but that audio is sampled at 48KHz — even higher than the 44.1KHz used for CD audio. If you import your audio at 48KHz, you save some time during the iDVD encoding process.

Recording narrations

iMovie includes a Record Voice button in its audio pane and, after you set up the hardware (or choose the Mac's built-in mic), you may think that you're just about done. You'd be wrong, though. Speaking into a microphone and getting good results is not as easy as TV shows make it seem. Here are a few tips for improving your recording:

- Clear your throat and do a little test count before you start recording to make sure that you're really ready.
- Test the microphone to make sure it is turned on and operational.
- Eliminate background noises wherever possible. This includes closing windows and turning off electronic devices (such as TVs, radios, and stereos).
- Get close to, but keep a few inches of separation between the mic and your lips.
- Have a script and practice it before you record. The first reading or two are likely to be somewhat stilted and artificial. Extemporaneous presentations tend to have *uhs*, *hmms*, and *ers*, besides being of unpredictable duration.
- Time your presentation so you know whether to speed up, slow down, or adjust the material in order to match the footage in length and timing.

Recorded audio clips are also limited by iMovie to just under 10 minutes. Where iMovie continues importing video and creating new clips seamlessly, recorded audio narrations terminate when the limit is reached. Plan your narration accordingly. Break it into separate recordings based upon your rehearsals. In addition to working around the length limit, limiting a session's length results in a clearer, more engaged voice.

Preparing the Shoot

You may think that preparing a storyboard, script, shot list, budget, and so forth are only applicable to commercial moviemaking. *Au conrtaire, mon frere!*

In fact, you'll find that equipment lists come in handy even for casual photography, such as when you take pictures of the kids at the park or the beach. Preparing a checklist of such items as extra batteries, additional memory cards, and whatever lenses and filters you may need prevents you from missing some possibly great memories.

The preparation and groundwork becomes even more critical when making movies. Unless you're just stringing together a haphazard collection of footage, you need to think about what message you want your project to convey. Similarly, you need to consider why you're making the movie and who your intended audience is. Answering these questions lays a solid foundation for the scenes you want to shoot and what sort of effects and soundtrack you employ.

Planning the scope

After you answer the fundamental questions, start planning your project. You can consolidate a plan in many ways, but all of them share one set of goals. They list the tasks you need to perform and show dependencies between the tasks as well as the costs arising from the tasks — you may have to license some audio, rent some equipment, pay an access fee, and consider travel costs in both time and dollars.

You can create an outline (something that would make your old schoolteachers beam with pride), chart the movie out the way a programmer or systems engineer flowcharts a software project, or use the bureaucrat's planning tool of choice, a *PMS* (Project Management System). Some tools in these categories include:

- ✦ **Outliners:** Microsoft Word and AppleWorks both include quite functional outliners and, if you're a regular user of either product, that may well be how you choose to go. If you want a clean, stand-alone outliner, though, check out Omni Group's OmniOutliner ($30, `www.omnigroup.com/applications/omnioutliner/`) or DEVONthink PE ($35, `www.devon-technologies.com/products/devonthink.php`).
- ✦ **Charting tools:** You can just draw and connect boxes using the AppleWorks Draw module, but updating a chart of this type is a tedious, manual operation where you have to rearrange all the subsequent boxes and connectors when something changes. If you're a visual person, consider OmniGraffle ($70) or OmniGraffle Pro ($120) from the Omni Group

or Kivio mp ($90 download or $100 on CD from theKompany.com, `www.thekompany.com/poducts/kivio`). A portion of an OmniGraffle project plan can be seen in Figure 3-12.

✦ **Project Management Software:** If you want to go the full Gantt and PERT chart route, with bill of materials, automatic cost tracking, and all the other amenities and intricacies of a professional project planning and tracking tool, then you want a Project Management System. If you don't know what those terms mean, then a PMS is probably not for you. A couple of inexpensively priced PMS products are Creative Manager Pro ($35, Creative Manager, Inc., `www.creative-manager.com/a10003/`) and Intellisys Project Desktop X ($89, Intellisys Inc., `www.webintellisys.com/project/desktop.html`).

Project Management Systems require tremendous discipline, extreme attention to detail, and fastidious maintenance to produce status reports, schedules, and budgets that are grounded in reality. Using a PMS and understanding its nuances is the subject of many books far thicker than this one. Failure to accurately account for every detail results in misleading or just plain crazy reports. But, if you have the experience and discipline, you'll be able to recognize problems well in advance — a major help in minimizing the problem's impact or avoiding it altogether.

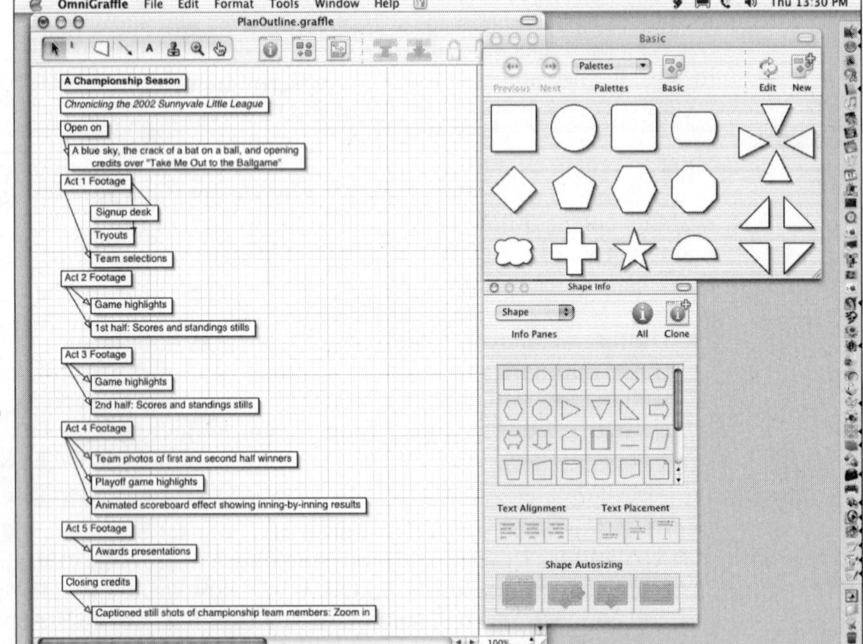

Figure 3-12: OmniGraffle helps the visual planner lay out a project.

Filling in the details

If your project requires narration, or if you're creating a non-documentary film, you need to write a script. In addition to providing the words your audience hears, a script also gives direction to the performer as to where to look, enter, exit, or pause. A script can be a casual text document created in TextEdit, Word, or AppleWorks (for example). If you want to be even more professional about it, consider professional scriptwriting software, such as Final Draft AV ($179, www.finaldraft.com).

Whether or not your movie has dialog, narration, or scripted action, you still need part of what a script provides: the shot list. Determine what scenes you're going to use as well as where, when, and how you're going to shoot them. Preparing a shot list helps you avoid missing any of the shots you need. Some scenes may end up on the cutting room floor, but you probably won't have to scramble at the last minute trying to fill in a gap.

Additionally, take your script and list the scenes where you want to set chapter markers. Play with rough menu designs until you get something that fits both your vision and the material you have on hand. This is often called a *storyboard*. To find out more about chapter markers in iMovie, see Book III.

Budgeting time and money

You've probably heard the adage, "Time is money." We don't think they're exactly the same, but when you're developing a project, they bear a lot of similarities. Both need to be budgeted (though budgeting time is usually called *scheduling*).

This is where your script and, in particular, the shot list come in handy. Go through the shot list and note any equipment you need to purchase or rent, any locations you need to rent or arrange, the tapes and discs you need to record and burn your project, and any people (actors, writers, or stage help) you need to hire. If you do a cost analysis before you start shooting, you can avoid running out of money partway through by either arranging more funding or refining the project so that you stay within your means.

Don't forget about miscellaneous items that require budgeting, such as tapes, cables, batteries, microphones, lights, and (probably) a tripod or gyro-stabilizer. Keeping an inventory of needed equipment and scheduling its use helps insure that you have what you need when you need it.

Similarly, after you have the list of shots itemized, figure in how long they require for shooting (including travel time and making allowance for multiple takes to make sure you get what you're after). You may find that you can't do everything you want to do in the time allotted for the project.

Planning for the DVD

Creating the DVD involves more than just exporting an iMovie, slapping a button or two on the screen, and telling iDVD to burn the disc. The storyboard is a big part of planning your DVD. It tells you how many menus you need and how to navigate them. This design also gives you a heads-up on which still images, audio, and video you want to extract from your iMovie to use as buttons and menu backgrounds.

If you're distributing your DVD to friends, family, or business associates, also consider the artwork you'll use for the DVD case cover, an insert, or even a label to place on the DVD. Still images extracted from the movie make great illustrations for such items.

Make sure that you know the precise running time of your movie. If you have high-action scenes, you want the highest bit-rate encoding iDVD has to offer. That means that you want the movie to be less than 60 minutes in length. Go over 60 minutes, even just a hair, and iDVD encodes at the 90 minute bit rate, which can show a quality loss in fast-moving scenes.

Keep in mind that a movie can have only 36 chapters when you're planning your scenes and menus. Prioritize wisely.

Index

Symbols

A

B

C

D

E

F

G

J

K

N

O

P

Q

R

S

T

U

V

W

X

Y

Z

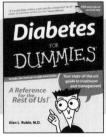

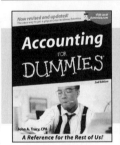

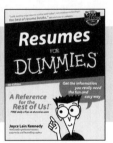

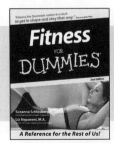

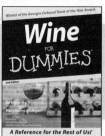

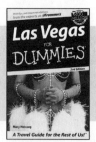

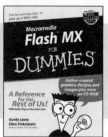

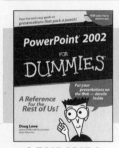